C000041255

INDIA'S FINANCIAL SYSTEM

Building the Foundation for Strong and Sustainable Growth

Editors

ALFRED SCHIPKE
JARKKO TURUNEN
NADA CHOUEIRI
ANNE-MARIE GULDE-WOLF

© 2023 International Monetary Fund
Cover design: IMF Creative Solutions

Cataloging-in-Publication Data
IMF Library

Names: Schipke, Alfred, 1959-, editor. | Turunen, Jarkko, editor. | Choueiri,
    Nada, editor. | Gulde-Wolf, Anne-Marie, editor. | International Monetary
    Fund, publisher.
Title: India's financial system : Building the foundation for strong and
    sustainable growth.
Edited by Alfred Schipke, Jarkko Turunen, Nada Choueiri, and Anne-Marie
    Gulde-Wolf
Other titles: Building the foundation for strong and sustainable growth.
Description: Washington, DC : International Monetary Fund, 2023. | 2023. |
    Includes bibliographical references.
Identifiers:
paper: 9798400223525
ePub: 9798400223822
Web PDF: 9798400223860
Subjects: Finance—India. | Fiscal policy—India. | India—Economic policy.
Classification: LCC HG185.I53.S3 2023

DISCLAIMER: The views expressed in this book are those of the
authors and do not necessarily represent the views of the IMF's
Executive Directors, its management, or any of its members. The
boundaries, colors, denominations, and any other information
shown on the maps do not imply, on the part of the International
Monetary Fund, any judgment on the legal status of any territory
or any endorsement or acceptance of such boundaries.

Recommended citation: Alfred Schipke, Jarkko Turunen, Nada Choueiri, and
Anne-Marie Gulde-Wolf, eds. *India's Financial System: Building the Foundation for
Strong and Sustainable Growth*. Washington, DC: International Monetary Fund.

ISBNs: 9798400223525 (paper)
        9798400223822 (ePub)
        9798400223860 (PDF)

Please send orders to:

International Monetary Fund, Publication Services
PO Box 92780, Washington, DC 20090, USA
Tel: (202) 623–7430 | Fax: (202) 623–7201
E-mail: publications@imf.org
Internet: www.elibrary.imf.org
www.bookstore.imf.org

Contents

Foreword

India's vibrant growth performance over the past three decades has lifted millions out of poverty. The country is now the third largest economy in the world (in terms of purchasing power parity), and developments in India have significant global and regional implications.

While the COVID-19 pandemic hit the country's economy hard, India's future remains bright, reflecting continued development opportunities and favorable demographics. Here, a financial system that is healthy and stable, but also vibrant—capitalizing on digital technologies and opportunities to support sustainable, green, and inclusive growth—will play a central role in enabling India's enormous potential and boosting the standard of living of all its citizens.

With all the promise this holds, this book takes a comprehensive look at India's financial system. In addition to providing the broad macro-financial setting, the book zooms in on key financial sector issues such as strengthening the banking and nonbank sectors, and fostering the development of capital markets to channel savings and investment to the most productive sectors of the economy. At the same time, the book analyzes how financial markets can contribute to the greening of the economy and how digitalization can foster financial inclusion—an area where India has been at the forefront, as I saw firsthand on my recent visit.

The development of India's financial system will, however, also depend on complementary reforms ranging from monetary policy communication to policies to maximize stable capital inflows, while minimizing volatility—all topics of critical importance that are explored in this book. Finally, as financial sector soundness depends on a healthy corporate sector, the book also discusses insights from corporate stress tests and measures to further enhance private debt resolution frameworks.

The IMF is partnering closely with the Indian authorities on these issues on a range of fronts—including our regular annual policy dialogue (Article IV), technical collaboration, and also via our Financial Sector Assessments Program (FSAP). Furthermore, we are enhancing our engagement on many emerging topics including fintech and digital money, bringing together Indian officials and IMF staff to share experiences and emerging good practices, some of which are relevant for the IMF's broader membership. The South Asia Regional Training and Technical Assistance Center (SARTTAC) in Delhi—generously supported by the Indian authorities—has hosted some of these engagements and thus been an important platform not only for capacity development in India but across the South Asia region.

I am so appreciative of the strong partnership the IMF enjoys with India. We look forward to continuing and building on this across all aspects of our cooperation, and notably as India embarks on its first ever G20 presidency in 2023.

Kristalina Georgieva
Managing Director
International Monetary Fund

Acknowledgments

As India leaves the COVID-19 pandemic behind, the economic recovery and the country's medium-term growth prospects will critically depend on the health of its financial system. This book provides a comprehensive review of India's financial system, analyzing both its development over time and its current structure with a view to identifying important strengths and areas for future reforms. It covers the nexus between growth in economic activity and the financial system and corporate sector vulnerabilities during the pandemic, as well as developments in the banking and nonbank sectors, corporate bond market, issues in green finance, fintech and financial inclusion, and capital flows and potential spillovers. The book also takes a look at supporting areas such as the role of recent reforms, including monetary policy communication during flexible inflation targeting regimes and the private sector debt resolution framework after the introduction of the Insolvency and Bankruptcy Code.

This book combines rigorous analysis with detailed institutional knowledge from authors from many IMF departments (Asia and Pacific, European, Monetary and Capital Markets, Research, Legal and Institute for Capacity Development), as well as the private sector and academia. The book has benefited from excellent contributions and insightful comments and feedback from many. In addition to the editors and authors of individual chapters, the book benefited from input and comments by Zamid Aligishiev, Elif Arbatli Saxegaard, Tamon Asonuma, Wouter Bossu, Luis Breuer, Carine Antoine Chartouni, Vu Thanh Chau, Hee Kyong Chon, Lorraine Pecarsky Coffey, Mariarosaria Comunale, Sonali Das, Udaibir Saran Das, Joy De Vera, Xiaodan Ding, Futoshi Narita, Russell Green, Alessandro Gullo, Naomi Griffin, Federico Grinberg, Phakawa Jeasakul, Joong Shik Kang, Nila Khanolkar, Romain Lafarguette, Sudip Mohapatra, Mico Mrkaic, Futoshi Narita, Hiroko Oura, Shanaka J. Peiris, Nathalie Pouokam, Cian Ruane, Damiano Sandri, Nimarjit Singh, Katrien Smuts, Sergio Sola, John Spray, Jan Strasky, Chia Yi Tan, Priscilla Toffano, Thierry Tressel, Filiz Derya Unsal, Laura Valderrama, and Rui Xu, and seminar participants at the Reserve Bank of India, the Indian Ministry of Finance, and the IMF's Asia and Pacific Department.

We would like to also thank IMF Executive Director Surjit Bhalla, for his support and inputs. We are grateful to Madelen Conde-Panesso, Ankita Goel, Khyati Chauhan, Yang Liu, Armaghan Naveed, and François-Clément Charbonnier for providing excellent research and editorial support.

We sincerely thank Linda Kean and Patricia Loo for getting the editorial process off the ground and their continued support, as well as the team at Absolute Service, Inc. led by Teresa Exley, for copyediting, proofreading, indexing, and typesetting. We are deeply indebted to Lorraine Coffey for managing the production of the book in record time.

Contributors

Faisal Ahmed is IMF Mission Chief for Bhutan and Senior Economist working on the IMF CD Strategy 2023. Previously, he served as Senior Desk on India. During 2015–19, he served as the Chief Economist and Senior Advisor to the Governor at the Bangladesh (Central) Bank. He has worked on a broad range of advanced, emerging, and developing economies at the IMF and also served as the IMF Resident Representative in Cambodia (2011–15). Previously, he worked as an actuary for a global reinsurance company and as an economist at the US Federal Reserve Bank. He has also taught at the University of Minnesota and the Royal School of Administration in Cambodia. He completed his graduate studies in economics and finance at the University of Minnesota and Princeton University.

Mahir Binici is a senior economist in the European Department of the IMF, where he covers Iceland and Malta. He previously worked in the Strategy, Policy, and Review Department on the external policy issues, also covering India, and at the Central Bank of Türkiye. His research interests include international finance, monetary policy, and banking. He holds a PhD in international economics from the University of California, Santa Cruz.

Marco Casiraghi is a Financial Sector Expert in the Monetary and Capital Markets Department of the IMF, where he works on monetary and macroprudential policies, with a focus on central bank communication. Prior to joining the IMF, he was an Advisor in the Monetary Analysis Division at the Bank of Italy. While at the Bank of Italy, Marco contributed to assessing macroeconomic, monetary, and financial conditions and determining the appropriate European Central Bank monetary policy stance. He has also conducted and published research on several topics, including the effectiveness of unconventional monetary policy measures and their impact on inequality. Marco holds a PhD in economics from Boston University, where his thesis focused on the macroeconomic effects of financial and banking crises.

Nada Choueiri has been the Mission Chief for India at the IMF since September 1, 2021. Before that, she was Mission Chief for Malaysia and Singapore. Her career at the IMF spans 23 years, during which she worked on a range of countries in Emerging Europe, the Middle East, and Asia and spent several years in the Office of the Deputy Managing Director as Advisor. While on leave from the IMF during 2014–15, she was Lead Economist for Algeria and Libya at the World Bank. Born in Lebanon, Ms. Choueiri received her BA in economics from the American University of Beirut and her PhD in economics from The Johns Hopkins University in Baltimore, Maryland.

José M. Garrido is the Supervisor of the Insolvency Working Group and a senior counsel at the Financial and Fiscal Law Unit of the Legal Department of the IMF. He is an internationally recognized specialist in insolvency and creditor rights and in financial and company law, with ample experience in legal analysis and the design of law reforms in numerous countries in Europe, Asia, Africa, and the Americas. He is a professor of commercial, corporate, and insolvency law at the University of Castilla-La Mancha in Spain and has written extensively on a wide range of legal topics, particularly on insolvency and debt restructuring. He holds a PhD from the University of Bologna, an LLM from the University of London, and a JD from the University of Alcalá (Spain).

Siddharth George is Presidential Young Professor in the Department of Economics at the National University of Singapore. Previously, he was an Assistant Professor of Economics at Boston University and Dartmouth College. His research interests include development economics and political economy. Siddharth earned his PhD at Harvard University and a BSc at the London School of Economics.

Rohit Goel, CFA, is the head of global macro research at Breakout Capital Partners. In his previous role, he was a Financial Sector Expert in the IMF's Monetary and Capital Markets Department. He contributed to sections of the *Global Financial Stability Report*, and focused extensively on financial stability risks in emerging markets, global rate markets, and quantitative modeling across asset classes. He has also contributed to the financial stability assessment programs for South Africa, the euro area, and China and worked briefly as the MCM economist for the Brazil desk. Prior to joining the IMF, he worked as an assistant vice president and a writing analyst at Barclays Asia Equities for four years. He holds a BTech in computer science from the Indian Institute of Technology, Delhi, and an MBA from the Indian Institute of Management, Bangalore. He is also a certified Chartered Financial Analyst and has completed Chartered Alternative Investment Analyst and Financial Risk Manager certifications.

Lucyna Górnicka is a senior economist in the Prices and Costs Division at the European Central Bank. She is currently on leave from the IMF, where she worked on a range of macro-financial projects, including Financial Sector Assessment Programs for Austria, Colombia, and New Zealand. Ms. Górnicka holds a PhD from the University of Amsterdam. Her research interests focus on financial stability and monetary and macroprudential policy issues. Her work has been published in the *Journal of International Economics, Journal of Financial Intermediation, Journal of Banking and Finance, and Economic Policy Journal.*

Anne-Marie Gulde-Wolf, a German national, is Deputy Director in the IMF's Asia and Pacific Department (APD). She is directly overseeing the department's work and policy priorities on South Asian countries (India, Bangladesh, Bhutan,

Nepal, Maldives, and Sri Lanka) and on several East Asian countries (Cambodia, Lao PDR, Myanmar, Thailand, and Vietnam), as well as the department's work on financial sector issues. Before joining APD in 2019, she was Deputy Director in the African Department and earlier in the European Department and previously held a division chief position in the Monetary and Capital Markets Department. She studied economics, political science, and history in Tübingen (Germany), St. Louis (United States), and Kiel (Germany) and holds a PhD in international economics from the Graduate Institute of International Studies in Geneva (Switzerland). She has published widely on different topics in international economics, with a focus on exchange rate regimes, currency boards, and financial stability and development issues.

Purva Khera is an economist in the IMF's Asia and Pacific Department, where she currently covers Japan and Timor-Leste. Previously, she worked in the IMF's Monetary and Capital Markets Department, where she worked on the IMF Financial Sector Assessment of China, Brazil, and Italy. Her research interests and publications have mainly focused on macro-financial linkages, financial inclusion, fintech, labor markets, informality, and gender economics. She holds a PhD and an MPhil in economics from the University of Cambridge, and a BA in economics from St. Stephen's College, University of Delhi.

Divya Kirti is an economist in the Research Department at the IMF. Previously, he worked in the Middle East and Central Asia Department. His research interests include financial intermediation, macro-finance, and corporate finance. His work has been published in the *Journal of Financial Intermediation* and the *Journal of Banking and Finance* and has also been covered by media outlets such as the *New York Times*. He holds a PhD in economics from Harvard University and a BA in economics and mathematics from Cornell University.

Margaux MacDonald is an economist in the Asia and Pacific Department of the IMF, where she covers India and Bhutan. Previously, she worked in the Research Department covering the G20 and contributing to the *World Economic Outlook*, and in the African Department on IMF program countries. Her research interests include international macroeconomics and finance, and her recent work focuses on cross-country spillovers from monetary policy, banking, and trade. She holds a PhD in economics from Queen's University (Kingston, Canada).

Maria Soledad (Sole) Martinez Peria is Assistant Director in the Research Department of the IMF. She manages the Macro-Financial Division, responsible for conducting research and policy work on macroeconomic and financial issues critical to IMF surveillance activities, with a focus on macro-financial linkages, financial flows, and financial systems. Her research addresses questions related to financial crises, bank competition, financial inclusion, small and medium size finance, macroprudential policies, and digital currencies. Before joining the IMF, she was a research manager at the World Bank. She also held short-term positions at the Brookings Institution, the Central Bank of Argentina, and the Federal Reserve Board. She has a PhD in economics from the University of California, Berkeley and a BA from Stanford University.

Fabio M. Natalucci is Deputy Director of the IMF's Monetary and Capital Markets Department, with responsibility for the IMF's global financial markets monitoring and systemic risk assessment functions. He is responsible for the *Global Financial Stability Report,* which presents the IMF's assessment of global financial stability risks. Before joining the IMF, he was a senior associate director in the Division of Monetary Affairs at the US Federal Reserve Board, where he conducted research and analysis on the relationship between monetary policy, financial regulatory policy, and financial stability. Between October 2016 and June 2017, he was Deputy Assistant Secretary for International Financial Stability and Regulation at the US Department of Treasury. His responsibilities included leading US engagement on financial regulatory cooperation in the G20, representing the US Treasury at the Financial Stability Board, coordinating between domestic and international post-crisis regulatory reforms, and monitoring developments and vulnerabilities in global financial markets. He holds a PhD in economics from New York University.

Natalia Novikova is the IMF's Resident Representative in Singapore. She joined the IMF in 2013. Before moving to Singapore, she was a senior economist in the IMF's European and Strategy Policy and Review Departments. She worked on debt sustainability and financial stability issues and participated in designing macroeconomic policies in a range of advanced, emerging, and low-income economies, including in the context of development and implementation of IMF-supported programs. Before joining the IMF, she was an economist at Citigroup, worked at the monetary operations department of the Central Bank of Russia, and led a market research team at PricewaterhouseCoopers. She holds a master's degree in economics from Erasmus University, The Netherlands, and from the State University—Higher School of Economics, Russia. For several years, she taught macroeconomics, monetary policy, and public debt management to graduate students. Her research interests and publications cover sovereign debt, capital flows, modeling of inflation, and exchange rates.

Sumiko Ogawa is Assistant to the Director in the Monetary and Capital Markets Department of the IMF. Previously, she worked on India, Japan, and Belarus covering financial sector issues, was Deputy Mission Chief for the Financial Sector Assessment Program for Thailand, and covered Bolivia and countries in the Caribbean in the Western Hemisphere Department. Before joining the IMF, she worked at the IMF's Regional Office in Tokyo, and at Merrill Lynch and JPMorgan in Tokyo. She has an MA in International Relations from the University of Tokyo.

Anjum Rosha is Senior Counsel at the Legal Department of the IMF and serves as the coordinator for the IMF's Working Group on Insolvency and Creditor Rights. She has extensive first-hand experience advising authorities on insolvency law reform in a number of European and Asian countries. In addition to insolvency law reform, she is responsible for overseeing the legal aspects of the IMF's engagement with more than a dozen of its member countries.

Alfred Schipke is Director of the IMF–Singapore Regional Training Institute for Asia and the Pacific in charge of technical assistance and training. Before that he was Assistant Director and Mission Chief for India and Senior Resident Representative and Mission Chief for China providing policy advice, spearheading analytical work, and coordinating capacity development. As Division Chief in the IMF Asia and Pacific Department, he led the department's work on fast-growing low-income countries in Southeast Asia (Frontier Economies) and was Mission Chief for Vietnam. In the IMF's Western Hemisphere Department, he negotiated several successful IMF programs including for El Salvador and St. Kitts and Nevis. He has taught international finance at Harvard Kennedy School and the National School of Development at Peking University and has authored and edited several books and articles. He holds a PhD from Duisburg-Essen University, an MPA from Harvard, and a BA from Indiana University of Pennsylvania.

Jay Surti is Chief of the IMF's Financial Supervision and Regulation Division. He previously served as Deputy Chief in this division, with responsibility for the work program on financial markets and NBFI supervision and regulation, and in the Global Financial Stability Analysis Division, where he led teams producing the thematic chapters of the IMF's Global Financial Stability Report. He has participated in several Financial Sector Assessment Program missions, most recently as mission chief of the 2018 Tanzania FSAP, and has served as economist in the IMF's African and European departments, covering a range of countries. During 2018–20, he served as special advisor to the Governor, Reserve Bank of India, advising the RBI's executive management in the areas of financial supervision and macro-financial risk surveillance. He holds a PhD in economics from Boston University.

Jarkko Turunen is Deputy Division Chief in the South Asia 1 Division and Mission Chief to Nepal in the Asia and Pacific Department of the International Monetary Fund. In addition to country work, his work covers cross-cutting financial sector issues in the Asia region. Earlier, Mr. Turunen was Deputy Mission Chief for India and Mission Chief to Solomon Islands and Cambodia, and worked on the United States (with focus on monetary policy), the Caribbean (also as Mission Chief to The Bahamas), as well as in the Strategy, Policy and Review Department on Egypt, Belarus, and various Fund policy issues, including conditionality in Fund programs, international trade and competitiveness, and jobs and growth. Before joining the Fund, he was Principal Economist at the

European Central Bank and a visiting scholar in the MIT economics department. He holds a PhD in economics from the European University Institute, in Florence, Italy. His main research interests are in macroeconomics, monetary policy, development economics, and labor economics, with articles published in *Journal of the European Economic Association, Journal of Economic Perspectives, IMF Economic Review, Journal of Economic Dynamics and Control, Empirical Economics,* and *Economics Letters.*

Rajesh Vijayaraghavan is an assistant professor of accounting at the University of British Columbia Sauder School of Business, Vancouver, Canada. His research focuses on risk management, disclosures, and corporate governance with a special interest in understanding financial institutions. Before his academic career, he worked in risk management at Bank of America-Merrill Lynch in New York. He earned his doctorate in accounting and management from Harvard Business School, Boston. He holds a BTech from the University of Madras, India, and a master of science from the Courant Institute of Mathematical Sciences, New York University.

TengTeng Xu is a senior economist in the Asia Pacific Department at the IMF, where she is a senior desk on the Japan team and mission chief for Nauru. Previously, she served as a senior desk on both the India and Bhutan teams. She participated in the Financial Sector Assessment Programs (FSAP) of Germany, Spain, and Poland in the Monetary and Capital Markets Department, including leading the risk analysis team for the Poland FSAP. She also worked on the IMF Program on Romania in the European Department. Prior to joining the IMF, Ms. Xu was a senior analyst in the International Economic Analysis Department at the Bank of Canada, covering China and Japan. She also worked at the Inter-American Development Bank, the Organisation for Economic Co-operation and Development (OECD), Goldman Sachs, and Morgan Stanley. She holds a PhD in Economics from the University of Cambridge, and an MPhil in Economics and a BA (First Class Honours) in Mathematics and Statistics from the University of Oxford.

Abbreviations

AUMs	assets under management
BIS	Bank for International Settlements
BRR	Business Responsibility Reporting
BRSR	Business Responsibility and Sustainability Report
CBDC	central bank digital currency
CD	certificate of deposit
CMIE	Centre for Monitoring Indian Economy
COVID-19	coronavirus disease 2019
DBIE	Database of Indian Economy
ECB	European Central Bank
EBIT	earnings before interest and taxes
EM	emerging market
ESG	environmental, social, and governance
FDI	foreign direct investment
FG	forward guidance
FY	fiscal year
GaR	growth-at-risk
GDP	gross domestic product
GVA	gross value added
IBC	Insolvency and Bankruptcy Code
IBBI	Insolvency and Bankruptcy Board of India
ICR	interest coverage ratio
IMF	International Monetary Fund
MPC	monetary policy committee
MSMEs	micro, small, and medium enterprises
NBFCs	nonbanking financial companies
NGFS	Network for Greening the Financial System
NPA	nonperforming asset
NPLs	nonperforming loans
OIS	overnight interest rate swap
PMJDY	Pradhan Mantri Jan Dhan Yojana
PSBs	public sector banks
RBI	Reserve Bank of India
Rs	rupees
SARFAESI	Securitisation and Reconstruction of Financial Assets and Enforcement of Securities Act
SEBI	Securities and Exchange Board of India
SD	standard deviation
TLTRO	targeted long-term refinancing operations
UNCITRAL	United Nations Commission on International Trade Law
UPI	Unified Payments Interface

PART I

Setting the Stage and Overview

CHAPTER 1

Macro-financial Setting and Overview

Alfred Schipke, Jarkko Turunen, Nada Choueiri, and Anne-Marie Gulde-Wolf

INTRODUCTION

India has experienced a prolonged period of strong economic growth since it embarked on major structural reforms and economic liberalization in 1991, with real GDP growth averaging about 6.6 percent during 1991–2019. Millions have been lifted out of poverty. With a population of 1.4 billion and about 7 percent of world economic output (in purchasing power parity terms), India is the third largest economy—after the US and China (see Annex Table 1.1.1, and Figure 1.1) and projected to be the most populous country in 2023 (see United Nations 2022). As such, developments in India have significant global and regional implications, including via spillovers through international trade and global supply chains. The Indian financial sector, the topic of the ten chapters in this volume,

Figure 1.1. India's Share of Global GDP
(Percent)

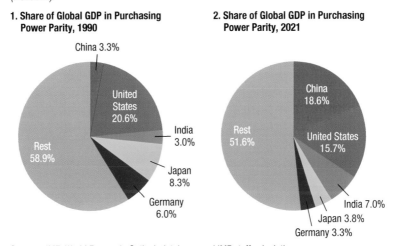

1. Share of Global GDP in Purchasing Power Parity, 1990

China 3.3%
United States 20.6%
India 3.0%
Japan 8.3%
Germany 6.0%
Rest 58.9%

2. Share of Global GDP in Purchasing Power Parity, 2021

China 18.6%
United States 15.7%
India 7.0%
Japan 3.8%
Germany 3.3%
Rest 51.6%

Sources: IMF, World Economic Outlook database; and IMF staff calculations.

plays a critical role in the country's economic development and has provided an important foundation for strong and sustainable economic growth over the past three decades.

At the same time, India's economic development has not been linear and has been impacted by external and domestic shocks, some directly related to the financial sector. Indeed, India was not spared from external regional and global shocks, such as the Asian financial crisis (1997), the global financial crisis (2008), and more recently, the devastating impact of the COVID-19 pandemic (from 2020) and the war in Ukraine (2022). The economy has also been hit by domestic shocks. These included, for example, a period of excessive bank credit growth resulting in misallocation of credit and a subsequent and much-needed tightening of banking regulation (2014 and 2015) and the broader financial sector fallout from the default of a few nonbanking financial companies (NBFCs) (2018) (see Figure 1.2).

Not all shocks to India's economy have been adverse, however. Economic development has been supported by important reforms, from increasing the role of the private sector in the banking sector (from 1993 onward) to the introduction of flexible inflation targeting and the Insolvency and Bankruptcy Code (IBC) (both in 2016). These reforms have contributed to financial deepening (see Figure 1.3) As such, the 30 years since 1991 highlight that even though external shocks are outside the direct control of domestic policymakers, continued structural reforms and maintaining the health of the financial sector are critically important for India's growth performance (see Annex Table 1.1.2).

Figure 1.2. Key Shocks and Reforms
(Credit and GDP growth, percent)

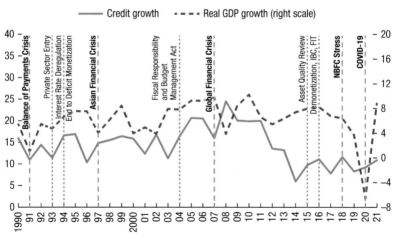

Sources: Country authorities; Haver Analytics; and IMF staff calculations.
Note: The data refer to total credit to the economy. Red vertical dashed lines refer to shocks and the light blue vertical dashed lines to reforms. FIT = Flexible Inflation Targeting; IBC = Insolvency and Bankruptcy Code; NBFC = nonbanking financial company.

Figure 1.3. Financial Deepening
(Credit to GDP, percent)

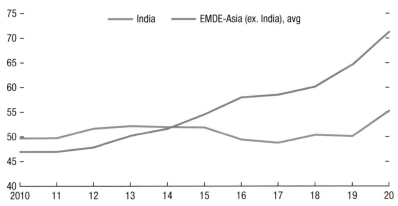

Source: World Bank, Global Financial Development Database.
Note: EMDE-Asia (ex. India) includes average of Bangladesh, Bhutan, Brunei Darussalam, Cambodia, China, Fiji, Indonesia, Japan, Malaysia, Maldives, Micronesia, Mongolia, Myanmar, Nepal, Papua New Guinea, Philippines, Solomon Islands, Sri Lanka, Timor-Leste, Tonga, Vanuatu, and Vietnam. 2019 does not include Micronesia, Sri Lanka, and Tonga. 2020 does not include Cambodia, Micronesia, Papua New Guinea, Sri Lanka, and Tonga. avg = average; EMDE = emerging market and developing economies; ex. = excluding.

Developments over the past few years illustrate this point. India's economy was already slowing prior to the COVID-19 pandemic, reflecting a decline in private sector demand. The pandemic and the initial, relatively stringent, lockdown caused a deep and broad-based economic downturn in 2020, followed by a further temporary slowdown in activity during the second pandemic wave in 2021, with potential for adverse social and longer lasting impact. To minimize the economic and social consequences of the pandemic shock, policymakers responded with fiscal support—including scaled-up support to vulnerable groups—wide-ranging monetary policy easing, liquidity provision, and accommodative financial sector and regulatory policies. Important financial sector measures included a temporary loan moratorium, financial support to firms through measures such as the Emergency Credit Line Guarantee Scheme, and the temporary suspension of firm resolution through the IBC (see Chapter 9 on addressing corporate sector vulnerabilities). Most pandemic-related support measures have by now expired.

The pandemic-related downturn has been followed by a strong rebound in economic activity, with output in most sectors (except for contact-intensive services) recovering to pre-pandemic levels by end-FY2021/22. Credit growth has increased, thus strengthening financial sector support to economic activity, and credit quality indicators have improved, reflecting stronger corporate and financial sector balance sheets. Despite the expiration of the pandemic-related support measures, banks have seen their nonperforming asset ratio decrease and capital ratio increase. The balance sheets of NBFCs have also improved.

India's long-term growth outlook is positive. Strong population growth in recent decades has delivered a young labor force with the promise of significant economic dividends. And India's lower-middle income status suggests the possibility of a significant catch-up in the years ahead. Realizing its medium-term growth potential (currently estimated at about 6 percent) and further growing that potential depend, however, on steadfast implementation of a broad structural reform agenda. For example, long-standing reform priorities include infrastructure investment to overcome bottlenecks, land and labor reforms, better governance, and improved education outcomes. Each of these will help maximize long-term growth. Structural reforms would need to be accompanied by a strengthening of social safety nets and adequate support to those that may be adversely impacted during the transition.

Alongside the above-mentioned reforms, further financial development and increasing financial sector efficiency and strength would also be needed to further expand India's growth potential. A well-functioning financial sector would help channel resources to their most productive uses, supporting the creation of physical capital and the buildup of human capital, thereby raising growth. This book digs deeper into the various facets of India's financial sector to understand its strengths and opportunities and to elicit policy actions that could help the financial sector better support India's growth potential.

INDIA'S FINANCIAL SYSTEM: AN OVERVIEW

In line with India's strong growth performance, the country's financial system has grown. At the same time, the structure of India's financial system has also changed, as reflected, among other things, in the growth of NBFCs, greater reliance on market-based financing, and the emergence of digital money and financing.

Financial intermediaries, especially public sector banks, still dominate India's financial system (see Figure 1.4). Twelve public sector banks accounted for 60 percent of total bank assets. The remaining 40 percent includes 22 domestic private sector banks and 46 foreign banks operating in India. There were also some 100,000 regional rural, urban cooperative, and rural cooperative banks, reflecting the regional diversity of the country.

Following the asset quality review and tightening of banking regulation in 2015 to deal with risks after years of strong bank credit growth, less regulated NBFCs grew rapidly. This resulted in NBFC credit growth in 2018 of about 30 percent, partly filling the gap created by slower bank credit growth.[1] Especially, micro, small, and medium enterprises (MSMEs) benefited from NBFC loans.

---

[1] As of January 2021, 9,507 NBFCs were registered with the Reserve Bank of India, of which 64 were deposit-taking (NBFCs-D) and 292 systemically non-deposit-taking NBFCs (NBFCs-ND-SI). Nonfood credit excludes credit provided (to state agencies) to ensure deep food distribution and is widely used to monitor credit growth in the Indian economy.

Figure 1.4. Financial Intermediaries
(Share of nominal GDP)

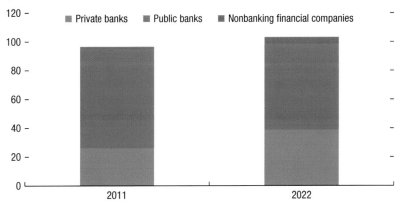

Sources: Haver Analytics; Reserve Bank of India; Statista; and IMF staff calculations.

In 2018, however, Infrastructure Leasing and Financial Services, a systemically important NBFC, defaulted, representing an important shock to the sector that led to further defaults and negative spillovers to the rest of the financial system and the real economy.[2] Since then, regulation and supervision has been tightened, with the new scale-based regulatory framework bringing regulation of NBFCs closer to bank regulation, especially for the 25–30 largest institutions. Given the nonsystemic position of smaller NBFCs and associated regulatory burden, the regulation for these institutions remains less onerous. The banking sector remains closely connected to, and has been an important source of financing for, the NBFC sector (see Chapter 3 on the development of bank and NBFC sectors). Ongoing NBFC regulatory reform agenda focuses on tighter capital, provisioning, and large exposure requirements for the largest NBFCs.

Market-based financing is also playing an increasingly important role in India's financial system. From a low base, the bond market has grown rapidly over the past 10 years and total outstanding debt amounted to about 80 percent of GDP at the end of 2021. The attractiveness of India's bond market for international investors has also increased, given the prospect of the inclusion of the country's bonds in global bond indices such as the Bloomberg, FTSE, and JPMorgan Chase & Co. bond indices, which by some estimates could lead to a passive inflow of $30–$40 billion.[3] While foreign bond holdings of 2 percent are currently low, that share could rise quickly, as China's inclusion in global bond indices a few years earlier has demonstrated. At the same time, the corporate debt market cur-

---

[2] Infrastructure Leasing and Financial Services default was followed by default of Dewan Housing Finance Corporation, resulting in broader concerns about the health of the NBFC sector as a whole.

[3] Estimates vary; see, for example, Morgan Stanley 2021: India: Primed for Bond Index Debut.

Figure 1.5. Outstanding Government and Corporate Debt Securities
(Percent of GDP)

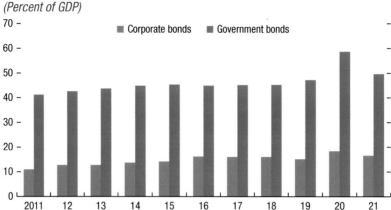

Sources: Haver Analytics; Ministry of Finance; Reserve Bank of India; and IMF staff calculations.
Note: Government bonds include market loans of state governments and union territories and marketable securities of central government.

rently accounting for about 18 percent of GDP still has a lot of room for development (see Chapter 5 on the development of the private debt market) (see Figures 1.5 and 1.6). India's equity market capitalization has also grown significantly, albeit with fluctuations, and recently became the fifth largest in the world in March 2022, after the US, China, Japan, Hong Kong SAR, and China, and ahead of the UK and Canada (see Figure 1.7).[4]

Measures of financial sector development, such as bank-credit-to-GDP ratios, equity market capitalization, and the value of outstanding bonds, however, do not fully capture India's financial sector development.[5] For example, measures to foster financial inclusion, including by strengthening the digital payment infrastructure, have significantly contributed to India's financial sector development. India has developed a sophisticated and efficient digital payments infrastructure. Among important innovations, the Unified Payments Interface, an interoperable payments platform, has fostered innovation and attracted the private sector with new technologies and products to different segments of the population, thus enhancing financial inclusion (see Chapter 7 on fintech and financial inclusion). Furthermore, the framework for payments is integrated into a broader digital platform that combines elements such as digital identity, data, and payments (known as the

---

[4] India breaks into world's top five club in terms of market capitalization | Business Standard News (business-standard.com), https://www.business-standard.com/article/markets/india-breaks-into-world-s -top-five-club-in-terms-of-market-capitalisation-122031200004_1.html#:~:text=India%27s%20 equity%20market%20has%20broken,and%20Canada%20(%243.18%20trillion).

[5] The discussion in this book does not cover a broader set of nonbanking financial companies, such as insurance companies, pension funds, and investment funds.

Figure 1.6. Outstanding Government and Corporate Debt Securities
(Percent of GDP)

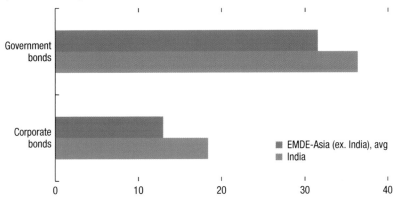

Sources: Haver Analytics; and IMF staff calculations.
Note: EMDE-Asia (ex. India) includes Bangladesh (2017), China (2021), Malaysia (2021), Philippines (2014), Thailand (2021), and Vietnam (2017). Data on India are for 2020. avg = average; EMDE = emerging market and developing economies; ex. = excluding.

Figure 1.7. Equity Market Capitalization
(Percent of GDP)

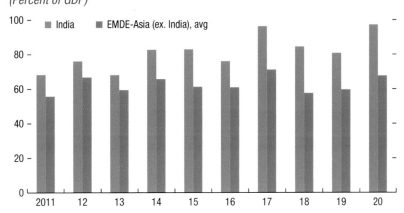

Sources: World Bank, World Development Indicators; and IMF staff calculations.
Note: EMDE-Asia (ex. India) includes Bangladesh, China, Indonesia, Malaysia, Philippines, Sri Lanka, Thailand, and Vietnam. avg = average; EMDE = emerging market and developing economies; ex. = excluding.

India Stack). Ongoing efforts, such as innovations that allow the use of low-tech cell phones to engage in financial transactions, will further strengthen financial inclusion. Progress has been achieved in a relatively short period of time, with strong synergies between the public and private sectors. Looking ahead, the Reserve Bank of India (RBI) is planning to begin the phased implementation of a central bank digital currency (CBDC) by March 2023, with potential to further enhance the digital payments landscape. More than 100 other countries are researching or piloting CBDCs in some manner. While CBDCs offer benefits, they may also raise risks, including risks to financial stability, so it is important to manage these risks with appropriate design of CBDC and within legal and regulatory systems that maximize its benefits and minimize its risks.

India's last financial sector assessment (FSAPs) in 2018 highlighted the rapidly changing structure and development of the system.[6] It also listed recommendations to (1) reduce vulnerabilities, (2) further strengthen the framework for financial sector oversight, and (3) foster market development. Since then, the country has made several advances in addressing the recommendations (see IMF 2018 and IMF 2021). For example, in the banking sector, the number of public sector banks was reduced from 20 to 12, and in 2021 the government announced plans to privatize two additional banks. Important progress has also been made in improving public sector bank governance; bank recapitalization; corporate debt restructuring; regulation, supervision, and oversight of financial market institutions; and crisis management.

In 2019, the government announced stronger governance measures allowing banks to recruit chief risk officers from the market, making management more accountable to boards of directors, increasing the role of externally appointed board directors, and increasing flexibility in adjusting compensation of management. To deal more effectively with nonperforming loans, new regulation was introduced in 2019 giving banks more flexibility in the loan resolution process, detailed restructuring schemes were reintroduced during COVID-19, and the authorities established National Assets Reconstruction Company Limited to deal with distressed assets (see Chapter 10 on strengthening private debt resolutions frameworks). Also, both public and private sector banks increased their capital. Despite these measures, the financial sector reform agenda remains substantial.

As in other countries, India's financial sector is also confronted with new challenges, including the impact of climate change and the need to adapt. Further digitalization of financial systems, in turn, brings many opportunities to build on progress in improving access to financial services to economically disadvantaged populations. Financial innovations and rapid financial sector development, however, also present continuous challenges for financial sector regulation and supervision, which constantly need to be upgraded to allow the healthy development of the financial sector while avoiding risk buildup.

STRENGTHENING INDIA'S FINANCIAL SYSTEM

What should be done to strengthen the financial system to support growth and reduce vulnerabilities? This book sets itself to answer that question through discussing the linkages between the financial sector and growth, how to improve

---

[6] IMF conducts FSAPs in G20 countries about every five years. The last FSAP was conducted in 2017 with the report published in January 2018. India's next assessment is currently planned for 2024.

bank lending to foster productivity, and measures to further develop India's corporate bond market. The book also reflects on India's success in leveraging digitalization to foster financial inclusion and highlights how the financial system can be helpful in addressing climate issues through the development of India's environmental, social, and governance (ESG) financial markets.

Chapter 2 discusses linkages between India's financial sector and growth. A country's financial sector plays a key role in the allocation of scarce resources and impacts the economy in the short and long term. Economic fluctuations can be amplified and directly linked to the financial sector given relationships (comovements) among credit, asset prices, and the real economy. Also, the health of the banking sector can constrain bank lending. Having a good understanding of these relationships can guide policymakers in increasing financial sector resilience and reducing bottlenecks to foster economic growth.

Two approaches are used to analyze the linkages between India's financial sector and growth. The first approach uses a framework—Growth-at-Risk—to relate contemporaneous macro-financial variables to future growth. The results suggest that higher credit and lower nonperforming loans are associated with higher real GDP growth. In fact, a negative shock to credit and leverage could imply lower growth in the short and medium term, as well as higher tail risks. Furthermore, policies to support credit growth and to strengthen balance sheets would be particularly important during periods of low economic growth.

The second approach focuses on whether bank capitalization plays a role in determining banks' ability to provide credit to the economy. Indeed, the results suggest that the level of capitalization is critical for credit and thus economic growth, especially for private sector banks. The relationship is weaker, however, for public sector banks, possibly reflecting a perception of implicit guarantees—that is, the government would step in to bail those banks out—as well as directed lending.

Both approaches, however, highlight the importance of resolving nonperforming loans (the focus of Chapter 10 on strengthening private debt resolution frameworks) and strengthening capital buffers to foster credit growth and, ultimately, real economic growth.

Chapter 3 discusses financial sector development and presents an overview of nonbanking financial companies. The importance of public sector banks in India's financial sector goes back to the nationalizations of 1969 and 1980. Since then, public sector banks have played a key role in the sector, including support for lending to priority sectors and efforts to foster financial inclusion. Following strong credit growth during the 2000s related to corporate lending to support infrastructure—which continued throughout the 2008 global financial crisis when domestic private and foreign bank credit growth slowed—public sector bank asset quality started to deteriorate. The RBI's Asset Quality Review in 2015 led to a sharp increase in nonperforming loans, a deceleration in credit growth, and a decline in profitability and capital. Subsequent banking reforms and recapitalizations facilitated balance sheet cleanup and mergers, which saw the number of public sector banks decline from 27 to 12.

The tightening of bank regulation and a slowdown in bank credit growth during the first half of the 2010s in turn were associated with regulatory arbitrage and a surge in lending by NBFCs. In 2021, the almost 10,000 NBFCs accounted for about 25 percent of commercial bank loans. NBFCs tend to rely more on bank borrowing and market funding. Given their specialization within a few loan segments, including real estate and infrastructure, NBFCs have less-diversified portfolios. Most NBFCs are private, while government-owned entities account for about 40 percent of assets.

The default of two NBFCs in 2018 highlighted the risk of spillovers and contagion, with negative feedback loops from NBFCs to financial intermediaries, a credit crunch, corporate defaults, and subsequent further weakening of NBFC balance sheets. Since 2019 and the subsequent COVID-19 shock, the RBI has taken steps to strengthen NBFC regulation and supervision. These included guidelines to enhance liquidity risk management and the introduction of a scale-based framework classifying NBFCs by characteristic, including size and whether they were deposit taking. This led to a regulatory convergence between banks and certain types of NBFCs. Given that today NBFCs play an important role in the financial sector, including financing to segments of micro, small, and medium-size enterprises, it is important to increase the resilience of NBFCs and to minimize potential spillovers to the banking sector. This calls for further strengthening of regulation to facilitate diversification of NBFC funding sources as well as limits on bank borrowing by NBFCs.

Chapter 4 examines whether banks deliver on their mandate to channel credit to productive activities. To maximize India's long-term growth potential, efficient allocation of factors of production (capital and labor) is paramount. Indeed, income and productivity gaps between advanced and emerging economies are frequently attributed to capital misallocation and related factors. Given the large role of banks in India's financial system, it is thus important to understand whether bank credit flows to the most productive sectors and firms.

Because India's banking sector is dominated by public sector banks, the empirical analysis focuses on the link between credit growth, firm productivity, and bank ownership. It uses firm-level data from the Centre for Monitoring Indian Economy's Prowess database and bank-level financial information from the Reserve Bank of India's Database on Indian Economy from 2005 to 2020. Key variables of interest include the stock of bank credit and sales scaled by physical capital (plant, property, and equipment) to measure firm capital productivity. The regression analysis controls for firm size, age, sector, asset quality, interest coverage, leverage, and whether banks are owned privately or publicly.

The analysis reveals that the link between productivity and bank credit growth is weaker for firms with significant ties to public sector banks, especially in years when public sector banks represent a large share of new credit. These results are driven by large firms, which account for the lion's share of credit in India. Large flows of credit to unproductive firms represent important missed growth opportunities for more productive firms. These insights suggest that in addition to important policies to strengthen India's public sector banks—such as continued recapitalization and the establishment of the National Asset Reconstruction Company Limited to alleviate problems with bad loans—further bank privatization, as envisaged by the government, and measures to improve governance of public sector banks would be important to reduce capital misallocation.

Chapter 5 takes a close look at India's corporate debt market. India's financial system is still largely bank based, and further reforming the banking system by improving governance and privatizing banks will foster access to credit to underserved sectors and companies. At the same time, India's capital markets are increasingly important in allocating savings and investment. Its corporate bond market in particular still has significant room to develop, which would increase competition, foster access to long-term financing, allow better risk management, and support lending to innovative sectors.

Government bonds accounted for 68 percent of the fixed-income market in 2021 and corporate bonds accounted for 20 percent. Prior to the failure of an NBFC in 2018 and the ensuing credit squeeze, and before the COVID-19 shock in 2020, the corporate bond market grew at an average annual rate of 17 percent (2011–18). The uncertainty triggered by these two shocks and the significant increase in issuance of government debt, however, contributed to a decline in corporate bond issuance as a share of the total fixed-income market in 2019 and 2020.

The Indian corporate bond market has several features that are worth mentioning. It is dominated by private placements rather than by public offerings. Smaller firms especially are likely to be challenged in meeting disclosure requirements for public issuance and listing of their debt and greater difficulties in absorbing the implied cost of credit rating agencies. Yet at the same time, concentration risk seems to have increased, in that larger issues are becoming more systemic. While the COVID-19 pandemic led to an unsurprising shortening of maturities, average maturities had increased in the decade leading up to the pandemic. India's bond market is dominated by local currency issuance (70 percent), but offshore issuance has been rising steadily, broadly in line with other emerging markets.

While much progress has been made over the past decade in strengthening legal and regulatory frameworks, scope exists for further improvements, including on implementation and enforcement. The corporate bond market would particularly benefit from better creditor rights, stronger market and rating infrastructures, measures to improve bond liquidity and credit risk management, and efforts to broaden the investor base.[7]

Looking at the sectors for corporate bond issuance highlights the potential for India's bond market to support growth. Almost 70 percent of all corporate bond issuance now takes place in the financial sector and, even within the industrial sector, almost 90 percent of issuance is related to financial services such as banking and housing finance. Hence, the potential for the nonfinancial sector to grow is large both in absolute and relative terms. Comparisons with emerging market peers also suggest significant potential for the market to grow. Further developing India's corporate bond market will increase access to finance and foster economic growth.

---

[7] In January 2023, the RBI issued its inaugural sovereign green bond in local currency raising about $1 billion.

Chapter 6 documents the evolution of green finance in India. Climate change is anticipated to have large economic and social costs, calling for policymakers and the private sector to react decisively in adapting to and mitigating its impacts. For the financial sector, climate-related events can undermine stability, yet the sector can also play a critical role in channeling resources to sustainable sectors. By considering ESG factors, for example, asset managers can be crucial to efforts combatting climate change and reducing carbon footprints. Although efforts to promote ESG in finance started some three decades ago, they have accelerated over the past few years, including in India.

India is highly vulnerable to the effects of climate change. In 2022, India pledged to reduce the emissions intensity of its GDP—that is, the amount of emissions produced per unit of output—by 45 percent by 2030 (from 2005 levels) and to achieve carbon neutrality by 2070. In this context, India's ESG market (equity and bonds) could play an important role in helping finance climate mitigation efforts. While ESG-related bond issuance surged in 2021, it is still only a small fraction of India's total bond issuance (accounting for about 2 percent). The same is true for assets under management of ESG-related equity funds. Within the universe of ESG bonds, green bonds accounted for 80 percent of issuance in 2019–2021, while social and sustainability-linked bonds accounted for the remaining 20 percent, a share that is broadly in line with other emerging markets. About 90 percent of Indian green bonds are issued in US dollars, which compares to 60 percent in other emerging markets (excluding China and India). This is quite notable given that, for the overall corporate bond market, most bonds are issued in local currency. In addition, Indian green bonds tend to have shorter maturities and higher coupon rates than other emerging markets, reflecting the weaker fundamentals of corporates (i.e., lower credit ratings) and more limited investor base.

How can India deepen and broaden the development of the sustainable finance market? Promoting the adoption of principles, in line with the International Capital Market Association green bond principles, would provide information about the environmental impact of investment. Critically important is the availability of reliable data for financial sector stakeholders to assess financial stability risk, properly price and manage ESG-related risks, and take advantage of opportunities arising from the transition to a green economy. Guidelines issued by the Securities and Exchange Board of India are likely to address some of the issues related to disclosure, such as India's relatively low ESG disclosure score (25 percent compared to 40 percent in the US).

Chapter 7 presents India's impressive progress in advancing financial inclusion, largely aided by digitalization. Both the theoretical and empirical literature suggests that financial inclusion—improved access to finance via payment systems, loans, savings, insurance, and wealth management—helps boost economic growth and reduce inequality. In this, India is a useful case study in how to leverage digital technology to foster financial inclusion and thus economic growth.

As recently as 2011 only 35 percent of the population had bank accounts, significantly below the average of other emerging markets. However, several important policies focusing on digitalization changed this significantly. Some of the measures included the following:

1. Introducing a biometric digital identification system (Aadhaar) in 2010

2. Rolling out a scheme to provide all households with bank accounts with convenient access through a debit card (RuPay) in 2014 (called Pradhan Mantri Jan Dhan Yojana or PMJDY, which in turn could be linked to Aadhaar and was subsequently also used for the transfer of government social benefits)

3. Launching the Unified Payments Interface in 2016, allowing interoperable and real-time interbank transactions through various payment platforms

The large scale and low unit cost of operating Aadhaar led to the enrollment of 1 billion people and increased access to financing. The PMJDY scheme has resulted in more than 450 million new bank accounts (33 percent of the population).

Despite the progress, the reform agenda remains large. A large share of the population, especially those who are economically disadvantaged and those in rural areas, still do not have access to financial services, and usage remains a major challenge. Based on the IMF Financial Access Survey, India had among the lowest mobile and internet transactions and debit card use among peers in Asia and the Pacific region in 2020.[8] A Reserve Bank of India subindex also shows low usage of digital services and limited progress for the period 2017–2021. A likely factor here is the lack of financial and digital literacy. Also, the digital divide remains large: men are more likely to own mobile phones than women (20 percentage points), digital penetration is largely limited to urban areas, and almost 57 percent of the poorest households do not own a smartphone. Estimates suggest that an increase in the adoption of digital financial payments to the level in China, for example, could increase India's GDP per capita by 3–4 percentage points. The impact is likely even greater given that other components of digital finance (such as savings, credit, and insurance) could positively impact growth.

Hence, it is of paramount importance to continue efforts to ensure equal access to digital infrastructure and to support reforms to foster usage, including by improving financial and digital literacy. These need to go hand in hand with the strengthening of policy frameworks for digital finance, including consumer protection, data privacy, and cybersecurity, to ensure financial stability.

LINKAGES AND SUPPORTING REFORMS

Apart from reducing financial sector vulnerabilities, increasing the system's resilience, and fostering its development, an efficient allocation of savings and investment calls for supporting reforms. These include measures to reduce vulnerabilities that originate in the private sector and the resolution of debt overhangs stemming from private companies and households. Also, to reduce financial market

---

[8] This may reflect in part the use of the Unified Payments Interface, which facilitates payments, for example, by scanning QR codes.

volatility, it is important to have a good understanding of spillovers and the role of policy frameworks, including monetary policy communication.

Chapter 8 reviews trends and risks in capital flows. Given India's still relatively low per-capita income, favorable growth prospects, demographic trends, and development needs, the country continues to benefit from foreign capital inflows supplementing domestic investment and allowing households to smooth consumption. Stable capital inflows can also alleviate any funding pressure stemming from higher COVID-19-related public debt levels.

Initially, India has been gradually focusing capital account liberalization on foreign direct investment (FDI) and equity. Recent FDI and portfolio inflows into equity markets have amounted to about 2.5 percent of GDP annually[9] and have been historically less volatile than regional peers. At the same time, foreign inflows into debt markets remain relatively small compared with peers. More recently though, authorities have gradually eased restrictions on debt flows, accompanied by more favorable investment regimes for government and corporate debt. The prospect of India's inclusion in global bond indices could lead to sizable passive inflows, with additional scope for ESG-related inflows.

Although capital inflows can bring benefits, they could also carry risks given that portfolio flows are more volatile and susceptible to changes in global risk appetite, with implications for financial system stability. Surges in inflows can arise during domestic credit booms and asset price bubbles. Sudden reversals in turn can lead to abrupt financial sector tightening, lower asset prices, and tighter bank lending conditions. Indeed, India has experienced episodes of strong inflows and sharp reversals, such as during the 2008 global financial crisis, the 2013 taper tantrum, the 2020 COVID-19 shock, and in 2022 the impact of the war in Ukraine and tightening on global financial conditions. Thus, it is important to analyze the level of flows as well as the cycle, that is, the nature of "extreme" flows, especially because domestic and external shocks impact them differently. Signs exist that since the global financial crisis, capital flow cycles in India have shortened and have been associated with greater capital flow volatility.

While some degree of capital flow volatility is unavoidable in times of shocks or stress, policies can help contain such volatility. To minimize adverse spillovers from external shocks, it is crucial that the authorities continue to strengthen domestic policy frameworks and communication about the direction of reforms and policies. For example, a clearly communicated medium-term fiscal consolidation strategy combined with enhancements in expenditure efficiency, improved public financial management, and revenue-enhancing measures, as well as the privatization agenda, would foster confidence in the financial markets. The government's plans to liberalize FDI policies related to strategic sectors are important steps to attract stable capital inflows. Finally, monetary policy communication, which can enhance the RBI's policy toolkit, improve predictability, and reduce uncertainties (see below) can also help.

---

[9] As reflected in the IMF External Sector Assessment (IMF 2021), current account deficits of about 2.5 percent of GDP should be financeable over time.

To assess the resilience of a financial system, it is useful to analyze the impacts of shocks via macro-financial linkages. *Chapter 9 takes a closer look at the corporate sector, which lies at the center of these linkages.* Here, stress testing the corporate sector can play a critical role. For example, the COVID-19 pandemic and related lockdowns and social distancing measures constituted a severe shock to corporate sector balance sheets and hence to the financial system. Such analysis can identify areas for reforms and provide insights into calibrating policies to maximize benefits while minimizing adverse implications in the future.

Following the 2008 global financial crisis and prior to the COVID-19 pandemic, India's corporate sector went through a gradual deleveraging process, with improvement in profitability. The median return on assets, for example, improved from 0.9 percent in 2009 to 2.2 percent in 2019. At the same time, the median interest coverage ratio increased to 2.8, almost reaching levels seen before the global financial crisis. The improvement was most noticeable in the manufacturing and contact-intensive trade, transport, and hospitality service sectors. By firm size, however, profits among micro firms (with sales below 50 million rupees) were persistently low throughout the period.

To assess the COVID-19 impact on the corporate sector, a series of sensitivity and stress tests (baseline, moderately adverse, and severely adverse) was conducted. The stress tests highlighted that without borrower relief measures and monetary easing, the COVID-19 shock would have led to a significant increase in the share of corporate debt issued by firms with earnings insufficient to cover their debt interest payments (that is, with an interest coverage ratio below 1). Sectors most affected include construction, manufacturing, and contact-intensive trade, transport, and hospitality services. The share of debt among micro, small, and medium enterprises with an interest coverage ratio below 1, consistent with their weaker pre-pandemic liquidity positions, would have increased more than large firms under the baseline and two adverse scenarios. Forward-looking multiyear analysis suggests that the overall impact of the COVID-19 shock would crucially depend on the speed of the economic recovery.

Borrower relief measures to firms and monetary easing provided in 2020 are found to have been effective in mitigating the liquidity impact of the COVID-19 shock. At the same time, the effects of policy measures on corporate solvency are found to be less pronounced, reflecting the focus of the implemented policy measures on supporting corporate liquidity.

Corporate stress could have a sizable impact on bank and nonbanking financial companies' balance sheets, particularly on public sector banks, due to their relatively weak starting capital positions. The results show that the policy support measures taken by the government have played an important role in mitigating the impact of the pandemic on the financial sector.

Chapter 10 looks at ways to strengthen private debt resolution frameworks. Effective resolution frameworks for corporate and household debt are particularly important for the financial system to ensure efficient allocation of credit and financial sector stability. Given that investment decisions are made under uncertainty and an economy can be hit by unanticipated shocks such as the COVID-19 pandemic, it is critically important to have frameworks in place that deal with issues of overindebtedness expeditiously to minimize costs and maximize reallocation of scarce economic resources to their most productive uses.

Such frameworks usually include procedures for debt enforcement, restructuring, and liquidation. They can be in the form of: (1) *in-court processes*, that is, through judicial supervision of creditors and debtors; (2) *out-of-court* debt restructurings that provide greater flexibility, are cheaper, and require voluntary compromises between parties; (3) *enhanced out-of-court* procedures, which use mechanisms such as creditor committees and arbitration/mediation under ex-ante framework agreements to facilitate the restructuring; and (4) *hybrid* procedures, which provide for negotiations and majority voting to take place out of court, with a plan then submitted for judicial ratification at the final stage.

The establishment of the IBC in 2016 was a milestone aimed at modernizing India's insolvency procedures. This has been complemented with the more recent introduction of the so-called "pre-pack" insolvency process, designed to address the overindebtedness of MSMEs. Prior to these reforms, India only had an antiquated and fragmentary insolvency legislation. As a result, debt recovery was time consuming, expensive, uncertain, and prone to abuse by debtors, hindering bank lending and depriving small and medium enterprises of credit. Also, in the case of a default, creditors had incentives to evergreen loans or to enforce collateral without any assessment of the viability of the debtor's business. Bank officials hesitated to write down loans out of fear of liability under anticorruption laws. Key components of the IBC are consistent with international best practices, and it has also introduced important improvements in the institutional framework, such as the establishment of an insolvency regulator as well as professional agencies and specialized commercial courts.

A number of areas can be strengthened further.[10] These include encouraging the use of out-of-court processes, especially for cases that require only adjustments of debt. For in-court restructurings, current timelines for corporate resolutions are ambitious and need additional resources and adjustments to be observed. Also, the corporate resolution process should include mechanisms for the participation of operational creditors and ensure that creditors are classified according to their position in the hierarchy of claims. These changes would also result in better decision making over resolution plans and more effective safeguards for dissenting minorities. In the institutional framework, a key component is staffing and capacity development, including filling vacancies at the National Company Law and the National Company Law Appellate Tribunals, increasing the number of insolvency judges, and specialized training for judges and court officials. Further reform could be beneficial for micro and small enterprises, since pre-pack processes only cover incorporated MSMEs. The implementation of insolvency procedures for natural persons should include provisions for both unincorporated MSMEs and consumer debtors.

---

[10] As this book went to press, the Ministry of Corporate Affairs had released a proposal to make the insolvency regime significantly more efficient and transparent.

Chapter 11 examines the impact of RBI's monetary policy communications on financial markets. Financial markets provide important information to policymakers about market expectations and are an important conduit of monetary policy signals to the real economy. Reforms that improve the functioning of financial markets will therefore make macroeconomic management more effective. In this, monetary policy communication can play an important role in reducing market volatility, which in turn makes financial markets more attractive to savers and investors.

Forward-looking monetary policy communication has become a key element of flexible inflation-targeting regimes across advanced and emerging market economies. In India, the RBI's flexible inflation targeting framework, introduced in 2016, has been associated with improved anchoring of inflation expectations and more predictable monetary policy. A set of communication tools, including monetary policy statements and minutes, press releases, and the governor's press conference, supports the RBI's implementation of this framework, aided by policy innovations such as forward guidance on policy rates and, more recently, asset purchases.

Indeed, a review of recent innovations in monetary policy communications suggests forward guidance on the monetary policy stance likely helped moderate uncertainty and support some asset prices during the pandemic. For example, the RBI's monetary policy committee decision on October 9, 2020 and the governor's statement on forward guidance, which introduced time-based forward guidance about the duration of the accommodative stance, contributed to a decline in 10-year rates on the same day. In line with the results for other emerging markets, the relationship between monetary policy surprises and yields for government and corporate securities across all maturities is found to be positive and statistically significant in India, but it is less so for exchange rate and equity prices.

The results support an important role for monetary policy communication in guiding market expectations about the role of policies impacting market liquidity and the central bank balance sheet, as well as the likely path of policy interest rates. At the same time, as in other emerging market economies, room exists to further refine communication tools, including forward-looking communication about the economic outlook and the RBI's policy reaction function. Monetary policy communication can and should help calibrate policy normalization amid the ongoing economic recovery and elevated domestic and global inflationary pressures.

CONCLUSION

India's economy expanded rapidly for long periods since it began a reform drive back in 1991. And even though growth had already slowed prior to the COVID-19 shock and was hit hard by the pandemic and corresponding severe lockdowns, India's economy is rebounding and its growth potential remains high. To fully realize this potential, the financial sector will play a critical role. The following chapters analyze key financial sector issues in depth to highlight progress made and identify important reform areas to foster growth.

ANNEX 1.1. SELECTED ECONOMIC AND FINANCIAL SECTOR INDICATORS

ANNEX TABLE 1.1.1.

India: Selected Economic Indicators, 1980/81–2021/22

Population (2020/21): 1.39 billion
Per capita GDP (2020/21 estimate): 2136 USD
Literacy rate (2018): 74.37%
Poverty rate $1.90 a day PPP (2011): 22.5%
Main products and exports: Petroleum, chemical and primary products, business and IT services.
Key export markets: EU, US, United Arab Emirates, China, Singapore, and Saudi Arabia.

Fiscal Year[1]	1980/81	1990/91	2000/01	2010/11	2018/19	2019/20	2020/21	2021/22
Output								
Real GDP growth (%)	5.3	5.5	4.0	10.3	6.5	3.9	−5.8	9.1
Prices								
Inflation, CPI-Combined (%)	11.3	11.2	3.8	10.5	3.4	4.8	6.2	5.5
General Government Finances								
Fiscal balance (% of GDP)			−8.3	−8.6	−6.4	−7.1	−12.9	−9.6
Public debt (% of GDP)			73.6	66.4	70.4	75.0	88.5	84.7
Money and Credit								
Broad money (% change)		15.1	16.8	16.1	10.5	8.9	12.2	8.8
Domestic credit (% change)		16.0	15.9	19.9	11.7	8.3	9.5	9.0
Credit to the private sector (% change)		13.2	15.8	21.3	12.7	6.3	5.7	8.1
Three-month Treasury bill interest rate (%)			8.7	5.0	6.1	4.4	3.3	3.8
Balance of Payments								
Current account (% of GDP)	−1.5	−2.9	−0.6	−2.8	−2.1	−0.9	0.9	−1.2
FDI, net inflow (% of GDP)	0.0	0.0	−0.7	−0.7	−1.1	−1.5	−1.6	−1.2
Reserves (months of imports)		2.8	7.3	6.3	8.2	11.1	9.0	8.1
Exchange Rate								
REER (% change)		−9.7	2.4	13.9	−4.6	3.1	−0.8	0.3

Sources: Bloomberg L.P.; CEIC Data Company Ltd; data provided by the Indian authorities; Haver Analytics; World Bank, World Development Indicators; and IMF staff estimates.
Note: CPI = consumer price index; FDI = foreign direct investment; REER = real effective exchange rate.
[1] Fiscal year is April to March (e.g., 2019/20 = Apr. 2019 to Mar. 2020).

ANNEX TABLE 1.1.2.

India: Financial Soundness Indicators, 2014/15–2020/21
(Percent, unless indicated otherwise)

	2014/15	2015/16	2016/17	2017/18	2018/19	2019/20	2020/21
I. Scheduled Commercial Banks							
Risk-Weighted Capital Adequacy Ratio (CAR)	**12.9**	**13.3**	**13.6**	**13.8**	**14.3**	**14.7**	**16.3**
Public sector banks	11.4	11.8	12.1	11.7	12.2	12.9	14
Private sector banks	15.1	15.7	15.5	16.4	16.3	16.5	18.4
Foreign banks	16.8	17.1	18.7	18.6	18.5	17.7	19.5
Number of Institutions Not Meeting 9 Percent CAR	**0.0**	**1.0**	**1.0**	**1.0**	**1.0**	**3.0**	**1**
Public sector banks	0.0	0.0	1.0	1.0	0.0	1.0	N/A
Private sector banks	0.0	1.0	0.0	0.0	1.0	2.0	N/A
Foreign banks	0.0	0.0	0.0	0.0	0.0	0.0	N/A
Net Nonperforming Assets (percent of outstanding net advances)[1]	**2.4**	**4.4**	**5.3**	**6.1**	**3.8**	**2.9**	**2.4**
Public sector banks	3.0	5.7	6.9	8.6	5.2	4.0	3.1
Private sector banks	0.8	1.4	2.2	2.0	1.6	1.4	1.4
Foreign banks	0.5	0.8	0.6	0.4	0.5	0.5	0.8
Gross Nonperforming Assets (percent of outstanding advances)	**4.3**	**7.5**	**9.6**	**11.5**	**9.3**	**8.4**	**7.3**
Public sector banks	5.0	9.3	12.5	15.6	12.6	10.8	9.1
Private sector banks	2.1	2.8	4.1	4.0	3.7	5.1	4.8
Foreign banks	3.2	4.2	4.0	3.8	3.0	2.3	3.6
Restructured Loans (percent of outstanding loans)[3]	**5.8**	**3.4**	**2.5**	**0.9**	**0.4**	...	**0.9**
Public sector banks	7.1	4.1	3.1	1.1	0.5	...	0.9
Private sector banks	2.4	1.8	1.1	0.4	0.2	...	0.8
Foreign banks	0.1	0.3	0.3	0.1	0.0	...	1.1
Return on Assets[2]	**0.8**	**0.4**	**0.4**	**−0.2**	**−0.1**	**0.2**	**0.7**
Public sector banks	0.5	−0.1	−0.1	−0.9	−0.9	−0.2	0.3
Private sector banks	1.7	1.5	1.3	1.3	1.2	0.7	1.2
Foreign banks	1.9	1.5	1.6	1.3	1.6	1.4	1.0
Balance Sheet Structure of All Scheduled Banks							
Total assets (percent of GDP)	96.5	95.3	92.3	89.2	87.3	88.6	90.8
Loan/deposit ratio	78.3	78.2	73.0	74.2	75.3	73.7	69.5
Investment in government securities/deposit ratio	25.9	26.8	26.3	27.9	26.5	27.8	28.9
II. Nonbanking Financial Companies[4]							
Total assets (percent of GDP)	...	...	13.5	14.3	15.1	16.6	15.5
Risk-weighted CAR	26.2	24.3	22.1	22.8	20.1	23.7	25.0
Gross nonperforming assets (percent of outstanding advances)	4.1	4.5	6.1	5.8	6.1	6.8	6.4
Net nonperforming assets (percent of outstanding net advances)[1]	2.5	2.5	4.4	3.8	3.3	3.4	2.7
Return on assets[2]	2.2	2.1	1.8	1.7	1.7	1.3	1.3

Sources: Bankscope; Reserve Bank of India; and IMF staff estimates.
Note: N/A = not available.
[1] Gross nonperforming assets less provisions.
[2] Net profit (+)/loss (−) in percent of total assets. Data for 2020/21 for NBFCs is as of September 2020.
[3] Data for 2020/21 are as of July 2021.
[4] As of July 31, 2022, there were 9,640 nonbanking financial companies (NBFCs), of which 49 were deposit-taking (NBFCs-D) and 415 systemically non-deposit-taking NBFCs (NBFCs-ND-SI).

REFERENCES

International Monetary Fund (IMF). 2018. *Financial System Stability Assessment.* Washington, DC.

International Monetary Fund (IMF). 2021. *India. Staff Report for the 2021 Article IV Consultation.* Washington, DC.

Morgan Stanley. 2021. "India: Primed for Bond Index Debut." October 13, 2021. https://www.morganstanley.com/ideas/india-global-bond-indices

United Nations (UN). 2022. World Population Prospects 2022. https://www.un.org/development/desa/pd/content/World-Population-Prospects-2022

CHAPTER 2

Financial Sector and Economic Growth

Margaux MacDonald and TengTeng Xu

INTRODUCTION

India's financial sector has faced many challenges in recent decades, including a rapid increase in nonperforming assets (referred to hereafter as nonperforming loans, NPLs) after the global financial crisis and the 2018–19 run on nonbanking financial companies. At the same time, credit growth has been weak for some time, with a large, negative, and *persistent* credit-to-gross-domestic-product (GDP) gap since 2012. Just as the balance sheets of the financial sector started to gradually improve, the COVID-19 shock hit the economy, raising concerns about a new wave of NPLs and corporate defaults.

This chapter examines the nexus between the financial sector in India and economic growth and analyzes the potential impact of financial sector weakness on India's economic growth and development. The financial sector could affect economic growth through multiple channels, with both cyclical and long-term effects. This chapter focuses on these two channels and abstracts from the question of whether financial sector development is important for growth.[1] Specifically, this chapter first examines how cyclical financial conditions affect GDP growth using a growth-at-risk (GaR) approach (Adrian, Boyarchenko, and Giannone 2019) and assesses how financial conditions and credit risks could be associated with expected GDP growth going forward. Second, the chapter analyzes the link among bank balance sheets, credit growth, and long-term growth using bank-level panel regressions for both public sector and private banks accounting for about 85 percent of total banking sector assets.

This chapter is related to two strands of literature on financial sector and economic growth. The first strand examines the cyclical perspective. Adrian, Boyarchenko, and Giannone (2019), Adrian and others (2018), Prasad and others (2019), and the October 2017 *Global Financial Stability Report* applied the GaR approach to use the information content of financial indicators to forecast risks to growth. Both fast-moving asset prices and slow-moving credit aggregates were found to be useful predictors of

We thank Faisal Ahmed, Marco Casiraghi, Nada Choueiri, Anne-Marie Gulde-Wolf, Romain Lafarguette, Alfred Schipke, Sergio Sola, John Spray, Priscilla Toffano, Jarkko Turunen, and seminar participants from the RBI and the IMF's Asia and Pacific Department for useful feedback. Ankita Goel provided excellent research assistance. All remaining errors are our own.

[1] For a discussion of this broader topic, see Demirgüç-Kunt and Levine (2018) and references therein.

future output growth. For example, Ang, Piazzesi, and Wei (2006) highlighted the importance of the yield curve, particularly short rate, in predicting GDP growth. Goodhart and Hofmann (2008) assessed the linkages among credit, money, house prices, and economic activity in 17 industrialized countries over the last three decades and found that shocks to credit have significant repercussions on economic activity. Furthermore, recessions associated with financial crises are shown to have more severe and prolonged impact on the economy than typical recessions (see, e.g., Claessens, Kose, and Terrones 2011a, 2011b). The second strand of the literature examines the link between the health of the banking sector and real growth. For example, Levine (2005) found that countries with large, privately owned banks tend to channel credit to private enterprises and liquid stock exchanges and experience faster economic growth. Using balance sheet data for international banks from a range of advanced economies, Gambacorta and Shin (2016) and Muduli and Behera (2021) showed that well-capitalized banks enjoy lower costs of debt financing compared with more lever-aged competitors, which in turn translates into higher annual credit growth and can impact monetary policy transmission.

The chapter is organized as follows. The first section examines the link between cyclical financial conditions and growth. The second section analyzes the link between financial sector and long-term growth. The final section offers some concluding remarks.

CYCLICAL FINANCIAL CONDITIONS AND NEAR-TERM GROWTH

Data and Stylized Facts

A quarterly database is constructed for macro-financial data for India from the first quarter of 2000 to the third quarter of 2021. The database covers key macro-financial variables, covering GDP growth, inflation, policy rate, bond yields, sovereign spreads, stock prices, credit growth, credit gap, the NPL ratio, world growth, oil prices, exchange rates, and so forth. The database draws from multiple sources, including Haver Analytics, Reserve Bank of India (RBI), Central Statistics Office, International Monetary Fund, Bank of International Settlements, Ministry of Statistics and Programme Implementation, Bombay Stock Exchange, Energy Information Administration/Chicago Mercantile Exchange, and Bloomberg. The detailed definition of the underlying data and sources can be found in Annex Table 2.1.1.

The analysis focuses on the broad definition of credit that covers both bank credit and debt securities. The credit-to-GDP ratio peaked at around 106 percent in 2012 and declined to around 90 percent in 2021, while the bank credit-to-GDP ratio currently stands at around 55 percent. Following a period of double-digit credit growth, the credit-to-GDP gap[2] turned negative from 2012 (Figure 2.1). The decline in credit since 2012 was mostly driven by the deleveraging process of

---

[2] The credit-to-GDP gap is based on BIS calculations, defined as the difference between the credit-to-GDP ratio and its long-term trend. According to the BIS, the long-term trend is computed using a one-side Hodrick-Prescott filter with lambda equal to 400,000, as credit cycles are on average longer than standard business cycles. For detailed methodology, please see https://www.bis.org/publ/qtrpdf/r_qt1609c.htm.

Figure 2.1. Credit and Leverage
(Percent)

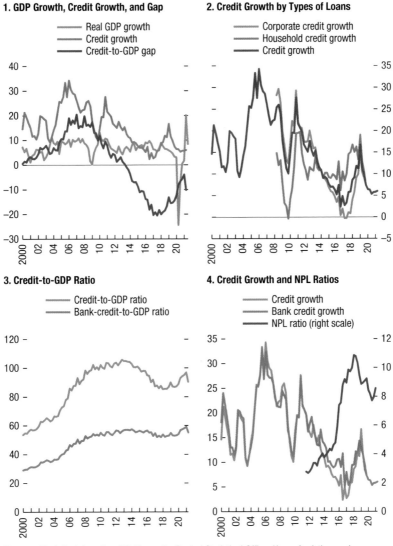

1. GDP Growth, Credit Growth, and Gap

Real GDP growth
Credit growth
Credit-to-GDP gap

2. Credit Growth by Types of Loans

Corporate credit growth
Household credit growth
Credit growth

3. Credit-to-GDP Ratio

Credit-to-GDP ratio
Bank-credit-to-GDP ratio

4. Credit Growth and NPL Ratios

Credit growth
Bank credit growth
NPL ratio (right scale)

Sources: Bank for International Settlements; Central Statistical Office; Haver Analytics; and
International Monetary Fund.
Note: NPL = nonperforming loan.

the corporate sector. Corporate credit growth slowed from a peak of close to 30 percent in 2008 to zero at its trough, with a sharper decline in corporate credit growth compared with the household segment. At the same time, the broad credit growth also experienced a sharper slowdown than bank credit growth, suggesting that the deleveraging process for corporates not only took place in the banking sector, but also in broader debt financing. The NPL ratio peaked at around 11 percent in 2017 but has since come down to around 8 percent.

Methodology

The GaR analysis in the India economy follows closely the approach of Adrian, Boyarchenko, and Giannone (2019) and Prasad and others (2019). GaR provides a tractable and robust estimation of the severity and the likelihood of a sharp economic slowdown. The model uses information contained in financial prices and aggregates to identify macro-financial linkages and gauge financial vulnerabilities. Importantly, GaR captures the entire growth distribution at different future horizons—reflecting both downside and upside risks—in addition to central-scenario growth forecasts. The concept helps better understanding of the relative importance of key drivers of future growth.

The first step of GaR analysis involves aggregating the set of macro-financial variables into economically meaningful groups ("partitions"). In this approach, five main partitions of macro-financial variables are considered (Table 2.1): (1) domestic prices, which capture the policy interest rate, 10-year Treasury bond yield, sovereign bond spread, and a change in stock prices; (2) credit and leverage, which includes credit growth, the credit-to-GDP ratio, the credit-to-GDP gap, and the NPL ratio; (3) macroeconomic vulnerabilities, which capture inflation, the current account-balance-to-GDP ratio, and the short-term external-debt-to-reserve ratio; (4) external prices, which include changes in oil prices and exchange rates; and finally (5) external macro that captures world GDP growth. These partitions are then computed using the principal component analysis that aggregates information about common trends among these macro-financial variables.

The second step of GaR uses a quantile regression approach to estimate the impact of financial conditions on different quantiles of real GDP growth in India. The following specification of the quantile regression is estimated:

$$y_{t+h}^q = \alpha^q + \beta_1^q X_{1,t} + \beta_2^q X_{2,t} + \beta_3^q X_{3,t} + \beta_4^q X_{4,t} + \beta_5^q X_{5,t} + \gamma^q y_t + \varepsilon_{t+h}^q \qquad (2.1)$$

TABLE 2.1.

Partition of Macro-financial Variables				
Domestic Prices	**Credit and Leverage**	**Macro Vulnerabilities**	**External Prices**	**External Macro**
• Policy rate	• Credit growth	• Inflation	• Oil price	• World GDP
• Treasury bill yields	• Credit-to-GDP ratio	• Current-account-	change	growth
(10-year)	• Credit-to-GDP gap	balance-to-GDP ratio	• Exchange	
• Sovereign spreads	• NPL ratio	• Short-term external-	rate change	
• Stock price change		debt-to-reserve ratio		

Source: Authors' calculations.
Note: NPL = nonperforming loans.

where y^q_{t+h} captures the h quarter ahead GDP growth (year-on-year) for quantile q, $X_{1,t}$ denotes the partition for domestic prices, $X_{2,t}$ captures the partition of credit and leverage, $X_{3,t}$ denotes the partition of macroeconomic vulnerabilities, $X_{4,t}$ represents the partition of external prices, and $X_{5,t}$ captures the partition of external macro conditions. Furthermore, ε^q_{t+h} denotes the residual, and α^q, β^q_1, β^q_2, and β^q_3, are the coefficients of the regression. In the analysis, five different quantiles (or percentiles) are considered, at 10 percent, 25 percent, 50 percent, 75 percent, and 90 percent, which capture the linkages between macro-financial conditions and growth at different points of the future growth distribution. For example, the 10 percent quantile captures low-growth periods (when growth rate is at the bottom 10th percentile), while the 90th percent quantile features high-growth periods. Multiple forecast horizons (e.g., 4 quarters ahead to 16 quarters ahead) are also considered to examine the impact of financial conditions on near- and medium-term growth.

Based on the results of the quantile regression, a t-skew distribution is then used to derive the probability density distribution of future GDP growth. The GaR framework could also be used to conduct scenario analysis, which examines the impact of shocks to the different partitions including credit and leverage, domestic prices, and macroeconomic vulnerabilities on the future growth distribution.

RESULTS

Macro-financial Partitions and Loadings

The relationship between different macro-financial partitions and real GDP growth in India is examined. As seen in Figure 2.2, the credit-to-GDP ratio, the credit-to-GDP gap, and credit growth have positive loadings on the first principal component[3] of credit and leverage indicators, while the NPL ratio has a negative loading. Therefore, an increase in the credit and leverage summary indicator would imply higher credit or more favorable credit conditions. After peaking in 2005/06, the credit and leverage indicator has been on a downward trend since 2011/12, coinciding with the period of negative credit-to-GDP gap.

On domestic prices, 10-year Treasury bill yields, policy interest rate, and sovereign yields have a positive sign in the principal component, while a change in stock prices has a negative loading. An increase in the principal component of domestic prices would then imply a tightening in price-based financial conditions. In the first half of the sample, there was an inverse relationship between real GDP growth and the summary domestic price indicator, where a tightening in the price-based financial conditions is associated with a decline in growth. More recently, there has been a continued loosening of financial conditions, with the link between price-based financial conditions and economic growth less pronounced.

On macroeconomic vulnerabilities, short-term external debt and inflation have positive loadings on the principal component, while the current account

---

[3] The first principal component of the credit and leverage partition (comprising the credit-to-GDP ratio, the credit-to-GDP gap, credit growth, and the NPL ratio) captures 77 percent of the variance.

Figure 2.2. Macro-financial Partitions and Loadings

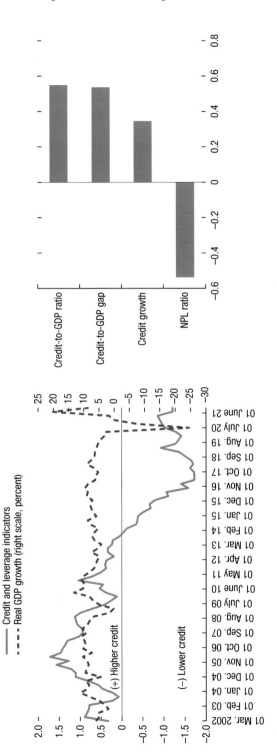

1. Credit and Leverage Indicators and Real GDP Growth

2. Credit and Leverage Indicators (Loadings)

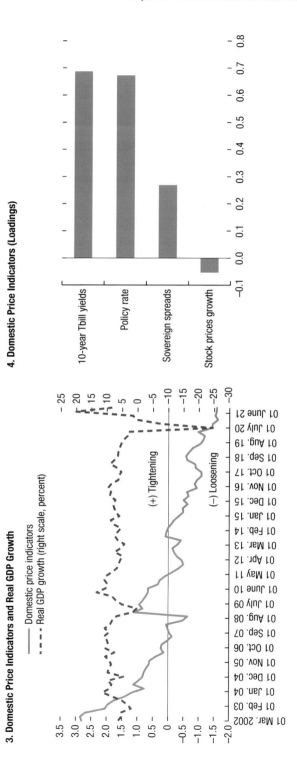

3. Domestic Price Indicators and Real GDP Growth

— Domestic price indicators
- - - Real GDP growth (right scale, percent)

4. Domestic Price Indicators (Loadings)

Figure 2.2 *(continued)*

5. Macroeconomic Vulnerabilities and Real GDP Growth

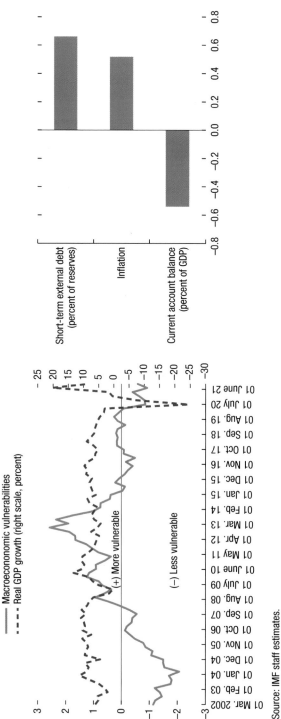

6. Macroeconomic Vulnerabilities (Loadings)

Source: IMF staff estimates.
Note: The blue lines in panels 1, 3, and 5 refer to the first principal component of each partition. NPL = nonperforming loan; Tbill = Treasury bill.

balance has a negative sign. A rise in the principal component of macroeconomic vulnerabilities would then imply higher vulnerabilities in the economy. Figure 2.2 shows that macroeconomic vulnerabilities peaked in 2012/13 but have been on a downward trend since then.

Scenario Analysis

A scenario analysis is conducted and considers a 2-standard deviation (SD) negative shock to the credit and leverage partition (Figure 2.3). A decline in the credit and leverage partition (here, referring to the principal component) would imply a tightening of the credit conditions and a worsening in credit quality, as measured by the NPL ratio. The green line captures the density before shock and the red line captures the one afterward. Following the negative shock, the entire distribution of GDP growth would shift to the left. The mode of the 4 quarterly ahead GDP growth would decline from 7.6 percent to 5.3 percent. Moreover, the tail risks would increase considerably, with the 5 percent GaR shifting from –5.7 percent to –12.2 percent. In other words, there was a 5 percent probability that growth could be below –5.7 percent prior to the shock. However, after the shock, there is 5 percent probability that growth could be below –12.2 percent, a much more severe tail outcome.

In addition, a 2 SD positive shock to the domestic prices partition and to the macro vulnerability partition are considered, respectively. An increase in the domestic prices partition would imply a tightening in the price-based financial conditions (Figure 2.4, left chart). The mode of the 4 quarter ahead GDP growth

Figure 2.3. Shock to Credit and Leverage

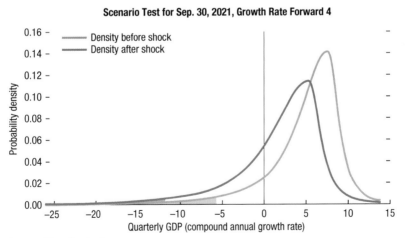

Scenario Test for Sep. 30, 2021, Growth Rate Forward 4

Source: IMF staff estimates.
Note: The results capture a two-standard-deviation negative shock to the credit and leverage partition, based on a growth-at-risk approach estimated using data from the fourth quarter of 2001 to the third quarter of 2021. The credit and leverage partition captures the credit-to-GDP ratio, the credit-to-GDP gap, credit growth, and the nonperforming loan ratio. The first three variables have positive loadings on the principal component, while the last variable has a negative loading.

Figure 2.4. Shocks to Domestic Prices and Macroeconomic Vulnerabilities

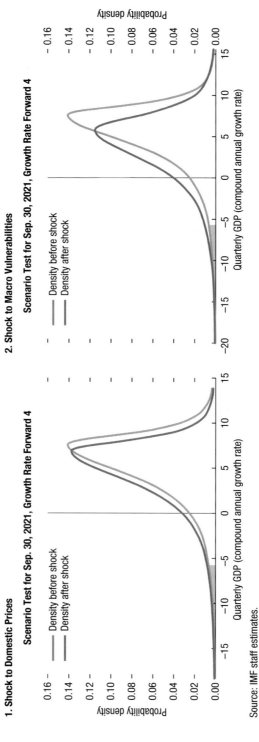

1. Shock to Domestic Prices

Scenario Test for Sep. 30, 2021, Growth Rate Forward 4

2. Shock to Macro Vulnerabilities

Scenario Test for Sep. 30, 2021, Growth Rate Forward 4

— Density before shock
— Density after shock

Source: IMF staff estimates.
Note: Panel 1 captures a two-standard-deviation (SD) positive shock to the domestic prices partition, which includes 10-year Treasury bill yields, policy interest rate, sovereign yields, and change in stock prices. Panel 2 features a two-standard-deviation positive shock to the macroeconomic vulnerability partition, which captures short-term external debt, inflation, and the current account balance. Both are computed based on the growth-at-risk approach estimated using data from the fourth quarter of 2001 to the third quarter of 2021.

would decline from 7.6 percent to 7 percent, with a slight shift of the growth distribution to the left following the shock. The relatively milder impact of the domestic price shock could be potentially attributed to the weaker relationship between domestic prices and growth in recent years. On macroeconomic vulnerabilities (Figure 2.4, right chart), a 2 SD positive shock (higher vulnerabilities) would imply a decline in 4 quarter ahead GDP growth from 7.6 percent to 5.9 percent (mode), with the growth distribution shifted to the left, capturing higher tail risks.

Term Structure of Credit and Leverage Indicators

Finally, the term structure of the credit and leverage indicators and the impact on GDP growth across different horizons is examined. Specifically, the 4 quarter, 8 quarter, 12 quarter, and 16 quarter ahead quantile regression results are considered. In Figure 2.5, the y-axis refers to the coefficient of the credit and leverage partition in the quantile regression (equation 2.1) and the x-axis refers to the different quantiles, capturing GDP growth at the 10th, 25th, 50th, 75th, and 90th percentiles. The results suggest that high credit and low NPLs have a positive and significant impact on GDP growth across all horizons. Furthermore, the impact is even larger at lower quantiles when GDP growth is lower. In other words, a favorable credit condition with higher credit and stronger credit quality is particularly important in supporting the economic recovery during periods of low growth.

Policy Discussions

The results from GaR highlight the importance of ensuring adequate credit growth and improving the balance sheets of banks, particularly through reducing problem loans. A negative shock to credit and leverage (lower credit and higher NPL ratio) could shift the distribution of growth to the left, with lower expected growth and higher negative tail risks.

During periods of low economic growth, policies to support credit growth and to strengthen balance sheets would be particularly important. In this regard, policy responses such as credit guarantee schemes for MSMEs and loan restructuring schemes for COVID-19–affected borrowers were important to support credit growth and cushion the economic impact of the pandemic.

Going forward, further efforts to make support measures even more targeted and facilitate the exit of nonviable firms may be warranted. In addition, financial regulators should continue to ensure that loans benefited from COVID-19–related restructuring schemes are closely monitored and property provisioned for, to safeguard the health of financial sector balance sheet to support the economic recovery.

FINANCIAL SECTOR AND LONG-TERM GROWTH

Several studies document that poor capitalization and weak asset quality negatively impact banks' ability to provide credit to the economy. Using balance sheet data for international banks from a range of advanced economies, Gambacorta and

Figure 2.5. Term Structure for Credit Indicators

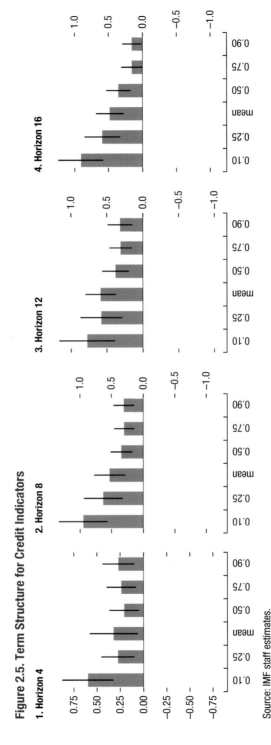

Source: IMF staff estimates.

Note: The horizons refer to quarters. The x-axis refers to the different quantiles q of the quantile regression. The y-axis refers to the coefficient β_2^q for the partition of credit and leverage in the quantile regression. The results are based on the growth-at-risk approach estimated using data from the fourth quarter of 2001 to the third quarter of 2021.

Shin (2018) show that well-capitalized banks enjoy lower costs of debt financing compared to more leveraged competitors, which in turn translates into higher annual credit growth. Muduli and Behera (2021) find similar evidence in India, of a positive correlation between bank equity and credit growth, and that this plays a role in monetary policy transmission. Blattner and others (2019) look at a macro angle and show that less-capitalized banks cut lending in response to higher capital requirements, which potentially contribute to weaker productivity growth. This section of the chapter builds on this literature by examining the role of balance sheets of Indian banks on credit growth, and ultimately overall output growth in the economy. The focus is, in particular, on the differential role of public and private sector banks in driving credit growth.

Data and Stylized Facts

Data for the main bank-level variables of interest (cost of funding, growth of debt funding, credit growth, and bank capitalization) as well as bank-level control variables (nonperforming assets, return on assets) are from FitchConnect. The sample is at an annual frequency from 1998 to 2021. Only public sector banks (PSBs) and private banks are kept in the sample, excluding such entities as non-banking financial companies, foreign banks, and development banks. The sample accounts for about 85 percent of total assets in the Indian financial sector in any given year of the sample. For the macro-level analysis, the data on GDP growth and various India-level or global controls are from the RBI via Haver Analytics and CEIC. Details of the data and sources are available in Annex Table 2.1.2.

The main explanatory variable is bank-level capitalization, which based on existing literature for banks in advanced economies as well as in India is an important driver of credit growth. This is defined in several different ways to determine the robustness of the results. First, capitalization is defined in turn as either common equity over total assets, total equity over total assets, or regulatory Tier 1 capital over total assets. The fourth measure of bank-level capitalization is the capital adequacy ratio, defined as Tier 1 regulatory capital over risk-weighted assets. Figure 2.6 shows the path of bank-level capitalization over time for PSBs and private sector banks, as defined by the simple ratio of equity to assets and by the capital adequacy ratio. While median bank capitalization was volatile and similar among bank types in the earlier years of the sample, since 2010 private sector banks have had consistently notably higher capitalization than PSBs, although both have been trending upward in recent years. Similarly, there has been a notable upward shift in the capital adequacy ratio since 2013, when India implemented the Basel III requirement (recommending a 9 percent capital adequacy ratio).

As has been documented in the literature, although banks may use their capital to fund lending, given the relatively low share of capital on their balance sheets, it is more likely that lending is funded through debt liabilities. This also appears to be the case for Indian banks, as depicted in Figure 2.7, that capital makes up a relatively small share of both private sector banks and PSBs.

Figure 2.6. Bank-Level Capitalization

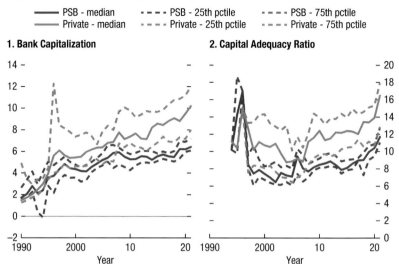

Sources: FitchConnect; and IMF staff estimates.
Note: Bank capitalization is defined as total equity over total assets. The capital adequacy ratio is defined as Tier 1 regulatory capital over risk-weighted assets. pctile = percentile; PSB = public sector bank.

At the same time, there is evidence of a relationship between bank equity and bank assets (a large part of which is lending) in India, as has also been identified for other countries (Gambaorta and Shin 2018). This is shown by estimating the simple correlation between total assets and total equity, both at the bank, i, year, t, level:

$$\log(assets_{it}) = a_i + \gamma_t + \beta \log(equity_{it}) + \delta X + e_{it} \tag{2.2}$$

where the model, in turn, includes the vector X of bank-level control variables (return on assets, NPLs), a set of bank-fixed effects, a_i, and a set of year fixed effects, γ_t. The coefficient β indicates the correlation between bank assets and bank equity, which is estimated separately for private banks and PSBs. These correlation estimates are reported graphically in Figure 2.8. Indeed, the results suggest that for private sector banks in India there is a correlation between assets and equity close to 1, even after including the full set of control variables—meaning the two variables move closely together over time. For PSBs, this correlation is much weaker once outside aggregate factors are controlled for (via time-fixed effects), which may affect bank assets.

Having established a link between bank assets (largely comprised of lending) and bank equity—at least for private sector banks—the question of whether there is a direct link between the capitalization of Indian banks and their lending growth, via debt funding, is formalized. The analysis proceeds in three steps,

Figure 2.7. Bank Balance Sheet Composition

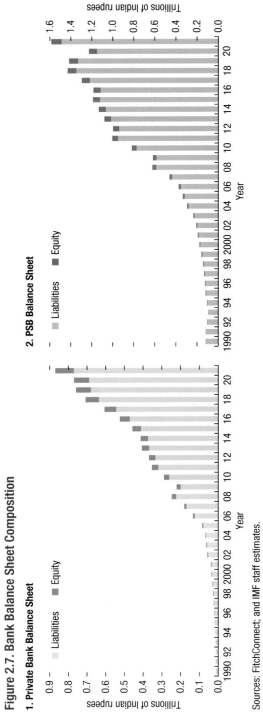

1. Private Bank Balance Sheet

2. PSB Balance Sheet

Sources: FitchConnect; and IMF staff estimates.
Note: PSB = public sector bank.

Figure 2.8. Correlation—Total Assets and Total Equity

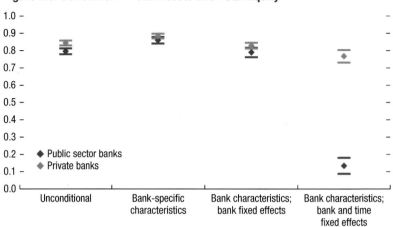

Sources: FitchConnect; and IMF staff estimates.
Note: Correlation estimated via ordinary least squares regression. The x-axis labels indicate control variables included in the regression. Diamonds indicate point estimates, and bars indicate the 90 percent (robust) confidence interval.

following the literature. First, ask whether a bank's capitalization reduces its cost of funding—this is important because it was previously established that most lending likely stems from debt funding. Second, investigate whether capitalization not only decreases funding costs but whether it is actually associated with an increase in debt funding. In Figure 2.9, the left and middle panels show these two simple correlations and suggest that for Indian banks, there is a strong association among higher bank capitalization, lower funding costs, and greater debt funding growth. Finally, as seen in the right panel, there is a strong positive correlation between lending growth and capitalization. Together, these suggest that better-capitalized banks lend more, possibly through a cheaper debt funding channel. Such a result would be consistent with the existing literature on international banks. In the next section, these relationships are formalized.

Finally, the chapter looks at the macro level and attempts to formalize the relationship between credit growth and real GDP growth. Because the distinction between public and private banks is made in the bank-level analysis, it is important to also understand how each contributes to aggregate credit growth in India. Figure 2.10 shows that throughout the period under analysis, PSBs have been responsible for the largest share of credit to the economy. However, since around 2013, private sector bank credit growth has been much faster than PSB credit growth, suggesting private banks are becoming an increasingly important player in the Indian banking sector.

Figure 2.11 reports the aggregate correlation between real GDP growth and credit growth for each type of bank, with both showing relatively strong positive correlations. This relationship is explored more carefully in the next sections.

Figure 2.9. Bank Capitalization, Funding, and Lending

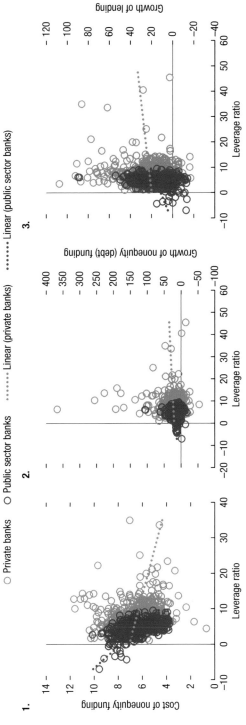

Sources: Fitch Connect; and IMF staff estimates.

Figure 2.10. Aggregate Bank Credit to the Economy

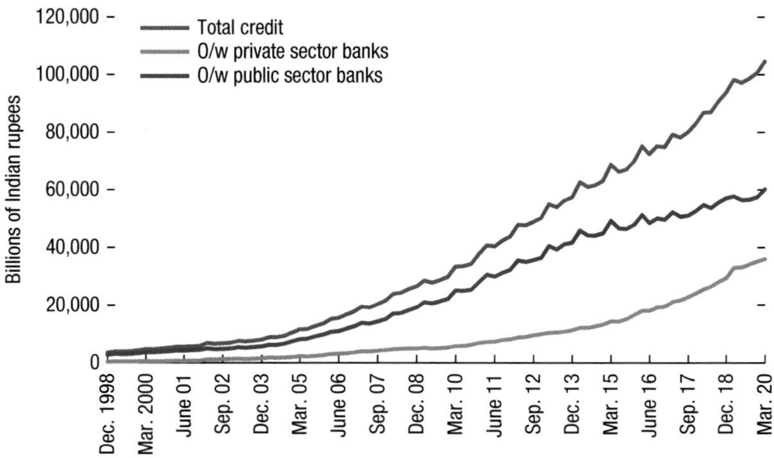

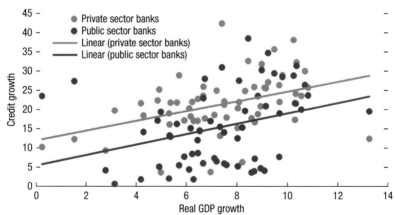

Sources: CEIC; and authors' calculations.
Note: Public sector bank credit is the sum of nationalized bank credit and State Bank of India credit for the period before June 2017. o/w = of which.

Figure 2.11. Real GDP Growth and Credit Growth

Sources: CEIC; and authors' calculations.
Note: Public sector bank credit is the sum of nationalized bank credit and State Bank of India credit for the period before June 2017.

Methodology

The methodology for the bank-level analysis follows the approach of two closely related papers, Gambacorta and Shin (2018) and Muduli and Behera (2021). It then extends the analysis to the macro level to analyze the impact of bank lending on real GDP growth in India. The approach will be in several stages. First, it examines whether bank capitalization leads to lower debt funding costs and higher debt funding—establishing whether the channel of debt funding for lending also exists in private and public banks in India in the sample period. Then, it turns to lending, to examine whether bank capitalization matters for lending, again distinguishing between private and public banks. Finally, it looks at the aggregate and examines whether bank lending is associated with higher real GDP growth in India. This latter step raises questions of causality—namely, whether lending boosts real GDP (for instance by increasing consumption and investment) or whether lending rises when real GDP growth is higher. Many papers have tried to tease out this relationship using data from other countries. Even though this chapter has insufficient data to carefully establish causality, it will nonetheless argue that the approach suggests there is a likely channel of transmission from bank lending to real GDP growth in India.

To estimate the role of bank capitalization on funding costs, debt funding costs of bank i in period t, $cost_{it}$, defined as the average cost of funding given by total interest rate paid over total level of debt (excluding equity and reserves), is regressed on bank capitalization ($Capitalization_{it-1}$) using various definitions described in the previous section. Time-fixed effects and bank-level controls, X_{it-1}, including return on assets and NPL ratio, are also included:

$$cost_{it} = \theta_t + \beta cost_{it-1} + \lambda Capitalization_{it-1} + \delta X_{it-1} + e_{it} \qquad (2.3)$$

The model is estimated using the dynamic generalized method of moments estimator (Arellano and Bond 1991), which ensures efficiency and consistency of the estimates. This is useful in this setting because the outcome variable likely depends on past realizations of itself. It is important to note that while this regression model can inform on the relationship between bank capitalization and funding costs, it cannot identify a causal relationship between these variables. Consistent with existing literature, it is expected that the results will show that lower capital levels are associated with higher prices for debt funding (i.e., higher equity reduces the cost of debt or that well-capitalized banks pay less for their funding).

Having established a link between bank capitalization and the cost of funding, the analysis then estimates the impact of bank capitalization on funding levels, using a similar setup, with the dependent variable this time being the growth of debt funding, $funds_{it}$:

$$\Delta \ln(funds_{it}) = a_i + \theta_t + \beta \Delta \ln(funds_{it-1}) + \lambda Capitalization_{it-1} + \delta X_{it-1} + e_{it} \qquad (2.4)$$

In this case, it is expected that better capitalization and an increase in asset quality will increase the rate of debt funding.

The final step in the bank-level analysis estimates the impact of bank capitalization on credit supply, again in a similar setup as the first three equations:

$$\Delta \ln(loans)_{it} = a_i + \theta_t + \beta \Delta \ln(loans)_{it-1} + \lambda Capitalization_{it-1} + \delta X_{it-1} + e_{it} \qquad (2.5)$$

In this case, it is expected that better capitalization increases the growth rate of loans.

With bank-level results established, the analysis turns to addressing the question of what the impact of banking lending, through bank balance sheets, is on the macroeconomy in India. This remains an open question because, while there is evidence that higher credit growth is often associated with higher GDP growth, in emerging markets this is sometimes the result of a boom–bust cycle, which can ultimately lead to lower growth. In such a case, it may indeed be that the health of bank balance sheets is particularly important to avoid these extreme swings. Also motived by the results from the GaR model, a measure of balance sheet health is controlled for directly, defined using the NPL ratio. The following regression model is estimated to determine the relationship between real GDP growth and credit growth (at the bank-year, *it*, level) in India:

$$
\begin{aligned}
\textit{Real GDP Growth}_t &= \alpha + \beta_1 \textit{Credit Growth}_{it-1} + \beta_2 \textit{NPL}_{it-1} \\
&+ \beta_3 \textit{Credit Growth}_{it-1} \cdot \textit{NPL}_{it-1} + \beta_4 \textit{Controls}_t + e_{it}
\end{aligned}
\tag{2.6}
$$

where the set of control variables are macro controls, including inflation, the real effective exchange rate, and world GDP growth. NPLs are defined as a dummy variable, equal to 1 if bank i's NPL ratio in year t is below the sample mean. Credit growth, in turn, is defined as actual credit growth or as a dummy variable for high credit growth equals to one if bank i's credit growth ratio in year t is above the sample mean. The credit growth variable is also winsorized at the 1st and 99th percentile, to account for extreme outliers.[4]

Results

The first results, based on estimating equation (2.2), are reported in Table 2.2. The sample is split between PSBs (columns 1 to 4) and private sector banks (columns 5 to 8) and shows results for the four different measures of bank capitalization. The results suggest that higher capitalization is associated with lower debt funding costs, especially and more so for private sector banks. This is consistent with what Gambacorta and Shin (2018) find for advance country banks. Muduli and Behera (2021) find a related, nuanced result for India, that (consistent with the results presented in this chapter) a higher level of bank capital is associated with lower funding costs but for PSBs it is only associated with lower funding costs if they have lower nonperforming assets. In contrast, the results here indicate there is some negative association on average, regardless of the level of NPLs, but it is not as strong as for private sector banks. This could be because PSBs often get public sector capital infusions, thus limiting the extent to which capital is indicative of risk for PSBs.

Next, the analysis asks whether capitalization matters for the overall growth of debt funding. The results for estimating this, as indicated in equation (2.3), are reported in Table 2.3, again separately analyzing public and private firms. Again, there is a similar distinction between the role of capitalization in public versus private sector banks. Private sector banks that have greater capitalization are associated with large and significantly greater debt funding growth. For PSBs, the relationship is not robust across the different measures of capitalization.

---

[4] Results are robust to not winsorizing and are available on request.

TABLE 2.2.

Bank Capitalization and Cost of Debt Funding							
	Impact of Leverage on the Cost of Funding—Full Sample						
	(1)	**(2)**	**(3)**	**(4)**	**(5)**	**(6)**	**(7)**	**(8)**
					Cost of Funding			
			PSBs				Private Banks	
Leverage ratio (total equity/ assets)	−0.0241 (0.0176)				−0.0521*** (0.0124)			
Leverage ratio (common equity/assets)		−0.0206 (0.0164)				−0.0494*** (0.0123)		
Leverage ratio (Tier 1/assets)			−0.0248 (0.0528)				−0.0531*** (0.0155)	
Capital adequacy ratio				−0.0177 (0.0138)				−0.0260*** (0.00777)
N	373	373	157	363	408	408	229	402
Year FE	Yes	Yes	Yes	Yes	Yes	Yes	Yes	Yes
Bank controls	Yes	Yes	Yes	Yes	Yes	Yes	Yes	Yes

Source: IMF staff estimates.
Note: Standard errors in parentheses. Sample period from 1998 to 2021. Model estimated using the dynamic generalized method of moments panel. FE = fixed effects; N = number; PSBs = public sector banks.
* $p < .05$; ** $p < .01$; *** $p < .001$.

The final exercise at the bank level, having established that better-capitalized Indian (private) banks are able to find cheaper debt funding and raise more funds relative to less well-capitalized banks, which can be a source of funds for lending, is to examine their lending practices directly. Table 2.4 reports results from estimating equation (2.4). With respect to private sector banks, there is some evidence of a positive relationship between capitalization and lending. PSBs show no evidence of any positive relationship between capitalization and lending. Isolating the

TABLE 2.3.

Bank Capitalization and Debt Funding Growth							
	Impact of Leverage on Growth in Debt Funding—Full Sample						
	(1)	**(2)**	**(3)**	**(4)**	**(5)**	**(6)**	**(7)**	**(8)**
					Growth in Debt Funding			
			PSBs				Private Banks	
Leverage ratio (total equity/ assets)	1.393*** (0.341)				2.276*** (0.456)			
Leverage ratio (common equity/ assets)		1.151*** (0.321)				2.205*** (0.451)		
Leverage ratio (Tier 1/assets)			0.529 (1.006)				4.755*** (0.686)	
Capital adequacy ratio				0.947*** (0.256)				1.393*** (0.323)
N	373	373	157	363	406	406	228	399
Year FE	Yes	Yes	Yes	Yes	Yes	Yes	Yes	Yes
Bank controls	Yes	Yes	Yes	Yes	Yes	Yes	Yes	Yes

Source: IMF staff estimates.
Note: Standard errors in parentheses. Sample period from 1998 to 2021. Model estimated using the dynamic generalized method of moments panel. FE = fixed effects; N = number; PSBs = public sector banks.
* $p < .05$; ** $p < .01$; *** $p < .001$.

TABLE 2.4.

Bank Capitalization and Lending Growth								
	Impact of Leverage on Credit Growth—Full Sample							
	(1)	(2)	(3)	(4)	(5)	(6)	(7)	(8)
					Growth of Gross Loans			
			PSBs				Private Banks	
Leverage ratio (total equity/ assets)	0.371 (0.392)				0.630 (0.484)			
Leverage ratio (common equity/ assets)		0.259 (0.366)				0.639 (0.480)		
Leverage ratio (Tier 1/assets)			0.0703 (1.102)				1.970** (0.798)	
Capital adequacy ratio				0.369 (0.294)				0.805** (0.349)
N	373	373	157	363	406	406	228	399
Year FE	Yes	Yes	Yes	Yes	Yes	Yes	Yes	Yes
Bank controls	Yes	Yes	Yes	Yes	Yes	Yes	Yes	Yes

Source: IMF staff estimates.
Note: Standard errors in parentheses. Sample period from 1998 to 2021. Model estimated using the dynamic generalized method of moments panel. FE = fixed effects; N = number; PSBs = public sector banks.
* $p < .05$; ** $p < .01$; *** $p < .001$.

period from 2011 to 2021, which is both when the RBI adopted the Basel II regulations and when private sector banks became much more prominent in India, there is an even stronger positive relationship between capitalization and lending, as shown in Table 2.5. Together, the results suggest that credit growth in India can be supported by ensuring that banks are adequately capitalized, which enables them to raise more debt funding, at cheaper rates, which is then ultimately

TABLE 2.5.

Bank Capitalization and Lending Growth, 2010–21								
	Sample Period 2011–21							
	(1)	(2)	(3)	(4)	(5)	(6)	(7)	(8)
					Growth of Gross Loans			
			PSBs				Private Banks	
Leverage ratio (total equity/ assets)	2.681** (1.148)				2.200*** (0.570)			
Leverage ratio (common equity/ assets)		3.024** (1.220)				1.970*** (0.562)		
Leverage ratio (Tier 1/assets)			−0.101 (1.527)				1.957*** (0.507)	
Capital adequacy ratio				0.432 (0.888)				1.369*** (0.335)
N	166	166	130	165	198	198	175	197
Year FE	Yes	Yes	Yes	Yes	Yes	Yes	Yes	Yes
Bank controls	Yes	Yes	Yes	Yes	Yes	Yes	Yes	Yes

Source: IMF staff estimates.
Note: Standard errors in parentheses. Sample period from 1998 to 2021. Model estimated using the dynamic generalized method of moments panel. FE = fixed effects; N = number; PSBs = public sector banks.
* $p < .05$; ** $p < .01$; *** $p < .001$.

used to support lending growth. This relationship is, however, particular to private sector banks and does not seem to hold for PSBs, which may have different funding models and different ability to lend.

Turing to the macro-level results, reported in Table 2.6, columns 3 and 4 suggest that there is a strong positive relationship between higher credit growth and real GDP growth, but only for those banks with a low NPL ratio. Furthermore, this result appears to be entirely driven by private sector banks (column 5), with public banks showing no relationships between credit growth and real GDP growth regardless of the level of NPLs. Although the methodology used here cannot speak to the reason for the lack of relationship between PSB lending and growth, the reasons could be varied. These may include that PSBs have different objectives than private sector banks and often engage in directed lending (also known as priority sector lending), or that it reflects implicit guarantees they have from the government. If real GDP growth is the overarching objective, then the results suggest private sector bank lending by banks with healthy balance sheets should be promoted. There may nonetheless be alternative reasons for continuing to promote PSB lending. It is also important to recall that this methodology does not speak to a causal relationship between bank lending and real GDP growth. The positive correlation may imply that private bank credit growth from banks

TABLE 2.6.

Real GDP Growth and Credit Growth

	(1)	(2)	(3)	(4)	(5)	(6)	(7)
				Sample Period 1990–2021			
Dependent Variable:				Real GDP Growth			
					Private Banks	PSBs	Large Banks
			Full Sample				
Credit growth	0.0421***	0.0105					
	(0.00949)	(0.0183)					
NPL ratio low		0.258	0.232	0.884*	0.376	3.069***	1.402
		(0.488)	(0.352)	(0.519)	(0.755)	(0.762)	(0.866)
Credit growth* NPL ratio low		0.0325					
		(0.0222)					
Credit growth high (dummy)			−0.196	−1.532	−1.861	−0.610	−2.352
			(0.389)	(0.936)	(1.341)	(1.399)	(1.582)
Credit growth high (dummy)*NPL ratio low			1.771***	1.797*	2.942**	−0.00683	2.206
			(0.486)	(0.961)	(1.402)	(1.345)	(1.660)
Inflation				−0.293***	−0.336***	−0.411***	−0.620***
				(0.0615)	(0.0898)	(0.0894)	(0.164)
Real effective exchange rate (RBI)				−0.199***	−0.263***	−0.0682	−0.343***
				(0.0330)	(0.0460)	(0.0517)	(0.0998)
World GDP				0.348***	0.358***	0.318***	0.406***
				(0.0276)	(0.0374)	(0.0403)	(0.0563)
Constant	5.753***	5.727***	5.807***	25.73***	32.00***	13.01**	41.78***
	(0.237)	(0.340)	(0.237)	(3.405)	(4.740)	(5.298)	(10.61)
N	807	807	824	588	309	279	221
R-squared	0.035	0.051	0.069	0.381	0.410	0.412	0.382

Source: IMF staff estimates.

Note: Robust standard errors in parentheses. Credit growth is winsorized at 1 and 99 percent. Low NPL ratio is defined as NPL ratio below the sample mean. High credit growth is defined as credit growth above the (winsorized) mean of the full sample. Large banks are defined as banks with total assets above the mean of the full sample. N = number; NPL = non-performing loan; PSBs = private sector banks; RBI = Reserve Bank of India.

* $p < 0.1$, ** $p < 0.05$ *** $p < 0.01$.

with low NPLs spurs real growth, but it may also indicate procyclical lending by private sector banks (and countercyclical lending by PSBs). Further analysis with micro-level data would be needed to disentangle this relationship, which is left to future research.

Policy Discussions

Results from this panel regression analysis, as with the results from the GaR, highlight the importance of ensuring adequate credit growth and improving bank balance sheets, particularly through reducing NPLs, to boost growth. It is only those banks with low NPLs and high credit growth that are associated with higher GDP growth.

At the bank level, to ensure high credit growth it is also imperative that banks are well capitalized. This allows them access to more and cheaper debt funding, which is in turn used to fund lending. These relationships, however, seem to exist primarily for private sector banks. PSBs, which may have different motivations for lending, appear to be less affected by their capital position in terms of their ability to lend.

Looking ahead, efforts to clean up bank balance sheets and boost capitalization—especially for private sector banks—will be critical in boosting credit growth, and thus GDP growth, over the medium term.

CONCLUSION

India's financial sector has faced many challenges in recent decades, with a large, negative, and persistent credit-to-GDP gap since 2012. This chapter examines how cyclical financial conditions affect GDP growth using a GaR approach and analyzes the link among bank balance sheets, credit growth, and long-term growth using bank-level panel regressions for both public and private banks. The results suggest that on a cyclical basis, a negative shock to credit or a rise in macro vulnerability could be associated with lower expected growth and higher negative tail risks; over the long term, the results indicate that higher credit growth, arising from better-capitalized banks with lower NPLs, is associated with higher GDP growth.

Using two distinct methodologies, the results provide consistent messages:

- On a *cyclical* basis, a negative shock to credit and leverage or a rise in macro vulnerability (measured by inflation, the current account-balance-to-GDP ratio, and the short-term external-debt-to-reserve ratio) could be associated with lower expected growth and higher negative tail risks;

- Over the *long term*, the results indicate that higher credit growth, arising from better-capitalized banks with lower NPLs, is associated with higher GDP growth.

Together, these results point to a number of policy considerations:

- First, the results highlight the importance of ensuring *adequate credit growth* and improving the *balance sheets of banks*, particularly through reducing problem loans. During periods of low economic growth, policies to support credit growth and to strengthen balance sheets would be particularly important.

- In addition, a focus on ensuring that *private sector banks* are *well capitalized*, either through new equity issuance or reducing cash dividends, is crucial, given the relationship between their balance sheets and credit to the economy.

ANNEX 2.1.

ANNEX TABLE 2.1.1.

Definitions of and Data Sources for Macro-financial Variables

Variables	Definitions	Sources
Real GDP growth	Real GDP at market prices, % change - YoY	Haver Analytics/Central Statistics Office
Policy rate	Repo rate (EOP, % per annum)	Haver Analytics/Reserve Bank of India
Treasury bill yields (10-year)	10-year government bond yield (EOP, % per annum)	Haver Analytics/Reserve Bank of India
Sovereign spreads	JPSSGINB Index	Bloomberg
Stock price change	Stock prices: BSE Sensex/BSE 30 Index (% YoY)	Haver Analytics/Bombay Stock Exchange
Stock price volatility	BSE Sensex Volatility Index: 3-month	Haver Analytics/Financial Times
House price change	House Price Index (% from previous period)	Haver Analytics/Reserve Bank of India
Inflation rate	Consumer Price Index % Change - YoY	Haver Analytics/Ministry of Statistics and Programme Implementation
Current account deficit	BOP: current account balance/real GDP at market prices	Haver Analytics/Central Statistics Office and Reserve Bank of India
Short-term external debt-to-reserve ratio	Short-term gross external debt/intl liquidity reserves	Haver Analytics/Reserve Bank of India
NPL ratio	Nonperforming loans to total gross loans (EOP, %)	Haver Analytics/International Monetary Fund
Capital adequacy ratio	Regulatory Tier 1 Capital to Risk-weighted Assets (EOP, %)	Haver Analytics/International Monetary Fund
Credit growth	Adj credit by all sectors to nonfin priv sector (% YoY)	Haver Analytics/Bank for International Settlements
Credit-to-GDP ratio	Adj credit to the private nonfinancial sector (% of GDP)	Haver Analytics/Bank for International Settlements
Credit-to-GDP gap	Private nonfinancial credit-to-GDP gap (EOP, %)	Haver Analytics/Bank for International Settlements
World GDP growth	Real GDP, seasonally adjusted, % YoY, World	International Monetary Fund, World Economic Outlook
Oil price change	West Texas Intermediate ($/barrel) (% YoY)	Haver Analytics/Energy Information Admin/Chicago Mercantile Exch
Exchange rate change	India: Rupee/US$ exchange rate (AVG) (% YoY)	Haver Analytics/Reserve Bank of India

Sources: See third column of the table.

Note: Adj = adjusted; AVG = average; BOP = balance of payments; BSE = Bombay Stock Exchange; EOP = end of period; intl = International; JPSSGINB = JP Morgan Sovereign Bond index for India; nonfin = nonfinancial; NPL = nonperforming loan; priv = private; repo = repurchase agreement; YoY = year over year.

ANNEX TABLE 2.1.2.

Definitions of and Data Sources for Panel Regression Variables		
Variable	**Definition**	**Source**
Leverage ratio (total equity)	Total equity divided by total assets (%)	FitchConnect/Reserve Bank of India
Leverage ratio (common equity)	Total common equity divided by total assets (%)	FitchConnect/Reserve Bank of India
Leverage ratio (Tier 1)	Tier 1 capital divided by total assets (%)	FitchConnect/Reserve Bank of India
Capital adequacy ratio	Tier 1 capital divided by risk-weighted assets (%)	FitchConnect/Reserve Bank of India
Cost of funding	Total interest expense divided by total debt funding excluding derivatives	FitchConnect/Reserve Bank of India
Debt funding growth	Growth rate of debt funding	FitchConnect/Reserve Bank of India
Growth of gross loans	Growth rate of gross loans (%)	FitchConnect/Reserve Bank of India
Return on assets	Net income divided by total assets (%)	FitchConnect/Reserve Bank of India
NPL	Total impaired loans divided by gross loans	FitchConnect/Reserve Bank of India
GDP growth	Real GDP growth (%)	International Monetary Fund
Policy rate	Repo rate (average %)	Haver Analytics/Reserve Bank of India
Real effective exchange rate	Real effective exchange rate against 10 currency basket	Haver Analytics/Reserve Bank of India
Exchange rate	Rupee/USD exchange rate, nominal	Haver Analytics/Reserve Bank of India
US policy rate	Effective Federal funds rate	Haver Analytics

Sources: See third column of the table.
Note: NPL = nonperforming loan; Repo = repurchase agreement; USD = US dollar.

REFERENCES

Adrian, Tobias, Nina Boyarchenko, and Domenico Giannone. 2019. "Vulnerable Growth." *American Economic Review* 109 (4): 1263–89.

Adrian, Tobias, Federico Grinberg, Nellie Liang, and Sheheryar Malik. 2018. "The Term Structure of Growth-at-Risk." IMF Working Paper 2018/180, International Monetary Fund, Washington, DC.

Ang, Andrew, Monika Piazzesi, and Min Wei. 2006. "What Does the Yield Curve Tell Us about GDP Growth?" *Journal of Econometrics* 131 (1–2): 359–403.

Claessens, Stijn, Ayhan Kose, and Marco Terrones. 2011a. "Financial Cycles: What? When? How?" CEPR Discussion Paper 8379, Centre for Economic Policy Research, London.

Claessens, Stijn, Ayhan Kose, and Marco Terrones. 2011b. "How Do Business and Financial Cycles Interact?" CEPR Discussion Paper 8396, Centre for Economic Policy Research, London.

Demirgüç-Kunt, Asli, and Ross Levine. 2018. *Finance and Growth, Volume 1.* Chaltenham, UK, Edward Elgar Publishing.

Gambacorta, Leonardo, and Hyun Song Shin. 2016. "Why Bank Capital Matters for Monetary Policy." BIS Working Paper 558.

Goodhart, Charles, and Boris Hofmann. 2008. "House Prices, Money, Credit, and the Macroeconomy." *Oxford Review of Economic Policy* 24 (1): 180–205.

Levine, Ross. 2005. "Finance and Growth: Theory and Evidence." In *Handbook of Economic Growth,* edited by Philippe Aghion and Steven Durlauf. Amsterdam, Elsevier.

Muduli, Silu, and Harendra Behera. 2021. "Bank Capital and Monetary Policy Transmission in India." *Macroeconomics and Finance in Emerging Market Economies.*

Prasad, Ananthakrishnan, Selim Elekdag, Phakawa Jeasakul, Romain Lafarguette, Adrian Alter, Alan Xiaochen Feng, and Changchun Wang. 2019. "Growth at Risk: Concept and Application in IMF Country Surveillance." IMF Working Paper 2019/036, International Monetary Fund, Washington, DC.

PART II

Changing Structure of India's Financial System

CHAPTER 3

Banking Sector and Nonbanking Financial Companies

Faisal Ahmed, Marco Casiraghi, and Sumiko Ogawa

INTRODUCTION

India's financial sector structure has changed over the last few decades. Banks still dominate, especially public sector banks (PSBs), but private sector banks as well as nonbanking financial companies (NBFCs) are playing an increasingly prominent role. Private banks have generally stronger balance sheets with lower nonperforming loan ratios, although some private banks have faced stresses in recent years as well. Outside the commercial banks and NBFCs, a number of smaller banks serve narrower groups of borrowers, including rural cooperative banks, small finance banks, local area banks, and payment banks that operate in narrower geographical areas and/or range of services and that target specific clientele.

Of particular importance in recent years are NBFCs and their growing links with banks, which is the focus of this chapter. This chapter briefly reviews the banking sector (in the first section) and discusses the role of NBFCs (in the second section). The third section describes recent changes to the regulatory framework to strengthen the NBFC sector, and the final section offers a conclusion.

BANKING SECTOR

PSBs continue to play a sizable role in the banking system, despite the significant transition over the past two decades, a result of two rounds of bank nationalizations in 1969 and 1980. PSBs have supported the government's efforts on financial inclusion through priority sector lending, the Pradhan Mantri Jan Dhan Yojana basic bank accounts program, and their networks with wide coverage, including in rural areas. Although priority sector lending and statutory liquidity ratio requirements apply to all scheduled commercial banks, regardless of the ownership, PSBs in the past held a higher level of liquid assets (e.g., government securities) that counted toward statutory liquidity ratios than did private banks.

Prior to the COVID-19 pandemic, India's banking sector, particularly PSBs, underwent balance sheet cleanup and reforms. This followed rapid credit expansion during the 2000s, which originated importantly from lending to corporates to support infrastructure investments. Strong credit growth among PSBs continued during the global financial crisis, even as credit growth among private sector banks and foreign banks decelerated significantly (Figure 3.1).

As asset quality issues emerged, however, prompting a necessary asset quality review by the Reserve Bank of India (RBI) in 2015, credit growth overall decelerated relative to the preceding years. With the subsequent tightening of nonperforming asset (NPA) criteria amid the weakening performance in infrastructure-related lending, gross NPA ratios among PSBs increased around threefold from 5.4 percent in 2015 to a peak of 15.6 percent in March 2018 (4 percent for private sector banks) before moderating to 14.6 percent in March 2021 (4.6 percent for private banks). PSB credit growth decelerated to 3.8 percent in March 2021 (25.0 percent on average in 2003–09) and profitability declined, while the large provisioning burden reduced PSBs' capital.[1]

The Government of India launched banking sector reforms and undertook a series of capital injections into the PSBs to address the banking sector challenges. The Banking Reforms Roadmap, announced in January 2018, focused on six themes, including strengthening PSBs, increasing credit supply, and deepening financial inclusion. With more than rupees (Rs) 2 trillion of capital (around 1 percent of gross domestic product [GDP]) injected in fiscal year (FY) 2016/17–FY 2018/19, the PSB capital adequacy ratio improved to 12.2 percent in March 2019 from 11.45 percent in March 2015 (and compared to 16.3 percent for private sector banks). Lower NPAs and better capital adequacy ratios helped five of the 11 PSBs exit the RBI's prompt corrective action framework in FY 2018/19, which was imposed in 2017 due to high net NPA and negative return on assets (ROA). And 10 PSBs were merged into four as of April 2020, reducing the number of PSBs from 27 in 2017 to 12.[2] During FY 2021/22, the government announced its intention to privatize two PSBs, which could help reduce the footprint of the state in the financial sector.

During the COVID-19 pandemic, credit growth moderated to below 6 percent despite significant monetary easing and financial sector measures, reflecting weak demand and amplifying pre-pandemic growth slowdown. Pandemic-related financial sector measures included the six-month loan payment moratorium, easing of regulatory measures, and the Targeted Long-Term Repo Operation (TLTRO) aimed at supporting banks to provide funding to corporates. Credit growth has subsequently picked up during FY 2021/22, with the gradual return of normalcy following the acute phase of the pandemic. Nonfood credit rose by 9.7 percent (year on year) as on end-March 2022, up from 5.5 percent a year ago, mainly driven by retail loans but also supported by recovery in credit to industry.

---

[1] Taking a longer view, cross-country analysis suggests efficiency gaps among Indian banks relative to peers widened during that period (Box 3.1).

[2] The reduction in the total number of PSBs includes a merger of three banks in April 2019 and mergers of associate banks to the State Bank of India in 2017.

Figure 3.1. Banking Sector Developments

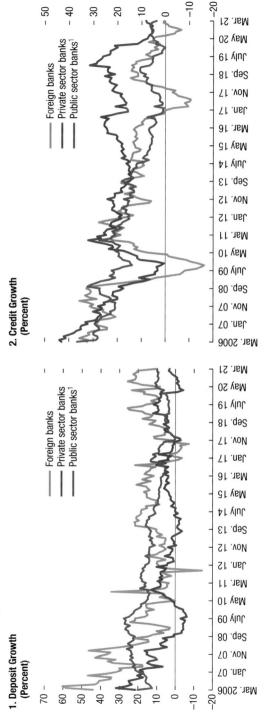

1. Deposit Growth
(Percent)

2. Credit Growth
(Percent)

Figure 3.1 *(continued)*

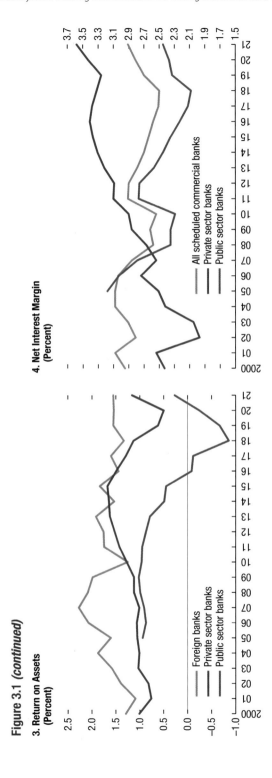

3. Return on Assets
(Percent)

4. Net Interest Margin
(Percent)

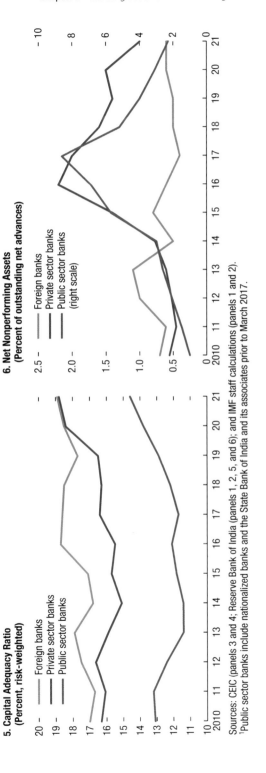

5. Capital Adequacy Ratio
(Percent, risk-weighted)

Foreign banks
Private sector banks
Public sector banks

6. Net Nonperforming Assets
(Percent of outstanding net advances)

Foreign banks
Private sector banks
Public sector banks
(right scale)

Sources: CEIC (panels 3 and 4; Reserve Bank of India (panels 1, 2, 5, and 6); and IMF staff calculations (panels 1 and 2).
¹Public sector banks include nationalized banks and the State Bank of India and its associates prior to March 2017.

Box 3.1. Assessment of Bank Efficiency by Ownership

We use data envelopment analysis to assess the efficiency of public sector banks (PSBs) compared with private sector banks, and to peer countries with significant state ownership of banks. The approach is a non-parametric linear programming method that can be applied to entities with common inputs and outputs to assess their efficiency (Charnes and others 1978). It has been widely used for analyzing banks' performance in turning multiple inputs into multiple outputs (Arena and others 2018; Kumar 2013; Kaur and Gupta 2015). It allows benchmarking individual institutions against the estimated efficiency frontier of the selected sample. Technical efficiency is estimated assuming that all entities operate at the optimal scale, which can be further disaggregated into purely technical efficiency (i.e., assuming variable returns to scale) and scale efficiency.

The analysis covers the largest 20 banks by assets for India and six comparator countries (Brazil, Russia, China, South Africa, Indonesia, and Vietnam) for 2000–17.[1] We consider various combinations of inputs and outputs, given the sensitivity of the results. Focusing on the banks' role as intermediators, we primarily look at variables related to funding and costs as inputs, and those related to profitability and assets accumulated as outputs (see Table 3.1.1). We present the results as simple averages of efficiency scores estimated for the 10 combinations of inputs and outputs.

TABLE 3.1.1.

Input/Output Combinations

	1	2	3	4	5	6	7	8	9	10
Inputs										
Interest exp				x	x	x	x	x		x
Noninterest exp	x	x	x						x	x
Personnel exp				x	x	x	x	x		
Other opr exp				x	x	x				
Deposits	x	x	x						x	x
Equity	x	x	x							
Fixed assets							x	x	x	
Outputs										
Opr profits	x	x		x	x					
Opr income			x			x	x			
Earnings assets	x		x							x
Net loans		x	x		x	x	x	x		x
Securities (liquid assets)		x	x		x	x	x	x		
Deposits								x		
Net interest income									x	
Noninterest income									x	

Source: IMF staff calculations.
Note: exp = expenses; opr = operating.

---

[1] The analysis covers up to 2017, to capture the period prior to the spillover from the NBFC stress and the impact from the COVID-19 pandemic.

Box 3.1. *(continued)*

We find that Indian banks' efficiency scores have declined relative to peers in the recent period (Figure 3.1.2). The average efficiency scores of the large Indian banks were the second highest after China in 2000–02. However, the distance of the Indian banks from the efficiency frontier estimated by the data envelopment analysis widened by 2015–17, with none of the top-20 Indian banks at the efficiency frontier. This finding is consistent with trends in some of the intermediation efficiency indicators: the decline in profitability and the increase in nonperforming assets in the Indian banking system, as well as the slowdown in credit growth in the mid-2010s.

The gaps between the average efficiency of the large PSBs and of the private sector banks in India has increased in recent years. Technical efficiency scores of private sector banks average higher than PSBs, except in 2003–05 and 2009–11 (Figure 3.1.1). The weaker performance of private sector banks in these two periods likely reflects the credit boom in the early 2000s, when PSB credit growth accelerated sharply, and private and foreign banks' credit growth slowed down during the global financial crisis. The higher PSB efficiency may also reflect the slow recognition of nonperforming assets and an increase in provisioning, which would have affected profitability and capitalization. The widening gaps in the most recent periods are consistent with the increase in nonperforming assets, slowing credit growth, declining profitability, and pressures on capital adequacy that have been more pronounced in PSBs. Breaking down technical efficiency into pure technical efficiency and scale efficiency, the wider gap observed for pure technical efficiency implies that PSBs benefit from economies of scale, partially offsetting the lag in pure technical efficiency. Indian banks' efficiency scores also have declined relative to peers in recent periods (Figure 3.1.2), consistent with the decline in profitability and the increase in nonperforming assets, as well as the slowdown in credit growth.

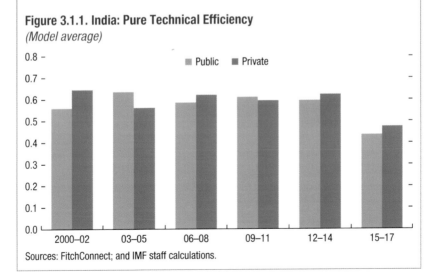

Figure 3.1.1. India: Pure Technical Efficiency
(Model average)

Sources: FitchConnect; and IMF staff calculations.

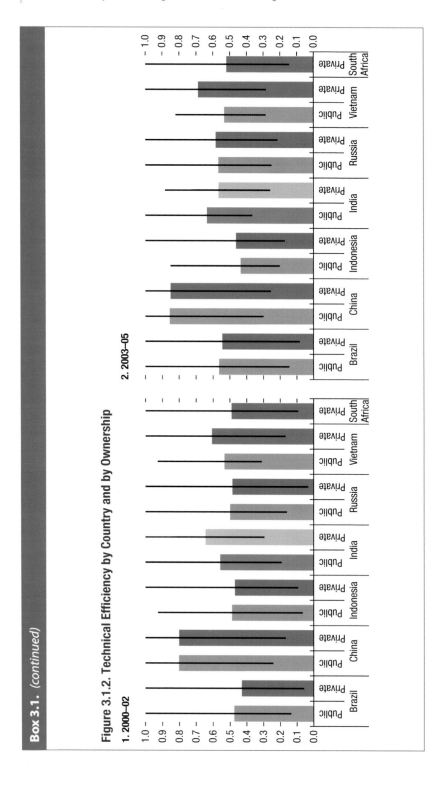

Box 3.1. *(continued)*

Figure 3.1.2. Technical Efficiency by Country and by Ownership

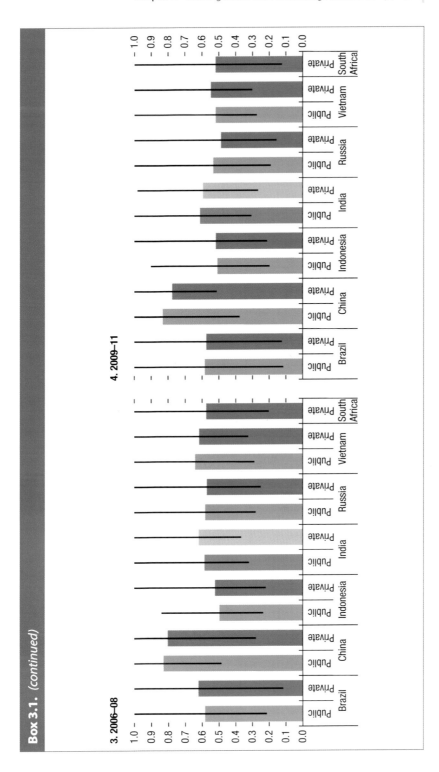

Box 3.1. *(continued)*

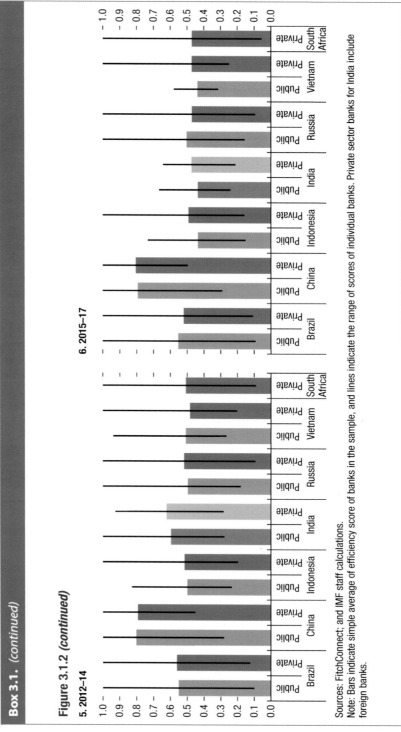

Box 3.1. *(continued)*

Figure 3.1.2 *(continued)*

5. 2012–14

6. 2015–17

Sources: FitchConnect; and IMF staff calculations.
Note: Bars indicate simple average of efficiency score of banks in the sample, and lines indicate the range of scores of individual banks. Private sector banks for India include foreign banks.

After significantly worsening in response to the pandemic, asset quality indicators have gradually improved, as banks have seen their NPA ratio decrease and capital ratio increase over time. In particular, the ratio of gross NPA decreased from 7.3 percent in March 2021 to 5.9 percent in March 2022, largely reflecting the recovery in the corporate sector, which is confirmed by the declining leverage of listed firms and falling delinquency rates across sectors and borrower types. Important differences in asset quality and capital adequacy persist between public and private banks, with the former performing significantly worse. Even if banks seem to have rebounded from the COVID-19 pandemic, structural vulnerabilities remain. For instance, NPAs remain high from an international perspective and could quickly increase in case of a faster-than-expected tightening in financial conditions. Moreover, regulation requires banks (e.g., high statutory liquidity ratio) to hold very large government portfolios, which increase the exposure to interest-rate risk and give rise to a strong sovereign-bank nexus. Although the share of government dated securities held by commercial banks has steadily declined from 45 percent in 2014 to 35 percent in December 2021, the exposure remains sizeable, exposing banks to market risks. The planned reduction in statutory liquidity ratio in a phased manner can help banks better manage their risks.

NONBANKING FINANCIAL COMPANIES

The NBFC sector in India comprises nonbanking financial institutions under a wide range of business models and regulated by the RBI.[3] It encompasses 11 categories based on activity, such as extending financing for physical assets and infrastructure loans (Table 3.1). In general, NBFCs tend to have less-diversified portfolios than banks, reflecting their specialization within one or a few loan segment types. For instance, as their name suggests, housing finance companies are NBFCs focusing on the real estate market.

According to the RBI definition, NBFCs must hold the majority of their total tangible financial assets toward housing finance to qualify as housing finance companies.[4] There were 9,680 NBFCs registered with the RBI in September 2021, including asset reconstruction companies and housing finance companies, of which 52 were deposit-accepting and 312 systemically important nondeposit-taking NBFCs with an asset size of Rs5 billion. The majority were private companies, with government-owned entities accounting for about 39 percent of assets.

---

[3] It does not include nonbanking financial institutions such as all-India financial institutions and primary dealers (regulated by RBI), insurance companies (Insurance Regulatory and Development Authority of India), merchant banking companies, venture capital fund companies, stock broking, and collective investment schemes (Securities and Exchange Board of India). The regulation of housing finance companies was transferred from the National Housing Bank to the RBI in 2019.

[4] The required share of assets for housing finance will gradually increase, reaching 60 percent in March 2024.

TABLE 3.1.

Classification of Nonbank Financial Companies by Activity	
Type of NBFC	**Activity**
1. Investment and credit company (ICC)	Lending and investment
2. NBFC-infrastructure finance company (NBFC-IFC)	Financing of infrastructure sector
3. Core investment company (CIC)	Investment in equity shares, preference shares, debt, or loans of group companies
4. NBFC-infrastructure debt fund (NBFC-IDF)	Facilitation of flow of long-term debt only into post commencement operations in infrastructure projects that have completed at least one year of satisfactory performance
5. NBFC-micro-finance institution (NBFC-MFI)	Providing collateral free small-ticket loans to economically disadvantaged groups
6. NBFC-Factor	Acquisition of receivables of an assignor or extending loans against the security interest of the receivables at a discount
7. NBFC-Nonoperative financial holding company (NBFC-NOFHC)	Facilitation of promoters/promoter groups in setting up new banks
8. Mortgage guarantee company (MGC)	Undertaking of mortgage guarantee business
9. NBFC-account aggregator (NBFC-AA)	Collecting and providing information about a customer's financial assets in a consolidated, organized, and retrievable manner to the customer or others as specified by the customer
10. NBFC–Peer-to-peer lending platform (NBFC-P2P)	Providing an online platform to bring lenders and borrowers together to help mobilize funds
11. Housing finance company (HFC)	Financing for housing

Source: Reserve Bank of India.
Note: NBFC = nonbanking financial company.

NBFCs have played an increasingly important role in credit, filling the gap created by slower bank credit growth (Figure 3.2). The growth of NBFC loans and advances outpaced that of bank credit during 2014–2021, except for one year, as the asset quality problem weighed on banks. As a result, NBFC loans are now almost equal to one-quarter of commercial bank loans, up from 17 percent in 2013. They are an important provider of credit to all major sectors, with the largest share of loans (about 39 percent) given to industry. Among corporates, NBFCs lend mainly to large firms, whose loans account for 80 percent of the sector's aggregate loans. Although NBFCs had intermediated about 11 percent of credit outstanding to micro, small, and medium enterprises as of 2021, the total share masks important differences in market share across micro, small, and medium enterprise with respect to size, sector, and regions and does not reflect trends in new loan disbursements.

An important characteristic of NBFCs is their reliance on bank borrowing and market funding (Figure 3.3). Unlike the banking sector, deposits play a limited role in NBFC sector funding, given the small and declining number of deposit-taking institutions (around 2–3 percent of liabilities).[5] Instead, bank borrowing and market funding (debentures and commercial paper) accounted for close to 33.1 percent

---

[5] No new deposit-taking NBFC has been licensed since 1997.

Figure 3.2. Nonfood Credit Growth
(Percent, year-over-year)

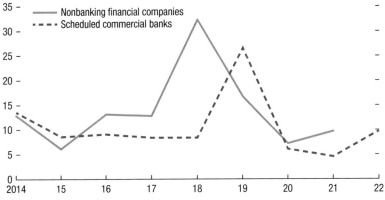

Sources: CEIC; Reserve Bank of India; and IMF staff calculations.

Figure 3.3. NBFCs: Sources of Funding
(Percent of total borrowings)

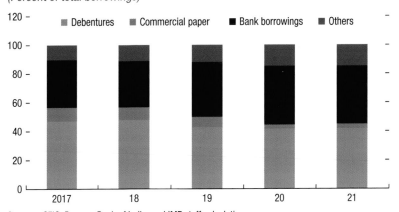

Sources: CEIC; Reserve Bank of India; and IMF staff calculations.
Note: NBFCs = nonbank financial companies.

and 45 percent of total liabilities, respectively, as of March 2021. There had been a shift toward market funding at the expense of bank borrowing in the mid-2010s, but the trend reversed after the liquidity shocks to the sector starting in the late 2010s (see Box 3.2).

NBFCs managed to achieve higher profitability than banks for many years, enjoying higher returns on assets until the late 2010s, when the sector faced severe distress (Figure 3.4, Box 3.2). High net interest margins have been a key contributor, and deposit-taking NBFCs have outperformed the rest of the sector.

Box 3.2. The 2018 Nonbanking Financial Companies Stress and Interlinkages

A series of defaults by an important core investment company, Infrastructure Leasing and Financial Services, in 2018 triggered a negative risk-aversion shock among investors and led to a flight to safety, starting with a systemwide run on the shadow banking system, mutual funds in particular. These intermediaries, especially those exposed to nonbanking financial companies (NBFCs), were forced to cut lending to NBFCs and the financial system more broadly. Faced with a fall in available funding, NBFCs responded by reducing lending to limit cash outflows. As a consequence, borrowers, including real estate developers, lost access to credit and their illiquidity soon turned into insolvency. Corporate defaults in turn further weakened NBFC balance sheets, reinforcing concerns about their soundness and leading to a flight to quality. A few months later, in June 2019, the default of another NBFC (Dewan Housing and Finance Corporation) amplified the shock, restarting the adverse dynamic that took place following the Infrastructure Leasing and Financial Services default.

The Dewan Housing and Finance Corporation default in turn had knock-on effects on the banking sector. Because commercial banks had increased lending to NBFCs, partly to meet their priority sector lending requirements and partly to relieve NBFCs' liquidity pressures, interlinkages also increased. Concerns also grew about the asset quality of some banks, as they had become increasingly exposed to troubled sectors—particularly real estate and infrastructure. Both factors raised uncertainty about hidden bank vulnerabilities, prompting investors to reduce their exposure to some banks and worsening liquidity conditions. Starting in June 2019, several commercial banks struggled to raise wholesale funding, and stress in the interbank market increased. Like NBFCs, banks responded by holding excess liquidity, reaching 2 percent of GDP by the first week of January 2020, equivalent to 40 percent of the fresh lending banks did in FY 2018/19.[1]

Amid the lack of granular data on individual institutions and risk aversion, the sector experienced a liquidity crunch. Except for large NBFCs with well-established and strong parentage, access to funding via mutual funds tightened, which had been a key source of funding. The share of long-term market debt (i.e., nonconvertible debentures) in total borrowings of the NBFC sector declined from 49.1 percent at end-March 2017 to 40.8 percent at end-December 2019. The consequent funding gap was met through new borrowing from banks, which rose from 23.1 percent of total (new) NBFC borrowings to 29.5 percent over this period. The share of NBFC loans over total nonfood bank credit has increased from 5.5 percent to 8.3 percent (Figure 3.2.1).

---

[1] The financial shock may have also contributed to the reduced transmission of monetary policy. With commercial banks competing for deposits, term deposit rates have increased—with the spread between the term deposit rates and repo rates spiking after the defaults of Infrastructure Leasing and Financial Services and Dewan Housing and Finance Corporation. Thus, competition for deposits is one of several factors that may help explain why the cut in the repo rates is not being transmitted one-for-one to deposit/lending rates

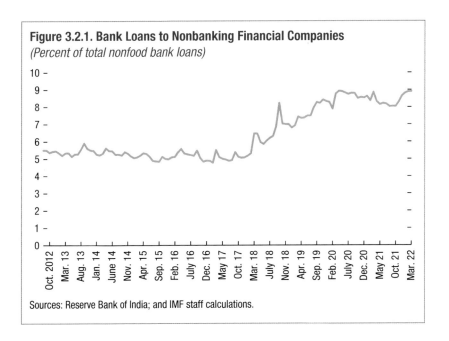

Figure 3.2.1. Bank Loans to Nonbanking Financial Companies
(Percent of total nonfood bank loans)

Sources: Reserve Bank of India; and IMF staff calculations.

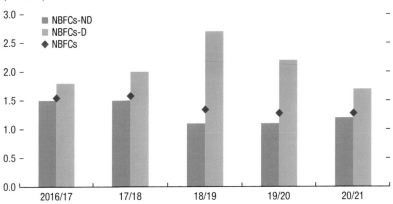

Figure 3.4. Return on Assets of Nonbanking Financial Companies
(Percent)

Sources: Reserve Bank of India; and IMF staff calculations.
Note: NBFCs-ND = nonbanking financial companies–nondeposit taking; NBFCs-D = nonbanking financial companies–deposit taking.

TABLE 3.2.

Asset Quality

(Percent of assets/RWA)

	Asset Quality/CRARs of NBFCs						
	2016	2017	2018	2019	2020	2021	2022
GNPA ratio	4.5	6.1	5.8	6.1	6.8	6.4	6.2
NNPA ratio	2.5	4.4	3.8	3.3	3.4	2.7	3.3
CRAR	24.3	22.1	22.8	20.1	23.7	25.0	26.9

Source: July 2022 *Global Financial Stability Report*.
Note: CRAR = capital-to-risk-asset ratio; GNPA = gross nonperforming asset; NBFCs = nonbanking financial companies;
NNPA = net nonperforming asset; RWA = risk-weighted asset.

In March 2021, the systemwide capital adequacy ratio stood at 26.5 percent, significantly above the 2017 level, before the sector experienced severe distress (see Box 3.2) and the ratio of gross NPAs was equal to 6.4 percent, slightly lower than the peak reached during the COVID-19 crisis in March 2020 (Table 3.2). Developments in NBFC balance sheets partly reflect the phased tightening of regulation aimed at closing potential regulatory arbitrage between these intermediaries and banks, as discussed in the following section.

Following the COVID-19 shock, the NBFC sector benefited from several targeted support measures. First, a government guarantee program envisaged government guarantee schemes to support investment by other financial institutions in securities issued by NBFCs. Specifically, the program included a full guarantee for investment-grade debt securities of NBFCs and a partial credit guarantee scheme on debt of lower-rated NBFCs, where government would bear the first 20 percent of any losses. Second, a resolution scheme for retail and corporate loans under distress due to the COVID-19 shock enabled NBFCs and housing finance companies (and banks) to continue classifying loans as standard if a successful restructuring had been carried out before December 31, 2020.[6] Finally, banks obtaining liquidity from the RBI via Targeted Long-Term Repo Operation 2.0 were obliged to invest in investment-grade bonds, commercial paper, and the nonconvertible debentures of NBFCs.

NBFC credit initially lagged behind bank credit post-COVID-19, but it quickly rebounded. Year-over-year credit growth stood at 1.9 percent for NBFCs and 6.1 percent for scheduled commercial banks as of end-March 2020. However, lending by NBFCs grew 9.7 percent in FY 2022, outpacing bank credit (up 5.5 percent). Support measures played a key role in supporting credit markets and it is still too early to determine whether NBFCs will keep growing at the rates observed before 2019. Moreover, it is crucial to closely and continuously monitor whether the support measures have intensified risks faced by the financial sector and act accordingly. In particular, TLTRO and government guarantees on NBFC-issued bonds have incentivized banks to further increase exposure to NBFCs, while the resolution scheme may have artificially and temporarily improved asset quality.

---

[6] There is a similar, but separate provision for restructured micro, small, and medium enterprise loans, if restructuring takes place before March 31, 2021.

EVOLUTION IN THE REGULATORY FRAMEWORK

RBI has been taking steps to strengthen the regulation and supervision of NBFCs. The regulatory framework was revised in 2014 to harmonize and strengthen the prudential norms. NBFCs accepting public deposits and systematically important nondeposit-taking NBFCs are subject to prudential regulation and supervision, while the nonsystemically important nondeposit-taking NBFCs are only subject to reporting requirement. Exemptions from regulations granted to government-owned NBFCs were withdrawn from June 2018, with phased-in timelines for compliance through FY 2022. Key features of the revised NBFC regulatory framework included the designation of systemically important NBFCs, the introduction of capital requirements, and the effort to harmonize NPA recognition norms with those for banks.

After 2019 and COVID-19, the RBI has been taking steps to strengthen regulation and supervision of NBFCs. Their historically higher capitalization and lower NPA ratios than banks in part reflect different and relatively looser prudential norms. To eliminate these sources of potential regulatory arbitrage and improve the resilience of NBFCs, the RBI has adopted several measures in recent years that address both credit and liquidity risks.

The central bank published guidelines to enhance liquidity risk management for all NBFCs in 2019. The guidelines identify granular maturity buckets and corresponding tolerance limits for net cumulative mismatches. The guidelines also recommend monitoring of liquidity by using a stock approach, in addition to measurement of structural and dynamic liquidity and extending the principles of sound liquidity risk management to various issues, including stress testing and diversification of funding. The framework requires that nondeposit-taking NBFCs with asset size of at least Rs 100 billion and all deposit-taking NBFCs maintain a minimum liquidity coverage ratio, which will progressively increase and reach 100 percent on December 1, 2024.

Another important change in the regulatorily environment of NBFCs was the introduction of a scale-based framework in 2021. The framework is based on a four-layered structure. The base layer consists of relatively small nondeposit-taking NBFCs and the middle layer mainly includes all deposit-taking NBFCs and larger nondeposit-taking NBFCs. The upper layer will comprise certain NBFCs specifically identified by the RBI based on a set of parameters. The top layer is expected to remain empty until specific NBFCs are identified as posing systemic risk.

Building on this scale-based framework, additional changes have led to further convergence in regulation between banks and NBFCs, specifically those in the upper layer. Although the capital-to-risk-weighted-assets ratio requirement for all NBFCs is 15 percent, NBFCs in the upper layer also need to have to maintain a Common Equity Tier 1 capital ratio of at least 9 percent. Moreover, a large exposure framework has been introduced, limiting credit concentration for NBFCs in the upper layer.

CONCLUSION

Banks have been the main providers of credit within India's financial system, accounting for around 60 percent of credit to the private sector. Since the 1970s, PSBs have played a pivotal role in India's development strategy by extending credit to sectors prioritized by the government. Although private banks are playing a more important role, NBFCs in particular have grown in recent years as alternative intermediaries of finance. NBFCs have provided an alternative source of credit for businesses and households, now accounting for about one-fifth of the credit of banks.

However, NBFCs also receive a significant share of their funding from banks, increasing the risk that stress in NBFCs can spill over to the banking system. During 2015–18, NBFCs expanded credit at around twice the pace of banks, partly prompted by constrained credit growth by the PSBs and accompanied by higher systemic risk. Subsequently, a high-profile NBFC default in 2018 significantly tightened funding conditions for NBFCs and reduced the flow of credit.

The change in the NBFC regulatory framework has increased the ability of the sector to withstand adverse shocks, but vulnerabilities remain. The introduction of a scale-based framework and the adoption of guidelines for liquidity management represent significant steps toward strengthening NBFCs and reducing the regulatory gap between them and banks. This progressive alignment in regulation could favor consolidation between banks and NBFCs, potentially generating efficiency gains and improving governance. At the same time, the increased interconnectedness between banks and NBFCs implies that shocks hitting either of these sectors would have immediate and direct spillover on the other. Regulation aimed at limiting bank borrowing by NBFCs, and in general favoring diversification in funding sources, would contribute to weakening interlinkages and preventing a diabolic loop from emerging in the future. Further strengthening the liquidity requirements for NBFCs would contribute to reducing the risk of adverse liquidity shocks leading to insolvency and sectoral stress, as it happened in the past. Closing macroprudential policy gaps, for instance by requiring NBFCs to maintain a net stable funding ratio, as has been the case for banks since 2021, would represent an important step.

REFERENCES

Arena, Marco, Alexander Culiuc, and Marzie Sanjani. 2018. "The Role of the State in the Russian Banking Sector." Selected Issues Paper, IMF Country Report 18/276, Washington, DC.

Charnes, A., W.W. Cooper, and E. Rhodes. 1978. "Measuring the Efficiency of Decision Making Units." *European Journal of Operational Research* 2: 429–44

Goyal, J., and A. Aggarwal. 2018. "Efficiency and Technology Gaps in Indian Banking Sector: Application of Meta-frontier Directional Distance Function DEA Approach." *Journal of Finance and Data Science* 5 (3): 156–72.

Kaur, S., and P.K. Gupta. 2015. "Productive Efficiency Mapping of the Indian Banking System using Data Envelopment Analysis." *Procedia Economics and Finance* 25: 227–38.

Kumar, Sanjeesh. 2013. "Total Factor Productivity of Indian Banking Sector: Impact of Information Technology." Reserve Bank of India Occasional Papers, Vol. 34, No. 1 and 2.

CHAPTER 4

Banks: Lending to Productive Firms?

Siddharth George, Divya Kirti, Maria Soledad Martinez Peria, and Rajesh Vijayaraghavan

INTRODUCTION

Capital misallocation—the allocation of capital to less productive rather than more productive firms—is widely thought to be an important factor underpinning productivity and income gaps between advanced and emerging economies.[1] In the case of India, several studies suggest that the extent of capital misallocation, reflected in an unusually high dispersion of productivity across firms, is large (Hsieh and Klenow 2009). The literature has examined a wide range of potential drivers of capital misallocation, ranging from property rights and contract enforcement to licensing rules and infrastructure.[2]

Capital misallocation could also be driven by credit market misallocation: credit flowing to less productive firms, and more productive firms facing credit constraints that impede growth. Moreover, credit misallocation might give rise to a large presence of zombie—i.e., unviable—firms, which can be a barrier to the entry and growth of other firms. This phenomenon has been shown not only for Japan (Caballero, Hoshi, and Kashyap 2008) and other Organisation for Economic Co-operation and Development countries (McGowan, Andrews, and Millot 2017), but also in the case of India (Chari, Jain, and Kulkarni 2021).

Because banks in India are an important source of finance for the economy (see Chapter 3 on bank and nonbanking financial companies), it is critical to understand how banks allocate credit, particularly public sector banks (PSBs), which are majority owned by the government and play an outsized role in credit markets. Banerjee, Cole, and Duflo (2004) examined the allocation of credit across sectors in India comparing the behavior of PSBs and private banks, finding that the former lend more to

---

Yang Liu, Armaghan Naveed, and François-Clément Charbonnier provided excellent research assistance.

[1] A survey of this literature can be found in Restuccia and Rogerson (2017).

[2] Prior work has examined the role of property rights and contract enforcement (Bloom and others 2013), land regulation (Duranton and others 2015), industrial licensing (Alfaro and Chari 2015; Chari 2011), privatization (Dinç and Gupta 2011; Gupta 2005), reservation laws (Garcia-Santana and Pijoan-Mas 2014; Martin, Nataraj, and Harrison 2017; Rotemberg 2019), highway infrastructure (Ghani, Goswami, and Kerr 2016), roads (Asher and Novosad 2020), electricity shortages (Allcott, Collard-Wexler, and Connell 2016), labor regulation (Amirapu and Gechter 2019), land market frictions (Sood 2020), and capital market integration (Bau and Matray 2020).

agriculture, rural areas, and the government and less to trade, transport, and finance. Research has also shown that bank lending allocation in India is sensitive to election cycles. Cole (2009) found that PSBs increase agricultural credit during election years, but that these lending booms are not associated with larger agricultural output. Kumar (2020) went further, showing that bank lending to farmers increases before elections at the expense of lending to manufacturing firms, which cut their production and operate below full capacity. D'Souza and Surti (2021) developed a model in which state-owned banks tend to lend excessively to previously bad borrowers when they benefit from public guarantees that are not dependent on the prompt recognition of loan losses. They argue that their model is consistent with credit dynamics in India. Finally, Chakraborty, Javadekar, and Ramcharan (2021) examined how branch deregulation affects bank lending in India and found that PSBs reduce their lending to poorly performing firms (i.e., those with low return on assets) when branching expands in a district, suggesting that competition has a positive impact on credit allocation. Despite this active literature, the link between bank lending and firm-level productivity in India is not well understood.

This chapter studies how well Indian banks allocate capital across firms with varying levels of productivity. It develops simple metrics to investigate whether firms' productivity is associated with more financing from banks, and then examines whether this association depends on the extent to which firms maintain banking relationships with PSBs and the share of new credit in the economy provided by these banks.

The analysis shows the following:

- There is a stark difference between firms with and without significant ties to PSBs in the importance of productivity in determining the allocation of credit in years where PSBs account for a large share of new credit.

- Credit growth is strongly associated with productivity for firms with limited reliance on PSBs.

- For firms that do heavily rely on PSBs, the relationship between credit growth and productivity is weaker.

- The findings are driven by large firms, which receive the bulk of corporate credit in India. While large firms that tend to have more ties with PSBs see stronger growth in years in which these banks account for a larger share of new credit, this credit growth is concentrated in unproductive firms.

- These results do not change when the analysis controls for the extent to which firms have ties with banks that are less capitalized, rely more on sticky deposit funding, and have higher ratios of nonperforming or restructured loans. This suggests that the effects of firms' reliance on PSBs are most likely related to these banks' governance and supervision as opposed to performance.

- Hence, adoption of policies that aim to improve the governance and supervision of PSBs or that reduce public bank ownership (via privatizations) may be necessary to address the misallocation of credit in the economy and hence foster economic growth.

The results imply that:

- Reallocating the credit channeled to large unproductive firms by Indian banks could markedly lift the amount of credit available to more productive large firms.

- A simple counterfactual exercise for 2010–14, a period during which PSBs had a large overall footprint that excludes the impact of the global financial crisis, indicates that shifting half of the credit allocated by banks to large unproductive firms to more productive large firms could have raised credit growth for the more productive firms from 9 to more than 13 percentage points per year. Credit growth would have risen to over 17 percentage points if all the credit to unproductive firms were to be allocated to more productive firms.

- In the context of meaningful credit constraints for firms (Banerjee and Duflo 2014), this represents an important missed opportunity.

In the remainder of the chapter, the first section describes the data and the second section presents stylized facts. The third section discusses empirical specifications and the fourth section summarizes empirical findings. The final section offers a conclusion.

DATA

The analysis combines firm-level balance sheet and income statement data for nonfinancial firms from CMIE Prowess with bank-level balance sheet and income statement data from the Database of Indian Economy (DBIE) from the Reserve Bank of India (RBI).[3] In addition to the financial statement items, DBIE also includes information on bank-level nonperforming assets and restructured loans, and selected performance and financial soundness ratios for scheduled commercial banks.[4]

The chapter matches firm-level bank information from Prowess to bank financial information from the DBIE database. Given that there is no common identifier between the Prowess and RBI databases, the chapter matches the list of firms' banks (reported in the variable "Banker") in the Prowess database to the banks in the RBI database using a name-matching approach. First, the list of all bank names in the RBI DBIE database is standardized to ensure consistency. The analysis then relies on descriptions provided by RBI of bank name changes to construct a list of bank names at the year level.[5] The chapter implements an algorithm that begins with a fuzzy match, by year, between bank names in the Prowess data and the list of banks in the RBI database. It then manually confirms the

---

[3] Bank-level data can be downloaded at https://dbie.rbi.org.in/DBIE/dbie.rbi?site=statistics.

[4] Commercial banks that maintain required cash reserves with RBI are listed on the second schedule of the Reserve Bank of India Act (1934) and hence referred to as scheduled commercial banks. See https://rbidocs.rbi.org.in/rdocs/Publications/PDFs/RBIA1934170510.PDF.

[5] See Notes on Tables at https://dbie.rbi.org.in/DBIE/dbie.rbi?site=publications#!4.

accuracy of this match. The approach matches over 99 percent of the bank–firm links reported by Prowess firms in the sample described below.[6]

The main variables of interest from Prowess for the analysis are the stock of bank credit and the variables used to measure firm capital productivity, namely: sales and physical capital (net plants, property, and equipment). The analysis also collects other variables from Prowess to control for firm characteristics beyond productivity, including firm size (log of assets), age (in years), sector (as measured by five-digit level National Industrial Classification codes),[7] location (measured at the district level), sales growth (log growth in sales), leverage (debt-to-assets ratio), and interest coverage (earnings before taxes to interest expenses). The chapter also collects information on the firm ownership type (including government ownership).

The focus is on studying how the link between firm productivity and the growth of bank credit changes depending on the characteristics of the banks that firms borrow from. Hence, the chapter uses RBI data to construct bank-level variables that identify banks' ownership (public, new private, and other),[8] capitalization (capital-to-asset ratio), funding mix (share of nondeposit liabilities), and asset quality (nonperforming plus restructured loans-to-assets ratio). In firm-level regressions, the analysis collapses these variables to the firm-year level by weighting by bank loans among the set of banks listed by the firm in that year.

The data sets cover 2005–20. In the regression analysis described below, the sample includes firms in the following sectors: manufacturing, electricity and gas supply, construction, wholesale and retail trade, transportation, accommodation and food services, information and communication, professional and scientific activities, administrative and support service activities, and other service activities.[9] The sample is restricted to firms with at least five years of nonmissing data on total assets, net plant, property and equipment, sales, total borrowing, and bank borrowing. The analysis also imposes the condition that there be at least five firms in each five-digit National Industrial Classification sector-year pair. Lenders not included in the RBI database are dropped from the analysis. The sample is also restricted to firms for which there is a nonmissing data on the firm-level controls and at least one bank reported by the firm with matched data from RBI.

---

[6] See Chari, Jain, and Kulkarni (2021) and Ghosh, Narayanan, and Garg (2021) for examples of other work matching Prowess and RBI based on bank names.

[7] Prowess provides National Industrial Classification codes based on the 2008 classification. Five-digit National Industrial Classification codes identify highly granular industries. Examples of five-digit National Industrial Classification industries in our sample include *manufacture of hot-rolled and cold-rolled products of steel* (24105), *finishing of cotton and blended cotton textiles* (13131), *sale of motor vehicle parts and accessories* (45300), and *publishing of newspapers* (58131).

[8] The chapter follows RBI (2021) in identifying Axis Bank, Bandhan Bank, DCB Bank Limited, HDFC Bank, ICICI Bank, IDBI Bank Limited, IDFC First Bank, IndusInd Bank Ltd, Kotak Mahindra Bank, and Yes Bank as new private banks.

[9] The chapter retains firms in Sections C, D, F, G, H, I, J, M, N, and S in the sample. Manufacturing firms (Section C) account for about 60 percent of assets and bank credit in the sample.

STYLIZED FACTS

The chapter presents four stylized facts about banks in India and the allocation of credit. First, it documents that PSBs account for a sizeable share of bank credit. Since 2005, PSBs have accounted for 60–80 percent of outstanding loans, with total loans growing to about 100 trillion rupees, more than 50 percent of GDP, by 2020 (Figure 4.1). Most of the remaining credit is disbursed by "new private banks." These banks commenced operations following banking sector reforms introduced in 1993 to allow private entry to induce greater competition. However, this average figure masks significant year-to-year variation in the share of new credit from PSBs relative to other banks (Figure 4.2). This number varies from less than 20 percent in some years (e.g., 2016, 2017) to over 90 percent in other years (e.g., 2009, 2010). The analysis in this chapter documents below that this appears to be associated with the efficiency of credit allocation in each year.[10]

Second, the analysis documents that PSBs have higher nonperforming asset ratios (including restructured loans, as in Chari, Jain, and Kulkarni 2021),

Figure 4.1. Outstanding Bank Credit by Bank Ownership Type

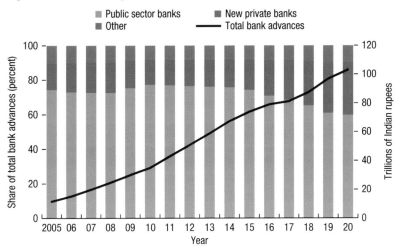

Sources: Reserve Bank of India; and authors' calculations.
Note: This figure shows the share of public sector banks, new private banks, and other banks in the total stock of advances outstanding by year (left-hand axis), as well as the total stock of advances (right-hand axis).

---

[10] While strong lending by PSBs in the aftermath of the global financial crisis appears to have had costs related to poor allocation of credit, it may also have supported broader economic performance by avoiding a credit crunch.

Figure 4.2. New Bank Credit by Bank Ownership Type

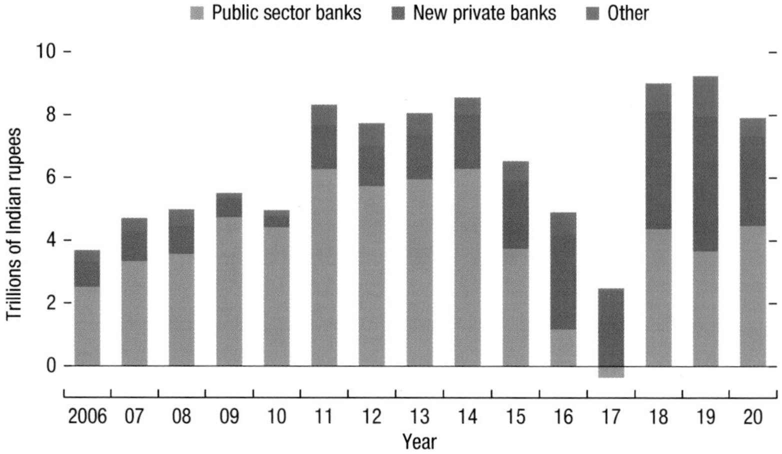

Sources: Reserve Bank of India; and authors' calculations.
Note: This figure shows new bank credit (change in stock of advances since the previous year) by year, breaking out bank types, in trillions (lakh crores) of rupees.

lower Tier 1 capital ratios, and a lower share of nondeposit liabilities than the new private banks (Figure 4.3). PSBs broadly operate at similar scales to new private banks; both are considerably larger than other banks (Figure 4.3).

Third, the analysis finds that a significant fraction of new bank credit is extended to unproductive firms (Figure 4.5). In an average year, around 45 percent of new bank credit is allocated to unproductive firms (firms with sales-to-physical-capital ratios in the bottom tercile within industry-year).[11] Moreover, since nearly all new credit goes to large firms (Figure 4.4), credit misallocation in India is a phenomenon that takes place within the sample of large firms (Figure 4.5).

Fourth, this average number belies significant year-to-year variation in the share of credit going to unproductive firms (Figure 4.5). In 2015, less than 10 percent of new credit went to unproductive firms, while this figure was over 80 percent in 2018. One important correlate of the quality of credit allocation, as Figure 4.5 shows, is the share of new credit in the year that is disbursed by PSBs.

The next section investigates the link between firm productivity and bank credit growth more systematically by examining the correlation within granular industries and districts and including a battery of bank and firm controls.

---

[11] Unreported analysis finds that credit allocated to state-owned firms does not account for a large share of credit allocated to unproductive firms in most years.

Figure 4.3. Differences between Banks of Different Ownership Types

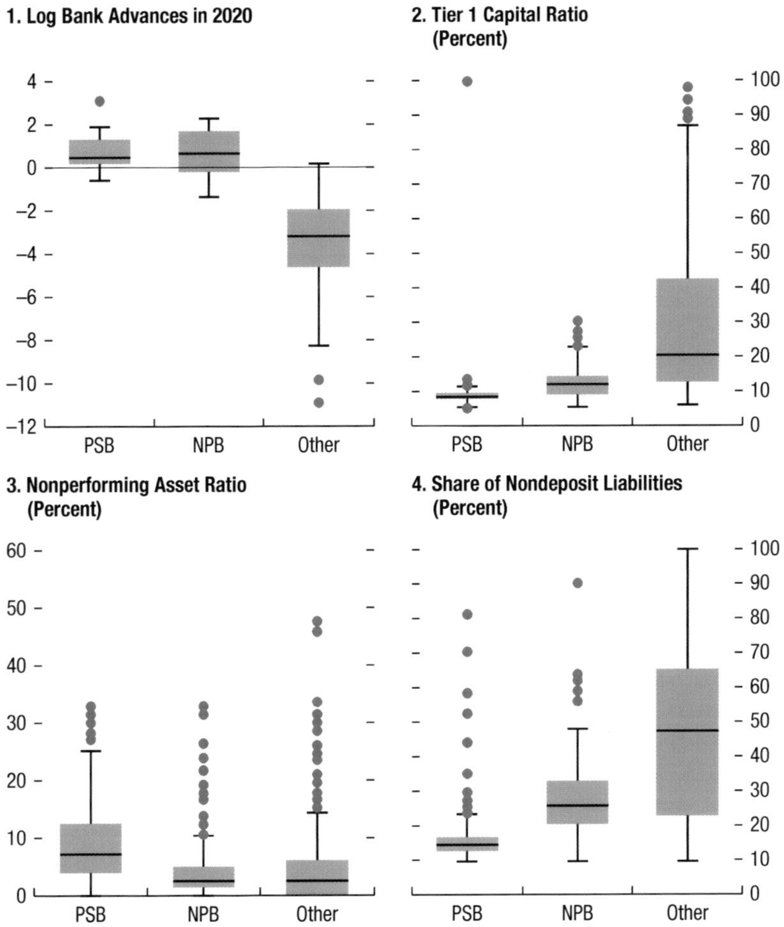

1. Log Bank Advances in 2020

2. Tier 1 Capital Ratio
(Percent)

3. Nonperforming Asset Ratio
(Percent)

4. Share of Nondeposit Liabilities
(Percent)

Sources: Reserve Bank of India; and authors' calculations.
Note: This figure shows how public sector banks (PSBs) differ from private banks and other Indian banks. Each panel shows box plots by type of bank showing the 10th, 25th, 50th, 75th, and 90th percentiles (as well as individual outliers). Panel 1 shows log bank advances in 2020 (prior to taking logs these advances are in trillions [lakh crores] of rupees). Panel 2 shows the Tier 1 capital ratio across 2005–20, in percentage points. Panel 3 shows the nonperforming asset ratio (defined as the sum of gross nonperforming assets and restructured loans as a fraction of advances) across 2005–20, in percentage points. Panel 4 shows the share of nondeposit liabilities across 2005–20, in percentage points. The ratios shown in Panels 2, 3, and 4 are winsorized at the 5th and 95th percentiles by year. NPB = new private bank.

Figure 4.4. Share of New Bank Credit to Large Firms

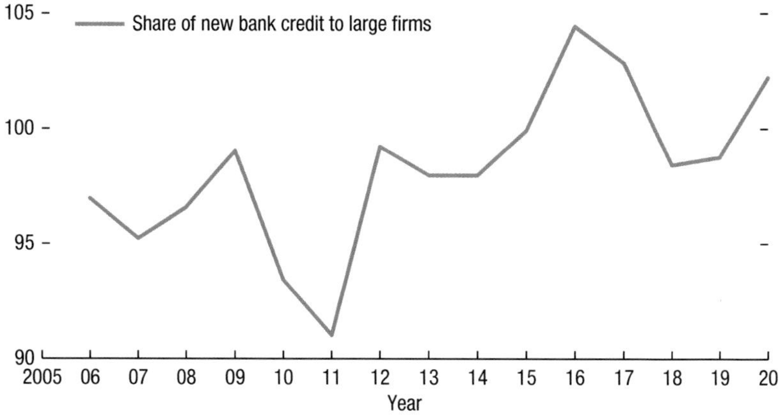

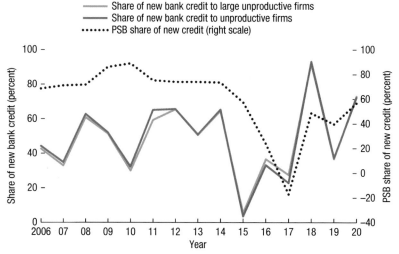

Sources: CMIE Prowess; and authors' calculations.
Note: This figure shows the percentage of new bank credit (change in the stock of bank credit since the previous year) that goes to large firms (top tercile of total assets within year). It is possible for new bank credit to fall for a group of firms in a given year. The sample of firm-years from Prowess is described in the text.

Figure 4.5. Share of New Bank Credit to Large Unproductive Firms and PSB Share of Credit

Sources: CMIE Prowess; Reserve Bank of India; and authors' calculations.
Note: This figure shows the share of new bank credit (change in stock of bank credit since the previous year) allocated to unproductive firms or to large unproductive firms (within large firms) by year in percentage points on the left vertical axis. Large firms are in the top tercile of assets within year. Unproductive firms are in the bottom tercile of productivity (lagged ratio of sales to physical capital). The figure shows public sector banks' share of new bank credit (change in advances since the previous year) in the economy by year in percentage points on the right vertical axis. The sample of firm-years from Prowess is described in the text. PSB = public sector bank.

EMPIRICAL SPECIFICATIONS

To explore the link between bank credit growth, firm productivity, and bank ownership, the analysis starts by estimating equation (4.1) below:

$$C_{it} = \alpha + \beta_1 \text{Productivity}_{it-1} + \beta_2 \text{PSB dependence}_{it-1} + \tag{4.1}$$
$$\beta_3 \text{Productivity}_{it-1} * \text{PSB dependence}_{it-1} + \beta_4 \text{Productivity}_{it-1} *$$
$$\text{PSB share of credit}_{t-1} + \beta_5 \text{PSB share of credit}_{t-1} *$$
$$\text{PSB dependence}_{it-1} + \beta_6 \text{Productivity}_{it-1} * \text{PSB share of credit}_{t-1} *$$
$$\text{PSB dependence}_{it-1} + \theta X_{it-1} + \delta_{st} + \mu_{dt} + \varepsilon_{it}$$

where the dependent variable, C_{it}, denotes the bounded annual growth in the stock of bank credit received by firm i (i.e., credit granted to firm i by all banks) at time t.[12] *Productivity*$_{it-1}$ is the lagged ratio of sales to physical capital.[13] The analysis identifies firm-level reliance on PSBs by combining two measures. First, *PSB dependence*, which varies by both firm and time, defined as the weighted share of PSBs with which a firm has banking relationships, where the weights are based on each bank's share of total lending in that year.[14] Second, *PSB share of credit*, which captures the importance of PSBs in new lending over time, defined as the proportion of new loans granted by PSBs in each year. In contrast to PSB dependence, which varies by both firm and time, the PSB share of credit captures the importance of PSBs in new lending over time.[15] X_{it-1} are firm level controls for size (log assets), sales growth (log growth in sales), leverage (debt-to-asset ratio), interest coverage ratio, and ownership.[16] δ_{st} are sector-time fixed effects and μ_{dt} are district-time fixed effects. Sector-time fixed effects are important: the ratio of sales to physical capital is a tighter proxy for productivity within industry (Bau and Matray 2020).

While the direct impact of productivity on credit growth (measured by β_1 and all interactions of productivity with other terms) is also relevant, the main coefficient of interest is β_6, which captures the extent to which firm credit growth varies depending on the extent to which the firm's banking relationships are concentrated among PSBs and the importance of these banks in providing new credit each year

---

[12] The bounded growth of credit is defined as $\dfrac{C_{it}-C_{it-1}}{\dfrac{(C_{it}+C_{it-1})}{2}}$ and can take values between −200 and 200 percentage points.

[13] To be precise, the ratio of sales to physical capital captures average revenue productivity of physical capital. Variation in this ratio within granular industries is used in the literature to proxy for the marginal revenue product of capital (e.g., Bau and Matray 2020).

[14] Because this analysis cannot rely on data on how much each bank lends to each firm, it uses the share of total advances outstanding for each bank in a given year as a weight because the expectation is that banks with a larger portfolio would have a greater ability to lend to firms with which they maintain relationships and on average are expected to account for larger shares of lending to these firms.

[15] PSB share of credit does not enter by itself in the equation because its effect is already captured by the sector-time fixed effects.

[16] To control for firm ownership, the analysis includes a state ownership dummy and an ownership excluding large private group dummy.

relative to other banks in the system. A negative sign on β_6 would indicate that during periods where a large share of new lending is provided by PSBs, productive firms that rely predominately on relationships with PSBs obtain lower credit growth relative to other firms.

Because large firms account for most of the new credit provided by banks in India, it is important to consider the role of firm size in examining the link between credit growth, firm productivity, firm dependence on PSBs, and the share of new credit provided by these banks. To do so the analysis estimates equation (4.2) below:[17]

$$C_{it} = \alpha + \text{Productivity}_{it-1} * [\beta_1 + \beta_2 \text{PSB dependence}_{it-1} + \qquad (4.2)$$
$$\beta_3 \text{PSB share of credit}_{t-1} + \beta_4 \text{PSB share of credit}_{t-1} *$$
$$\text{PSB dependence}_{it-1} + \text{Log of assets}_{it-1} * (\beta_5 + \beta_6 \text{PSB dependence}_{it-1} *$$
$$+ \beta_7 \text{PSB share of credit}_{t-1} + \beta_8 \text{PSB dependence}_{it-1} * \text{PSB share of}$$
$$\text{credit}_{t-1})] + \text{PSB dependence}_{it-1} [\beta_9 + \beta_{10} \text{PSB share of credit}_{t-1} +$$
$$\text{Log of assets}_{it-1} (\beta_{11} + \beta_{12} \text{PSB share of credit}_{t-1})] + \theta X_{it-1} + \delta_{st} + \mu_{dt} + \varepsilon_{it}$$

In estimating equation (4.2), the interest is in comparing β_4 to β_8. In other words, the goal is to determine whether credit growth among productive firms that depend on PSBs, during periods where the latter account for a large share of new credit, changes depending on the size of the firm.

Finally, even though the focus is on the impact of bank ownership in shaping the relationship between firm credit growth and productivity, it is important to allow for the possibility that other bank characteristics (e.g., capitalization, funding mix, and asset quality) might also matter. To do so an expanded version of equation (4.2) is estimated in which *Bank characteristics* and the corresponding interactions are added, in a similar fashion to the way *PSB dependence* above is treated.

$$C_{it} = \alpha + \text{Productivity}_{it-1} * [\beta_1 + \beta_2 \text{PSB dependence}_{it-1} + \qquad (4.3)$$
$$\beta_3 \text{PSB share of credit}_{t-1} + \beta_4 \text{PSB share of credit}_{t-1} *$$
$$\text{PSB dependence}_{it-1} + \beta_5 \text{Bank characteristics}_{it-1} + \beta_6$$
$$\text{PSB share of credit}_{t-1} * \text{Bank characteristics}_{it-1} + \text{Log of assets}_{it-1} *$$
$$(\beta_7 + \beta_8 \text{PSB dependence}_{it-1} * + \beta_9 \text{PSB share of credit}_{t-1} +$$
$$\beta_{10} \text{PSB dependence}_{it-1} * \text{PSB share of credit}_{t-1} +$$
$$\beta_{11} \text{Bank characteristics}_{it-1} + \beta_{12} \text{Bank characteristics}_{it-1} *$$
$$\text{PSB share of credit}_{t-1})] + \text{PSB dependence}_{it-1} [\beta_{13} + \beta_{14} *$$
$$\text{PSB share of credit}_{t-1} + * \text{Log of assets}_{it-} 1 (\beta_{15} +$$
$$\beta_{16} \text{PSB share of credit}_{t-1})] + \text{Bank characteristics}_{it-1} [\beta_{17} + \beta_{18}$$
$$\text{PSB share of credit}_{t-1} + \text{Log of assets}_{isdt-1} (\beta_{19} +$$
$$\beta_{20} \text{PSB share of credit}_{t-1})] \theta X_{it-1} + \delta_{st} + \mu_{dt} + \varepsilon_{it}$$

The purpose of equation (4.3) is to test whether the association between productivity, PSB dependence, and the share of new credit provided by PSB banks changes once other bank characteristics are controlled for capturing capitalization, asset quality, and funding mix.

---

[17] In equation (4.2) log of assets is included among the firm characteristics represented by X.

RESULTS

Table 4.1 shows the formal empirical results on how the extent of firms' links with PSBs affect the allocation of bank credit. As discussed in the Empirical Specifications section, Table 4.1 presents regressions in which the dependent variable is bounded growth in firms' bank credit, in percentage points. The first column examines the role of links to PSBs in shaping the allocation of bank credit without separating firms by size. The second column allows for differences between small and large firms. The final column accounts for the impact of bank characteristics beyond ownership. This section describes the results from each of these exercises in turn.

The first column of Table 4.1 relates bank credit growth to firm characteristics, relying on within industry-year and within district-year variation following equation (4.1). The main firm-level characteristics of interest are productivity (sales per unit of physical capital), PSB dependence (fraction of links with PSBs, weighted by the share of credit at the bank level), and their interaction. The combination of PSBs' share of overall bank credit in each year and PSB dependence at the firm-year level provides a time-varying proxy for the importance of PSBs for each firm over time. The Empirical Specifications section discusses additional firm-level characteristics that are included as controls.

When and where PSBs are more important sources of bank credit, a weaker link is found between productivity and bank credit growth at the firm level. The interaction between PSBs' share of credit in each year and PSB dependence at the firm-year level provides the sharpest proxy of the importance of PSBs. Importantly, the first column of Table 4.1 shows that firms with higher PSB dependence see considerably stronger credit growth in years where PSBs account for a larger share of overall credit (positive and statistically significant interaction coefficient between PSB share of credit [t–1] and PSB dependence [i,t–1]). However, this credit growth is not concentrated in productive firms: the link between productivity and credit growth is weaker for PSB-dependent firms in years when PSBs account for a large share of overall credit (negative and statistically significant interaction coefficient between PSB share of credit [t–1], Productivity [i, t–1], and PSB dependence [i,t–1]). While these coefficients have a clear connection to the link between the presence of PSBs and allocation of credit, other coefficients in the first column of Table 4.1 are hard to interpret in isolation. For example, the small negative and statistically insignificant coefficient for Productivity (i, t–1) alone does not imply that productive firms generally see slower credit growth, as the specification includes several terms interacted with Productivity (i, t–1). The chapter therefore now turns to figures that illustrate the combined implications of all coefficients in this specification for credit growth for different groups of firms.

More precisely, the analysis finds that the combination of a larger footprint of PSBs over time and across firms is associated with greater misallocation of bank credit. Panels 1 and 2 of Figure 4.6 show the estimated sensitivity of bank credit to productivity at the firm level for firms with different levels of productivity and for different combinations of firm-level PSB dependence and PSB share of overall credit considering all of the estimated coefficients in the first column of Table 4.1,

TABLE 4.1.

Sensitivity of Growth in Bank Credit to Firm-Level Productivity

	(1)	(2)	(3)
Productivity (i,t−1)	−0.60	3.06***	2.36
	(0.39)	(0.62)	(3.71)
PSB dependence (i,t−1)	−1.59**	3.05**	2.15
	(0.66)	(1.24)	(2.84)
PSB share of credit (t−1) × Productivity (i,t−1)	2.10**	−1.09	−0.25
	(0.82)	(2.05)	(6.04)
PSB share of credit (t−1) × PSB dependence (i,t−1)	3.97***	−6.56**	−5.12
	(1.04)	(2.37)	(4.00)
Productivity (i,t−1) × PSB dependence (i,t−1)	1.17***	−2.72**	−3.90***
	(0.27)	(1.12)	(0.73)
PSB share of credit (t−1) × Productivity (i,t−1) × PSB dependence (i,t−1)	**−1.97*****	5.33**	6.94***
	(0.61)	(2.27)	(2.25)
Log assets (i,t−1) × Productivity (i,t−1)		−0.58***	−0.61***
		(0.15)	(0.15)
Log assets (i,t−1) × PSB dependence (i,t−1)		−0.71***	−0.76***
		(0.22)	(0.22)
Log assets (i,t−1) × PSB share of credit (t−1) × Productivity (i,t−1)		0.54	0.55
		(0.33)	(0.32)
Log assets (i,t−1) × PSB share of credit (t−1) × PSB dependence (i,t−1)		1.58***	1.62***
		(0.39)	(0.40)
Log assets (i,t−1) × Productivity (i,t−1) × PSB dependence (i,t−1)		0.62**	0.68***
		(0.21)	(0.20)
Log assets (i,t−1) × PSB share of credit (t−1) × Productivity (i,t−1) × PSB dependence (i,t−1)		**−1.13****	**−1.20*****
		(0.37)	**(0.37)**
District × Year FE	Y	Y	Y
National Industrial Classification × Year FE	Y	Y	Y
Firm controls	Y	Y	Y
Bank controls and interactions			Y
R^2	0.227	0.229	0.229
Within R^2	0.019	0.021	0.022
N (firm-years)	21,409	21,409	21,409
Firms	4,753	4,753	4,753
Districts	177	177	177
National Industrial Classifications	282	282	282

Sources: CMIE Prowess; Reserve Bank of India; and authors' calculations.

Note: This table shows regressions where the dependent variable is bounded growth in bank credit (see the chapter text for a definition), winsorized at the 5th and 95th percentiles within year, in percentage points. All three columns include District × Year and five-digit National Industrial Classification Industry × Year FEs. Productivity is the ratio of sales to physical capital limited to between 0 and 30, winsorized at the 5th and 95th percentiles within year, and standardized to have unit variance. Public sector bank (PSB) dependence is the share of reported bank links to PSBs, weighted by total advances for each bank as a share of advances of all banks listed by the firm. PSB share of credit is the share of new bank credit (change in stock since previous year) attributable to PSBs (based on aggregate Reserve Bank of India data, varying only over time). All specifications include a set of firm-level controls (log assets, log growth in sales, debt-to-asset ratio, interest coverage ratio, state ownership dummy, and ownership excluding large private group dummy). The final column includes weighted averages of Tier 1 capital ratios, nondeposit funding, and asset quality ratios in all terms included for PSB dependence in the second column. Standard errors, double-clustered by firm and year, are shown in parentheses. FE = fixed effect; N = number of observations.

*p < .10; **p < .05; ***p < .01.

Figure 4.6. Sensitivity of Growth in Bank Credit to Firm-Level Productivity

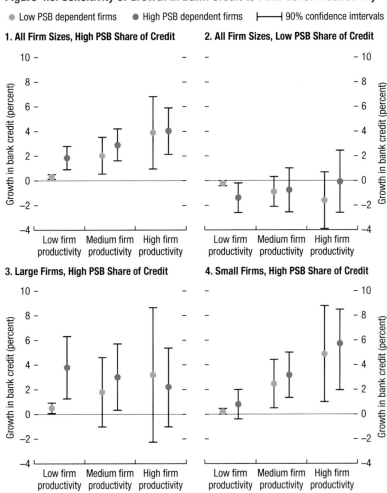

● Low PSB dependent firms   ● High PSB dependent firms   ├———┤ 90% confidence imtervals

Sources: CMIE Prowess; Reserve Bank of India; and authors' calculations.

Note: This figure shows how credit growth varies with firm productivity using all coefficients shown in Table 4.1, evaluated at appropriate points. Ninety percent confidence intervals are shown for each point. Panels 1 and 2 use coefficients from a specification that does not split firms by size (first column of Table 4.1). Panels 3 and 4 use coefficients from a specification that does split firms by size (second column of Table 4.1). Low, medium, and high productivity are evaluated at sales-to-physical-capital ratios (standardized to have unit variance) of 0.1, 1.5, and 3, respectively (this range spans roughly the 10th to the 95th percentiles in the data). Years with high and low public sector bank (PSB) shares of credit are evaluated at 90 percent and 0 percent PSB share of credit in year, respectively. High and low PSB dependence are evaluated at PSB dependence of 10 percent and 90 percent, respectively. Large and small firms are evaluated at log assets of 5 and 10, respectively (assets in millions of rupees prior to logs).

evaluated at appropriate points.[18] Panel 1 focuses on periods when PSBs account for a large share of overall credit. Credit growth for firms with high PSB dependence is shown in red, while credit growth for firms with low PSB dependence is shown in blue. In years in which PSBs account for a large share of overall credit, low-productivity firms with low dependence on PSBs see very low credit growth, while high-productivity firms with low dependence on PSBs see strong credit growth. In other words, credit growth strongly responds to productivity for firms with low PSB dependence. Crucially, the link between productivity and credit growth is weaker for firms with high PSB dependence. Low-productivity firms with high PSB dependence obtain credit growth to about the same degree as medium-productivity firms with low PSB dependence. This credit growth for low-productivity firms represents a missed opportunity to channel credit to more productive firms. In contrast, panel 2 shows that in years where PSBs account for a small share of credit, while all firms struggle to obtain credit, there is little difference in the importance of productivity in determining credit growth between firms with high PSB dependence and firms with low PSB dependence.

Importantly, the link between PSBs' footprint and misallocation of credit is concentrated in larger firms. As discussed in the Stylized Facts section, large firms dominate overall volumes of new credit, and high shares of credit allocated to large, unproductive firms constitute an important signal of credit misallocation. The second column of Table 4.1 introduces interactions of all of the coefficients included in the first column with firm size (log of assets), following equation (4.2). The results are concentrated in large firms. Large firms with higher PSB dependence see stronger credit growth in years where PSBs account for a larger share of overall credit (positive and statistically significant interaction coefficient between Log assets [i,t–1], PSB share of credit [t–1], and PSB dependence [i,t–1]). Again, this credit growth is not concentrated in productive firms: the link between productivity and credit growth is weaker for large PSB-dependent firms in years when PSBs account for a large share of overall new credit (negative and statistically significant interaction coefficient between Log assets [i,t–1], PSB share of credit [t–1], Productivity [i,t–1], and PSB dependence [i,t–1]). As discussed previously, other coefficients in the second column of Table 4.1 are hard to interpret in isolation. For example, the positive and statistically significant coefficient on Productivity (i,t–1) does not imply that all productive firms see stronger credit growth, as the specification includes several terms interacted with Productivity (i,t–1). The chapter therefore turns to figures that illustrate the combined implications of all coefficients in this specification.

A greater role of PSBs is associated with stark differences in the allocation of credit for large firms. Panels 3 and 4 of Figure 4.6 show the estimated sensitivity of bank credit to productivity at the firm level for firms with different sizes and

---

[18] Low, medium, and high productivity are evaluated at sales-to-physical-capital ratios (standardized to have unit variance) of 0.1, 1.5, and 3, respectively. Years with high and low PSB shares of credit are evaluated at 90 percent and 0 percent PSB share of credit in year, respectively. High and low PSB dependence are evaluated at PSB dependence of 10 percent and 90 percent, respectively.

levels of productivity and for different combinations of firm-level PSB dependence and PSB share of overall credit considering all of the estimated coefficients, evaluated at appropriate points, in the second column of Table 4.1.[19] Both panels focus on periods when PSBs account for a large share of overall credit. Panel 3 shows that large low-productivity firms with high PSB dependence obtain stronger credit growth than large high-productivity firms with high PSB dependence—nearly 4 percent credit growth per year. For large firms with low PSB dependence, on the other hand, credit growth is driven much more strongly by productivity. Again, the final quadruple interaction term in the second column of Table 4.1 shows that this difference is statistically significant. Panel 4 of Figure 4.6 shows a strong positive link between credit growth and productivity for small firms regardless of the level of PSB dependence. The analysis therefore finds a link between the footprint of PSBs in channeling credit and the quality of the allocation of credit with data at the firm level that corresponds to the aggregate patterns in the time series discussed in the Stylized Facts section.

Improved allocation of credit could substantially increase the supply of credit to available firms. Figure 4.6 shows that when PSBs account for a large share of overall credit, large firms with low productivity with high PSB dependence are able to obtain meaningful credit growth. In contrast, large firms with low productivity but low PSB dependence obtain very little credit growth. Shifting some of the credit channeled to large unproductive firms by Indian banks could markedly lift the amount of credit available to more productive large firms. Figure 4.7 shows a simple counterfactual exercise between 2010 and 2014 (as Figures 4.2 and 4.5 show, this period is of interest because it represents years with a large overall footprint of PSBs and excludes the impact of the global financial crisis). Over these years, more productive large firms saw credit growth of 9 percentage points per year on average. Shifting even half of the credit allocated by banks to large unproductive firms during this period to more productive large firms could have raised credit growth for these more productive firms by nearly 50 percent (to 13.3 percentage points per year). Shifting all credit allocated to unproductive firms to more productive firms could have almost doubled credit growth for the more productive firms (to 17.3 percentage points per year). Efforts to improve the manner in which Indian banks allocate credit could therefore have important implications for aggregate productivity and economic growth.

The link between the importance of PSBs and the allocation of credit appears to reflect fundamental differences between PSBs and other banks. As discussed in the Stylized Facts section, PSBs differ from other banks on a variety of dimensions that could, in principle, matter for the allocation of credit. PSBs are less well capitalized, have weaker asset quality, and are more reliant on sticky deposit funding. The third column of Table 4.1, following equation (4.3), shows that characteristics more fundamental to the way PSBs operate—rather than these observable

---

[19] Large and small firms are evaluated at log assets of 5 and 10, respectively (assets in millions of rupees prior to logs). See footnote 19 for details on evaluation in other dimensions.

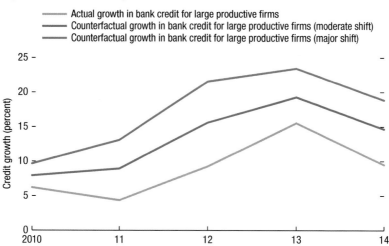

Figure 4.7. Room for Improvement in Allocation of New Bank Credit

—— Actual growth in bank credit for large productive firms
—— Counterfactual growth in bank credit for large productive firms (moderate shift)
—— Counterfactual growth in bank credit for large productive firms (major shift)

Sources: CMIE Prowess; and authors' calculations.
Note: This figure shows actual and counterfactual growth in bank credit (in percentage points, based on change in stock of bank credit relative to previous year) for large productive firms (top tercile of assets within year, and top two terciles of sales to physical assets within five-digit National Industrial Classification industry and year) using the sample of firm-years described in the text. Credit growth is value weighted by the lagged stock of bank credit across firms. The lowest line shows actual growth in bank credit for large productive firms. The middle and top lines show counterfactual growth in bank credit if 50 percent and 100 percent of the new credit, labeled as moderate and major shift, respectively, were allocated to large unproductive firms (top tercile of assets within year, and bottom tercile of sales to physical assets within five-digit National Industrial Classification industry and year) were instead allocated to large productive firms, split proportionately to the lagged stock of bank credit.

differences—appear to drive the results. For each characteristic (a loan-weighted average at the firm level for banks the firm has links to), the specification adds all terms and interactions included for PSB dependence in the second column of Table 4.1. The analysis continues to find a role for PSB dependence in explaining the flow of credit to large unproductive firms: the interaction coefficient between Log assets $(i,t-1)$, PSB share of credit $(t-1)$, Productivity $(i,t-1)$, and PSB dependence $(i,t-1)$ continues to be negative and statistically significant, with a similar magnitude to the second column of Table 4.1.

CONCLUSION

The Indian banking sector is characterized by a large presence of PSBs. This chapter has examined credit allocation in India by assessing the link between firm productivity and credit growth. It investigated how this link depends on (1) the extent to which firms maintain banking relationships with PSBs; and (2) the share of new credit in the economy provided by these banks.

The estimations show that:

- The link between productivity and credit growth is weaker for PSB dependent firms in years when PSBs represent a large share of new credit in the economy.

- This result is driven by large firms, which account for most of the credit in India, and is robust to controlling for other important bank characteristics.

From a policy perspective, the findings suggest that:

- In addition to important policies to strengthen PSBs such as through further recapitalization and the establishment of the National Asset Reconstruction Co (NARCL) to resolve bad PSB assets, plans announced by the government and RBI to privatize additional PSBs and to improve the quality of governance at PSBs more broadly could have an important role to play (IMF 2021).[20] Acharya and Rajan (2020) reviewed a broad range of options to improve governance of PSBs, including independent and representative boards, both partial and full privatization, and more market-based implementation of policy mandates for the banking sector.

- Similarly, as suggested by D'Souza and Surti (2021), improving RBI's supervisory powers vis-à-vis PSBs might also help to reduce credit misallocation. In particular, as with private banks, RBI should have the ability to replace management and board members from PSBs, withdraw their bank licenses and commence the resolution of failing PSBs.

REFERENCES

Acharya, Viral, and Raghuram Rajan. 2020. *Indian Banks: A Time to Reform?* Mimeo.

Alfaro, Laura, and Anusha Chari. 2015. "Deregulation, Misallocation, and Size: Evidence from India." *Journal of Law and Economics* 57 (4): 897–936.

Allcott, Hunt, Allan Collard-Wexler, and Stephen D. O. Connell. 2016. "How Do Electricity Shortages Affect Industry? Evidence from India." *American Economic Review* 106 (3): 587–624.

Amirapu, Amrit, and Michael Gechter. 2019. "Labor Regulations and the Cost of Corruption: Evidence from the Indian Firm Size Distribution." *Review of Economics and Statistics* 102 (1): 1–48.

Asher, Sam, and Paul Novosad. 2020. "Rural Roads and Local Economic Development." *American Economic Review* 110 (3): 797–823.

Banerjee, Abhijit, Shawn Cole, and Esther Duflo. 2004. "Banking Reform in India." In *India Policy Forum.* Vol. 1, edited by Arvind Panagariya, Barry Bosworth, and Suman Bery, 277–323. Washington, DC: Brookings Institution Press.

Banerjee, Abhijit, and Esther Duflo. 2014. "Do Firms Want to Borrow More? Testing Credit Constraints Using a Directed Lending Program." *Review of Economic Studies* 81 (2): 572–607.

Bau, Natalie, and Adrien Matray. 2020. "Misallocation and Capital Market Integration: Evidence from India." NBER Working Papers 27955, National Bureau of Economic Research, Cambridge, MA.

---

[20] For more information on NARCL, see https://economictimes.indiatimes.com/topic/national-asset-reconstruction-co and https://economictimes.indiatimes.com/topic/narcl.

Bloom, Nicholas, Benn Eifert, Aprajit Mahajan, David McKenzie, and John Roberts. 2013. "Does Management Matter? Evidence from India." *Quarterly Journal of Economics* 128 (1): 1–51.

Caballero, Ricardo, Takeo Hoshi, and Anil K. Kashyap. 2008. "Zombie Lending and Depressed Restructuring in Japan." *American Economic Review, American Economic Association* 98 (5): 1943–77, December.

Chakraborty, Indraneel, Apoorva Javadekar, and Rodney Ramcharan. 2021. *The Real Effects of Bank Branching: Evidence from India.* Mimeo.

Chari, Anusha. 2011. "Identifying the Aggregate Productivity Effects of Entry and Size Restrictions: An Empirical Analysis of License Reform in India." *American Economic Journal: Economic Policy* 3 (2): 66–96.

Chari, Anusha, Lakshita Jain, and Nirupama Kulkarni. 2021. "The Unholy Trinity: Regulatory Forbearance, Stressed Banks and Zombie Firms." NBER Working Paper 28435, National Bureau of Economic Research, Cambridge, MA.

Cole, Shawn. 2009. "Fixing Market Failures or Fixing Elections? Agricultural Credit in India." *American Economic Journal: Applied Economics* 1 (1): 219–50, January.

Dinç, I. Serdar, and Nandini Gupta. 2011. "The Decision to Privatize: Finance and Politics." *Journal of Finance* 66 (1): 241–69.

D'Souza, Errol, and Jay Surti. 2021. *Public Bank Guarantees, Credit Allocation and Aggregate Investment.* Mimeo.

Duranton, Gilles, Ejaz Ghani, Arti Goswani, and William Kerr. 2015. "The Misallocation of Land and Other Factors of Production in India." World Bank Policy Research Working Paper 7221, World Bank, Washington, DC.

Garcia-Santana, Manuel, and Josep Pijoan-Mas. 2014. "The Reservation Laws in India and the Misallocation of Production Factors." *Journal of Monetary Economics* 66: 193–209.

Ghani, Ejaz, Arti Grover Goswami, and William R. Kerr. 2016. "Highway to Success: The Impact of the Golden Quadrilateral Project for the Location and Performance of Indian Manufacturing." *Economic Journal* 126 (591): 317–57.

Gupta, Nandini. 2005. "Partial Privatization and Firm Performance." *Journal of Finance* 60 (2): 987–1015.

Hsieh, Chang-Tai, and Peter J. Klenow. 2009. "Misallocation and Manufacturing TFP in China and India." *Quarterly Journal of Economics* 124 (4): 1403–48.

International Monetary Fund (IMF). 2021. "Staff Report for the 2021 Article IV Consultation." IMF Country Report 21/230, Washington, DC.

Kumar, Nitishi. 2020. "Political Interference and Crowding Out in Bank Lending." *Journal of Financial Intermediation* 43: July.

Martin, Leslie A., Shanthi Nataraj, and Ann E. Harrison. 2017. "In with the Big, Out with the Small: Removing Small-scale Reservations in India." *American Economic Review* 107 (2): 354–86.

McGowan, Muge Adalet, Dan Andrews, and Valentine Millot. 2017. "The Walking Dead? Zombie Firms and Productivity Performance in OECD Countries." OECD Economics Department Working Paper 1372, Organisation for Economic Co-operation and Development, Paris.

Reserve Bank of India. 2021. "Macrofinancial Risks." Chapter 1, Financial Stability Report, July.

Restuccia, Diego, and Richard Rogerson. 2017. "The Causes and Costs of Misallocation." *Journal of Economic Perspectives* 31 (3): 151–74.

Rotemberg, Martin. 2019. "Equilibrium Effects of Firm Subsidies." *American Economic Review* 109 (10): 3475–3513.

Sood, Aradhya. 2019. *Land Market Frictions and Manufacturing in India.* Mimeo.

CHAPTER 5

Corporate Debt Market: Evolution, Prospects, and Policy

Jay Surti and Rohit Goel

The availability of a deep and liquid market for private sector debt can be a significant contributor to both growth and financial stability. It provides firms with a stable alternative to bank loan finance for long-term and working capital investments and investors with better portfolio optimization opportunities. India's onshore corporate debt market has grown rapidly over the decade prior to the pandemic, although access to firms in lower-investment-grade buckets and outside the financial sector remains limited and key institutional investors are allocating significantly lower funds than their statutory limits permit them to. This chapter reviews the evolution of the Indian corporate debt market, drawing comparisons with peer emerging market economies, and evaluates factors that may be inhibiting the pace and breadth of its growth. In particular, the first section reviews the key benefits of domestic corporate bond markets, the second section discusses the evolution of India's bond market, the third section benchmarks India's corporate bond market with those in other emerging markets, the fourth section proposes policies to further develop the markets, and the final section offers a conclusion.

BENEFITS OF DOMESTIC CORPORATE BOND MARKETS

The benefits offered by deep and liquid corporate bond markets are many and well recognized, including fostering access to long-term finance for the corporate and financial sectors, allowing better risk management, and supporting lending to innovative sectors. By broadening the investor base, they provide an invaluable "spare tire" during times of stress when bank (re)financing gets clogged by asset quality and liquidity challenges and other creditors such as insurers and pension funds may be able to continue funding debt issuing firms. Capital market funding can provide the spare tire because it can bring in creditors who are in a better position to meet firms' stable, long-term financing needs, either because they are

We thank Viral Acharya, Leena Chacko, Sanjay Nayar, and staff of the Reserve Bank of India and the Securities and Exchange Board of India for insightful conversations, and Caroline Wu for excellent research support.

not liability driven (e.g., sovereign wealth funds) or because they themselves have long-term liabilities and, therefore, are relatively immune to immediate liquidity pressures (e.g., life insurers and pension funds). By choosing a wider mix of credit providers, firms can distribute the tenor of their external financing more evenly between short-, medium-, and long-term liabilities, reducing concentration risk and cliff effects.[1] In turn, this may increase their expected net present value and the number of firms assessed as viable for external funding by banks and markets, serving the important goal of inclusive financial markets and growth. Intimately connected to this final point is that unlike bank lending, which often tends to be extended on a collateralized basis, most corporate bonds are unsecured debt, which increases economic efficiency.[2]

EVOLUTION OF THE CORPORATE BOND MARKET IN INDIA

The Indian corporate debt market is a core segment of the Indian financial system. It constitutes more than 20 percent of the Indian fixed-income universe (Figure 5.1, panel 1); it is the second largest segment, following government securities (68 percent).[3] It has grown significantly through the last decade, with total outstanding debt volumes increasing from 9 trillion Indian rupees (Rs) in 2011 to almost Rs40 trillion now, an impressive cumulative annual growth rate of 14.5 percent (Figure 5.1, panel 2). This compares with a cumulative annual growth of real GDP of approximately 5.5 percent, reflecting the rising role of corporate bonds in the Indian financial system. Looking closer, however, this growth tapered off during 2019–21, with outstanding volumes growing by just 8.5 percent per year during the last two fiscal years (FY) compared to 17 percent per year over the previous eight fiscal years. During FY 2019/20, short-term corporate debt issuance fell off sharply in the commercial paper and certificates of deposit (CD) markets, probably reflecting the strain in the nonbanking financial company segment after the default of Infrastructure Leasing & Financial Services on September 27, 2018 (Goel 2020). During FY 2020/21, CD issuance shrank further, but this was dominated by growth in corporate bond and commercial paper issuance. During the time, the stress and the uncertainty related to the COVID-19 pandemic led to a sharp increase in government debt issuance globally. This was also true for India and is potentially one of the key reasons why corporate debt issuance fell as a share in India's total fixed-income market during this period

---

[1] This implies a situation where a significant proportion of the debt matures at a single date, which increases the risk of a default and inherently increases the cost of funding.

[2] This is, however, not true in the current Indian context where most corporate bonds are issued on a secured basis.

[3] Government securities include both debt securities of the central government and state development loans outstanding. But debt securities issued or placed by state-owned enterprises, including public sector banks, are included in the corporate bonds category.

Figure 5.1. Size and Evolution of the Indian Corporate Debt Market

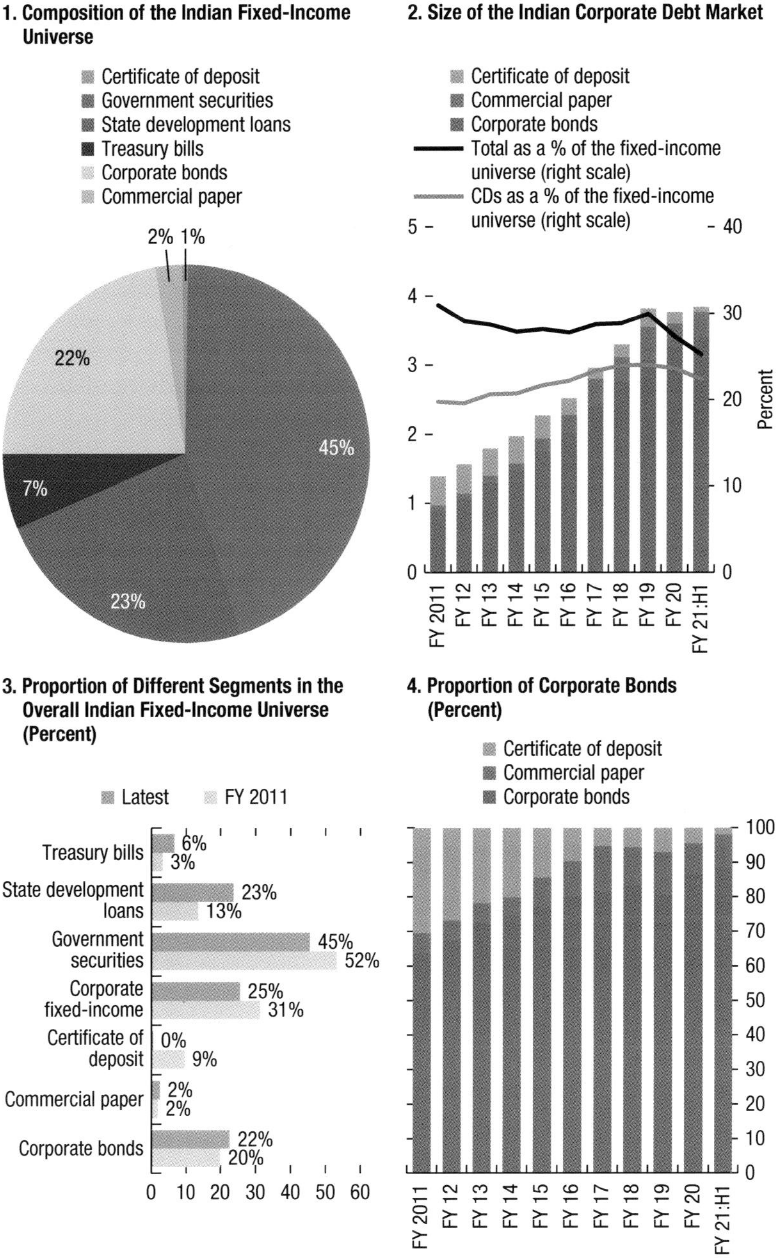
1. Composition of the Indian Fixed-Income Universe
Certificate of deposit
Government securities
State development loans
Treasury bills
Corporate bonds
Commercial paper
2% 1%
22%
45%
7%
23%
2. Size of the Indian Corporate Debt Market
Certificate of deposit
Commercial paper
Corporate bonds
Total as a % of the fixed-income universe (right scale)
CDs as a % of the fixed-income universe (right scale)
Percent
FY 2011
FY 12
FY 13
FY 14
FY 15
FY 16
FY 17
FY 18
FY 19
FY 20
FY 21:H1
3. Proportion of Different Segments in the Overall Indian Fixed-Income Universe (Percent)
Latest
FY 2011
Treasury bills
6%
3%
State development loans
23%
13%
Government securities
45%
52%
Corporate fixed-income
25%
31%
Certificate of deposit
0%
9%
Commercial paper
2%
2%
Corporate bonds
22%
20%
4. Proportion of Corporate Bonds (Percent)
Certificate of deposit
Commercial paper
Corporate bonds

Sources: Bloomberg L.P.; Haver Analytics; Haver; Reserve Bank of India; and authors' calculations.
Note: CDs = certificates of deposit; FY = fiscal year; H1 = first half.

Because of this strong growth in the corporate bond market, its share in the total Indian fixed-income universe rose 2.5 percentage points in the last 10 years. However, CD issuance has fallen steeply over the last decade, resulting in an overall decrease in the fixed-income market share of corporate debt from 31 percent in FY 2011 to 25 percent now (Figure 5.1, panel 3). Outstanding volumes of CDs have decreased at a cumulative annual growth rate of 16 percent during the last decade, from a total of 9 percent of the Indian fixed-income universe to almost negligible now. CDs are an important source of funds for the banks, which use them to meet their temporary asset-liability mismatches. CD rates are also higher than retail fixed deposit rates, as they are raised when banks face a liquidity crunch. Increasing ability to issue medium-term notes is one factor behind this sharp decline in CD issuance, among others. As a result, corporate bonds now constitute 86 percent of the Indian corporate fixed-income universe, followed by commercial paper, at around 9 percent (Figure 5.1, panel 4). The rest of the chapter thus focuses on corporate bonds as a proxy of the overall Indian corporate fixed-income market.

Financial Services Dominate Corporate Bond Issuance

The financial services sector dominates issuance of corporate bonds at almost 60 percent of the total (Figure 5.2). The industry sector and public sector undertakings account for the rest of the total. Even within the industry sector, financial (and related) services—particularly banking and housing finance—account for

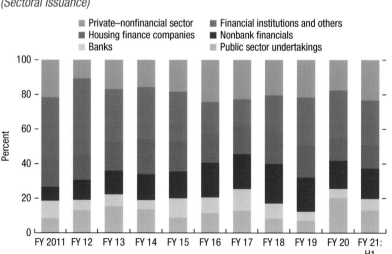

Figure 5.2. Composition of the Indian Corporate Bond Market
(Sectoral issuance)

Sources: Bloomberg L.P.; Haver Analytics; Reserve Bank of India; and authors' calculations.
Note: FY = fiscal year; H1 = first half.

almost 90 percent of the total issuance and the number of issues. Outside financial services, real estate and power generation supply make up the rest. Consequently, corporate bond issuance from manufacturing and (nonenergy) infrastructure sectors is a very small proportion of the overall bond market. Longer-term trends point to a steady rise in the proportion of issuance from nonbanking financial companies, reflecting the growing importance of these institutions in the Indian financial system.

Private Placements Are Overwhelmingly Preferred to Public Issuance

Funds in the bond market can be raised through either public issuance or private placements. The main differences in the two placement routes are as follows.[4]

- **Investor set:** In a public issue, an offer is made to the general public to subscribe to the bond. While, in general, issuance can be structured to target institutional and/or retail investors in the primary market (e.g., through minimum bid size and other features), in India, there are strict requirements under Securities and Exchange Board of India (SEBI) norms for public issuances that significantly limit structuring public issuances to, for example, cater only to institutional investors. In a private placement, the securities are issued to a select group of people.[5] The potential benefits offered by public issuance include access to a wider and more diversified investor base, which may also provide greater scope for secondary market liquidity of the bonds—to the extent that not all may be buy-and-hold investors. In turn, greater liquidity can contribute to lower funding costs.[6]

- **Disclosure requirements:** Disclosure is standardized for public issuance and is guided by statutory and regulatory requirements. This places an onus on smaller firms in particular to organize their operational and financial affairs so as to facilitate disclosure at low cost. Moreover, going for the public issuance option implies preparedness of a firm to disclose hitherto private information regarding its business and finances to the general public. For firms whose equity is publicly listed and for regulated (financial) institutions, such compliance and disclosure may already be the norm, but for other (nonfinancial) corporations, it may represent a significant departure and require them to be at an inflection point in their growth and maturity.

---

[4] More precisely, the difference between the two most typically lies in the mode of issuance of the debt securities rather than their listing on an exchange; that is, privately placed corporate debt is also often subsequently listed on an exchange, reflecting tax and regulatory incentives and publicly issued debt is always listed.

[5] Even for private placement, the issuer has to raise amount through the Electronic Bidding Platform (EBP) of exchanges. This is mandatory for firms raising more than Rs. 100 crores in a year.

[6] This is particularly important to note in light of the argument that is often made that private placement lowers costs due to targeting a niche investor segment, thereby saving time and resources in fund raising.

By contrast, in a private placement, the disclosure and documentation requirements can, like the financial terms and covenants, be negotiated between the debt issuing firm and the targeted investors and contractual requirements (as opposed to regulatory) guide what is disclosed.[7] Moreover, disclosure is limited to investors funding the bonds and does not go beyond them. In the Indian context, there are a couple of caveats to this broad description. First, disclosure requirements for only-debt listed companies are a subset of those mandated for equity listed companies, reflecting priority given to deepening the bond market. Second, if privately placed debt is subsequently listed, SEBI-issued (basic) disclosure norms apply.

The Indian corporate bond market is dominated by private placements. However, because a majority of privately placed bonds are subsequently listed, it would appear that rather than disclosure aversion, cost advantages offered by private placement through customization of debt structures to preferences of key investor segments dominate cost benefits of public issuance due to access to a wider investor base. The total number of issuers opting for private placement rose sharply from about 1,900 in FY 2011/12 to almost 2,500 in FY 2018/19, reflecting the expanding corporate bond market and increasing prominence of the private placement route.[8] The increasing prominence of this route is also reflected in total issuance. Data reveal that the total amount issued in the private market is almost 50 times that issued in the public market. Furthermore, this ratio has increased more than 3.5 times from 10 times in FY 2014/15. One aspect of private placements in the Indian context that is deserving of further analytical attention is the subsequent impact on liquidity of the debt issued through this approach because, under the Companies Act, private placements can target only a maximum of 200 investors in a single fiscal year.

Rising Prominence of Small Issuance and in Diversification of Ratings

The expansion of the Indian corporate bond market and the sustained preference for private placements appear, in part, to be driven by sharp growth in the smallest issue bracket (size of Rs100 million and below). Such issuance grew at a cumulative annual growth rate of 20 percent during the last decade (Figure 5.3, panel 1), around four times that of the largest issues (size of Rs 1 billion and above). An important open question is whether this reflects an increase in the share of total issuance by smalls (issuance by the smallest bracket has risen by 6 percentage points—Figure 5.3, panel 2, blue bars—to almost one-third of total issuance—Figure 5.3, panel 3, inner bar). On the one hand, the fact that the size of the smallest issues is declining (Figure 5.3, panel 4) may point to the greater ability of ever smaller firms to successfully raise external funding outside of bank credit through the bond market. If true, this is a positive development from

---

[7] Though information may be available on the electronic bidding platform.

[8] However, the total number of issuers has declined in the last few years.

Figure 5.3. Rise in the Smaller Issuers Shows That the Market Is Expanding

1. Growth in the Number of Issues
(Percent; 10-year cumulative annual growth rate)

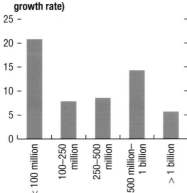

2. Change in the Proportion of Different Segments in the Last Decade
(Percent)

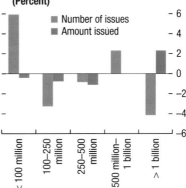

3. Composition of the Indian Corporate Bond Market
(Percent)

- < 100 million
- 100–250 million
- 250–500 million
- 500 million–1 billion
- > 1 billion

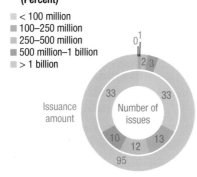

4. Average Size of the Issuance in the Two Extreme Categories

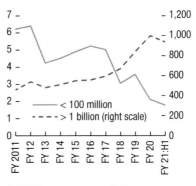

5. Number of Issuers in Different Rating Buckets
(Percent)

AAA   AA   A   BBB
BB   B and below   NR

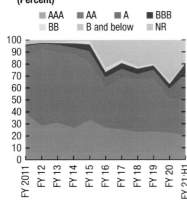

6. Total Issuance across Ratings
(Percent)

AAA   AA   A   BBB
BB   B and below   NR

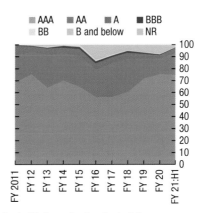

Sources: Bloomberg L.P.; Haver Analytics; Reserve Bank of India; and authors' calculations.
Note: FY = fiscal year; H1 = first half; NR = not rated.

market depth and financial inclusion perspectives, and it may also provide a partial explanation for the continued prominence of private placements—such small firms are unlikely to be well placed to meet disclosure and other requirements and the costs of the external credit ratings process required for public issuance. On the other hand, these aggregate numbers and trends may reflect fragmented issuance, whereby large firms are choosing to issue in small amounts through multiple tranches.[9] The largest firms continue to dominate the market in issuance amount, accounting for 95 percent of the market (Figure 5.3, panel 3, outer bar). To the extent that ever-smaller firms are indeed being able to successfully tap the bond market for financing, the growing size of average issuance in the largest bracket may potentially indicate increasing bifurcation of the market.

One piece of evidence supporting expansion of market access to smaller firms is the growing share of the number of bond issues by nonrated and lower-rated issuers over the last few years and a corresponding decline in the share of AA- and AAA-rated issuers[10] (Figure 5.3, panel 5). On the other hand, a breakdown of the total amount issued continued to show the high and increasing dominance of the higher-rated issuers, with a steady rise in their proportion (Figure 5.3, panel 6). Taken together, this evidence points to the greater access to market by smaller, unrated, and mid-size lower (investment grade) rated issuers (the latter particularly in the A–BBB bracket) even as larger, top-rated firms continue to dominate volumes coming to the market. Although the growing systemic importance of larger firms points to potential for rising concentration risk, a rise in access by small firms, if true, is a positive development from an inclusive growth perspective.

Maturity

Indian firms have successfully extended maturities over the last decade. The market was dominated by issuance in the 0- to 3-year maturity bracket, constituting well over 50 percent of the annual total through FY 2015. Starting FY 2016, the 3- to 5-year bucket became predominant and medium-term notes and long-term bonds also picked up, totaling 25 percent or above during FY 2018–FY 2020 (Figure 5.4, panel 1). The pandemic has, unsurprisingly, been associated with a swing back in favor of the short end, with the share of the 0- to 3-year issuance rising in FY 2021 largely at the expense of medium-term notes and long-term bonds.[11] The smallest maturity bucket has also risen steadily by proportion of trading (Figure 5.4, panel 2), albeit as overall trading volumes have increased sharply for Indian corporate bonds since FY 2016.

---

[9] One factor that may be behind multiple small-sized issuances being bunched up over time is the need to meet the annual limit on the number of ISINs issued by SEBI.

[10] The trend has changed a little in the last two years, as risk aversion environment has led to the issuance moving back to the higher-rated issuers.

[11] The recent swing back is likelier to reflect the pandemic than other developments weighing on credit quality (e.g., nonbanking financial company sector following the default of Infrastructure Leasing & Financial Services) because it is largely confined to FY 2021. For instance, the taper tantrum episode also saw issuance moving significantly to lower-maturity buckets.

Figure 5.4. Maturity Structure
(Percent)

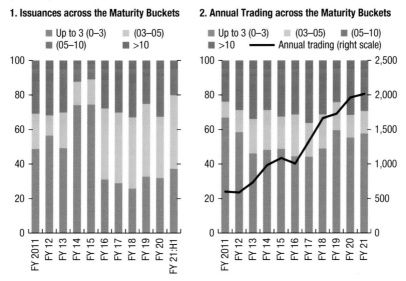

1. Issuances across the Maturity Buckets

2. Annual Trading across the Maturity Buckets

Sources: Bloomberg L.P.; Haver Analytics; Reserve Bank of India; and authors' calculations.
Note: FY = fiscal year; H1 = first half.

Currency

Local currency remains the dominant choice for Indian firms, accounting for almost 70 percent of total issuance (Figure 5.5, panel 1, blue bars). To an important degree, this reflects policy choices seeking to limit exchange rate and aggregate national balance sheet risks, such as limits on external commercial borrowing under the automatic route.

The proportion of offshore issuance is rising steadily, having risen 10 percentage points from 20 percent in 2012 (Figure 5.5, panel 1, green bars). Offshore issuance was at a record pace in 2021, amounting to almost $10 billion in the first nine months. The last three years have seen historically high total offshore issuance of $35 billion (Figure 5.5, panel 3), the trend broadly in line with trends for the overall emerging markets.[12] The US dollar remains the preferred currency of choice for Indian issuers, staying with trends in rest of the emerging market issuers, except Poland and Hungary (Figure 5.5, panel 2).

Coupon costs for Indian firms' offshore bonds started creeping up in FY 2018/19 after being flat for a number of years, although they rose slower than the emerging market median over this period. The year 2020 saw a sharp spike, with Indian firms' coupon costs significantly overshooting emerging market peer firms before a sharp downward correction in 2021 back to emerging market

---

[12] EMs' offshore corporate bond issuance was historically high in 2021 after an insipid 2020.

Figure 5.5. Currency Profile

1. Issuances across Currency Denomination
(Percent)

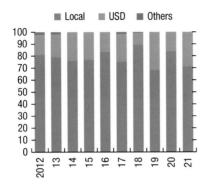

2. Currency Denomination in
Offshore Issuance
(Percent)

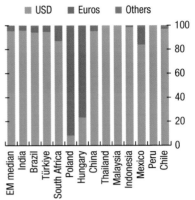

3. Average Coupon in Offshore Issuance

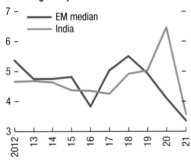

4. Average Tenor in Offshore Issuance

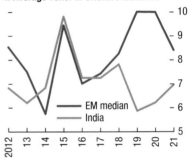

5. Indian Offshore Corporate Issuance,
by Rating

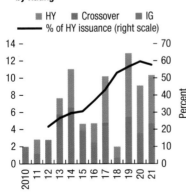

6. Indian Offshore Corporate Issuance,
by Sector

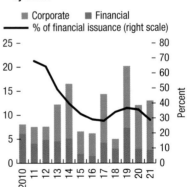

Sources: Bloomberg L.P.; Haver Analytics; Reserve Bank of India; and authors' calculations.
Note: EM = emerging market; HY = high yield; IG = investment grade.

median levels (Figure 5.5, panel 3). Digging deeper, Indian firms may have actively managed coupon costs by reducing the average issuance maturity of offshore bonds through 2018/19 unlike their emerging market peers. However, they increased issuance maturity during the pandemic, unlike emerging market peers (Figure 5.5, panel 4).

Interestingly, lower-rated firms have more actively sought bond funding in the offshore, hard-currency market as opposed to local currency issuance, which, as noted above, remains dominated by AAA–AA rated firms (Figure 5.4, panel 6). Even though issuance was dominated by investment-grade issuers in earlier years (70–80 percent of total offshore issuance from 2012 to 2014), the picture has reversed itself in the last three years, when lower-rated, high-yield issuers have accounted for almost 60 percent of offshore hard currency issuance (Figure 5.5, panel 5).

Another disconnect between the local currency and offshore hard currency market is in the economic diversity of bond issuing firms. The local currency market is dominated by firms from the financial services sector, including banks and nonbank financial corporations. In the offshore hard currency market, non-financial corporates dominate issuance—firms from the financial sector issue 20 percent of offshore hard currency bonds and this proportion has been declin-ing over time (Figure 5.5, panel 6).

This disconnect between the local currency and the hard currency markets could reflect the interest of the different investor base, or the crowding out of the local currency market by the higher-rated and the financial issuers.

COMPARISON OF INDIAN CORPORATE BOND MARKET WITH OTHER EMERGING MARKETS

Size

India's corporate bond market is just 25 percent of GDP, in line with the emerg-ing market median, but significantly smaller than its larger emerging market peers including Brazil, China, and Mexico (Figure 5.6, panel 1). India also lags several emerging market peers in growth of issuance in the last five years (Figure 5.6, panel 2).

Currency

Indian corporate bonds are predominantly local currency denominated, in line with Asian emerging markets (China, Malaysia, and Thailand) but in contrast with the rest of the emerging market universe, where hard currency issuance is significant; for example, at the other extreme, emerging markets like Brazil, Mexico, and Peru issue predominantly in US dollars (Figure 5.7, panel 1).

Sectors

Financials dominate Indian local currency corporate bond issuance (Figure 5.7, panel 2). The energy sector is a major issuer for commodity-exporting emerging markets (Brazil, Indonesia, Mexico).

Figure 5.6. Cross–Emerging Market Comparison of Size

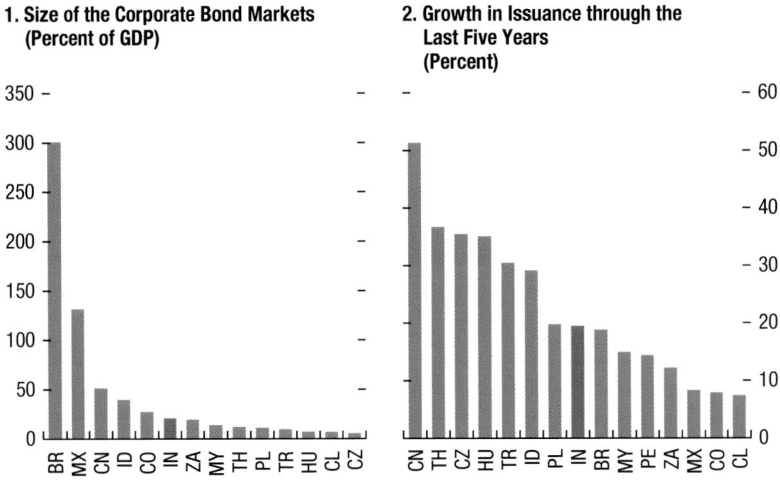

1. Size of the Corporate Bond Markets (Percent of GDP)

2. Growth in Issuance through the Last Five Years (Percent)

Sources: Bloomberg L.P.; Haver Analytics; Reserve Bank of India; and authors' calculations.
Note: BR = Brazil; CL = Chile; CN = China; CO = Colombia; CZ = Czech Republic; HU = Hungary; ID = Indonesia; IN = India; MX = Mexico; MY = Malaysia; PE = Peru; PL = Poland; TH = Thailand; TR = Türkiye; ZA = South Africa.

Financial Engineering

Eighty-five percent of outstanding Indian corporate bonds are bullet payment, expiration-at-maturity debt securities without embedded options. Embedded options are rare—sinkable and callable bonds are 5 percent of outstanding. This is in line with most emerging markets, barring a few (Brazil, Mexico, and Peru) that issue a significant amount of bonds with embedded options.

PROMOTING GROWTH OF THE MARKET

A combination of actions and strategies would serve to promote the further growth of India's corporate bonds market. Strengthening creditor rights and incentives underpinning the credit ratings process and outcomes would serve to improve ability and quality of investor risk management thereby expanding market access to lower-rated issuers, at longer maturities and reduced costs. Accompanying enhancements to trading infra- and micro-structures would serve to increase market depth and liquidity, thereby potentially widening the investor base. Finally, there may be scope for significant gains arising from deepening markets in a stable and safe manner through the introduction of new products and financial structures and by reassessing the case for certain regulations.

Creditor Rights

Difficulties faced by bond holders on recovering on outstanding debt of defaulting firms have been extensively documented and discussed (IMF 2018).

Figure 5.7. Cross–Emerging Comparison on Key Features
(Percent)

1. Currency Composition of the Corporate Bond Universe

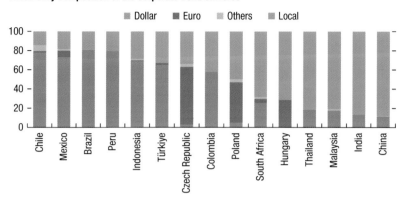

2. Sectoral Composition of the Corporate Bond Universe

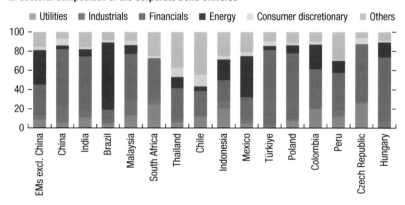

3. Types of Corporate Bonds

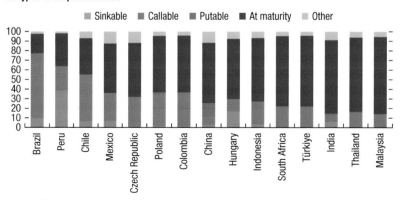

Sources: Bloomberg L.P.; Haver Analytics; Reserve Bank of India; and authors' calculations.
Note: excl. = excluding.

Delays in the recovery process, followed by poor recovery rates, are especially problematic in the local currency bond market, where external credit ratings themselves are perceived to have low reliability and a public credit registry providing sufficient equivalent information to assess ex-ante credit risk is unavailable (Acharya 2017). In such circumstances, secured debt, information-intensive bank lending, and private placements that can be contractually structured in bespoke fashion to provide additional security to creditors are likely to become the norm, as is the case in the local currency debt market.

Policy action has focused on improving the legal and regulatory frameworks for bad debt recovery. Until about five years ago, bond holders did not have recourse equivalent to banks in the event borrowers reneged on repayment obligations, covenants, or other contract terms. A 2016 amendment to the 2002 Securitisation and Reconstruction of Financial Assets and Enforcement of Securities (SARFAESI) Act changed this state of affairs for secured bond holders. Most local currency bond holders, however, continue to exercise recourse through the 2016 Insolvency and Bankruptcy Code (IBC). Traditionally, bankruptcy resolution proceedings could be triggered through collective action of at least 75 percent of bond holders/creditors under the IBC code. Recently, the Securities and Exchange Board of India (SEBI) resolved key impediments limiting bond holders' options under the IBC code, notably by allowing the tradability of claims on nonconvertible debentures in default; reducing collective action to 50 percent; and allowing negative consent for private placements, albeit not for publicly issued bonds.

From a market development perspective, however, many of these creditor-friendly actions may have limited benefits. As noted earlier, one of the principal advantages offered by corporate bonds is the ability to borrow on unsecured terms at reasonable cost. The SARFAESI Act amendment did not provide bond holders recourse under the special bankruptcy statute. By limiting its purview to secured debt holders, it may have increased preference for lending on a secured basis over holding bonds. The decision to limit negative consent to privately placed corporate bonds and not extend it to publicly issued bonds may have further increased market participants' preference for private placements. While not a cause of the already miniscule share of public issuance, this exclusion may nonetheless have adverse marginal impact on standardization of securities, which is important for bond trading and liquidity.

Implementation and enforcement continue to leave a lot to be desired. Bank recoveries outside of SARFAESI-based resolutions (e.g., through the *Lok Adalats*, debt recovery tribunals, and under the IBC code) were low and often averaged in single digits. Even though the IBC offers the incentive of a time-bound process for resolution (to avoid transition to liquidation), legal certainty is lacking about whether courts will not, in fact, declare liquidation after expiration of the resolution window if they do not view it as representing a binding legal mandate or would they extend the timeline on the basis of suspensions following an appeal by the debtor (Patel 2020). Reflecting some of these factors, debt restructuring history has been spotty and proposals for new asset restructuring companies keep cropping up to resolve legacy bad debts. Other significant issues hampering recovery of bad debts, including claims of bond holders, are capacity problems of debt recovery tribunals due to infrastructure shortcomings; legal uncertainties regarding insolvency resolution of corporate groups; excessive influence of promoters who may remain key decision makers in firms where they have lost ownership;[13] and weaknesses in the institutional framework that constrains effective use of the new insolvency process, especially with respect to large firms in default (IMF 2018).

In summary, much progress has been made on strengthening legal and regulatory frameworks. But, in order for corresponding benefits to accrue in full to bond holders, full implementation of such reforms is needed and effective enforcement of creditor rights is critical.

Market and Rating Infrastructure—Bond Liquidity and Credit Risk Management

Market infrastructure, in general, is a positive factor in financial market development in India, as is reflected in the presence of well-established securities depository (National Securities Depository Ltd.); the wide range of trading, clearing, and settlements services provided by the Central Clearing Corporation of India covering money, government securities, foreign exchange, and derivatives markets (e.g., the Negotiated Dealing System-Order Matching for government securities, dematerialization of equities and electronic trading thereof, among others). However, the market infrastructure for corporate bonds has some notable gaps that together impinge on primary issuance and secondary market liquidity (RBI 2016; SEBI 2017):

- The absence of a well-developed corporate repo market.
- Prohibitions on certain investors from trading bonds unless they are downgraded by two or more notches.
- Lack of robust secondary market infrastructure such as credit default swaps and interest rate futures. The Reserve Bank of India has issued the revised CDS Directions in February 2022.
- Lack of standardization of tax rules across states. However, with the objective of bringing uniformity in the stamp duty levied on securities transactions across states, the Government of India amended the Indian Stamp Act, 1899 (revised Act), through Finance Act, 2019, and the relevant Stamp Rules, 2019 were notified on December 10, 2019.[14]
- As is the case in most countries barring few exceptions like Israel, the prominence of over-the-counter trading of corporate bonds (despite potential for robust electronic, exchange-based trading), which is reliant on concentrated provision of intermediation services by a few dealers.

---

[13] The degree to which the IBC has successfully addressed this, by not allowing promoters to come back in, remains an open empirical question.

[14] Source: https://www.rbi.org.in/Scripts/BS_PressReleaseDisplay.aspx?prid=50033.

SEBI recently permitted bond-issuing firms to consolidate and reissue debt securities to increase the volume of on-the-run securities, which have higher liquidity than older, off-the-run bonds (SEBI 2017).[15] SEBI's new regulation was limited to allowing reissuance of privately placed bonds on the basis of a fresh credit rating from a single credit rating agency. The limitation to private placements is likely to increase the preference of firms for this mode of issuance over public issuance. Moreover, because contractual customization in private placements may reduce the liquidity of the bonds, this change in regulation may not have the intended effect on secondary market liquidity. Finally, to fully reap the benefits of this change, tax rules will need to be amended, that is, not treating reissuance as fresh issuance for the purpose of charging stamp duty.

The credit rating process is beset with significant incentive problems (Ganguly 2014; Prakash, Ayachit, and Garg 2017), ranging from (1) conflicts of interest arising from the "issuer pays" model, (2) rating shopping by issuers, (3) lack of accountability of ratings agencies to investors, and (4) mechanistic reliance on ratings by investors despite all of these issues. The severity of incentive problems is clear from the implication of Grant Thornton's forensic audit in the wake of the Infrastructure Leasing & Financial Services default that pointed to alleged collusion by several major credit ratings agencies staff and staff of the failed nonbank financial corporation. Weaknesses in the rating process and outcomes can have a deep adverse impact on credit risk management, on costs of debt issuance, and on the ability to issue unsecured liabilities in the open market. Regulatory actions could aim at removing conflicts of interest (rotation of employees, analysts, and credit rating agencies; exploring the feasibility of alternative payment models such as *exchange-pays*) and reducing rating shopping (establishing a platform to disclose all ratings given to an issuer, permitting withdrawal of ratings in a larger number of situations). The 2016 report of the H.R. Khan Committee (RBI 2016) made a number of recommendations, including for strict adherence by credit rating agencies to regulatory requirements for timely disclosure of corporate defaults on their websites and to stock exchanges and for the RBI to consider allowing these agencies access to its central repository of information on large credits (Central Repository of Information on Large Creditors).

In summary, policy priorities on the trading infra- and micro-structures are common to most countries—promoting electronic, exchange-based trading of corporate bonds can strengthen market liquidity, relieve pressure on a narrow set of bank dealers making markets, and thereby also reduce concentration risk. On the other hand, addressing incentives in the credit ratings process and improving its information base are top priorities specific to the Indian context.

---

[15] This was in line with action taken in the past by other Asian countries, such as Korea, that had followed this strategy in 2000 to enhance liquidity in its onshore government bonds market (Black-Rock 2017).

Investor Base

Nonbank financial institutions have increased their share in the investor base for local currency corporate bonds, but holdings of insurance companies and pension/provident funds remain well below investment limits mandated by their regulators. Indeed, a significant factor in the growth of nonbank financial institution investors is the growing holdings of debt mutual funds rather than these long-term investors. Moreover, although investment limits of insurers and pensions have been raised, ratings requirements largely constrain their holdings to AA–AAA rated bonds. This significantly narrows the investor base for investment grade local currency bonds for firms in the BBB–A range and constrains the size of the market and availability of funds for private sector capital expenditure and production. It also introduces potential cliff effects for firms that meet the AA floor at a point in time but may face a downgrade in the event of an idiosyncratic or systemic shock. In a context of endemically low secondary market liquidity, such a cliff effect will likely also create significant challenges for insurers and pensions to sell out of illiquid corporate bonds, potentially only possible at steep discounts, resulting in large losses. This constellation of factors may, in part, explain the reticence of these investors to step up investments in bonds issued by AA–AAA up to their regulatory investment limits.

It is of interest to explore how many elements of the current corporate bond market equilibrium are connected to these factors. One hypothesis is that the pressure on credit ratings agencies comes not only from the usual incentive issues of getting paid by the firms they are rating and who want to retain their AA–AAA ratings to maintain a stable investor base and low debt financing costs. However, it also comes from investors who wish to avoid cliff effects.

This discussion does inject a note of caution to unqualified recommendations to removing ratings constraints on bond holdings of Indian nonbank financial institutions (at least to firms rated lower investment grade). It is probably unrealistic to expect that the risk management function, particularly the middle office desks, at insurers and pensions are comparable at this time to those of Indian banks and nonbank financial corporations. Consequently, allowing them to go down the credit curve—even if within the investment-grade categories—may need to await resolution of the weaknesses in credit ratings infrastructure noted above.

In summary, the striking disparity between ratings diversity in hard currency debt issued by Indian corporates relative to local currency bonds indicates potential scope for broadening the investor base and increasing supply for lower-rated firms. However, improvements to the ratings infrastructure and to institutional risk management and its oversight remain key prerequisites.

Other Factors

First, an important driver of financial institutions having the lion's share in corporate debt issuance may be that they are exempt from maintaining financially onerous liquidity buffers. Traditionally, all firms except banks and nonbank financial corporations (who are exempt) were required to set aside a *debenture redemption reserve* of 25 percent of the value of outstanding local currency bonds. Moreover, nonfinancial corporates must invest an additional 15 percent of the value of bonds maturing within the year in eligible assets (bank deposits and government securities). The relative cost of external financing via corporate bonds is, therefore, very high for Indian nonfinancial firms (e.g., relative to bank credit). As consistent with SEBI (2018), doing away with such requirements is likely to significantly increase the incentives of these firms to issue bonded debt without adding much on the margin to credit risk for the investor.

Second, from the perspective of widening the investor base for corporate bonds, scope should be explored for growth of local currency corporate bond exchange traded funds. A widely acknowledged benefit of this fund structure is that it transforms over-the-counter, less-liquid debt securities into exchange-traded equities, facilitating rapid growth in the (retail) investor base and potentially increasing secondary market trading and liquidity. Operational feasibility would need to be assessed with respect to incentives of authorized participants to arbitrage between the primary (debt) and secondary (equity) markets. In turn, this points to a potential chicken-and-egg issue; that is, for the creation and redemption process to work and incentivize authorized participants to play their critical role, local currency bond liquidity may need to rise to some threshold level.

Third, from the perspective of promoting long-term stable funding for certain nonbank financial corporations, consideration could be given to secured debt instruments, specifically covered bonds, to be issued under a statutory framework.[16] Credit enhancement through access to a dedicated cover pool of high-quality mortgage, infrastructure, or other assets, overcollateralization, and bankruptcy remoteness of the collateral, could be beneficial to the nonbank financial corporations. This could facilitate issuance to a wider set of (institutional) investors at longer tenors and at lower cost, contributing not only to stabilizing the funding situation and reducing asset–liability mismatch risk, but also allowing them to access higher-quality credit exposures by increasing their loan pricing competitiveness vis-à-vis banks.

Finally, scope exists to revisit the differential regulatory treatment of credit exposures of banks and nonbank financial corporations via loans and local currency corporate bonds in their market risk capital charge. Although loans are held to maturity and, therefore, do not carry market risk from a regulatory perspective, local currency bonds of the same firms held by banks and nonbank financial corporations are marked to market. This is despite low liquidity significantly hindering the ability to trade these bonds for profits or liquidity in the market, although it may be generating a preference for holding debt via the loan route over bonds because the capital cost is lower for the former.

---

[16] Such covered bonds are distinct from *structured* covered bonds, which have been contractually issued using special purpose vehicle structures and are in line with mortgage-covered bonds issued, for example, under the Pfandbrief framework in Germany or under the statutory rules governing such bonds in Denmark. For example, see Surti (2010).

CONCLUSIONS

Deepening corporate bond markets can offer India several benefits in terms of inclusive growth, including fostering access to long-term finance for the corporate and financial sectors, allowing better risk management, and supporting lending to innovative sectors. From a financial stability perspective, in common with several emerging market economies, deeper onshore corporate debt markets with a wider domestic investor base at home can increase resilience to capital flow surges in the face of external shocks and reduce opportunistic short-term borrowing in global markets. For India, key policy priorities to move in this direction include strengthening credit rights and ratings, improving trading infrastructure, and promoting safe financial innovation.

REFERENCES

Acharya, Viral. 2017. "A Case for Public Credit Registry in India." Speech at the 11th Statistics Day of the Reserve Bank of India.

Acharya, Viral. 2020. *Quest for Restoring Financial Stability in India.* Sage.

BlackRock. 2017. "Addressing Market Liquidity: A Perspective on Asia's Bond Markets." January 2017.

Ganguly, Shromona. 2014. "India's Corporate Bond Market: Issues in Market Microstructure." *RBI Bulletin* 19–30, January.

Goel, Rohit. 2020. "Challenges in India's NBFC Sector." IMF Special Features Series. Washington DC.

International Monetary Fund (IMF). 2018. *India—Financial Sector Stability Assessment.* Country Report. Washington, DC.

Patel, U. 2020. *Overdraft: Saving the Indian Saver.* Harper India.

Prakash, Shreya, Aditya Ayachit, and Shreya Garg. 2017. *Regulation of Credit Rating Agencies in India.* Delhi, India: Vidhi Centre for Legal Policy.

Reserve Bank of India (RBI). 2016. *Report of the Working Group on Development of Corporate Bond Market in India* (H.R. Khan Committee). Mumbai.

Securities and Exchange Board of India (SEBI). 2017. *Consolidation and Re-issuance of Debt Securities under the SEBI (Issue and Listing of Debt Securities) Regulations, 2008.* Consultation Paper, February 2.

Securities and Exchange Board of India (SEBI). 2018. *Designing a Framework for Enhanced Market Borrowing by Large Corporates.* Consultation Paper, July 18.

Surti, J. 2010. "Can Covered Bonds Resuscitate Residential Mortgage Finance in the United States?" IMF Working Paper 10/277, International Monetary Fund, Washington, DC.

CHAPTER 6

Development of Environmental, Social, and Governance Financial Markets

Fabio Natalucci and Rohit Goel

INTRODUCTION

Sustainable finance is growing in importance globally, as is the focus on the related financial stability risks. India has significant issues related to climate and sustainability, and green finance can play an important role in mitigating these risks and strengthening the financial sector.

Sustainable finance is defined as the incorporation of environmental, social, and governance (ESG) principles into business decisions, economic development, and investment strategies. Recent work and research have well established that sustainable finance can generate public-good (Principles for Responsible Investment 2017; Schoenmaker 2017; United Nations 2016) in which actions on an extensive set of issues generate positive impacts on society. It also plays a significant role in global financial stability issues (October 2019, October 2020, and October 2021 *Global Financial Stability Report*).

Sustainability dynamics impact financial stability through multiple channels: (1) Environmental risk exposures can lead to large losses for firms, and climate change may entail losses for financial institutions, asset owners, and firms (October 2020 *Global Financial Stability Report*). (2) Governance failures at banks and corporations have contributed significantly to past financial crises, as was evident during the global financial crisis in 2008. (3) Social risks in the form of inequality may contribute to financial instability by triggering a political response of easier credit standards to support consumption, despite stagnant incomes for middle- and lower-income groups (Rajan 2010). On the other end of the spectrum, analysis also shows that participation in these markets can spur positive changes. For instance, firms borrowing in green bond, green loan, and

---

The data in this chapter is as of the end of 2021.

sustainability-linked borrowers lower their emission intensity over time faster than other firms (Schmittmann and Han Teng 2021).[1]

Participants in sustainable finance are focusing significantly on climate-related issues globally (October 2021 *Global Financial Stability Report*). Globally, the financial sector has recognized climate change as a systemic risk to financial stability (Bolton and others 2020), with the climate change risks being classified into (1) physical risks and (2) transition risks (TCFD 2017).[2] The Network for Greening the Financial System (NGFS), a group of central banks and financial supervisors, has expressed concern that financial risks related to climate change are not fully reflected in asset valuations and has called for integrating these risks into financial stability monitoring (NGFS 2019).

These issues are becoming increasingly important for emerging markets, which has led to 2021 being a breakout year for the sustainable finance markets in emerging markets (Gautam, Goel, and Natalucci 2022; Goel, Natalucci, and Gautam 2022). These issues are also particularly relevant for India. Studies have shown that India is ranked the fifth most vulnerable nation to the effects of climate change, with 2.5–4.5 percent of its GDP at risk annually. As a result, India has pledged to reduce the carbon intensity of its GDP by 45 percent by 2030 from its 2005 levels (MoEFCC, 2022). The World Bank estimates that, unchecked, climate change will reduce India's GDP by nearly 3 percent and adversely affect the living standards of almost half the country's population by 2050 (Mani and others 2018). Another study shows how economic losses due to extreme weather have been drastically increasing over the years and stood at $45 billion in 2008–17 versus $20 billion over 1988–2007 (Singh 2019).

To achieve this target, India needs to mobilize a total of $2.5 trillion over 2016–2030 (MoEFCC 2015). The financial sector can play a vital role in mitigating the overarching climate change risks by diverting capital from the carbon-emitting sectors to the carbon-mitigating sectors (Krogstrup and Oman 2019). In 2021, India pledged to reduce carbon intensity—that is, the amount of goods produced per unit of energy—by 45 percent by 2030 (from 2005 levels) and to achieve carbon neutrality by 2070. Green finance could be one of the primary mechanisms to achieve this,[3] allowing the financial sector to strategically increase capital allocation to climate mitigation and adaptation measures that would achieve the most environmental, social, and economic benefits. While efforts to promote ESG in finance started some 30 years ago, they have accelerated more

---

[1] The authors note that a likely interpretation of the results is that green debt issuers pursue green debt to signal their green credentials, as argued by Flammer (2021) for green bonds. Other reasons could be for engagement with investors, organizational learning, and mainstreaming of green considerations and may potentially play a role as well.

[2] Physical risks arising from climate change can be event-driven or occur as longer-term shifts in climate patterns. This could result in direct damage to assets or cause indirect impacts through supply chain disruptions and resource unavailability. Transition risks refer to the potential risks incurred by the financial system due to policy, regulation, legal, and market changes in a country that is transitioning toward a low-carbon economy.

[3] Green finance refers to the financial arrangements specific to the use for environmentally sustainable projects or projects that adopt the aspects of climate change.

recently (October 2019 *Global Financial Stability Report*). The Reserve Bank of India (RBI 2019) has also acknowledged that climate change risks could undermine the stability of India's financial system and the important role the RBI needs to play in disclosures and prudential regulations (RBI 2019). The central bank further states that green finance could be an opportunity to diversify financial assets and enable mobilization of private capital for sustainable development in India. This was reflected in India issuing its inaugural sovereign green bond in January 2023 and raising $1 billion.

This chapter is one of the first studies to look at the evolution of green finance in India and to benchmark it for other emerging markets. In this chapter, the first section discusses the evolution of the ESG financial markets in India. The second section analyzes the key characteristics of the Indian green bond market. The third section compares the Indian green bond market with other emerging markets, on size as well as the key characteristics. The fifth section discusses key development areas in the Indian sustainable finance market, including ESG score and data disclosure-related issues. The final section concludes with a few policy implications and the latest guidelines from Indian regulators.

EVOLUTION OF THE ESG FINANCIAL MARKETS IN INDIA

The growing recognition of sustainability linked assets has also led to a gradual development of ESG-related financial subsectors in India. Assets under management of ESG-related equity funds have picked up sharply in the last few years. Related funds (as per the EPFR database) now number 16, with total assets under management crossing $2 billion (Figure 6.1, panel 1).[4] ESG-related products have also been increasing in Indian bond markets. While yearly issuance levels are volatile (and contingent on the external risk sentiment), 2021 has seen a sharp acceleration with almost $8 billion in issuance in year to date. This has led to cumulative issuance of almost $20 billion since the first ESG-related bond issuance in 2015 (Figure 6.1, panel 2). This is equivalent to 1 percent of the total bond issuance since 2015 but amounted to almost 2 percent of the total bond issuance in 2021—reflecting the escalation recently.

The development of the Indian ESG financial market is also supported by ESG outperformance of regular assets, in both equities and bonds. The ESG version of the Indian equity index has outperformed the broader index (Figure 6.1, panel 3) by 2 percentage points (annualized) in the last five years, with this outperformance accelerating in the last two years (to 4 percentage points per year). This is also evident in the credit market, where green bonds have traded at a notable premium to the regular version from the same issuer.[5] Trends are broadly consistent with

---

[4] These numbers are based on the EPFR data and are likely to underreport the actual data given the sample and reporting issues.

[5] Other analysis shows that this *greenium* (premium for green bonds) exists for other major emerging markets as well (JP Morgan 2021).

Figure 6.1. Development of Green Finance in India

1. ESG-Related AUMs for Indian Equity Funds and the Number of Such Funds
(Billions of dollars; number, right scale)

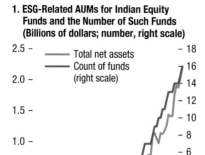

2. Indian ESG Bond Issuance
(Billions of dollars)

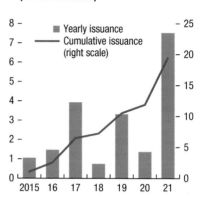

3. Indian Equity Performance: ESG vs. Regular Index
(Annualized returns)

4. Proportion of ESG Issuance across the Various Categories
(Percent)

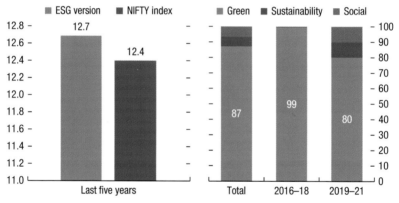

5. Number of Entities That Have Issued Bonds
(Number)

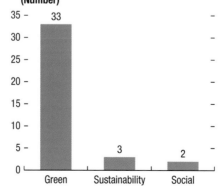

Sources: Bloomberg L.P.; and authors' calculations.
Note: AUMs = assets under management; ESG = environmental, social, and governance.

global developments, where ESG-related assets have been the source of notable outperformance. Despite this outperformance, green bonds are issued at significantly higher financing costs in India versus the other nongreen issuers (RBI 2019), which points to the ongoing challenges in developing this market.

As the name suggests, the ESG segment has multiple sectors covering green bonds, as well as social and sustainability-linked bonds, with corresponding subsectors (ESG Risk AI 2021). The Indian ESG bond market has been dominated by green bonds,[6] which accounted for almost 100 percent of total issuance in 2016–19. More recently, though, that share has fallen, with other subsectors, such as social and sustainability-linked bonds, comprising almost 20 percent of total issuance in 2019–21 (Figure 6.1, panel 4). This trend is in line with what we saw in the rest of the emerging markets (October 2021 *Global Financial Stability Report*). Despite the rising penetration in total issuance, very few corporates (Figure 6.1, panel 5) have participated in these markets (low single digits for social and sustainability-linked bonds as compared with almost 30 for green bonds).

The next section describes characteristics of the Indian green bond market.

KEY CHARACTERISTICS OF THE INDIAN GREEN BOND MARKET

Currency Denomination

Green bond issuance in India has primarily been denominated in US dollars, with cumulative issuance in local currency down to about 10 percent in 2021, from around 25 percent in 2016 (Figure 6.2, panel 1). This partly reflects the stage of development of the Indian green bond market. The difference in the two segments is also reflected in issuance characteristics. While the maturity profile is broadly similar between US dollar–denominated and local currency–denominated issues, coupon rates differ notably, at 4.8 percent and 7.9 percent, respectively (Figure 6.2, panel 2). This is in line with the experience in other countries at the same stage of bond market development and might partially explain the inclination to issue more in US dollar denominations. The liberalized External Commercial Borrowings (ECB) norms of RBI have enabled Indian renewable energy companies and other firms to tap the ECB route for raising finance through green bonds and sustainable bonds, reflecting the growing attractiveness of this route for raising finance.

Credit Rating Profiles of Issuers

Issuers across rating profiles have tapped the green bond market in India. However, profiles have changed, reflecting rising market access from even

---

[6] Green bonds are bonds issued by any sovereign entity, intergovernmental group or alliance, and corporates that aim to use proceeds for projects classified as environmentally sustainable.

Figure 6.2. Key Characteristics of the Green Bond Market in India

1. Green Bond Issuance by Currency Denomination
(Percent, cumulative since 2015)

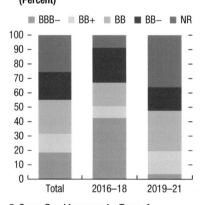

2. Key Metrics for the Indian Green Bond Issuance by Currency Composition
(Percent; number of years)

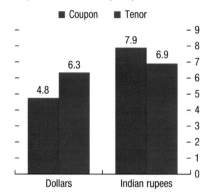

3. Green Bond Issuance by the Rating of the Issuer
(Percent)

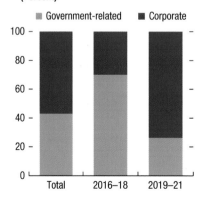

4. Key Metrics for the Indian Green Bond Issuance by Currency Composition
(Percent; number of years)

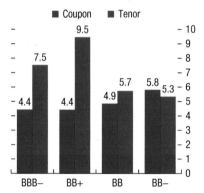

5. Green Bond Issuance by Type of Issuer
(Percent)

6. Key Metrics for the Indian Green Bond Issuance by Type of Issuer
(Percent; number of years)

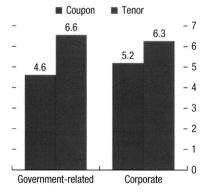

Figure 6.2 *(continued)*

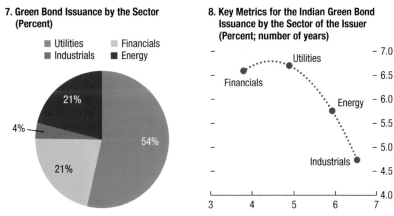

7. Green Bond Issuance by the Sector
(Percent)

■ Utilities   ■ Financials
■ Industrials   ■ Energy

8. Key Metrics for the Indian Green Bond
Issuance by the Sector of the Issuer
(Percent; number of years)

Sources: Bloomberg L.P.; and authors' calculations.
Note: NR = not rated.

lower-rated issuers (Figure 6.2, panel 3). Higher-rated issuers (proxied through BBB– and BB+ ratings) accounted for almost 50 percent of total issuance over 2016–18. However, these issuers accounted for a marginal 10 percent of total issuance over 2019–21, with lower-rated issuers comprising a significant proportion.[7] Expanding market access is encouraging and highlights improving investor comfort in this nascent segment. As expected, investors continue to differentiate, across issuers, as the lower-rated issuers pay a much higher coupon (Figure 6.2, panel 4). Average coupon rate for a BB-rated issuer is 5.8 percent, versus 4.8 percent for a BBB-rated issuer. Differentiation exists across the maturity profile, with lower-rated issuers having significantly lower tenors (at 5.3 years for BB-rated issuers vs. 7.6 years for BBB-rated issuers).

Types of Issuers

Within total issuance in India, 45 percent of the total issuance has been dominated by quasi-sovereign corporates,[8] reflecting the significant role played by public sector entities in the Indian financial sector. However, trends have changed over time. While quasi-sovereigns accounted for almost 70 percent of total issuance in

---

[7] The findings are true even adjusting for the nonrated category.

[8] There is no green bond sovereign issuance in India. However, it was announced in the February 2022 budget speech that the government would issue sovereign green bonds in the domestic market as part of its overall market borrowing program for the 2022–23 fiscal year. As announced in the Issuance Calendar for Marketable Dated Securities for H1:2022–23, the government and the RBI are working jointly in bringing out a framework for issuance of sovereign green bonds. Issuance of sovereign green bonds is likely to take place in H2:2022–23 (October 2022–March 2023) after finalization of the sovereign green bond framework.

2016–18, their share dropped to just 30 percent in 2019–21 (Figure 6.2, panel 5). The increasing role played by the nonquasi corporates also corroborates the finding that market interest and access for sustainable finance have improved over the last few years. Investor differentiation, as with previous characteristics, is also evident in key metrics. Quasi-sovereigns, as expected, enjoy much better coupon rates (at 4.7 percent vs. 5.5 percent for nonquasi corporates) even though the maturity profile seems broadly similar for both (Figure 6.2, panel 6).

Economic Sectors of Issuers

While market access is improving across categories, only a handful of economic sectors have issued green bonds, with utilities, energy, and financials accounting for 49 percent, 24 percent, and 23 percent of total green bond issuance, respectively (Figure 6.2, panel 7). Green bond markets differ slightly from the overall corporate bond market, where the financial sector accounts for over 80 percent of issuance (see Chapter 5 on India's corporate bond markets). Within these categories, around 55 percent of issuance is dominated by companies associated with renewable sectors, in line with their core business models. However, this also implies that a significant number of firms not directly related with sustainable finance are issuing green bonds to venture into sustainable finance activities and to tap into a new investor base. These economic sectors, however, differ significantly with respect to the trade-off between average tenor and the average coupon rate (Figure 6.2, panel 8). Financials have the lowest coupon rate, with a significantly longer maturity profile. This contrasts with the industrial sector, which has the lowest tenor and the highest coupon rate.

INDIAN GREEN BOND MARKET, BENCHMARKED VERSUS OTHER EMERGING MARKETS

Benchmarking in Terms of Size

While the green bond market has been developing steadily in India, it accounts for a small proportion (about 7 percent) of the emerging-market-wide green bonds, dominated by China, which accounts for 75 percent of the total (Figure 6.3, panel 1). However, most of China's dominance is because of its issuance in local currency. The US dollar–denominated green bond market potentially plays a more important role for global investors. India accounts for a relatively meaningful 20 percent of total issuance, while China accounts for closer to half (Figure 6.3, panel 2). India's importance in the emerging market green bonds can also be seen through the numbers of issuers participating. While India has the third-largest number of issuers, it remains low compared with some major advanced economies, indicating the still-relative underpenetration (Figure 6.3, panel 3). In relation to its size, India has issued 0.5 percent of GDP equivalent in green bonds. While this is lower than Chile's and China's issuance of 3.5 percent and 1 percent, respectively, it is higher than most other emerging markets (Figure 6.3, panel 4).

Figure 6.3. Comparison of Indian Green Bond Market vs. Other Emerging Markets—Size

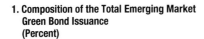

1. Composition of the Total Emerging Market Green Bond Issuance (Percent)

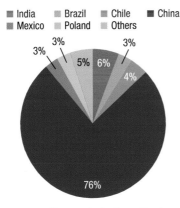

2. Composition of the Total Emerging Market Green Bond Issuance, Denominated in Dollars (Percent)

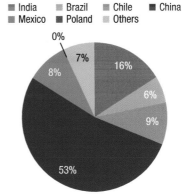

3. Number of Issuers in the Green Bond Space (Number; billions of dollars on right scale)

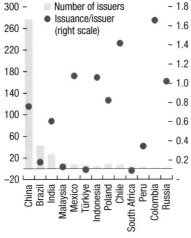

4. Total Green Bond Issuance, as a Percent of GDP (Percent)

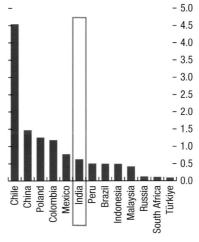

Sources: Bloomberg L.P.; and authors' calculations.

Benchmarking on Key Characteristics

It is also useful to benchmark India on key features.

Currency Denomination

More than 90 percent of Indian green bonds are denominated in US dollars, compared with 60 percent for other emerging markets (excluding China and India).

The emerging market universe is also more diversified because of issuance denominated in euros (24 percent of total issuance) and others (including Swiss francs, Hong Kong dollars, and others). Local currency denominations account for 75 percent of issuance in China, almost 15 percent in other emerging markets, and just 8 percent for India (Figure 6.4, panel 1). This potentially reflects the stage of development of the Indian green bond market. It could also indicate the fact that sustainable finance is a nascent though growing asset class. Thus, global investors provide a better pool for the issuers to tap into. Second, the higher-risk premiums in the local bonds, especially for a new asset class, might result in the dollar bonds becoming a relatively cheaper source of funding.

Sectoral Composition

Utilities comprise almost 50 percent of total green bond issuance in India, with the rest broadly divided into energy and financials. The high sectoral concentration contrasts sharply with other emerging markets, which are a lot more diversified (Figure 6.4, panel 2). This may also reflect corporates continuing to rely primarily on bank loans instead of the bond market. This is also true for overall corporate bonds in India, where issuance is concentrated in just a few sectors, unlike the rest of the emerging markets.

Tenors

Indian green bonds, with an average maturity of 6.4 years, are of significantly lower tenor than the rest of the emerging markets (excluding China), where the average tenor is 12.2 years (Figure 6.4, panel 3, y-axis).

Coupon Rate

India green bonds are launched at a relatively higher coupon rate of 4.9 percent, which compares with the emerging market (excluding China) average of 4.2 percent (Figure 6.4, panel 3, x-axis). The findings remain consistent even when analyzing different currency denominations (Figure 6.4, panel 4). For local currency–denominated issuance, Indian green bonds pay an average 7.9 percent coupon, one of the highest among emerging market peers (except Türkiye and South Africa). The divergence is relatively less stark for US dollar–denominated issuance, where Indian green bonds have an average coupon rate of 4.8 percent, which is broadly in line with the median of emerging market peers.

Analysis notes that Indian green bonds are issued at a comparatively higher coupon and at significantly lower tenors. This could be due to multiple reasons: (1) Indian corporate bonds generally embed significantly higher risk premiums than other emerging markets, reflecting the comparatively weaker fundamentals of the corporates (October 2019 *Global Financial Stability Report*); (2) India's credit rating is also weaker than an average emerging market, which might explain the overall higher risk premiums; (3) the Indian green bond market is at an early stage of development; and (4) investor base difference between the various emerging markets might also play a very important role in driving these decisions. Lack of

Figure 6.4. Indian Green Bond Market vs. Other EMs—Key Characteristics

1. Comparison of India with Other Major Emerging Markets—on the Currency Composition of the Issuance
(Percent)

2. Comparison of India with Other Major Emerging Markets—on the Sectoral Composition of the Issuance
(Percent)

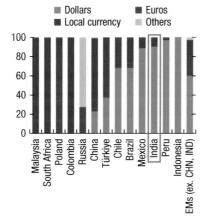

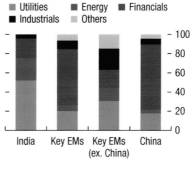

3. Average Tenors and Coupons for Green Bond Issuances across the Major Emerging Markets
(Percent; number of years–Red dot is India)

4. Coupon Rates for USD and Local Currency Issuance
(Percent)

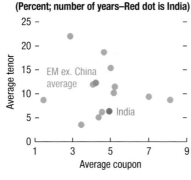

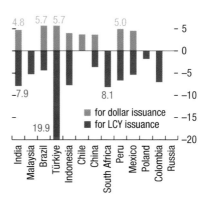

5. Comparison of India with Other Major Emerging Markets—on the Type of Corporates
(Percent)

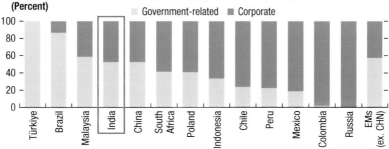

Sources: Bloomberg L.P.; and authors' calculations.
Note: CHN = China; EMs = emerging markets; ex. = excluding; IND = India; LCY = local currency.

data precludes us from doing a detailed deep dive on this topic, reiterating the importance of increased data transparency.

Types of Issuers

Emerging markets vary remarkably in type of issuer, and India is broadly in line with the median emerging market peer with an almost equal participation from quasi and nonquasi corporates (Figure 6.4, panel 5).

KEY DEVELOPMENT AREAS

The following are a few key areas for development that may help further deepen and broaden the development of the sustainable finance market in India:

- **Promoting the adoption of green bond principles.** The International Capital Market Association's Green Bond Principles (ICMA 2022) are voluntary guidelines that recommend transparency and disclosure and promote integrity in the development of the green bond market.[9] The proportion of India's green bond issuance adhering to these principles has declined over the last few years, on three of four major metrics (Figure 6.5, panel 1). This could be because more, lower-rated issuers are accessing the green bond market (see the section on benchmarking on key characteristics), or because there are less bond disclosures in general. India also scores less favorable on all of these parameters when compared to other emerging markets (Figure 6.5, panel 2). For project selection and reporting, India is at the lower end of the interquartile range, reflecting significant scope for improvement.

  While adherence to these principles is voluntary, it can help develop the market in multiple ways: (1) aiding investors by promoting availability of information to evaluate environmental impact of green bond investments, and (2) assisting underwriters by offering vital steps to facilitate transactions and market integrity.

- **Strengthening Data Disclosure.** A key challenge with the development of green bond markets globally is progress on data disclosure. Reliable and comparable data are crucial for financial sector stakeholders to assess financial stability risks, properly price and manage ESG-related risks, and take advantage of opportunities arising from the transition to a green economy (NGFS 2021). Figure 6.6, panel 1, plots the extent of data disclosure by major corporates across a few economies. With a median ESG disclosure

---

[9] (1) Project selection: The issuer of a green bond should outline the decision-making process it follows to determine eligibility of the projects. (2) Management of proceeds: The net proceeds of the green bond should outline the decision-making process it follows to determine the eligibility of the projects. (3) Assurance: The issuer should obtain third-party verification of green credentials as either a second-party opinion, third-party certification, green bond audit, or green rating. (4) Reporting: Issuers should report on the projects financed, project performance, and, preferably, environmental impact at least once a year.

Figure 6.5. Key Issues Part 1: Green Bond Principles

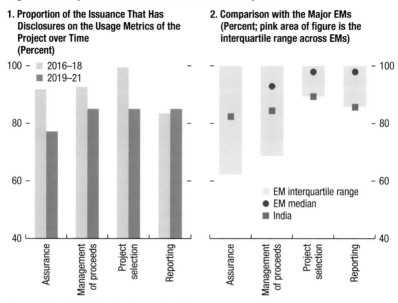

1. Proportion of the Issuance That Has Disclosures on the Usage Metrics of the Project over Time
(Percent)

2. Comparison with the Major EMs
(Percent; pink area of figure is the interquartile range across EMs)

Sources: Bloomberg L.P.; and authors' calculations.
Note: EMs = emerging markets.

score of 25, Indian corporates lag major advanced economies (e.g., the United States at 40, the euro area at 60, and the United Kingdom at 45). They lag even those of EMs (Goel, Gautam, and Natalucci 2022). Securities and Exchange Board of India's (SEBI) latest set of guidelines (Business Responsibility and Sustainability Reporting [BRSR]; refer to Box 6.1) are a very helpful next step to address this issue. Within the disclosure metrics in India, it is highest for the governance segment followed by the social segment (Figure 6.6, panel 2). Disclosure metrics related to the environment are notably lower, which is especially relevant given the significant climate-related risks India faces (ranked fifth most vulnerable nation to effects of climate change, with 2.5–4.5 percent of GDP at risk annually; see Jena and Purkayastha 2020). Data by the company ESG Risk AI show a very strong correlation between data disclosure transparency and actual ESG scores (Figure 6.6, panel 3). This may show that firms with weak progress on the ESG front also do not disclose these metrics, which may potentially amplify the investor concerns and risk premiums in these markets.

- **Achieving Higher ESG Scores.** Corporates are also scored on the various ESG-related parameters (e.g., external corporates by JP Morgan 2021, overall corporates in India by ESG Risk AI 2021). JP Morgan's data on external corporates show that the ESG score for India has declined sharply in the last few years and is touching historical lows (Figure 6.7, panel 1). The decline potentially reflects the challenged fundamentals of Indian corporates

Figure 6.6. Key Issues Part 2: ESG-Related Data Disclosures

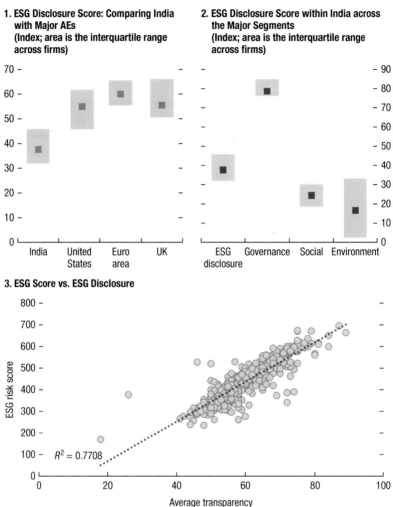

1. ESG Disclosure Score: Comparing India with Major AEs
(Index; area is the interquartile range across firms)

2. ESG Disclosure Score within India across the Major Segments
(Index; area is the interquartile range across firms)

3. ESG Score vs. ESG Disclosure

$R^2 = 0.7708$

Sources: Bloomberg L.P.; ESG Risk AI; and authors' calculations.
Note: AEs = advanced economies; ESG = environmental, social, and governance.

(GFSR 2019). India has significant room to improve compared with other emerging markets and is at the lower end of the interquartile range (Figure 6.7, panel 2). In addition, data show a considerable heterogeneity across corporates, as seen through the wide kernel distributions in Figure 6.7, panel 3. The heterogeneity is particularly notable across the environment and government categories (standard deviations of 66 and 60, respectively) versus the social category (standard deviation of 48)—potentially reflecting the different economic sectors (and private vs. public ownership) corporates are involved in. Variation is also notable across the three categories, with corporates scoring

Figure 6.7. Key Issues Part 3: Weak ESG Scores

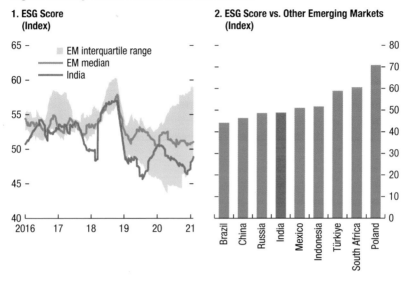

1. ESG Score
   (Index)

2. ESG Score vs. Other Emerging Markets
   (Index)

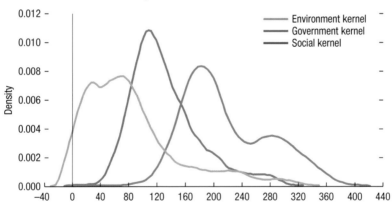

3. ESG Score across Different Categories

Sources: Bloomberg L.P.; ESG Risk AI; JPMorgan Chase; and authors' calculations.
Note: EM = emerging market; ESG = environmental, social, and governance.

weakest on the environment category and highest on the government category. This reiterates the potential risk that issues related to climate (and environment) can pose for Indian corporates and financial stability.

KEY POLICY RECOMMENDATIONS

- Data disclosure requirements are critical to enable investors to price risks appropriately and develop the sustainable finance market in India. In this respect, the latest BRSR guidelines in India are encouraging (see Box 6.1)

Box 6.1. New Set of Guidelines Help with the Disclosure Requirements

Earlier in 2021, India's security market regulator (SEBI) introduced new guidelines to extend the corporate environmental, social, and governance (ESG) disclosure requirements. The new guidelines (called Business Responsibility and Sustainability Reporting [BRSR]) will replace the current business sustainability report and are mandatory from 2022 to 2023. The move from Business Responsibility Reporting (BRR) to BRSR is expected to provide greater transparency in companies' sustainability risk management practices and extend the current framework on multiple dimensions (ESG Risk AI 2021). See Figures 6.8 and 6.9.

- **Firm coverage:** Contrary to the business sustainability report requirements, which mandated the disclosure for the top-100 listed firms, BRSR mandates it for the top 1,000 National Stock Exchange of India–listed companies, which will include many small to medium-sized firms as well. This has made India one of the few countries with an explicit taxonomy and mandated disclosures.
- **Closer to the global standards:** While BRR India's existing reporting standards cover a good part of the Global Reporting Inititive standards, BRSR brings India's sustainability reporting closer to Global Reporting Inititive's global reporting standards and shows a meaningful improvement.
- **Wider coverage:** Multiple new areas have been integrated into the framework, including board diversity, ESG reporting, board structuring, and functioning, among others.
- **Deeper coverage:** BRSR covers more data points than BRR, especially in the governance category. It covers 2 percent more in the environment, 6 percent more in the social, and 2 percent more in the governance categories, as well as 88 percent data points.

---

but also highlight areas for improvement. For instance, mandatory disclosures on both targets as well as the performance against these targets will be especially helpful for industries with high emissions and water consumption/pollution. Data from ESG Risk AI show that industries that are water and carbon intensive have an average overall transparency of 56 percent. In contrast, transparency in nonintensive sectors like the financial industry (not water or energy intensive) is considerably better at 77 percent.

- RBI 2019 also notes that higher financing costs for green bond issuers is a significant impediment to market development, and information asymmetry is a key reason behind that. In line with other major economies (Shen and others 2020), India could develop a better information management system that may help reduce maturity mismatches and borrowing costs and lead to a more efficient resource allocation in this segment.

- Company disclosures will also expand policy and research analysis. As Schmittmann and Han Teng (2021) noted, most research and analysis so far are focused on green bond markets. Data constraints prevent analysis of bank-based green products and issuer-based instruments.

- A formal green finance definition could also mitigate the risks of "greenwashing" and bring better reporting and disclosure to investors and financiers (European Commission 2017). NGFS 2019 also notes that a definition would also improve the financial sector's ability, in general, to

Figure 6.8. Extension of the Current Disclosure Guidelines by SEBI: Difference between Old (BSR) and New (BRSR) Guidelines

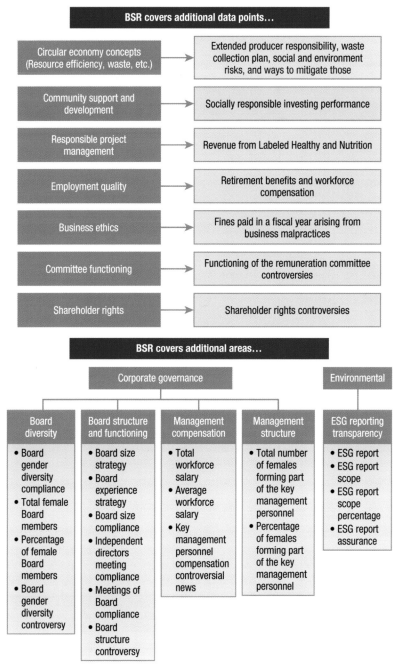

Source: ESG Risk AI.
Note: BRR = Business Responsibility Reporting; BRSR = Business Responsibility and Sustainability Report; ESG = environmental, social, and governance; SEBI = Securities and Exchange Board of India.

identify, assess, and control financial risks emanating from climate change. Adherence to the International Capital Markets Association's green bond principles can also help strengthen investor confidence in these products and establish a local market. SEBI's recent consultation paper (SEBI 2022) for ESG rating providers and the directives for issuance of green debt securities (SEBI 2017) are very helpful in this context.

- ESG issues can have a material impact on corporate risk profile and the system's financial stability (October 2019, October 2020, and October 2021 *Global Financial Stability Report*). The integration of ESG factors into firms' business models—prompted either by regulators or by investors— may help mitigate some of these risks.

- There is a strong need to sensitize India's financial sector about the importance of green finance and the need for accelerating capital. Only a handful of institutions are participating in the sustainable finance market and are signatories of the Principles for Responsible Investment, for instance.

- Incentivizing green projects can also help develop the market and the awareness in the market. This can be achieved through subsidies or sanctions for firms not aligned with the Paris Accords.

CONCLUSION

The Indian sustainable finance market is growing in size (for both equities and fixed income) but remains smaller compared to other emerging markets (both in absolute issuance and in the number of issuers). At the same time, the market is expanding across multiple dimensions, indicating rising awareness and interest among corporates and investors, in particular:

- In addition to green bond market, the issuance of social and sustainability bonds is increasing.

- While primarily quasi-sovereigns dominated the market in the past, increasingly private sector corporates issue green bonds.

- Lower and nonrated issuers are increasingly coming to the market.

A comparison with other emerging markets highlights some unique features of the Indian green bond market (Figure 6.9). For example, Indian green bonds are shorter in maturity and pay higher coupon rates, issuance is predominantly in US dollars and its share significantly higher than in other emerging markets, and the market is a lot more diversified. This is particularly notable, because the majority of overall corporate issuance in India is in local currency (for more details, refer Chapter 5 on India's corporate bond market). The greater use of USD green bonds is probably due to the larger offshore green bond market.

The chapter also notes a few development areas that can help further expand the sustainable finance market in India, including promotion of green bond principles, improvement of data disclosure requirements, and achievement of higher ESG scores. SEBI's new data disclosure framework (BRSR) (Figure 6.8) is a step

Figure 6.9. Comparison between Indian ESG and Non-ESG Corporate Bond Market: Proportion of Issuance in Different Currencies
(Percent of total issuance)

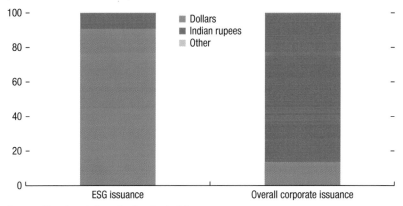

Sources: Bloomberg L.P.; and authors' calculations.
Note: ESG = environmental, social, and governance.

in the right direction that helps significantly improve the data disclosure requirements and granularity across a large number of corporates. More concrete improvements, including creating an information management system, a more concrete definition of "green" bonds to prevent green washing, and incentivizing green projects, might help further the interest in and scope of these activities.

REFERENCES

Bolton, Patrick, Morgan Despres, Luiz Awazu Pereira da Silva, Frederic Samama, and Romain Svartzman. 2020. "The Green Swan: Central Banking and Financial Stability in the Age of Climate Change." Bank for International Settlement. https://www.bis.org/publ/othp31.pdf.

ESG Risk Assessments and Insights (ESG Risk AI). 2021. "The ESG Yearbook 2021: Indian Landscape."

Flammer, Caroline. 2021. "Corporate Green Bonds." *Journal of Financial Economics* 142 (2021): 499–516.

Gautam, Deepali, Rohit Goel, and Fabio Natalucci. 2022. "Sustainable Finance in Emerging Markets Is Enjoying Rapid Growth, but May Bring Risks." IMF Blog. https://www.imf.org/en/Blogs/Articles/2022/03/01/sustainable-finance-in-emerging-markets-is-enjoying-rapid-growth-but-may-bring-risks.

Goel, Rohit, Deepali Gautam and Fabio Natalucci. 2022. "Sustainable Finance in Emerging Markets: Evolution, Challenges, and Policy Priorities." IMF Working Paper 22/182, International Monetary Fund, Washington, DC.

International Capital Market Association (ICMA). 2022. "Green Bond Principles (GBP) 2021." ICMA, Zurich. https://www.icmagroup.org/sustainable-finance/the-principles-guidelines-and-handbooks/green-bond-principles-gbp/.

Jena, Labanya Prakash, and Dhruba Purkayastha. 2020, June. "Accelerating Green Finance in India: Definitions and Beyond." Climate Policy Initiative (CPI) Discussion Brief. https://www.climatepolicyinitiative.org/wp-content/uploads/2020/07/Accelerating-Green-Finance-in-India_Definitions-and-Beyond.pdf.

JP Morgan. 2021. "Asia ESG Credit: A Fast-Growing Space with a Slowly Emerging Spread Premium," March.

Krogstrup, Signe, and William Oman. 2019. "Macroeconomic and Financial Policies for Climate Change Mitigation: A Review of the Literature." IMF Working Paper 19/185, International Monetary Fund, Washington, DC.

Mani, Muthukumara, Sushenjit Bandyopadhyay, Shun Chonabayashi, Anil Markandya, and Thomas Mosier. 2018. "South Asia's Hotspots: and Precipitation Changes on Living Standards." South Asia Development Matters. Washington, DC: World Bank Group.

Ministry of Environment, Forest and Climate Change (MoEFCC). 2015. Government of India. Press Information Bureau. https://pib.gov.in/newsite/PrintRelease.aspx?relid=128403.

Network for Greening the Financial System (NGFS). 2019, April. "A Call for Action: Climate Change as a Source of Financial Risk." Technical document. https://www.ngfs.net/sites/default/files/medias/documents/ngfs_first_comprehensive_report_-_17042019_0.pdf.

Network for Greening the Financial System (NGFS). 2021, May. "Progress Report on Bridging Data Gaps." https://www.ngfs.net/sites/default/files/medias/documents/progress_report_on_bridging_data_gaps.pdf.

Principles for Responsible Investment. 2017. "The SDG Investment Case." PRI Association, London.

Rajan, Raghuram G. 2010. "How Inequality Fueled the Crisis." Project Syndicate, July 9.

Reserve Bank of India (RBI). 2019. "Opportunities and Challenges of Green Finance." Report on Trend and Progress of Banking in India 2018–19, 17–18.

Schmittmann, Jochen, and Chua Han Teng. 2021. "How Green Are Green Debt Issuers?" IMF Working Paper 21/194, International Monetary Fund, Washington, DC.

Schoenmaker, Dirk. 2017. "From Risk to Opportunity: A Framework for Sustainable Finance" (September 20, 2017). RSM Series on Positive Change, Volume 2. Rotterdam School of Management, Netherlands.

Securities and Exchange Board of India (SEBI). 2017, May 30. "Disclosure Requirements for Issuance and Listing of Green Debt Securities." SEBI. https://www.sebi.gov.in/legal/circulars/may-2017/disclosure-requirements-for-issuance-and-listing-of-green-debt-securities_34988.html.

Securities and Exchange Board of India (SEBI). 2022, January 24. "Consultation Paper on Environmental, Social and Governance (ESG) Rating Providers for Securities Markets." SEBI. https://www.sebi.gov.in/reports-and-statistics/reports/jan-2022/consultation-paper-on-environmental-social-and-governance-esg-rating-providers-for-securities-markets_55516.html.

Singh C. 2019. "Assessing India's Mounting Climate Losses to Financial Institutions." *PreventionWeb*. https://www.preventionweb.net/files/63287_climatelossesrevised.pdf.

Task Force on Climate-related Financial Disclosures. (TCFD). 2017. "The Use of Scenario Analysis in Disclosure of Climate-Related Risks and Opportunities—Technical Supplement." TCFD.

United Nations. 2016. *The Sustainable Development Goals Report 2016*. https://unstats.un.org/sdgs/report/2016/The%20Sustainable%20Development%20Goals%20Report%202016.pdf.

CHAPTER 7

Digital Financial Services and Inclusion

Purva Khera

INTRODUCTION

Financial inclusion has featured prominently in India's public policy agenda for a long time and is recognized as one of the most critical aspects of inclusive growth and development. Financial access allows firms to invest and households to smooth their consumption and build capital over time, fostering the creation of businesses and helping to improve people's livelihoods. It also helps households and firms protect themselves against shocks and better manage risk.

As such, universal financial inclusion has always been a national commitment and public policy priority in India (Chakrabarty 2011). It has been defined as "the process of ensuring access to financial services, timely and adequate credit for vulnerable groups such as weaker sections and low-income groups at an affordable cost" (Reserve Bank of India [RBI] 2008).

India has much to gain from broadening access to finance while maintaining financial stability. In addition to enhancing individual opportunities, it has positive macroeconomic effects: International Monetary Fund (IMF) research shows that financial inclusion supports growth and lowers inequality, and provided the financial sector is well regulated, it does not hurt financial stability (Sahay, Čihák, N'Diaye, Barajas, Bi, and others 2015; Sahay, Čihák, N'Diaye, Barajas, Mitra, and others 2015; Sahay and Čihák 2020). It also improves the effectiveness of macroeconomic policies, further supporting growth and stability (Loukoianova and Yang 2018). However, financial inclusion of less-productive agents can also hurt growth (Dabla-Norris and others 2015). Financial stability risks increase when access to credit expands without proper regulation and supervision.

Technological developments are changing the way people access financial services. Digital financial services are faster, more efficient, and typically cheaper than traditional financial services and therefore increasingly reach lower-income households and micro, small, and medium enterprises (MSMEs).[1] Although digital financial services are still small relative to traditional services, they are growing rapidly and at varying speeds across regions and countries (Khera and others

---

[1] Digital financial services are financial services accessed and delivered through digital channels, including mobile devices.

2021a; Sahay and others 2020). Moreover, the COVID-19 pandemic and its need for social distancing have put a spotlight on digital financial services, which helped improve social distancing and allowed governments to disburse funds to those in need quickly and effectively, and enabled many households and firms to rapidly access online payments and financing.

Beyond promoting financial inclusion, digital financial services can also provide impetus to growth and employment (Philippon 2017; Sahay and others 2020). Empirical work based on survey data at the household and firm level points to the economic benefits of digital financial inclusion (primarily mobile money) arising from improved risk sharing, consumption smoothing, and saving (Jack and Suri 2014; Mbiti and Weil 2016; Riley 2016). Based on a cross-country empirical study consisting of data for 52 developing and emerging economies, one IMF study (Khera and others 2021b) found that in recent years, digital financial inclusion in payments has had a positive impact on economic growth.

This chapter focuses on two leading factors in financial inclusion in India—access to payments and credit—with a special focus on digitalization. This reflects that payments, followed by credit, are often the first step and the gateway to gaining access to financial services. While the other dimensions of financial inclusion—saving, insurance, and wealth management—are equally important, they are still nascent, and adequate data are lacking.

In this chapter, the first section reviews developments and trends in financial inclusion in India in the past decade, focusing on the role of digitalization in closing India's financing gaps. The second section quantifies the impact of digital financial services on financial inclusion through a new digital financial inclusion index. The third section summarizes the empirical evidence of the economic impact of digital financial inclusion, and the fourth section provides a cross-country comparison and analyzes the remaining financial inclusion gaps in India. The final section concludes with related policy implications.

INDIA'S FINANCIAL INCLUSION JOURNEY OVER THE PAST DECADE

Improving Financial Inclusion of Households

Financial inclusion in India was very low as recently as 2011, when only 35 percent of adults possessed a bank account, well below the average of other emerging market economies (Demirgüç-Kunt and others 2018). Even fewer adults saved with (12 percent) or borrowed from (8 percent) a financial institution (Figure 7.1). Cash was used extensively, with currency in circulation at about 12 percent of gross domestic product (GDP), even though holding cash carried high opportunity cost and availability of ATMs was just 21 per 100,000 adults (IMF Financial Access Survey).

Since then, several government initiatives have focused on laying a digital foundation for improvements in financial inclusion. The first major step was the launch of Aadhaar, the biometric digital ID system, in 2010. This has been a game changer because it facilitated access to bank accounts by reducing the time and the cost of the "know your customer" (KYC) process. Within three years of

Figure 7.1. Access to Financial Services a Decade Ago, 2011
(Percent)

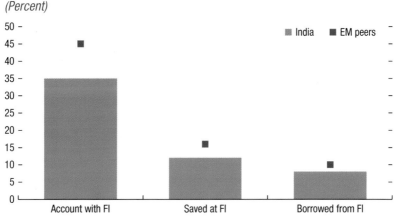

Source: World Bank, Global Findex database.
Note: EM = emerging market; FI = financial institution.

its launch, about 600 million Aadhaar digital ID numbers had been issued, equivalent to roughly half the Indian population. By 2017, over 90 percent of the population possessed an Aadhaar and half of the identity holders had linked their bank accounts to their Aadhaar number (Figure 7.2).

Notably, India is neither the only nor the first country to adopt a digitally verifiable unique identity system; similar digital ID schemes exist in countries such as Estonia and Uruguay (OECD 2019). According to the 2017 World Bank

Figure 7.2. Biometric Digital ID System Improved Access to Bank Accounts

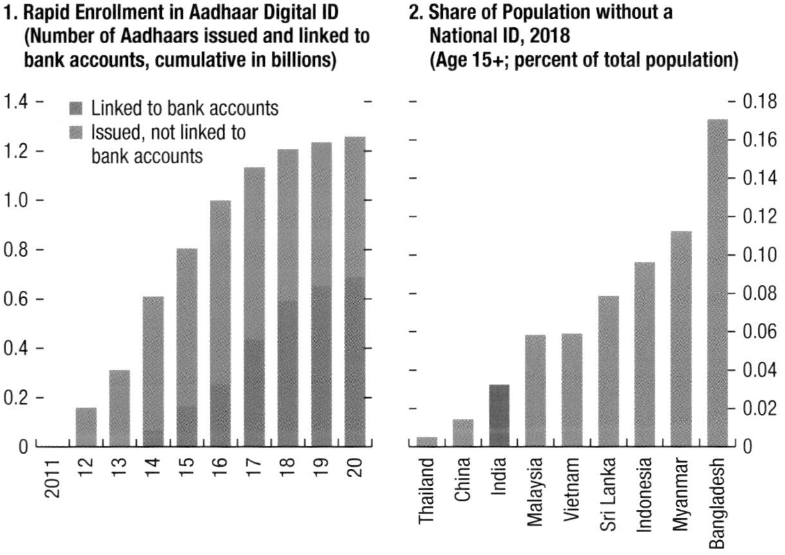

1. Rapid Enrollment in Aadhaar Digital ID
(Number of Aadhaars issued and linked to bank accounts, cumulative in billions)

2. Share of Population without a National ID, 2018
(Age 15+; percent of total population)

Sources: Unique Identification Authority of India; and World Bank, ID4D Findex Survey data.

Figure 7.3. New Account Opening Following the PMJDY Scheme
(Account at financial institutions)

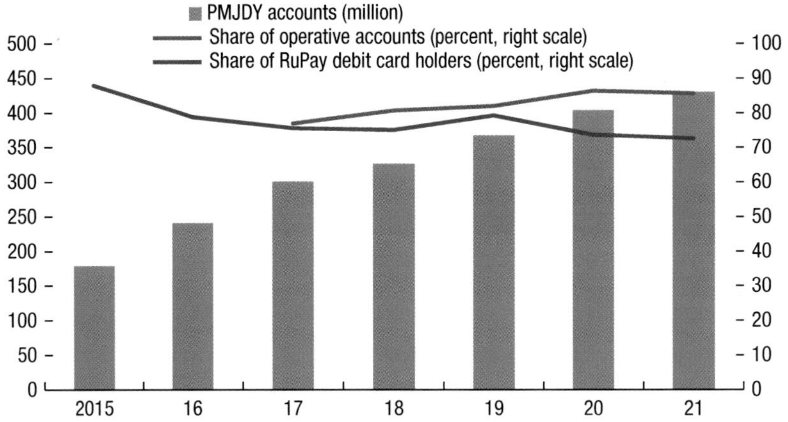

Source: Pradhan Mantri Jan Dhan Yojana (PMJDY) website.

ID4D Global Dataset, 83 countries collect fingerprints or biometrics for issuing digitized ID. What sets India apart is the large scale and low unit costs of operating the program, which enabled its billion-plus population to enroll in the program and quickly acquire a national ID that could be used in all aspects of economic life, including swift access to financial services.

The biggest structural shift in access to finance came with the rollout of the Pradhan Mantri Jan Dhan Yojana (PMJDY) scheme in August 2014.

- This was an ambitious financial development policy to provide bank accounts to all households in India and convenient access to saving accounts through a debit card (called RuPay) and mobile banking. A variety of features distinguished this financial inclusion program from previous and similar programs. These include a no-frills, zero-balance account with a debit card, access to mobile banking for funds transfer, overdraft facilities, and built-in basic life insurance coverage (about $440) for all account holders (Agarwal and others 2019). Bank accounts under this scheme could be opened using the Aadhaar ID and subsequently linked to it for the transfer of government benefits.

- In just one year after its launch, 180 million Indians, about 15 percent of the population, had opened accounts as part of the program, and 404 million had accounts by 2020 (30 percent), with 86 percent of the accounts still operative and 73 percent of the account holders using the RuPay debit card (Figure 7.3).[2] Moreover, about 13 percent of PMJDY account holders receive direct benefit transfers from the Indian government under various schemes.

---

[2] As per RBI guidelines, a PMJDY account is treated as inoperative if there are no customer-induced transactions in the account for over a period of two years.

Figure 7.4. Gaps in Access to Financial Services across Income Groups and Gender Have Narrowed

1. Gap in Financial Access between the Poor and Rich
(Percent with FI account)

2. Gender Gaps in Financial Access
(Percent with FI account)

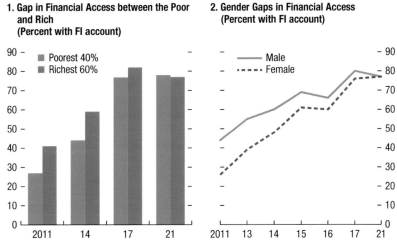

Sources: World Bank, Global Findex database; and Finclusion database.
Note: FI = financial institution.

This facilitated a rapid increase in financial inclusion while also narrowing gaps across different dimensions (Figure 7.4). Even though up to a third of PMJDY accounts appear to have been opened for customers who already had a bank account, the scheme does seem to have effectively lifted the accessibility constraint for a large section of the population who were financially excluded in 2014.[3] Between 2014 and 2017, the percentage of the Indian population with an account at a financial institution increased from 53 to 80 percent; that is, more than 300 million people were brought into the formal financial sector.[4] This is considerably above the world average (68.5 percent), South Asia (70 percent), and lower-middle-income countries (58 percent). Based on cross-country comparison, D'Silva and others (2019) underscored that this represented an impressive leapfrogging of traditional financial development, as similar expansions in financial access elsewhere have taken almost half a century. Moreover, the gap in financial access between the rich and poor narrowed, and the gender gap in financial access also improved—55 percent of PMJDY account holders are women and 67 percent of accounts are in rural and semiurban areas.

---

[3] See MicroSave PMJDY Wave III Assessment for more information. More details can be found here: https://www.microsave.net/files/pdf/PMJDY_Wave_III_Assessment_MicroSave.pdf.

[4] Improvement since then has been slow, as this percentage remains close to 80 percent even in 2021 according to the recent release of the Global Findex database.

Digital financial services have played a major role in achieving this progress, supported by unique digital infrastructure and an enabling regulatory environment:

- The linking of PMJDY bank accounts with Aadhaar and mobile phone numbers—the so-called J-A-M trinity—provides the foundational digital infrastructure for increasing digital financial inclusion.

- Affordability and access to smartphones have improved significantly in recent years. This reflects increased competition among mobile service providers and affordable smartphones from Chinese manufacturers (available for $20–$30).[5] The number of mobile money accounts in India has grown rapidly, and these now serve more than half the population (GSMA 2018).

Demonetization led to the first surge in use of digital payments, particularly mobile money (Figure 7.5). On November 8, 2016, the Government of India unexpectedly announced the demonetization of major banknotes from circulation, effectively withdrawing 86 percent of currency from circulation and constraining the use of cash. While the effectiveness of demonetization in meeting its other stated objectives of addressing corruption and counterfeit bills and increasing the formal tax base is not clear, it did lead to a spike in the use of digital payments instruments.

India's largest mobile money payments provider since 2010, Paytm, witnessed a large spike in transaction volumes immediately following the policy announcement, which contrasts with the relatively lower level of transaction activity in the days right before.[6] Chodorow-Reich and others (2020) also document a large increase in mobile money use following demonetization, which was persistent in the increase in the growth rate of the user base (Crouzet, Gupta, and Mezzanotti 2019). This is comparable to international data sets, with the IMF Financial Access Survey reporting growth of 83 percent in the number of mobile money transactions per 1,000 adults between 2016 and 2018 and World Bank Global Findex reporting a 50 percent increase in the share of adults who made or received digital payments between 2014 and 2017. Relatedly, the growth of debit cards transactions around this period (October–December 2016) was 129 percent (RBI 2017).

The launch of interoperable payments, through the Unified Payments Interface (UPI) in 2016, played a major role in sustaining use of digital financial services (Figure 7.6). The UPI allows instant and real-time interbank transactions through various payments platforms, and enabled banks and nonbanks to operate with each other. While demonetization contributed as an immediate trigger to growth in digital payments, the longer-term growth seen since the start of 2016 appears to be explained much more by the growth of UPI—which coincided with increased business formalization and digital acceptance since the launch of the goods and services tax in 2017.

---

[5] Smartphone users numbered an estimated 450 million, allowing them to leapfrog computers as a way to access the internet.

[6] In India, Paytm has been the largest mobile money payments firm since 2010, serving more than 400 million users and 14 million businesses as of 2019.

Figure 7.5. Impact of Demonetization and GST on Digital Payments

1. Growth in Digital Transactions
(Monthly value of transactions, billions of Indian rupees)

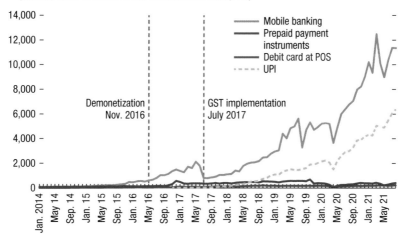

2. Paytm Use around the Demonetization Policy Period
(Daily transaction volume)

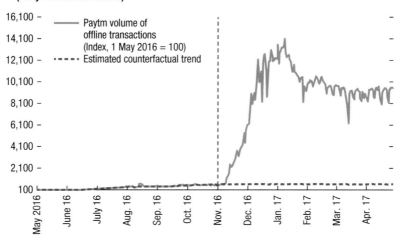

Sources: Patnam and Yao (2020); Paytm; and Reserve Bank of India.
Note: Panel 2 shows daily transaction volume from Paytm in blue (as an index with May 1, 2016 as base). The vertical dotted line corresponds to the date of demonetization. The counterfactual prediction calculated based on a Bayesian structural time-series model is shown in red, using proxies for economic/financial market activity growth in the post-demonetization period (based on daily industrial production index, stock market index, and consumption index). GST = goods and services tax; POS = point of service; UPI = Unified Payments Interface.

Figure 7.6. Rising Retail Payments through Digital Wallets
(Millions of transactions)

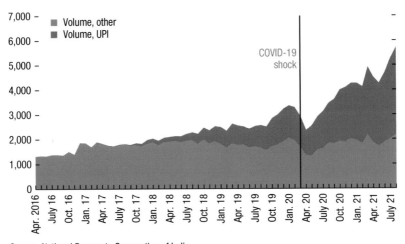

Source: National Payments Corporation of India.
Note: UPI = Unified Payments Interface.

These different layers of digital infrastructure introduced gradually over the last decade together constitute the "India Stack," which has helped widen access to digital financial services. Carriere-Swalloy, Haksar, and Patnam (2021) analyze India Stack's four layers of digital infrastructure. The first is the "presence-less layer" featuring the Aadhaar digital ID system that allows identity verification and mapping of information across data sets. The second is the "cashless layer" built on the UPI's interoperable payments system. The third is the "paperless layer," which allows verification of digital documents that can replace traditional paper analogs (e-know your customer, e-signature). The fourth is the "consent layer"—which is yet to become fully operational—that will involve the operation of data fiduciaries who act as intermediaries between individuals and financial companies. These fiduciaries will be charged with facilitating aggregation of individuals' financial data across their accounts at multiple financial institutions and sharing that data with interested third parties subject to the individual's consent.

Differentiated types of financial institutions leveraging technology were also licensed to deepen access to financial services. India's financial sector landscape is dominated by the public sector, with more than 70 percent of banking assets held by public sector banks in 2010, down to 60 percent in 2021. To deepen access to formal banking to the unserved and underserved population through high-technology and low-cost operations, payments banks and small finance banks were set up. In 2014–15, new payments banks were licensed and set up to deepen access to digital savings account, payments, and remittance services by leveraging technology, but they are not allowed to undertake lending activities (this includes Paytm as discussed above).[7] Starting in 2015–16, existing nonbank financial institutions and microfinance institutions could apply to become small finance banks with the aim to supply small savings and credit products to disadvantaged sectors.[8]

In 2020, the RBI released its National Strategy for Financial Inclusion 2019–24, which lays out its objectives for financial inclusion policies in India. The strategy aims to provide universal access to financial services—savings, credit, insurance, and pension products—to every eligible adult. It highlights the use of technology and adoption of a multistakeholder approach for achieving its financial inclusion goals and notes that the bank-led model of financial inclusion adopted by the RBI through issuance of differentiated banking licenses (small finance banks and payments banks) is helping bridge the gap in last-mile connectivity.

The COVID-19 pandemic increased momentum in the uptake of digital payments, including through fintech platforms (Figure 7.7). Lockdowns and social distancing accelerated use of digital financial services (Agur and others 2020; Sahay and others 2020). While fintech firms initially suspended operations during the lockdown due to the uncertain impact of COVID-19 on their risk and business models, stresses diminished later in the year and considerable optimism remains about the sector. Data from Tracxn show that despite the global economic slowdown in 2020–21, nearly $3 billion was invested in Indian fintech (compared to about $4.5 billion in 2019), indicating a tempering of investor sentiment due to the economic slowdown. Nevertheless, monthly trends indicate a revival of sentiment as the economic shock of the pandemic wears off.[9]

Improving credit availability

In terms of expanding access to credit for businesses, the following initiatives have been undertaken to expand access to credit for businesses.[10] The Pradhan Mantri MUDRA Yojana scheme was launched in April 2015 to enable access to formal finance for MSME businesses by providing collateral-free loans. Close to 1 percent of GDP in loans has been disbursed under the scheme, over one-third to new entrepreneurs. Moreover, the Pradhan Mantri MUDRA Yojana has enabled women-led businesses to access finance—they accounted for about

---

[7] They were initially mandated to accept only demand deposits with a maximum daily balance of Indian rupee (Rs) 0.1 million ($1,300), which was increased to Rs0.2 million ($2,600) in April 2021.

[8] Small finance banks are required to (1) extend 75 percent of adjusted net bank credit to the sectors eligible for classification as priority sector lending by the RBI, and (2) ensure that 50 percent of its loan portfolio should constitute loans and advances of up to Rs2.5 million.

[9] During 2020–21 (April–March), $56.1 billion was invested in the fintech sector globally, compared with $84.8 billion in 2019 and $77.8 billion in 2018.

[10] Under Priority Sector Lending, first introduced in 1972, the RBI mandates that 40 percent of banks' net bank credit must be lent to the priority sectors, including agriculture and small industries.

Figure 7.7. COVID-19 Pandemic Led to an Acceleration in Adoption of Digital Payments

1. Digital Payments

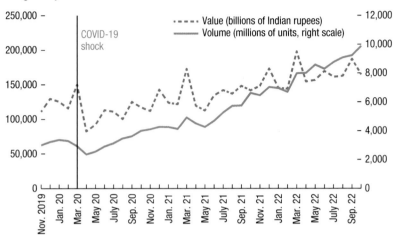

2. Fintech Funding in India
(Billions of dollars)

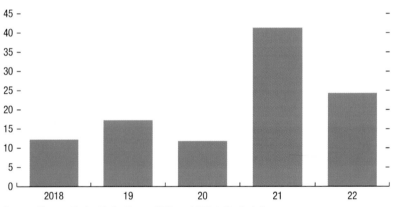

Sources: Reserve Bank of India; Tracxn 2021; and IMF staff calculations.

one-half of the total amount lent under the scheme and about four-fifths of the number of loans. Small finance banks, mandated to extend 75 percent of adjusted net bank credit to the sectors eligible for classification as priority sector lending by the RBI, are also growing. However, their share in the total banking system remains small at less than 1 percent of total banking assets so far.

At the same time, digital lending, facilitated by fintech, is helping fill the gap in MSME financing. Fintech firms are also finding niches in the huge untapped

Figure 7.8. Portion of Adults Who Borrowed in the Last Year by Source
(Percent, 2017)

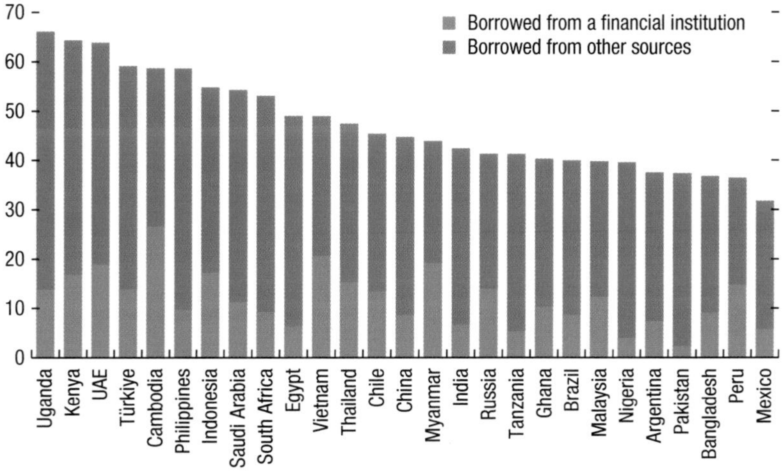

Source: World Bank, Global Findex Database.
Note: UAE = United Arab Emirates.

market across diverse regions in India for credit to MSMEs and individuals that are new to credit (Figure 7.8). The banking sector is dominated by public sector banks with balance sheet challenges and legacy technology, leaving a huge untapped market for fintech firms. Some nonbank financial companies are adopting technology and using alternative data sets (e.g., transaction data from supply chains) to overcome the lack of credit history and to improve credit assessments.[11] Fintech firms in the payments area are also expanding into lending and insurance, leveraging their networks and transaction data. These products are typically developed in partnership with regulated entities (i.e., banks, nonbank financial companies, and insurance companies) and offered on fintech companies' platforms. Banks and fintech firms are moving toward a "co-creation" model, in which banks take advantage of data available at fintech firms for better credit assessment and monitoring. Fintech firms see benefit in partnering with banks, allowing them access to credit and insurance products without becoming regulated entities themselves. However, a growing number of fintech firms are also offering credit products on their own balance sheets. Activities are less advanced in savings and wealth management areas, although some fintech firms are offering investment platforms with innovative approaches.

---

[11] All peer-to-peer lending platforms are required to be registered with the RBI as nonbank financial institutions, and the central bank regulates them.

Digital lending remains small but is growing at a rapid pace. Total digital loans in India have grown tenfold from 0.07 percent of GDP in fiscal year 2017 to 0.7 percent in fiscal year 2020.

- According to the data collected by the RBI (2021a), even though the share of digital lending by commercial banks is small at 2 percent of their total loan amounts disbursed, it entails more than 10 percent of the loan portfolio of nonbank financial institutions as of the end of 2020 (Figure 7.9, left chart). Digital loans by private sector banks have the largest share, at 55 percent. The share of nonbank financial companies, which includes fintech firms, in digital lending has increased from 6.3 percent in 2017 to 30.3 percent in 2020, indicating their increasing adoption of technological innovations (Figure 7.9, right chart). During the same period, public sector banks have also increased their share significantly, from 0.3 percent to 13.1 percent. The majority of the digital loans extended by nonbank financial companies are found to be short-term, small-sized personal loans and business loans to MSME clients largely for operational use, such as working capital loans.

- Based on cross-country data collected by the Cambridge Centre for Alternative Finance (2021), India is considered a major alternative finance

Figure 7.9. Digital Loans Are Being Adopted by Various Types of Lenders

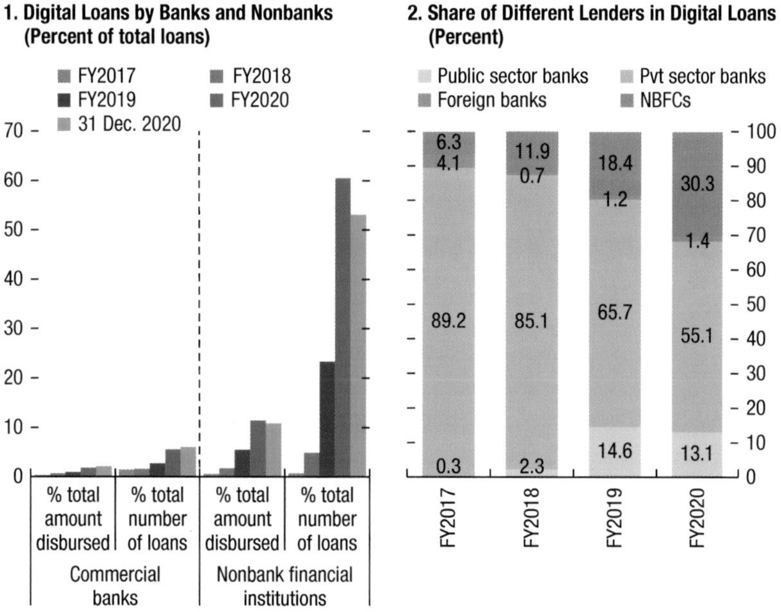

1. Digital Loans by Banks and Nonbanks (Percent of total loans)

2. Share of Different Lenders in Digital Loans (Percent)

Sources: *Report of the Working Group on Digital Lending including Lending through Online Platforms and Mobile Apps;* and Reserve Bank of India.
Note: FY = fiscal year; NBFCs = nonbank financial companies; pvt = private.

Figure 7.10. Top Three Countries in Asia-Pacific
(Millions of dollars)

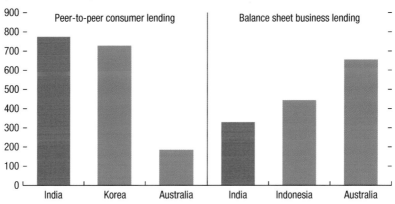

Source: Cambridge Centre for Alternative Finance.

market (i.e., credit through fintechs and bigtechs) in the South and Central Asia regions, contributing 89 percent of recorded digital loan volumes for 2020. In 2019 and 2020, India has ranked among the highest by volume of peer-to-peer and balance sheet consumer/business lending (Figure 7.10).

- This is also comparable to the data set put together by the Bank for International Settlements (Figure 7.11), which shows that while China, the UK, and the US had the highest total global alternative credit in 2019, fintech and bigtech lenders in India and other emerging and developing economies are attaining economic significance in specific segments such as small and medium enterprises (Cornelli and others 2020).

Central bank digital currency and crypto assets

Interest is also growing in new crypto assets. No official estimates exist of the size of the Indian crypto market, but informal data collated by the central bank indicate concentrated holdings by a few people, mainly as speculative investments to make high returns and tax incentives. Crypto assets are also being used as collateral/security to obtain loans from emerging so-called "crypto financial institutions." The rapid growth of the crypto ecosystem and the increasing adoption of crypto assets also pose challenges to financial stability. Moreover, the RBI has stated that it does not consider cryptocurrency a valid payment method (RBI 2022).

This growing interest has motivated the authorities to issue its own central bank digital currency (CBDC). Along with stated benefits such as improving the efficiency of payments by reducing transaction costs and fostering financial inclusion, another key motivation of the RBI has been to offer a risk-free virtual currency, i.e., an alternative to private crypto assets. This is because the central bank

Figure 7.11. Digital Lending Is Gaining Prominence

1. Market Share of Alternative Finance
   (Percent)

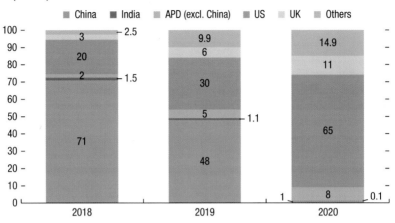

2. Total Alternative Online Credit, 2019
   (Millions of dollars; percent, right scale)

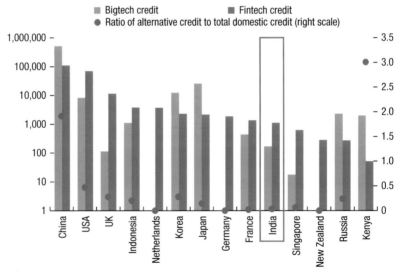

Source: Cambridge Centre for Alternative Finance.
Note: APD = Asia-Pacific; excl. = excluding.

is concerned about the latter's potential risks to the banking system, financial market stability, monetary policy transmission, implications for the capital account, and monetary sovereignty. The RBI issued a concept note on CBDC in October 2022 and has launched pilots of CBDC in both wholesale and retail segments.[12]

---

[12] https://pib.gov.in/PressReleaseIframePage.aspx?PRID=1882883

MEASURING THE IMPACT OF DIGITALIZATION ON FINANCIAL INCLUSION

To quantitatively assess the impact of digitalization in payments on financial inclusion, this chapter uses a new comprehensive measure of digital financial inclusion introduced in Khera and others (2021a). Their sample covers 14 indicators across 52 emerging and developing economies from 2014 to 2017. Instead of relying on a single indicator, they combine data from a variety of sources,[13] which presents a comprehensive picture of financial inclusion combining multiple aspects. The "digital" financial inclusion index aggregates financial inclusion facilitated by digital payments services provided through mobile phone and the internet, combining indicators of both access and usage. On the other hand, they also compute a "traditional" financial inclusion index, which captures financial inclusion driven by access to and usage of traditional financial services provided by banks (including debit cards). These two indices are then combined into a comprehensive financial inclusion index using three-stage principal component analysis. The value of the indices ranges between 0 and 1, with 1 being the highest level of digital financial inclusion. They further calculate male and female financial inclusion indices using the same method, based on gender disaggregated underlying indicators. Gender gaps in financial inclusion are measured as the percentage difference of the respective female-to-male indices.

Results confirm that digital financial payments services have led to an increase in India's financial inclusion: the improvement between 2014 and 2017 (the difference between the traditional/digital financial inclusion index in 2017 vs. 2014) is driven by both digital and traditional financial services (Figure 7.12). The access and usage subcomponents of the digital financial inclusion index indicate that the increase in digital financial access has played a key role: rapid growth in access to digital financial service agents, high mobile subscriptions, and improvements in internet penetration are the main factors driving digital financial inclusion.

Evidence also suggests that digital financial services can help close gender gaps faster in India. Digital financial services are helping address constraints that affect women in particular—such as mobility and time constraints—by allowing them to access mobile banking accounts from home and having minimum balance requirements that may be more binding for women, among others. Although gender gaps in fintech in 2017 are higher than in traditional financial inclusion, gender gaps have been narrowing and have declined more in fintech-based financial inclusion in comparison with traditional financial inclusion between 2014 and 2017 (Figure 7.13). This is not the case everywhere—the gender gap in fintech instead has widened in some other countries (Bangladesh, Kenya, Ghana, Sri Lanka, and others).

---

[13] The data sources include IMF Financial Access Survey, the World Bank Global Findex database, the International Telecommunication Union, and GSMA data.

Figure 7.12. Improvement in Financial Inclusion Driven by Expansion of Access to Digital Infrastructure

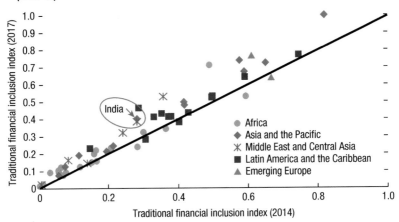

1. Progress in Traditional Financial Inclusion (2014–17)

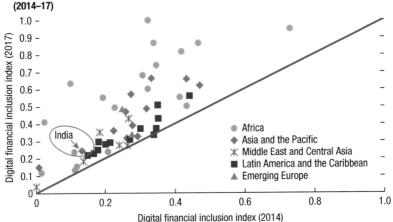

2. Progress in Digital Financial Inclusion (2014–17)

Source: Financial inclusion indices computed by Khera and others (2021a).

These findings are consistent with the RBI's computed measure of India's overall and digital financial inclusion, which covers more recent data from 2017 to 2021:

- RBI computes a multidimensional composite annual Financial Inclusion Index based on 97 indicators representing access, usage, and quality dimensions of financial inclusion. A unique feature of this index, in comparison to the one in Khera and others (2021a), is the quality parameter, which captures quality aspects of financial inclusion, such as financial literacy, consumer protection, and inequalities in services. Moreover, it covers other

Figure 7.13. Gender Gap in Financial Inclusion: Traditional vs. Fintech-Driven

(2014–17, higher value indicates larger gender gap)

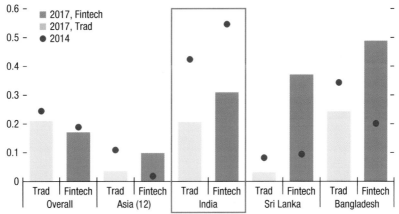

Source: Khera and others (2021b).
Note: Trad = traditional.

financial services beyond payments, such as credit, insurance, and pensions. However, the index is only computed for India and does not provide a cross-country perspective. Ranging from a scale of 0 (complete financial exclusion) to 100 (full financial inclusion), the index increased from 43.4 in 2017 to 53.9 in 2021. This improvement is largely driven by the access subindex, which stood at 73.3, reflecting substantial progress so far in scaling up financial infrastructure (Figure 7.14).

Figure 7.14. RBI Financial Inclusion Index, 2017–21

(Ranges from 0 to 100)

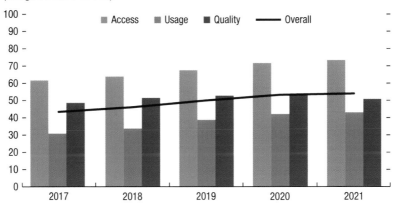

Source: Reserve Bank of India (RBI).

Figure 7.15. RBI Digital Payments Index
(March 2018 is the base year)

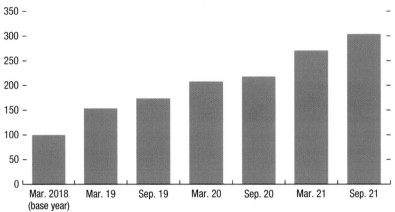

Source: Reserve Bank of India (RBI).

- RBI also recently released its biannual Digital Payments Index, covering 2018–21, which measures the extent of digitization in payments in India (with March 2018 as the base year).[14] It is composed of five broad parameters including (1) payment enablers (access to mobile, internet, Aadhar, and so on), (2) payments infrastructure—demand-side factors (debit and credit cards, prepaid payments instruments), (3) payments infrastructure—supply-side factors (bank branches, ATMs, business correspondents, and so on), (4) payment performance (volume and value of digital payments, currency in circulation), and (5) consumer centricity (literacy, complaints, frauds). The index shows that adoption of digital payments during 2018–21 grew a significant 40 percent, on average, year-over-year (Figure 7.15).

ECONOMIC IMPACT OF DIGITAL FINANCIAL INCLUSION

The positive macroeconomic impact of traditional financial inclusion is well documented, both theoretically and empirically. A number of studies have found that greater financial inclusion boosts growth and reduces poverty and inequality. Financial inclusion impacts macroeconomic performance through various channels: for instance, access to savings instruments helps households smooth consumption during unforeseen shocks, and access to credit enables corporates to improve productivity and competitiveness and promotes entrepreneurship for individuals. Demirgüç-Kunt, Klapper, and Singer (2017) discuss the benefits of financial

---

[14] For information, see https://www.rbi.org.in/Scripts/BS_PressReleaseDisplay.aspx?prid=50901.

inclusion in reducing poverty and inequality. Sahay and Čihák (2020) find that higher financial inclusion in payments is associated with a reduction in inequality, particularly for those at the low end of the income distribution and when female financial inclusion is high. On growth, Sahay, Čihák, N'Diaye, Barajas, Mitra, and others (2015) find that, for a country with low levels of financial inclusion (25th percentile), improving financial inclusion to the 75th percentile would lead to a 2- to 3-percentage point increase in GDP growth on average. Loukoianova and others (2018) find that a 1 percent increase in their financial inclusion index (equivalent to an increase from the fourth to the third quartile) is associated with a 0.2 percent cumulative increase in per capita income growth over a five-year period for low-income developing countries (and Asia and the Pacific).

This chapter instead focuses on the empirical evidence regarding the economic impact of digital financial inclusion, which although growing is still nascent as a subject in the literature. The bulk of recent empirical work that assesses the economic impact of digital financial inclusion was based on survey data at the household or firm level for specific countries (mainly in Africa). They focused on the economic benefits of digital financial inclusion (primarily mobile money), including from improved risk sharing, consumption smoothing, and saving.

Jack and Suri (2014) found that consumption of households in Kenya that use mobile money is unaffected by shocks, while households that do not use mobile money saw a 7 percent decline in consumption.

Riley (2016) also found similar results on consumption smoothing by mobile money users after rainfall shocks in Tanzania, while the consumption of nonusers from the same village was hurt.

Demombyne and Thegeya (2012) documented the widespread use of mobile money systems for savings in Kenya, and they found that mobile money users are 32 percent more likely to have some savings.

Mbiti and Weil (2016) found a positive relationship among the adoption of mobile money and frequency of sending and receiving transfers, as well as with bank use, formal savings, and employment.

Even fewer papers examine the impact of digital financial services using macro-data. To the best of our knowledge, only one study measured the macroeconomic growth impact of digital financial inclusion. Based on a general equilibrium macroeconomic model, McKinsey (2016) predicted that digital finance (includes both mobile money and mobile banking) could boost the GDP of emerging economies by 6 percent by 2025, informed by field research in seven large countries.

Both macro- and micro- empirical studies by the IMF pointed to significant economic gains from greater digital financial inclusion in India:

- Expansion of digital payments has helped stabilize incomes in India's rural areas. Patnam and Yao (2020) used district-level data combined with large-scale data on monthly mobile money transactions of about half a billion users in India, and found evidence that access to mobile money increased resilience to rainfall shocks by improving the efficiency of risk-sharing arrangements and dampening the impact on economic activity (the latter proxied by

Figure 7.16. Effect of Rainfall Shock by Intensity of Mobile Use Index

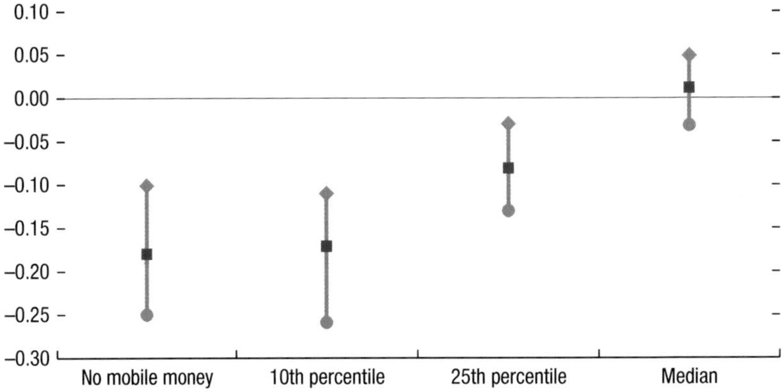

Source: Patnam and Yao (2020).
Note: This figure plots the predicted marginal effects of rainfall shock at different cross-sectional percentile level of a district's mobile money adoption (10th, 25th, and 50th percentiles together with no mobile adoption). The effects with their 95 percent confidence bands are reported in the graph.

night lights). A 10 percent increase in mobile money use in districts hit by a rainfall shock reduces the negative effect of the shock by 3 percent. The risk-sharing effects vary by the intensity of mobile money use. For instance, a district in the lower 10th percentile value of transactions can reduce the negative effects of rainfall shock from 18 percent to 16 percent. A district with the median value of transactions, on the other hand, can reduce the negative effects of rainfall shock from 18 percent to 1 percent (Figure 7.16).

- Digital payments have also helped boost sales for Indian firms in the informal sector. Patnam and Yao (2020) also analyzed the impact of mobile-based payments technology on firm sales by taking advantage of a phased targeting intervention that incentivized firms to adopt the technology. Results showed that firms adopting the novel payments technology improve their sales by about 26 percent relative to nonadopting firms.[15]

- An increase in the adoption of digital payments in India is associated with higher economic growth. Analysis conducted using data prior to the COVID-19 crisis, in Khera and others (2021b), indicated that an increase in India's adoption of digital financial payments to the level in China could raise India's real GDP growth rate by 3–4 percentage points (Figure 7.17).[16]

---

[15] Results are overall robust to different methods of identification and placebo tests for validating assumptions.

[16] There is significant uncertainty around these estimates as data constraints limit the sample period. The impact on growth may be underestimated as the analysis only captures payments and does not cover several other components of digital finance (savings, credit, and insurance) that may have more direct impact on consumption smoothing and investment.

Figure 7.17. Impact of Increase in Adoption of Digital Payments on Growth
(Percentage points of average GDP per capita growth)

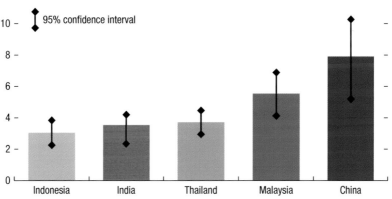

Source: Author's calculations.

This is based on a cross-country regression that related the growth rate of the real per-capita GDP against usage of digital financial services (measured by the digital financial usage index in Khera and others 2021a), along with a broad set of variables that serve as conditioning information, including the measure of traditional financial inclusion.[17] Economic activity is assumed to be more directly affected by the actual usage of financial services, which allows consumption smoothing and saving rather than the availability of access. The sample includes 52 emerging and developing economies covering data from 2011 to 2019. To establish causality, an instrumental variable approach is used in which access to mobile money agents and to the internet are used as instrument variables to control for the simultaneity bias and to extract the exogenous components of the digital financial usage index.

Digital payments have helped improve the ability to target government support to households during COVID-19, particularly to women. According to a survey conducted by the National Payments Corporation of India,[18] the Direct Benefit Transfers delivery system worked exceedingly well during the pandemic-related lockdown, as about 90 percent of low-income households eligible for direct benefit transfers received government support post lockdown. Moreover, under the Pradhan Mantri Garib Kalyan Yojana scheme, more than about 200 million PMJDY accounts of women were credited with a total of Rs0.3 trillion.

---

[17] Control variables include level of economic development, government consumption, foreign direct investment, private-credit-to-GDP ratio, population growth rate, and regional dummies.

[18] See the following for more information: https://www.npci.org.in/PDF/npci/press-releases/2021/NPCI-Press-Release-Digital-Payments-well-entrenched-in-Indian-household.pdf.

REMAINING GAPS: A CROSS-COUNTRY COMPARISON

Notwithstanding the recent progress and economic benefits, considerable gaps remain. In absolute terms, India has a large unbanked population; indeed, close to 17 percent of global unbanked adults reside there, according to the 2021 World Bank Findex (Figure 7.18). Significant inequality and regional disparities exist in the distribution of financial infrastructure, and a large proportion of the Indian unbanked belong to the poorer and rural populations, including women. This section delves deeper into identifying the existing gaps in India's financial inclusion journey, including by comparing its progress to other emerging and developing economies. This can guide further measures that need to be undertaken.

In comparison to other economies, India's financial inclusion in payments—both traditional and fintech based—is lower than the average for Asian and the Pacific countries (Figure 7.19). The 2017 financial inclusion index compiled by Khera and others (2021a) shows that although India has made a lot of progress in traditional financial inclusion over time—thanks to PMJDY—the progress in fintech-driven financial inclusion is lower than the Asia and Pacific average, thus leaving ample scope for improvement. More recent disaggregated data available until 2021 from the IMF's Financial Access showed that although there have been further improvements in digital access in recent years, reflected in greater access to mobile money accounts, gaps persist in use of financial services compared with peer countries.

Facilitating the use of financial services remains the biggest challenge. Although access to financial services and number of new accounts has surged, use of financial services has not (Figure 7.20). For instance, the level and increase in savings and borrowing remain very low even as access to financial services has widened. According to the World Bank Global Findex database, the share of adults in India who save with a financial institution increased only from 12 percent in 2011 to 20 percent in 2017 and then decreased to 13 percent in 2021.

Figure 7.18. Share of Global Unbanked Adults, 2021

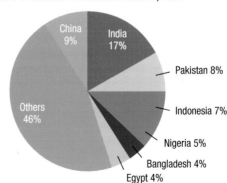

Source: World Bank, Findex.

Figure 7.19. Financial Inclusion: Traditional vs. Digital, 2017
(0–1, higher value indicates higher financial inclusion)

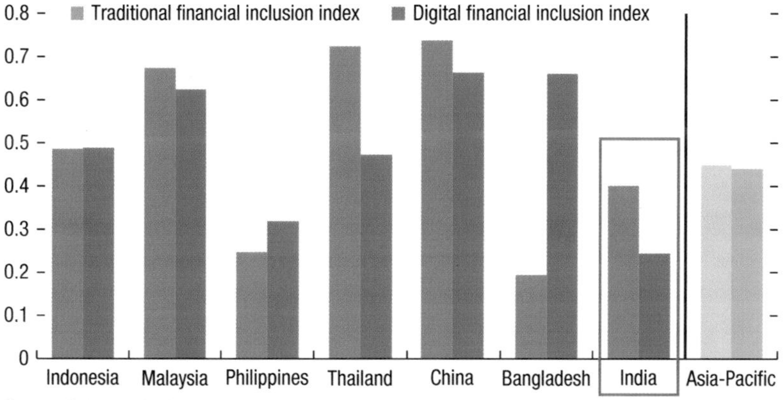

Source: Sahay and others (2020).

Adults who borrow actually decreased from 8 percent in 2011 to 7 percent in 2017, but has increased to 12 percent more recently in 2021. Even among the population with a bank account, nearly half (48.5 percent) of the accounts remained inactive in 2017, making India the country with the highest inactivity rate in the world.[19] More recent data from the IMF Financial Access Survey also shows that in 2021 India had among the lowest usage of debit cards and mobile and internet banking transactions among peer countries in the Asia and Pacific region, despite having high numbers of mobile money accounts. One of the reasons for the low activity/usage could be the low level of financial and digital literacy. For instance, Sahay and others (2020) found that use of digital financial services is low in countries with lower digital and financial literacy. Shen and others (2019) and Hasan and others (2020) also find that financial literacy increased the likelihood of using digital financial products and services in China. These findings are also comparable with the RBI's more comprehensive measure of financial services usage subindex, which shows that use remains low, with minimal improvement over 2017–21.

A digital divide is also emerging within the country (Figure 7.21). Only one-third of Indian households use digital payments, and a gap exists between the rich and the poor—a report by the National Payments Corporation of India (2021) showed that whereas one in two of India's richest 20 percent of households use digital payments, as many as one in four households in the poorest 40 percent use them. This is driven by lower financial literacy, awareness, and access among the poor to digital infrastructure. Digital penetration is limited largely to urban areas (RBI 2021b). For instance, whereas smartphone use is near universal, at 90 percent

---

[19] An inactive account is defined as one in which no deposits or withdrawals were made within a year.

Figure 7.20. Usage of Financial Services Remains Low

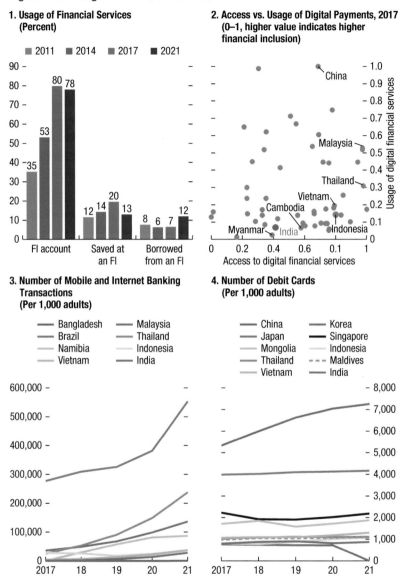

1. Usage of Financial Services
(Percent)

2. Access vs. Usage of Digital Payments, 2017
(0–1, higher value indicates higher financial inclusion)

3. Number of Mobile and Internet Banking Transactions
(Per 1,000 adults)

4. Number of Debit Cards
(Per 1,000 adults)

Sources: IMF, Financial Access Survey (panels 3 and 4); Sahay and others (2020) (panel 2); and World Bank Global Findex Database (panel 1).
Note: FI = financial institution.

Figure 7.21. India's Digital Divide

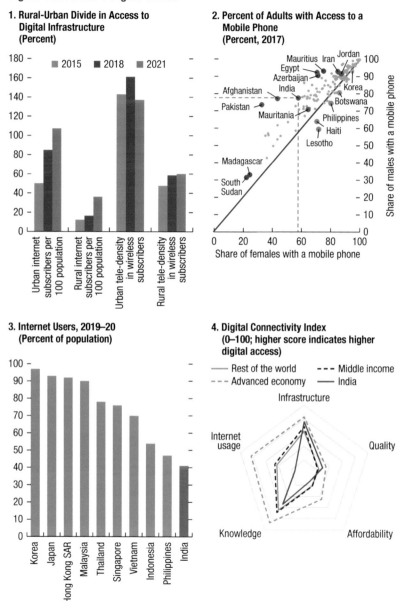

1. Rural-Urban Divide in Access to Digital Infrastructure
(Percent)

■ 2015 ■ 2018 ■ 2021

2. Percent of Adults with Access to a Mobile Phone
(Percent, 2017)

3. Internet Users, 2019–20
(Percent of population)

4. Digital Connectivity Index
(0–100; higher score indicates higher digital access)

—— Rest of the world   – – – Middle income
– – – Advanced economy   —— India

Sources: International Telecommunication Union; Telecom Regulatory Authority of India, *Annual Report;* and IMF staff estimates.

Figure 7.22. Outstanding Small and Medium Enterprise Loans from Commercial Banks
(Percent of GDP)

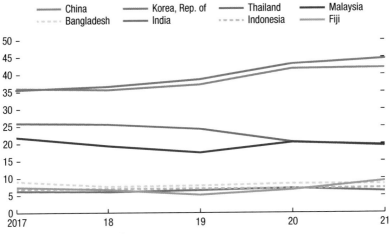

Source: IMF, Financial Access Survey.

among the richest 20 percent of Indian households, just 57 percent in the poorest households have a smartphone. According to the Telecoms Regulatory Authority of India, only 36 of 100 rural dwellers use the internet—compared to 107 in urban areas—and only 60 mobile subscribers per 100 people as opposed to 137 in urban areas.[20] Moreover, gender gaps in digital financial inclusion are high in India: for instance, men are 20 percentage points more likely than women to own a mobile phone. Moreover, RBI's "quality" financial inclusion subindex suggests that inequality and regional disparity in access to credit and deposits, measured using the Gini coefficient, is significantly high.

Access to finance remains a key constraint to entrepreneurship, especially for women (IFC 2018). MSMEs are considered engines of growth in the Indian economy, with about 62 million in the country contributing nearly 30 percent to GDP, 50 percent to exports, and providing employment opportunities to more than 110 million workers. Despite their economic importance, close to 35 percent of MSMEs are credit constrained (compared to 38 percent average in South Asia). The total addressable demand for formal credit is estimated at $37 million and overall supply of finance from formal sources at $14 million. The overall credit gap in the MSME sector is thus estimated at about $23 million, or 11 percent of GDP (compared to 13 percent in South Asia). Among Asia and Pacific countries, India has one of the lowest levels of small and medium enterprise loans as a share of GDP (Figure 7.22; IMF Financial Access Survey). This is despite several years of government-mandated lending programs (e.g., priority sector lending).

[20] For information, see Telecom Regulatory Authority of India Annual Report 2020–21. https://dot. gov.in/sites/default/files/Annual%20Report%202020-21%20English%20Version.pdf.

THE WAY FORWARD: POLICY PRIORITIES

This section lays out the key policy recommendations that could help expand and close India's remaining gaps in financial inclusion, particularly in the usage of financial services, while maintaining financial stability.

Ensuring equal access to digital infrastructure for all segments of the population, particularly in rural areas and for women, is key to closing the existing digital divide. For instance, the government can incentivize telecom operators to establish stable network connectivity in rural areas and private mobile manufacturers to offer smartphones at subsidized prices targeting the underserved and vulnerable. This would help build trust and regular usage of digital financial services, and it would increase women's financial inclusion because it lowers constraints such as the need for physical travel to a bank branch. In this regard, the Payments Infrastructure Development Fund scheme launched by the RBI in January 2021, which subsidizes both physical and digital Point of Sale infrastructure (e.g., QR code-based payments such as UPI) in underdeveloped areas, is a welcome initiative. Other such incentives for promoting usage of digital financial services could also be considered—for example in the Republic of Korea, wage earners are allowed to claim tax deductions for purchases made using digital payments when they file their year-end income taxes (Klapper and others 2019). At the same time, strengthening the implementation of policies that equalize sociocultural norms, and legally backing them up, would help narrow gender gaps in digital financial inclusion (e.g., household mobile phones are disproportionately owned or controlled by men).

Strengthening and developing the regulatory framework for digital finance will help expand safe digital financial inclusion. It is important to adapt regulatory approaches to balance support for financial innovation with addressing challenges and risks to financial stability. Although India's current share of digital lending in overall credit remains small and is not significant enough to affect financial stability, it is growing rapidly. Eliminating the current state of regulatory arbitrage in India's digital lending space is needed to ensure financial stability. For instance, even though digital lending by and in collaboration with banks and nonbank financial institutions is regulated, a large and growing number of entities and platforms in the digital lending space are not currently regulated (i.e., not registered or layered under regulated entities) and/or operating illegally (i.e., shadow digital lenders). Data compiled by the RBI suggest that 60 out of 100 lending apps in India operated illegally in 2021.

Need is also urgent for stronger data and consumer protection and cybersecurity to bolster people's confidence to make digital transactions. Even though the mandated two-factor authentication for digital payments and the 2019 Ombudsman Scheme for Digital Transactions[21] are positive steps, more needs to

---

[21] The scheme is designed for resolution of complaints relating to deficiency in customer services in digital transactions undertaken by customers. For information, see https://rbidocs.rbi.org.in/rdocs/Content/PDFs/OSDT31012019.pdf.

Figure 7.23. Incidents of Cyber Attacks across India
(Millions)

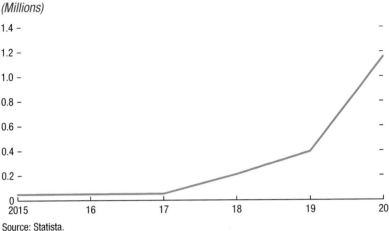

Source: Statista.

be done to safeguard consumer confidentiality and avoid unauthorized transactions and cyberattacks.[22] For instance, concerns related to unfair lending practices are rising as demand for quick digital loans rose during the pandemic. Many digital lenders charge exorbitant interest rates; have additional hidden charges; use data without customer permission, capitalizing on borrowers' lack of financial literacy; and have used improper or aggressive loan recovery mechanisms. More than 2,500 registered complaints were lodged against such digital lending platforms over 15 months during the pandemic from January 2020 to March 2021. Measures are needed to reduce the risk of "excessive" financial inclusion—which is when access to credit grows under insufficient regulation and supervision—such as the US subprime lending crisis, the more recent rise in default rates to nearly 20 percent on mobile bank loans in Kenya, or the 2010 microfinance crisis in Andhra Pradesh.

Moreover, as digitalization increases, cybersecurity is becoming a key concern. According to the data by Statista, India was among the top-five countries with the most cybersecurity incidents in 2020. More than 1.1 million cyberattacks were reported across India in 2020, up sharply from 0.4 million in 2019 (Figure 7.23). Even though India implemented a National Cyber Security Policy in 2013, which laid down several strategies to counter cybersecurity threats, its implementation has been limited.

Focusing on improving overall literacy rates, which remain considerably low in comparison to peers,[23] including financial and digital literacy, will help India

---

[22] Some other safeguards include facilities to switch on/off as well as set limits on various types of digital transactions.

[23] See World Bank data, https://data.worldbank.org/indicator/SE.ADT.LITR.ZS.

achieve its financial inclusion goals and fully utilize its economic benefits. Citizens should be made financially aware of the technological regulations put in place to protect them and must be taught about the safe practices in digital payments and lending. People should be educated on existing and new government schemes providing low interest lending, and regulators must ensure related services are delivered successfully. Recognizing the importance of inculcating financial literacy, the National Strategy for Financial Education 2020–25 was launched. The primary objective is to develop adequate financial knowledge and skills among the Indian population, including through integrating financial literacy curriculum in schools and through collaboration across various stakeholders. Such efforts should continue, including through a robust mechanism of monitoring its implementation and effectiveness.

CONCLUSIONS

This chapter has looked at India's growth in financial inclusion over the last decade, identifying key drivers and economic impact, focusing on digital financial services as a tool for expanding financial inclusion. Facilitated by unique digital infrastructure and enabling regulatory environment, digitalization is helping close India's financial inclusion gap. It is also improving targeting of government support to households, as witnessed during COVID-19.

The expansion of digital payments is also an important driver of economic development and has helped stabilize incomes in rural areas and boost sales for firms in the informal sector. Using data prior to the pandemic shows that wider adoption of digital payments could increase India's GDP per capita by 3 to 4 percentage points.

Even though the country has made immense progress in widening accessibility for the majority of the excluded population, including through a strong supply-side push for digital financial services, policies should focus more on addressing demand-side constraints to promote use of financial services, which remains low. Improving financial and digital literacy, internet and smartphone access, and expanding digital government payments to households (government to person) will help close the emerging digital divide. At the same time, strengthening consumer protection, data privacy, and cybersecurity remain crucial to promoting safe financial inclusion.

REFERENCES

Agarwal, Sumit, Shashwat Alok, Pulak Ghosh, Soumya Ghosh, Tomasz Piskorski, and Amit Seru. 2019. "Banking the Unbanked: What Do 255 Million New Bank Accounts Reveal about Financial Access?" Research Paper 2906523, Georgetown McDonough School of Business.

Agur, Itai, Soledad Martinez Peria, and Celine Rochon. 2020. "Digital Financial Services and the Pandemic: Opportunities and Risks for Emerging and Developing Economies." IMF COVID-19 Special Series. International Monetary Fund, Washington, DC.

Cambridge Centre for Alternative Finance. 2021. "The 2nd Global Alternative Finance Market Benchmarking Report." June 2021. University of Cambridge. Judge Business School.

Carriere-Swallow, Yan, V. Haksar, and Manasa Patnam. 2021. "India's Approach to Open Banking: Some Implications for Financial Inclusion." IMF Working Paper 21/52, International Monetary Fund, Washington DC.

Chakrabarty, K. C. 2011. "Financial Inclusion: A Road India Needs to Travel." *RBI Bulletin*, Reserve Bank of India, November.

Chodorow-Reich, Gabriel, Gita Gopinath, Prachi Mishra, and Abhinav Narayanan. 2020. "Cash and the Economy: Evidence from India's Demonetization." *Quarterly Journal of Economics* 135 (1): 57–103.

Cornelli, Giulio, Jon Frost, Leonardo Gambacorta, Raghavendra Rau, Robert Wardrop, and Tania Ziegler. 2020. "Fintech and BigTech Credit: A New Database." BIS Working Paper 887, September.

Crouzet, Nicolas, Apoorv Gupta, and Filippo Mezzanotti. 2019. "Shocks and Technology Adoption: Evidence from Electronic Payment Systems." Technical report, Northwestern University Working Paper.

Dabla-Norris, Era, Yan Ji, Robert M. Townsend, and D. Filiz Unsal. 2015. "Distinguishing Constraints on Financial Inclusion and Their Impact on GDP, TFP, and Inequality." NBER Working Paper 20821, National Bureau of Economic Research, Cambridge, MA.

Demirgüç-Kunt, Asli, Leora Klapper, and Dorothe Singer. 2017. "Financial Inclusion and Inclusive Growth:" A Review of Recent Empirical Evidence." Policy Research Working Paper 8040, World Bank Group, Washington, DC.

Demirgüç-Kunt, Asli, Leora Klapper, Dorothe Singer, Saniya Ansar, and Jake Hess. 2018. "The Global Findex Database: Measuring Financial Inclusion and the Fintech Revolution." World Bank Group, Washington, DC.

Demombynes, Gabriel, and Aaron Thegeya. 2012. "Kenya's Mobile Revolution and the Promise of Mobile Savings." Policy Research Working Paper Series 5988, World Bank Group, Washington, DC.

D'Silva, Derryl, Zuzana Filková, Frank Packer, and Siddharth Tiwari. 2019. "The Design of Digital Financial Infrastructure: Lessons from India." BIS Papers 106. Basel: Bank for International Settlements.

Global FinTech Adoption Index. 2019. EY Global Financial Services. https://assets.ey.com/content/dam/ey-sites/ey-com/en_gl/topics/banking-and-capital-markets/ey-global-fintech-adoption-index.pdf.

Global System for Mobile Communications (GSMA). 2019. "State of the Industry Report on Mobile Money 2018." https://www.gsma.com/r/wp-content/uploads/2019/05/GSMA-State-of-the-Industry-Report-on-Mobile-Money-2018-1.pdf.

Hasan, Md. Morshadul, Lu Yajuan, Appel Mahmud (2020). "Regional Development of China's Inclusive Finance through Financial Technology." SAGE Open 10 (1):215824401990125.

International Finance Corporation (IFC). 2018, November. "Financing India's MSMEs: Estimation of Debt Requirement of MSMEs in India." Washington, DC: The World Bank Group. https://www.ifc.org/wps/wcm/connect/dcf9d09d-68ad-4e54-b9b7-614c143735fb/Financing+India%E2%80%99s+MSMEs+-+Estimation+of+Debt+Requirement+of+MSMEs+in+India.pdf?MOD=AJPERES&CVID=my3CmzlIMF.

International Monetary Fund. Financial Access Survey Database. Washington, DC: IMF. https://data.imf.org/?sk=E5DCAB7E-A5CA-4892-A6EA-598B5463A34C.

Jack, William, and Tavneet Suri. 2014. "Risk Sharing and Transactions Costs: Evidence from Kenya's Mobile Money Revolution." *American Economic Review* 104 (1): 183–223.

Khera, Purva, Stephanie Ng, Sumiko Ogawa, and Ratna Sahay. 2021a. "Measuring Digital Financial Inclusion in Emerging Market and Developing Economies: A New Index." IMF Working Paper 21/90, International Monetary Fund, Washington, DC.

Khera, Purva, Stephanie Ng, Sumiko Ogawa, and Ratna Sahay. 2021b. "Is Digital Financial Inclusion Unlocking Growth?" IMF Working Paper 21/167, International Monetary Fund, Washington, DC.

Klapper, Leora, Margaret Miller, and Jake Hess. 2019. "Leveraging Digital Financial Solutions: To Promote Formal Business Partnership." The World Bank Group Report, Washington, DC.

Loukoianova, Elena, and Yongzheng Yang. 2018. "Financial Inclusion in Asia-Pacific." IMF Asia and Pacific Departmental Paper 18/17, International Monetary Fund, Washington, DC.

Mbiti, Isaac, and David N. Weil. 2016. "Mobile Banking: The Impact of M-Pesa in Kenya." In *African Successes, Volume III: Modernization and Development*, edited by Sebastian Edwards, Simon Johnson, and David N. Weil. University of Chicago Press.

McKinsey & Company. 2016. "Digital Finance for All: Powering Inclusive Growth in Emerging Economies." McKinsey Global Institute.

National Payments Corporation of India. 2021. "Digital Payments Well Entrenched in Indian Households across Income Groups, Reveals PRICE and NPCI Pan India Survey." https://www.npci.org.in/PDF/npci/press-releases/2021/NPCI-Press-Release-Digital-Payments-well-entrenched-in-Indian-household.pdf.

Organisation of Economic Cooperation and Development (OECD). 2019. "Digital Government in Chile—Digital Identity." OECD Digital Government Studies. OECD Publishing, Paris.

Patnam, Manasa, and Weijia Yao. 2020. "The Real Effects of Mobile Money: Evidence from a Large-Scale Fintech Expansion." IMF Working Paper 20/138, International Monetary Fund, Washington, DC.

Philippon, Thomas. 2017. "The FinTech Opportunity." BIS Working Paper 655, Bank for International Settlements.

Reserve Bank of India. 2008. "Report on Financial Inclusion." September 4, 2008. https://www.rbi.org.in/scripts/PublicationsView.aspx?id=10494.

Reserve Bank of India. 2017. "Report of the Working Group on FinTech and Digital Banking." November, 2017. RBI Central Office Mumbai.

Reserve Bank of India. 2020. "National Strategy for Financial Inclusion 2019–2024: India." https://rbidocs.rbi.org.in/rdocs/content/pdfs/NSFIREPORT100119.pdf.

Reserve Bank of India. 2021a. "Report of the Working Group on Digital Lending Including Lending through Online Platforms and Mobile Apps." November 18, 2021.

Reserve Bank of India. 2021b. "Responsible Digital Innovation—T. Rabi Sankar." *RBI Bulletin*. October 18, 2021. https://www.rbi.org.in/Scripts/BS_ViewBulletin.aspx?Id=20564.

Reserve Bank of India. 2022. "Cryptocurrencies—An Assessment." Keynote address delivered by Shri T. Rabi Sankar, Deputy Governor, Reserve Bank of India, February 14, 2022, at the Indian Banks Association 17th Annual Banking Technology Conference and Awards. https://rbi.org.in/Scripts/BS_SpeechesView.aspx?Id=1196.

Riley, Emma. 2016. "Mobile Money and Risk Sharing against Village Shocks." *Journal of Development Economics* 135: 43–58.

Sahay, Ratna, and Martin Čihák. 2020. "Finance and Inequality." IMF Staff Discussion Note 20/01, International Monetary Fund, Washington, DC.

Sahay, Ratna, Martin Čihák, Papa N'Diaye, Adolfo Barajas, Ran Bi, Diana Ayala, Yuan Guao, and others. 2015. "Rethinking Financial Deepening: Stability and Growth in Emerging Markets." IMF Staff Discussion Note 15/08, International Monetary Fund, Washington, DC.

Sahay, Ratna, Martin Čihák, Papa N'Diaye, Adolfo Barajas, Srobona Mitra, Annette Kyobe, Yen Nian Mooi, and Seyed Reza Yousefi. 2015. "Financial Inclusion: Can It Meet Multiple Macroeconomic Goals?" IMF Staff Discussion Note 15/17, International Monetary Fund, Washington, DC.

Sahay, Ratna, Ulric Eriksson von Allmen, Amina Lahreche, Purva Khera, Sumiko Ogawa, Majid Bazarbash, and Kimberly Beaton. 2020. "The Promise of Fintech: Financial Inclusion in the Post COVID-19 Era." IMF Departmental Paper 20/09, International Monetary Fund, Washington, DC.

Shen Yan, C., James Hueng, and Wenxiu Hu. 2019. "Using Digital Technology to Improve Financial Inclusion in China." *Applied Economic Letters* 27 (1): 30–34.

Tracxn. 2022. "Fintech Startups in India." https://tracxn.com/explore/FinTech-Startups-in-India.

World Bank. 2021. Global Findex Database. https://www.worldbank.org/en/publication/globalfindex.

World Bank. 20201. ID4D Dataset. https://id4d.worldbank.org/global-dataset.

PART III

Linkages and Supporting Reforms

CHAPTER 8

Capital Flows: Trends, Risks, and New Investor Bases

Rohit Goel and Natalia Novikova

INTRODUCTION

Foreign investment in India accelerated prominently in the early 2000s. Liberalization of the capital account and a dynamic economy made the country an important destination for investment in emerging market economies. India enters the top-five destinations for foreign direct investment (FDI) among emerging market and developing economies,[1] and capitalization of its equity market exceeded $3.5 trillion in 2022, ranking fifth globally by market size.

Cross-border capital flows bring important benefits but also carry risks. India's integration into the global financial system and capital inflows, alongside broader market opening, helped promote economic development by addressing funding gaps and expanding opportunities, including by opening access to modern technology. At the same time, however, the country became more exposed to capital flows' procyclicality and volatility, which may have implications for financial stability and complicate macroeconomic management. Despite a gradual and staggered capital liberalization approach in India, capital flows surged and reversed several times over the last two decades.

This chapter takes stock of trends in the structure and volatility of nonresident inflows to India since the global financial crisis (GFC) and looks at potential implications of evolving foreign investor base. The following analyzes the nature of capital flows (in the first section), discusses capital flow volatility and financial stability (in the second section), highlights the advent of a new investor base (in the third section), and makes recommendations about how to maximize benefits while minimizing risks (in the fourth section). The final section offers a conclusion.

CHANGING NATURE OF CAPITAL FLOWS

India started gradually liberalizing its capital account, accompanied by financial deepening, in the 1990s. Its approach to liberalization involved a hierarchy of capital flows with more openness introduced for foreign direct investment over portfolio investment and equity over debt flows.

The authors are grateful to Tian Yong Woon for research assistance.
[1] UNCTAD Handbook of Statistics 2022.

In the early 2000s, the limits on FDI were either removed or increased for selected sectors, and limits on the share of portfolio equity held by foreigners were also raised (Gupta 2016, Mohan and Ray 2017). According to OECD measures, FDI-related restrictions were relaxed on aggregate between 2003 and 2020 with indices for India getting closer to OECD average, especially in manufacturing, where India scores more open compared to other emerging and developing economies (Figure 8.1, panel 1). As of 2022, an automatic route for foreign investment up to 100 percent ownership was allowed for most of the sectors.[2] However, significant restrictions, including approval requirements and caps on capital ownership, remain in the financial sector, petroleum refinery, telecommunications, and some others.

Debt flows are subject to a complex set of legal and regulatory requirements. Two main multilayered frameworks include Foreign Portfolio Investor (FPI) and External Commercial Borrowing (ECB) schemes, which are adjusted frequently.[3] FPI framework defines quotas for portfolio debt investment by nonresidents and a list of certain specified government securities, which could by purchases by foreign investors without any limit or macro-prudential control. The restrictions were eased progressively, with investment limits increased for both corporate and government debt.[4] Nevertheless, the limits remain underutilized (Figure 8.1, panels 2 and 3). In addition, corporate access to foreign funds is subject to caps and currency conversion restrictions.

The complexity of the frameworks makes it challenging to measure the impact of multiple adjustments on capital account openness with de jure indices; for example, Chinn-Ito Index remained unchanged since 1970s. Meanwhile, studies using price-based de facto measures, which allow to capture the net impact of adjustments, found that India became much more integrated with global financial markets in recent years. For example, Aggarwal, Arora, and Sengupta (2021) analyzed covered interest parity deviations between onshore-offshore rupee marks and found that such deviations became generally smaller over time reflecting less binding aggregate capital flow restrictions, albeit the trend was not always linear and smooth.

Over the last two decades, FDI and equity portfolio inflows have totaled about 2.5 percent of GDP annually and proved less volatile than regional peers over the

---

[2] Automatic route, as opposed to an alternative government route, implies foreign investment does not require a prior approval of the Reserve Bank of India or the Central Government. See India's Consolidated FDI Policy here: https://www.investindia.gov.in/foreign-direct-investment.

[3] See, for example, data sets of de jure changes to capital flow management frameworks compiled by Pandey and others (2021) on measures related to the ECB scheme and Pandey and others (2020) covering measures with respect to foreign institutional investment in India.

[4] FPI includes three routes. Medium Term Framework, introduced in 2015, defines a percentage of the total outstanding stock of government securities and corporate bonds that could be purchased by eligible investors subject to certain macroprudential limits. Since 2019, Voluntary Retention Route introduced a combined limit to be invested in either government or corporate debt with limited macroprudential controls, but subject to a minimum retention period of three years. In 2020, India established a program that allows foreign investors to buy specified government bonds via its Fully Accessible Route (FAR) without any restrictions.

Figure 8.1. India: Restrictions on Foreign Investment

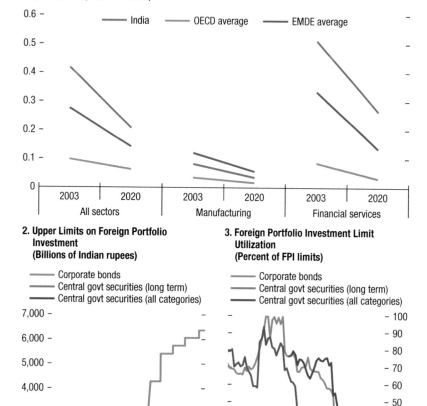

1. India: FDI Restrictiveness
   (Index; 0 = open, 1 = closed)

2. Upper Limits on Foreign Portfolio Investment
   (Billions of Indian rupees)

3. Foreign Portfolio Investment Limit Utilization
   (Percent of FPI limits)

Sources: Haver Analytics; Organisation for Economic Co-operation and Development (OECD); and IMF staff calculations.
Note: For panel 1, foreign direct investment (FDI) restrictiveness index takes into account four main types of restrictions: foreign equity restrictions; discriminatory screening or approval mechanisms; restrictions on key foreign personnel; and operational restrictions. Implementation issues and factors such as the degree of transparency or discretion in granting approvals are not considered.
EMDE = emerging market and developing economy; FPI = foreign portfolio investment; govt = government.

last two decades (Figure 8.2, panel 1). By contrast, foreign portfolio flows into debt markets were less than a half-percent of GDP per year, much smaller than in regional peers. After the GFC, nonresident flows slowed significantly, while resident outflows increased.[5] Average total nonresident flows declined after the taper tantrum, from 4.5 percent of GDP to 3.2 percent (Figure 8.2, panel 2), reflecting lower portfolio equity and other investment flows, which include bank loans. FDI flows have remained relatively stable and portfolio debt flows have increased but remained small. Meanwhile, resident outflows reached close to 3 percent of GDP, driven by growing direct investments by Indian firms and the other investment (Figure 8.2, panel 3). This increase in resident outflows reflects the liberalized capital flow regime and better performance of the overseas markets (including in advanced economies).

The cycle of foreign portfolio flows shortened over time, even though volatility remained lower than during the GFC (Figure 8.3). Episodes of portfolio outflows, especially debt flows, have become more frequent, leading to smaller surges. For example, a surge in inflows ahead of the GFC led to an almost quadrupling of central banks' foreign exchange reserves and rising inflationary pressures. Reversals, including the 2013 Federal Reserve "taper tantrum," were associated with sharp movements in the exchange rate.[6] Like other emerging market economies, India saw large portfolio outflows in early 2020, at the start of the COVID-19 pandemic,[7] and in 2022 amid synchronized tightening of global financial conditions.

CAPITAL FLOWS AND FINANCIAL STABILITY

Capital flows can provide substantial direct and indirect benefits. Foreign savings can be an important source of funding for investment, adding to domestic sources and allowing countries to "insure" themselves to some extent against fluctuations in their national incomes (Kose and Prasad 2020). The presence of nonresident investors can help financial sector development, foster the development of local bond markets, as well as reduce domestic funding costs including due to better domestic market liquidity and functioning[8] (April 2020 *Global Financial Stability Report*; Goel and Papageorgiou 2021, Peiris 2010, Ebeke and Kyobe 2015). The empirical evidence of relationship between countries'

---

[5] This trend is consistent with developments in global capital flows; see, for example, the Bank for International Settlements (BIS) 2021.

[6] The taper tantrum refers to market movements set off after the US Federal Reserve said it would begin "tapering" quantitative easing.

[7] In the first quarter of 2020, India—among a few selected emerging markets including Brazil—suffered the brunt of the portfolio rebalancing by multisector bond funds. In the first half of 2020, the share of such funds in foreign holdings of government debt dropped from above 10 percent to just above zero (Cortes and Sanfilippo 2021).

[8] Limited market liquidity is an amplifier of market pressures during stress and may impair monetary policy transmission in some cases.

Figure 8.2. Capital Flows to India in 2002–22

1. India vs. Regional Peers: Capital Inflows and Volatility

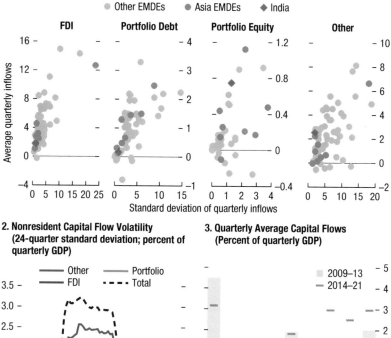

2. Nonresident Capital Flow Volatility
(24-quarter standard deviation; percent of quarterly GDP)

3. Quarterly Average Capital Flows
(Percent of quarterly GDP)

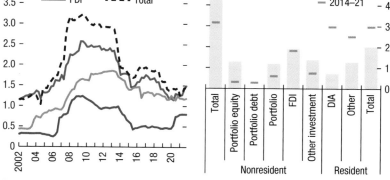

Sources: CEIC; Haver Analytics; and IMF staff calculations.
Note: In panel 1, Asia EMDEs (emerging and developing economies) pertain to China, Indonesia, Malaysia, Mongolia, the Philippines, Sri Lanka, Thailand, and Vietnam. DIA = domestic investment abroad; EMDEs = emerging market and developing economies; FDI = foreign direct investment.

Figure 8.3. India: Foreign Capital Flow Cycle

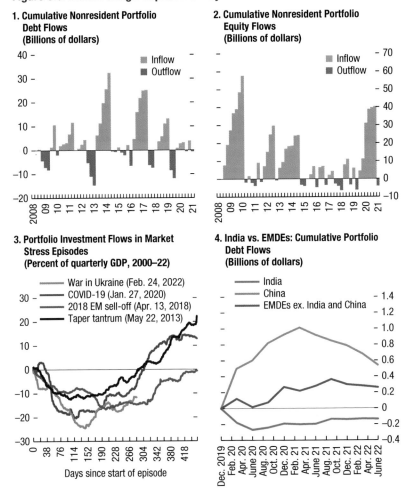

1. Cumulative Nonresident Portfolio Debt Flows
(Billions of dollars)

2. Cumulative Nonresident Portfolio Equity Flows
(Billions of dollars)

3. Portfolio Investment Flows in Market Stress Episodes
(Percent of quarterly GDP, 2000–22)

4. India vs. EMDEs: Cumulative Portfolio Debt Flows
(Billions of dollars)

Days since start of episode

Sources: CEIC; Haver Analytics; and IMF staff calculations.
Note: Following the April 2020 *Global Financial Stability Report* and Goel and Miyajima (2020), capital flow cycle is measured as the period during which flows continue to remain either positive or negative. Panels 1 and 2 show the sum of quarterly net flows until a change in flow direction occurs. EM = emerging market; EMDEs = emerging markets and developing economies; ex. = excluding.

long-term growth and their overall openness to capital flows is inconclusive. Nevertheless, there is a broad agreement that foreign investment could facilitate access to the latest technology (particularly FDI), promote competition and inclusion into global value chains, help introduce macroeconomic policy discipline, and strengthen governance. All of the above are critical for boosting economic growth potential.

At the same time, large and volatile capital flows can impact financial stability and give rise to systemic risk through multiple channels (IMF 2017, Gelos and others 2019). Rapid buildup of foreign liabilities, or surges in capital flows, tend to be accompanied by a domestic credit boom and currency appreciation, which can in turn lead to asset price bubbles and increase financial sector vulnerabilities, including via currency mismatches, non-core funding, and interconnectedness. In contrast, sudden stops can cause a tightening of financial conditions, a decline in asset prices, and tighter bank lending conditions (Guidotti and others 2004, among many others). These extreme flows tend to have different sensitivities to domestic and external shocks. Meanwhile, the growing importance of benchmark-driven and investment-fund intermediated flows could lead to more volatility in capital flows (Arslanalp and others 2020) and amplify potential spillovers (BIS 2021).

Strong implications of capital flows for exchange rate dynamics may affect countries' competitiveness, balance sheets, and inflation dynamic. In case of India, Dua and Sen (2017) found that net capital flows and their volatility are important determinants of real-effective exchange rate after controlling for government expenditures, monetary supply, and current account balance. In turn, in volatile times and during negative shocks, exchange rate depreciations can be an important driver of corporate vulnerability (Finger and Lopez Murphy 2019) and tend to have contractionary effects on economies via financial and trade channels and global investors (BIS 2020).

Capital flows may also act as a transmission channel of global financial conditions to domestic financial systems. Surprise tightening, particularly in the United States, has been associated with capital flow reversals from emerging market and developing economies, widening spreads, currency depreciations, and tighter external financial conditions (April 2021 *World Economic Outlook*).[9] Banerjee and Mohanty (2021) found that in India, tightening of monetary policy in the United States leads to a significant downturn in the domestic credit and business cycles via the financial channel of the exchange rate.

Capital flows can also exacerbate domestic macroeconomic weakness as external risk sentiment can transmit to domestic financial conditions via upward pressures on the domestic bond yields (Goel and Miyajima 2021; Goel

---

[9] Arteta, Kamin, and Ruch (2022) showed that increases in US interest rates associated with inflation or shocks triggered by forward-looking reassessment of the Federal Reserve monetary policy stance are likely to lead to more adverse spillovers compared to rate hikes in response to an anticipated improvement of the US economic activity.

and Papageorgiou 2021). Countries with higher debt levels and larger gross financing needs have usually been vulnerable to more extreme stress and capital flow pressures in such episodes. A highly volatile component of capital flows, like short-term debt, can be disruptive, leading to spikes in funding costs and posing challenges for policymakers by complicating monetary and exchange rate policies, and creating pressure on other types of flows. Financial stability risks from capital flows can become even more important in an environment where fiscal needs are high and domestic fundamentals remain challenged.

Moreover, BIS (2021) noted increasing selectiveness among international investors when assessing invetsment opportunities. GDP growth and fiscal and current accout balances are important cyclical pull factors used to differenciate countries. Structural elements like credibility of macroeconomic policies, financial openness and trade intergation, and development of local financial markets have improved on average in many emerging economies post-GFC and remain a precondition for attracting a broad group of investors. The episode of large capital outflows from emerging market and developing economies in 2022 also showed more differentiation across borrowers compared with previous stress cases (greater dispersion of spreads than in 2013 or 2018); among other factors, this could reflect assessment of vulnerabilities related to the buildup of private debt and contingent liabilities including via financial–sovereign nexus (April 2022 *Global Financial Stability Report*).

India, being one of the fastest growing economies with a large and mainly unsaturated domestic market, continues to draw interest from the global investors. The COVID-19 pandemic, however, has amplified some of the existing vulnerabilities in India. The country's fiscal balance has declined significantly more than Asian and emerging market economy peers, and its fiscal position remains worse relative to both pre-pandemic levels and emerging market peers (Figure 8.3). Local currency debt issuance has risen almost 50 percent since the time before the pandemic. In the absence of foreign investors, domestic investors had to step in and absorb the sovereign debt issuances. In India, domestic banks and insurers are the majority owners of government bonds (Figure 8.4). Large holdings of government debt by banks (over 20 percent of bank assets) expose this sector to significant risk, especially in a tightening cycle (IMF 2022a). India also saw a sharp rise in asset purchases by the Reserve Bank of India, including due to purchases of state loans along with the central government bonds. Even though the experience with emerging market asset purchase programs was fairly positive during COVID-19 (April 2020 *Global Financial Stability Report*; Sever and others 2021), large-scale and open-ended asset purchase programs may lead to important consequences including (1) potential weakening of institutional and central bank credibility, (2) fiscal dominance concerns, (3) distorting capital market dynamics, and (4) intensification of capital outflow pressures by crowding out foreigners and through negative risk sentiment if currency pressures persist due to fiscal dominance concerns.

Figure 8.4. Fiscal Needs and Government Bond Market

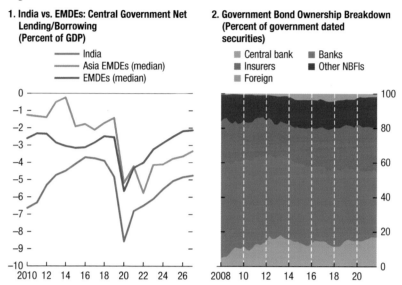

1. India vs. EMDEs: Central Government Net Lending/Borrowing (Percent of GDP)

2. Government Bond Ownership Breakdown (Percent of government dated securities)

Sources: Haver Analytics; IMF, April 2022 *World Economic Outlook;* and IMF staff calculations.
Note: EMDEs = emerging markets and developing economies; NBFIs = nonbank financial institutions.

ADVENT OF NEW TYPES OF INVESTORS

The importance of capital flows and evolving global investor base imply many emerging markets, including India, may also have to deal with an increasing role of certain types of investors in both debt and equity markets.

Investments Driven by Environmental, Social, and Governance Concerns

Sustainable finance is growing globally (IMF 2023). Although advanced economies historically have been the main driver of this segment, 2021 was a breakout year for emerging market economies, with a total of almost $200 billion in issuance of sustainable debt (up threefold compared to the last few years) and almost $25 billion in sustainability-led equity flows (a record high and up 25 percent year over year; Goel and others 2022). The Indian sustainable finance markets for both private debt and equity also accelerated sharply recently (see Chapter 6); further, in January 2023, India raised $1 billion via its inaugural sovereign green bond.

Sustainable finance markets could be another avenue to tap into a new and growing investor base. However, the rising importance of environmental, social, and governance (ESG) factors in shaping investment decision may also introduce financial vulnerabilities (April 2020 *Global Financial Stability Report*), some of which may be more prominent for emerging markets. ESG disclosures for emerging markets lag those of advanced economies, especially in Asian economies (notably India, Indonesia, and Thailand). It could prove a challenge for financial sector stakeholders to assess, properly price, and manage ESG-related risks.

Benchmark-Driven Debt Flows

Since the global financial crisis, benchmark-driven asset managers have played a major role in the surge in cross-border portfolio flows into emerging market economies and frontier markets. Total assets under management of the global debt emerging market benchmarks have quadrupled in the past 10 years to almost $1 trillion in 2021 (April 2021 *Global Financial Stability Report*).[10] Benchmark indices affect both passive and active fund portfolio allocations with benchmark-driven investment accounting for, on average, about 70 percent of country allocations (Raddatz, Schmukler, and Williams 2017).

India's local currency bond market is one of the largest among peers, but access to foreign investors remains limited. Introduction of FAR in 2020 paved the way for government bonds to be eligible for inclusion in global bond indices. As of September 2022, FAR-eligible bonds accounted above one quarter of government bonds outstanding, with a total value of about $280 billion. As a result, India has been put on multiple index watchlists including the JP Morgan Government Bond Index-Emerging Markets (GBI-EM) and the Bloomberg Global-Agg.

Benchmark inclusion and exclusion decisions could have significant implications for capital flows, and eventually for financial stability. First, index inclusion typically means larger capital inflows for the country added to the index and outflows for other economies due to recalibration of investor positions. Under a scenario in which India is assigned a maximum possible cap of 10 percent in JP Morgan's GBI-EM with assets under management tracking this benchmark between $250–$300 billion, incremental passive flows could reach $25–$30 billion.[11] Second, periodic index adjustments can significantly impact the cost and supply of financing for real activity and domestic financial market volatility. Finally, benchmark-driven investment strategies are found to induce greater correlation in portfolio flows (as well as the funding costs) within the cross-section of emerging

---

[10] The rising role of benchmarks has occurred in step with the doubling of the number of countries in the main emerging market indices (EMBIG) since 2007, which is currently 70. In addition, the growing size and liquidity of local bond markets in many emerging markets have allowed the number of countries in the main local-currency bond index (GBI-EM) to increase from 12 to almost 20. China's inclusion in the global benchmark indices in 2019 has been a notable development that has garnered significant investor attention (Chen, Drakopoulos, and Goel 2019).

[11] This section focuses the ongoing debate about country's inclusion in global bond indices. Benchmark-driven equity investment could be important as well, especially for individual stocks. MSCI India Index, for example, covers about 85 percent of the country's equity universe, while India accounts for more than 14 percent of MSCI EM index. However, the impact of foreign flows on aggregate market dynamic is mitigated by a high share of retail investors in additions to a solid base of domestic institutional investors.

market recipients and across emerging market economy bond yields. Miyajima and Shim (2014) showed that asset managers investing in emerging market economies tend to behave in a correlated manner. Some of this behavior is because of common or similar portfolio benchmarks and the directional co-movement of end-investor flows. As a result, benchmark-driven flows are estimated to be, on average, about three-to-five times more sensitive to common global risk factors than the total portfolio flows as benchmark-driven investors tend to treat emerging markets as an asset class focusing on factors that affect them as a group rather than on country-specific developments (April 2019 *Global Financial Stability Report*; Arslanalp and others 2020). Importantly, this sensitivity has been rising over time.

REAPING BENEFITS AND MITIGATING RISKS

India remains dependent on foreign capital flows for driving investment, while openness and penetration in some sectors are below peers. Persistent use of capital flow restrictions could lead to adverse consequences in the long run, including by hampering market development and leading to resource misallocation. IMF (2022b) argues, however, that planning and sequencing of liberalization should be aligned with a country's level of financial and institutional development. Changing flow patterns and structure of investors creates new challenges strengthening the case for a gradual approach. Here, sound domestic policies and institutions will be crucial to maximize the benefits of stable access to global financial markets and minimize negative spillovers from exposure to potentially volatile foreign capital flows.

Monetary and Fiscal Policy Based on Clear Communication and Focused on Creating Conditions for Sustainable Growth

The credibility of both policies will be important for building investor confidence, which is critical in both attracting foreign capital and dealing with increased volatility in times of stress. Fiscal policy should aim to support private-sector-led growth and be consistent with medium-term sustainability. This implies rebuilding fiscal policy space via revenue mobilization and expenditure efficiency, as well as improving fiscal transparency and reducing crowding out (IMF 2022a). Monetary policy should focus on ensuring price stability, while communication can be enhanced to reduce uncertainty and help guiding market expectations. Ahmed, Binici, and Turunen (2022) found that Reserve Bank of India's forward guidance played an important role in moderating uncertainty and supporting asset prices during the pandemic.

Structural Reforms to Improve the Efficiency of the Public Sector, Further Liberalize Trade and Investment, and Boost Growth Potential

India continued to make progress in liberalizing of FDI and portfolio flows in recent years. However, further reforms are needed to ensure external financial intermediation helps to support investment and capital accumulation. Privatization has long been identified as an important reform priority in India. Agarwal and others (2022) found there is scope to rationalize government ownership of enterprises in India. Well-designed privatization involving a medium-term strategy and reforms to improve governance in state-owned companies would help boost efficiency in government assets, create fiscal space, and attract investment. Government reforms such as privatization of public enterprises in nonstrategic sectors and important steps to liberalize FDI policies related to agriculture, telecommunication services, and the insurance sector are important. In addition, further efforts toward liberalization of trade regime, including reduction of tariffs and addressing non-trade barriers, could help deepen India's integration in global value chains and attract FDI (IMF 2022a, Salgado and Anand 2022). More broadly, steps to address growth bottlenecks and enhance India's competitiveness, including strengthening education, improving labor force participation, and reducing administrative burden and complexity of tax and capital flow restrictions, would help broaden investor base.

Measures to Maintain Financial Stability, to Enhance the Efficiency of the Financial Sector, and to Strengthen Financial Market Infrastructure

The financial sector can become an important shock transmitter and amplifier as discussed above. Thus, the regulatory framework should promote a strong and efficient financial sector (see Chapters 1 and 2). Further efforts are required to expand and improve functioning of domestic capital markets, especially for corporate debt (Chapter 5).

CONCLUSIONS

Cross-border capital flows have facilitated India's development by supplementing domestic investment and allowing households to smooth consumption. India's capital account liberalization has been gradual with priority given to non-debt creating and long-term capital flows. More recently, the authorities have eased restrictions on debt flows further, accompanied by more favorable investment regimes for government and corporate debt, increasing the prospects of India's inclusion in global bond indices, which in turn would lead to important inflows, but also affect the structure of the investor base.

As the literature and country experiences suggest, capital inflows can bring both benefits and risks. Portfolio flows can be volatile and susceptible to changes in global risk appetite, with implications for financial system stability. Surges in inflows can exacerbate domestic credit booms and asset price bubbles. Sudden reversals in turn can lead to abrupt financial sector tightening, lower asset prices, and tighter bank lending conditions. Indeed, India has experienced episodes of strong inflows and sharp reversals, such as during the 2008 global financial crisis, the 2013 taper tantrum, and the 2020 COVID-19 shock. While some degree of capital flow volatility is unavoidable in times of shocks or stress, policies can help contain such volatility. Among others, a further strengthening of domestic policy frameworks and good communication about the direction of reforms will be critical.

REFERENCES

Agarwal, Ruchir, Elif Saxegaard, Lesley Fisher, and Xuehui Han. 2022. "India's State-Owned Enterprises." IMF Working Paper 22/165, International Monetary Fund, Washington, DC.

Aggarwal, Nidhi, Sanchit Arora, and Rajeswari Sengupta. 2021. "Capital Account Liberalization in a Large Emerging Economy: An Analysis of Onshore-Offshore Arbitrage." WP-2021-013. Indira Ghandi Institute of Development Research, Mumbai.

Ahmed, Faisal, Mahir Binici, and Jarkko Turunen. 2022 "Monetary Policy Communication and Financial Markets in India." IMF Working Paper 22/209, International Monetary Fund, Washington, DC.

Arslanalp, Serkan, Dimitris Drakopoulos, Rohit Goel, and Robin Koepke. 2020. "Benchmark-Driven Investments in Emerging Market Bond Markets: Taking Stock." IMF Working Paper 20/192. International Monetary Fund, Washington, DC.

Banerjee, Shasadri, and M S Mohanty. 2021. "US Monetary Policy and the Financial Channel of the Exchange Rate: Evidence from India." BIS Working Paper No 975.

Bank for International Settlements (BIS). 2020. "Capital Flows, Exchange Rates and Policy Frameworks in Emerging Asia." Report by a Working Group established by the Asian Consultative Council of the BIS, November.

Bank for International Settlements (BIS). 2021. "Changing Patterns of Capital Flows." Committee on the Global Financial System Papers 66. Basel.

Chen, Sally, Dimitris Drakopoulos, and Rohit Goel. 2019. "China Deepens Global Finance Links as It Joins Benchmark Indexes." IMF Blog, Washington, DC. https://www.imf.org/en/Blogs/Articles/2019/06/19/blog061919-china-deepens-global-finance-links-as-it-joins-benchmark-indexes.

Cortes, Fabio, and Luca Sanfilippo. 2021. "Multi-Sector Bond Funds in Emerging Markets—Easy Come, Easy Go." IMF Global Financial Stability Note 2021/05, International Monetary Fund, Washington, DC.

Dua, Pami, and Partha Sen. 2017. "Capital Flows and Exchange Rates: The Indian Experience, India Studies in Business and Economics." In *Perspectives on Economic Development and Policy in India*, edited by K.L. Krishna, Vishwanath Pandit, K. Sundaram, and Pami Dua. New York: Springer.

Ebeke, Christian, and Annette Kyobe. 2015. "Global Financial Spillovers to Emerging Market Sovereign Bond Markets." IMF Working Paper 15/141, International Monetary Fund, Washington, DC.

Finger, Harald, and Pablo Lopez Murphy. 2019. "Facing the Tides: Managing Capital Flows in Asia." IMF Departmental Paper 19/015. International Monetary Fund, Washington, DC.

Gelos, G., Lucyna Górnicka, Robin Koepke, Ratna Sahay, and Silvia Sgherri. 2019. "Capital Flows at Risk: Taming the Ebbs and Flows." IMF Working Paper 19/279, International Monetary Fund, Washington, DC.

Goel, Rohit, Deepali Gautam, and Fabio M Natalucci. 2022. "Sustainable Finance in Emerging Markets: Evolution, Challenges, and Policy Priorities," IMF Working Paper 22/182

Goel, Rohit, and Ken Miyajima. 2021. "Analyzing Capital Flow Drivers Using the 'At-Risk' Framework: South Africa's Case." IMF Working Paper 21/253, International Monetary Fund, Washington, DC.

Goel, Rohit, and Evan Papageorgiou. 2021. "Drivers of Emerging Market Bond Flows and Prices." IMF Global Financial Stability Note 21/04. International Monetary Fund, Washington, DC.

Guidotti, Pablo, Federico Sturzenegger, Agustin Villar, Jose de Gregorio, and Ilan Goldfajn. 2004. "On the Consequences of Sudden Stops." *Economia* 4 (2, Spring): 171–214.

Gupta, Poonam. 2016. "Capital Flows and Central Banking: The Indian Experience." Policy Research Working Paper 7569. World Bank Group, Washington, DC.

International Monetary Fund (IMF). 2022a. *India 2022 Article IV Consultation*. IMF Country Report No. 22/386, Washington, DC.

International Monetary Fund (IMF). 2022b. *Review of The Institutional View on The Liberalization and Management of Capital Flows*. IMF Policy Paper No. 2022/008. Washington, DC.

International Monetary Fund (IMF). 2023. *Climate Finance Monitor*. Washington, DC.

Kose, M. Ayhan, and Eswar Prasad. "Capital Accounts: Liberalize or Not?" *Finance and Development*, February 2020. International Monetary Fund, Washington, DC.

Miyajima, Ken, and Ilhyock Shim. 2014. "Asset Managers in Emerging Market Economies." *BIS Quarterly Review* September. Basel, Switzerland: Bank for International Settlements.

Mohan, Rakesh, and Partha Ray. 2017. "Indian Financial Sector: Structure, Trends and Turns." IMF Working Paper 17/7, International Monetary Fund, Washington, DC.

Pandey, Radhika, Gurnain Pasricha, Ila Patnaik, and Ajay Shah. 2021. "Motivations for Capital Controls and Their Effectiveness." *International Journal of Finance and Economics* 26 (1): 391–415.

Pandey, Radhika, Rajeswari Sengupta, Aatmin Shah, and Bhargavi Zaveri. 2020. "Legal Restrictions on Foreign Institutional Investors in a Large, Emerging Economy: A Comprehensive Dataset." *Data in Brief* 28 (2020): 104819.

Peiris, Shanaka. 2010. "Foreign Participation in Emerging Markets' Local Currency Bond Markets." IMF Working Paper 10/88, International Monetary Fund, Washington, DC.

Raddatz, Claudio, Sergio Schmukler, and Tomas Williams. 2017. "International Asset Allocations and Capital Flows: The Benchmark Effect." *Journal of International Economics* 108 (September): 413–30.

Salgado, Ranil, and Rahul Anand. 2022. *South Asia's Path to Resilient Growth*. International Monetary Fund, Washington, DC.

Sever, Can, Rohit Goel, Dimitris Drakopoulos, and Evan Papageorgiou. 2020. "Effects of Emerging Market Asset Purchase Program Announcements on Financial Markets During the COVID-19 Pandemic." IMF Working Paper 20/292, International Monetary Fund, Washington, DC.

CHAPTER 9

Addressing Corporate Sector Vulnerabilities

Lucyna Górnicka, Sumiko Ogawa, and TengTeng Xu

INTRODUCTION

The COVID-19 pandemic has impacted the corporate sector in India, with contact-intensive services, and micro, small, and medium enterprises (MSMEs) being the most affected. A wide range of policy measures have been introduced to mitigate shocks to the corporate sector, including a moratorium on loan repayments, credit guarantee schemes, and resolution frameworks for distressed assets.

In this chapter, we first examine the evolution and current financial performance of the corporate sector in India, focusing on indicators related to profitability, leverage, liquidity, and debt repayment capacity. We then conduct a series of sensitivity analyses and stress tests to assess corporate resilience against COVID-19–related shocks. Specifically, we consider three single-year scenarios, where the sectoral decline in corporate net sales is proportional to the change in gross value added (GVA) in fiscal year 2020/21 (baseline), the second quarter of 2020 (severely adverse), and their average (moderately adverse), respectively. Second, we use the resulting increase in stressed debts to assess the impact of heightened credit risk in the corporate portfolio on aggregate balance sheets of banks and nonbanks. Finally, we consider two forward-looking multiyear scenarios covering a four-year period: one following the 2021 July *World Economic Outlook* projections and another one where the recovery is more protracted. By considering both single-year and multiyear stress scenarios, we hope to capture both the short-term and the medium-term impact of the COVID-19 shock, including through potential future waves of infections.

Our chapter is related to three strands of literature on corporate vulnerability. The first strand examines corporate sector stress in India using firm-level data.

We thank Faisal Ahmed, Zamid Aligishiev, Elif Arbatli Saxegaard, Xiaodan Ding, Shanaka J. Peiris, Hiroko Oura, Alfred Schipke, Katrien Smuts, Thierry Tressel, Jarkko Turunen, Laura Valderrama, Rui Xu, and seminar participants from the Reserve Bank of India, the Indian Ministry of Finance, and IMF's Asia and Pacific Department for useful feedback. Nimarjit Singh provided excellent research assistance.

For example, Oura and Topalova (2009) and Iorgova (2017) review the evolution of financial performances of corporates and assess their sensitivity to various types of shocks (e.g., interest rate, foreign exchange, and profits). Lindner and Jung (2014) find that growth in corporate leverage in India has been associated with a notable increase in the vulnerabilities of firms carrying high-interest-payment burdens. The second strand of literature considers corporate stress tests in the aftermath of the COVID-19 shock. For example, Tressel and Ding (2021) conduct a cross-country study on the impact of COVID-19 shock on listed companies. Diez and others (2021) quantify the rise in solvency and liquidity risks among small and medium enterprises for advanced economies. Caceres and others (2020) assess the solvency risks and liquidity needs facing the US corporate sector associated with the COVID-19 crisis. The Bank of Japan (2020 and 2021) examined the liquidity impact of the COVID-19 shock on the corporate sector in Japan, including the impact of policy measures and with a multiyear simulation. Finally, several studies have investigated the impact of policy responses including corporate relief measures following the pandemic in advanced economies (see, e.g., Bank of England 2020; Core and De Marco 2021; Ebeke and others 2021; Elenev, Landvoigt, and Van Nieuwerburgh 2020; and October 2020 *Regional Economic Outlook: Europe*). To our knowledge, our chapter is one of the first to examine the impact of COVID-19–related shocks on corporate resilience in India using a comprehensive firm-level database including MSMEs and to assess quantitatively the role of announced policy measures including moratorium and credit guarantee schemes.

The results from our stress testing exercise reveal that without policy support, the COVID-19 shock could have led to a significant increase in firms with earnings insufficient to cover their debt interest payments (i.e., with an interest coverage ratio [ICR] below 1). The share of corporate debt issued by these firms (debt-at-risk) rises from 23 percent to over 36 percent under the baseline scenario and to about 50 percent under the severe adverse scenario. Sectors most affected include construction, manufacturing, and contact-intensive services (i.e., trade, transport, and hospitality). Consistent with their weaker liquidity position prior to the pandemic, the share of MSME debt-at-risk increases more than for large firms under the baseline and two adverse scenarios.

We find that policy support measures provided to firms in 2020 were effective in mitigating the liquidity impact of the COVID-19 shock. For example, debt-at-risk based on ICR in the baseline scenario falls to 26 percent from 36 percent, and the share of debt issued by firms with negative cashflow goes down from about 35 percent to 8.6 percent. At the same time, the effects of policy measures on corporate solvency are found to be less pronounced, reflecting the focus of the implemented policy measures in supporting corporate liquidity. The results suggest that corporate stress could have a sizable impact on the balance sheets of banks and nonbanking financial companies (NBFCs), particularly for public sector banks (PSBs) due to their relatively weak starting capital position, although the policy support measures played an important mitigating role.

Finally, the forward-looking multiyear corporate stress tests suggest that the overall impact of the COVID-19 shock on the corporate sector will crucially depend on the speed of the economic recovery. Under the baseline path, the overall corporate performance improves gradually, with debt-at-risk returning to close to pre–COVID-19 levels by the end of 2023. However, a slower pace of recovery could lead to persistently high levels of debt-at-risk and prolonged scarring, especially in contact-intensive services, construction, and manufacturing sectors.

This chapter is organized as follows. The first section discusses the underlying data and provides some indicators of corporate sector performance prior to the pandemic. The second section describes the stress testing methodology used for the single-year analysis and presents results, including the impact of policy measures. The third section discusses the implication of corporate stress on aggregate balance sheets of banks and NBFCs. The fourth section presents the methodology and results of the multiyear stress tests. The final section offers some concluding remarks.

DATA

Data Sources

The analysis of corporate vulnerability in this chapter uses the Prowess database from the Centre for Monitoring Indian Economy (CMIE). The database covers over 20,000 listed and unlisted nonfinancial corporates on a standalone basis in India.[1] The database includes information on firm characteristics (e.g., industry, ownership, and the year of establishment) and detailed data on financial performance and balance sheets.

We base our analysis using the annual standalone financial database, given the greater coverage of MSMEs[2]; see Figure 9.1. Roughly two-thirds of the companies covered by the database for 2007–20 have sales of less than 1 billion rupees (Rs). By sector, those affected most by the pandemic are well-represented in terms of the share of assets and debt. Manufacturing firms account for about 40 percent and 32 percent of total assets and debts, respectively, followed by trade, hotels, transport, and communication (about 20 percent) and construction (about 10 percent). It should be noted that the share of the utilities sector is relatively high in total debt compared with total assets in the sample (24 percent and 15 percent, respectively), reflecting their high leverage.

For the analysis of corporate sector resilience, we use annual financial results for the fiscal year ending in 2019 (the December 2020 vintage of the Prowess database)

---

[1] About 4,000 firms are covered in the consolidated database in the Prowess database. The unconsolidated Prowess database has the largest coverage of corporate sector balance sheets in India at a granular level compared with other databases such as S&P Capital IQ (about 3,360 nonfinancial corporates) and RBI (2,608 listed nongovernment and nonfinancial corporates by industrial aggregates).

[2] The classification of MSMEs follows the turnover threshold defined by Ministry of Micro, Small, and Medium Enterprises.

Figure 9.1. Composition of Firms by Size and by Sector

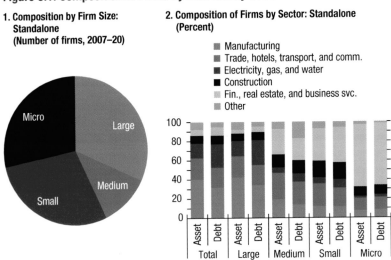

1. Composition by Firm Size: Standalone
(Number of firms, 2007–20)

2. Composition of Firms by Sector: Standalone
(Percent)

- ■ Manufacturing
- ■ Trade, hotels, transport, and comm.
- ■ Electricity, gas, and water
- ■ Construction
- ▨ Fin., real estate, and business svc.
- ■ Other

Sources: CMIE Prowess database; and authors' calculations.
Note: comm. = communication; Fin. = financial; svc. = services.

as the pre-shock starting point.[3] There are several benefits of using the 2019 data instead of 2020 as the starting point. First, the coverage of firms is more comprehensive and representative. The number of firms for 2019 (more than 21,000) is in line with previous years, whereas the smaller size for 2020 (about half of previous years as of August 2021) may introduce bias in the sample. Second, the financial performance for 2020 may already be partially affected by the economic impact of the pandemic. Third, we are interested in assessing the mitigating impact of policy measures introduced in 2020, and, therefore, data from the end of 2019 are more appropriate as a starting point. To focus on viable firms in our analysis, we trimmed the sample by removing the firms that were making losses for the last three consecutive years including 2019.

Stylized Facts: Pre–COVID-19 Conditions

The corporate sector in India went through a gradual process of deleveraging with an improvement in profitability prior to the pandemic (Figure 9.2). The median return on assets improved to 2.2 percent in 2019, from a trough of 0.9 percent following the global financial crisis in 2009. The median debt-to-equity ratio (leverage ratio) declined in the past five years, from 1.1 percent in 2015 to 0.8 percent in 2019, possibly reflecting the enhanced resolution under the

---

[3] Most firms in the database have fiscal year ending on March 31, i.e., the data used as pre-shock variables are as of the end of March 2019.

Figure 9.2. Profitability and Leverage of Firms by Sector and by Size

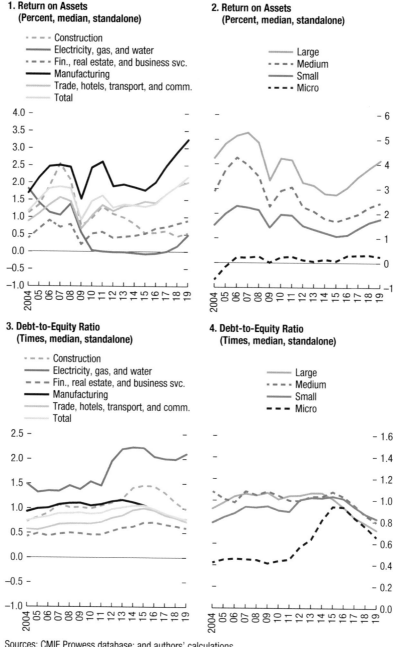

1. Return on Assets
(Percent, median, standalone)

- - - - Construction
───── Electricity, gas, and water
- - - - Fin., real estate, and business svc.
───── Manufacturing
───── Trade, hotels, transport, and comm.
───── Total

2. Return on Assets
(Percent, median, standalone)

───── Large
- - - - Medium
───── Small
- - - - Micro

3. Debt-to-Equity Ratio
(Times, median, standalone)

- - - - Construction
───── Electricity, gas, and water
- - - - Fin., real estate, and business svc.
───── Manufacturing
───── Trade, hotels, transport, and comm.
───── Total

4. Debt-to-Equity Ratio
(Times, median, standalone)

───── Large
- - - - Medium
───── Small
- - - - Micro

Sources: CMIE Prowess database; and authors' calculations.
Note: comm. = communication; Fin. = financial; svc. = services.

Insolvency and Bankruptcy Code of 2016. The improvement was most notable in manufacturing and contact-intensive sectors, whereas the construction and utility sectors continued to see stagnant levels of profitability and elevated leverage. By firm size, micro firms (defined as those with sales less than Rs50 million) experienced persistent low profitability throughout the sample period, with an uptick in leverage in 2015 followed by a gradual decline in recent years.

Against this backdrop, the median interest coverage ratio (ICR) of the firms in our sample recovered to 2.8 in 2019, close to the pre–global financial crisis levels (Figure 9.3). The improvement was more pronounced for larger firms and firms in manufacturing and contact-intensive sectors, whereas micro firms and those in construction and utilities sectors saw limited improvement. Debt-at-risk (defined as the share of debt owed by companies with ICR less than 1) declined to 25 percent in 2019 from a peak of 36 percent in 2016 but remained above the pre–global financial crisis levels. Furthermore, the share of debt of firms with ICR less than 2 stood at about 60 percent compared to about 40 percent prior to the global financial crisis, indicating a decline in the share of firms with large buffers to withstand shocks overtime. By sector, all sectors except wholesale and retail trade saw an increase in the median debt-at-risk in 2015–19 compared with 10 years earlier (2005–09). Consistent with the weaker performance as seen in low profitability and high leverage, the debt-at-risk for micro firms stood at about 80 percent, the highest among all segments of firms.

SINGLE-YEAR CORPORATE STRESS TESTS

Scenarios

One important objective of our stress testing exercise is to assess the impact of the pandemic on corporate liquidity and solvency. At the time of writing, the COVID-19 pandemic is still ongoing, with the full impact on the corporate sector and the economy yet to fully materialize. The nature of the COVID-19 shock makes the stress testing exercises particularly challenging because the selection of appropriate stress scenarios is subject to considerable uncertainty.

In the single-year stress tests, we consider three scenarios: "baseline," "moderately adverse," and "severely adverse." We calibrate the baseline scenario to be the realized outcome in GVA observed in different economic sectors in 2020. The other two single-year scenarios are more severe and are aimed at assessing corporate vulnerability to even larger but plausible negative shocks. The severely adverse scenario matches the realization of the sharp GDP contraction in the second quarter of 2020 (extrapolated to the whole year). The moderately adverse scenario is a simple average of growth outcomes in the baseline and the severely adverse scenarios. Figure 9.4 presents the sectoral growth assumptions for the single-year stress tests under each of three scenarios.

We consider shocks to net sales as the main channel through which firms are affected by the economic impact of COVID-19 pandemic. Ideally, we would empirically estimate the relationship between the GVA and changes in the firms'

Figure 9.3. Interest Coverage and Debt-at-Risk of Firms by Sector and by Size

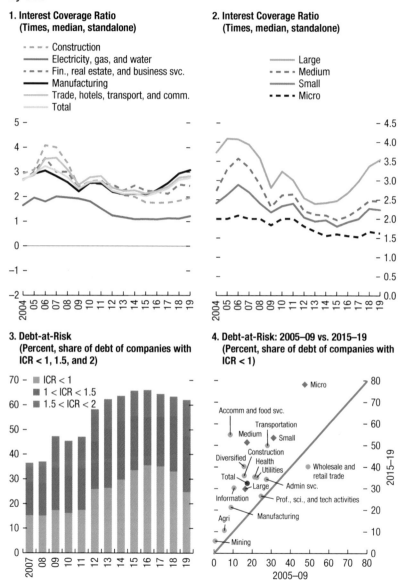

1. Interest Coverage Ratio
(Times, median, standalone)

- - - - Construction
——— Electricity, gas, and water
- - - - Fin., real estate, and business svc.
——— Manufacturing
——— Trade, hotels, transport, and comm.
——— Total

2. Interest Coverage Ratio
(Times, median, standalone)

——— Large
- - - - Medium
——— Small
- - - - Micro

3. Debt-at-Risk
(Percent, share of debt of companies with ICR < 1, 1.5, and 2)

■ ICR < 1
■ 1 < ICR < 1.5
■ 1.5 < ICR < 2

4. Debt-at-Risk: 2005–09 vs. 2015–19
(Percent, share of debt of companies with ICR < 1)

Micro
Accomm and food svc.
Transportation
Medium   Small
Construction
Diversified   Health
Utilities
Total   Wholesale and retail trade
Large   Admin svc.
Information   Prof., sci., and tech activities
Agri   Manufacturing
Mining

2005–09
2015–19

Sources: CMIE Prowess database; and authors' calculations.
Note: Accomm = accomodations; Admin = administrative; Agri = agriculture;
comm. = communication; Fin. = financial; ICR = interest coverage ratio; Prof. = professional;
sci. = science; svc. = services.

Figure 9.4. Sector Assumptions for Single-Period Stress Test Scenarios
(Percent)

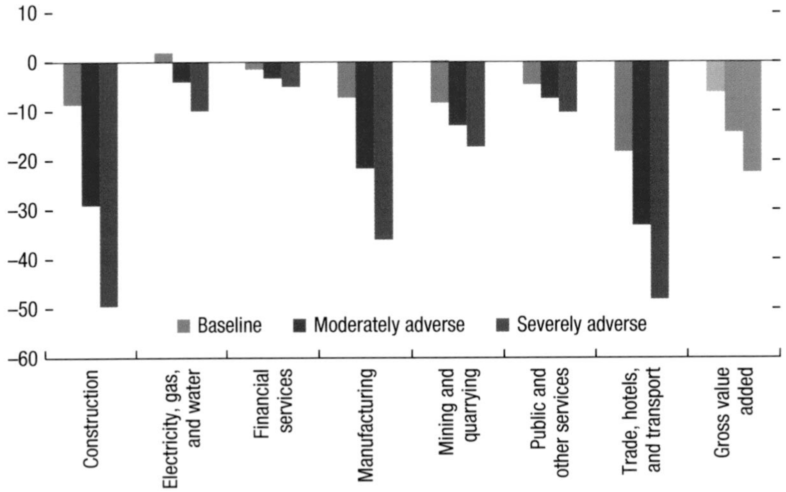

Sources: IMF, *World Economic Outlook*; and authors' estimates.

net sales. However, a lack of sufficiently long historical time series makes such an estimation infeasible. We therefore follow the standard approach in the literature by assuming that firms' sales decline by the same rate as GVA at the sectoral level. This approach has been applied frequently in other analyses of corporate balance sheets following the COVID-19 shock (e.g., see the October 2020 *Regional Economic Outlook: Europe*). An alternative approach could be to use projections of firms' sales by market analysts (e.g., see Tressel and Ding 2021). However, analysts' projections of sales tend to focus primarily on larger listed corporates (therefore, a smaller subset of firms), whereas our exercise aims to cover all firms for which data are available, including MSMEs. Furthermore, sales projections for large, listed firms may not be as relevant for those of MSMEs. In our analysis, we conduct robustness checks using alternative assumptions regarding the link between the GVA and net sales (see the section Liquidity Stress Test: ICR Metric, on the following page).

Methodology

We conduct two types of liquidity stress tests and one solvency stress test. The liquidity stress tests allow us to consider the impact of the COVID-19 and related shocks on corporate liquidity, measured by the ICR and end-of-period cash flows. The solvency stress test examines the impact of these shocks on firm equity. Whereas the two liquidity tests aim at capturing the short-term impact of the shocks on firms' ability to generate cash flows and cover expenses, the solvency stress test helps assess the potentially more persistent impact on firms' viability.

Liquidity Stress Test: ICR Metric

The first liquidity stress test is based on the concept of the IRC, which is the ratio of earnings before interest and taxes (EBIT) to the interest expenses. Formally, for a firm i in year t, the ICR is equal to:

$$ICR_{i,t} = \frac{EBIT_{i,t}}{interest\ expenses_{i,t}}, \tag{9.1}$$

where:

$$EBIT_{i,t} = net\ sales_{i,t} - (material\ costs_{i,t} + wage\ costs_{i,t} + other\ operational \tag{9.2}$$
$$expenses_{i,t}) + other\ income_{i,t} + interest\ expenses_{i,t}.$$

In what follows, we assume that the adverse shock affects a firm's ICR through a decline in net sales while allowing firms to adjust their wage and material costs in response. The ICR of a firm i in period $t + 1$, after a shock hits, is equal to:

$$ICR_{i,t+1|shock} = \frac{EBIT_{i,t} + x\%*[net\ sales_{i,t} - y\%*material\ costs_{i,t}] + z\%*wage\ costs_{i,t}}{interest\ expenses_{i,t+1}}, \tag{9.3}$$

where x captures a *negative* shock to sales, y captures firms' ability to reduce material costs in response to the sales shock, and z captures firms' ability to reduce wage costs in response to the sales shock.

In the absence of policy interventions, we assume that the interest expense in year $t + 1$ is the same as interest expense in the year before: *interest expenses*$_{i,t+1}$ = *interest expenses*$_{i,t}$. In addition, in absence of shocks to sales and costs, $x = y = z = 0$.

For the pass/fail criteria, we assume that a firm fails the ICR stress test if $ICR_{i,t+1|shock}<1$. The threshold of 1 is frequently used in the literature to identify firms with unsustainable debt levels. When reporting the results, we compute the share of total corporate debt issued by firms with a post-shock ICR below 1, by economic sector or by firm size. We call this metric "debt-at-risk" because it captures the share of unsustainable corporate debt in total corporate debt outstanding.

Liquidity Stress Test: Cash Flow–Based Stress Metric

The second liquidity stress test captures the ability of a firm to generate positive cash flows following an adverse shock to its net sales while accounting for principal debt payments and other short-term obligations. At the same time, any cash buffers and easy-to-liquidate current assets are counted toward the firm's ability to repay its debts. Formally:

$$cash\ balance_{i,t+1|shock} = cash\ balance_{i,t} + retained\ earnings_{i,t+1}$$
$$+ current\ assets_{i,t+1} - current\ liabilities_{i,t+1}, \tag{9.4}$$

where the retained earnings after shock are equal to:

$$retained\ earnings_{i,t+1} = (EBIT_{i,t+1} - interest\ expenses_{i,t+1})*$$
$$(1 - tax\ rate_{i,t+1}) \tag{9.5}$$

The applicable tax rate$_{i,t+1}$ is positive if $EBIT_{i,t+1}$ – $interest\ expenses_{i,t+1} > 0$, that is, if the pretax earnings are positive. Otherwise, firms do not pay taxes. Consistent with the ICR test, the EBIT after the shock is equal to:

$$EBIT_{i,t+1} = EBIT_{i,t} + x\%*[net\ sales_{i,t} - y\%*material\ costs_{i,t}] + z\%*wage\ costs_{i,t}. \quad (9.6)$$

Finally, in absence of policy intervention, we assume $interest\ expense_{i,t+1} = interest\ expense_{i,t}$. We also assume that $current\ assets_{i,t+1} = current\ assets_{i,t}$ and $current\ liabilities_{i,t+1} = current\ liabilities_{i,t}$.

On pass/fail criteria, a firm fails the cash flow stress test if it has negative cash balance at the end of the stress period, $cash\ balance_{i,t+1\backslash shock} < 0$. A negative cash balance means that a firm has a negative gap between available cash and its liquidity needs. As in the ICR stress test, we summarize results by computing the share of total corporate debt outstanding issued by firms with negative cash balance at the end of the stress period.

Solvency Stress Test

The objective of the solvency stress test is to capture a firm's ability to generate positive profits after paying long-term obligations. To measure solvency, we follow the literature and examine the behavior of a firm's equity after shock: if a firm's equity becomes negative, a firm is assumed to be insolvent. The post-shock equity is computed as:

$$equity_{i,t+1\backslash shock} = equity_{i,t} + retained\ earnings_{i,t+1}, \quad (9.7)$$

where the retained earnings are given by equation (9.5). We summarize the results of the solvency stress test by computing the share of corporate debt (by firm size and by sector) issued by firms with negative equity after the shock. The calibration of the parameters and the detailed mapping between the Prowess database and the variables in equations (9.1) to (9.7) are presented in Annex Tables 9.1.1 and 9.1.2.

The Impact of Policy Interventions

In response to the COVID-19 shock, Indian authorities introduced a range of policies aimed at supporting the flow of credit to the economy and at providing relief to borrowers. The policy measures included (1) a broad-based monetary easing, including through sovereign bond purchases; (2) a six-month moratorium on loan repayments; and (3) measures to facilitate funding to corporates, including targeted long-term refinancing operations (TLTRO), credit guarantee schemes for loans to MSMEs, and lending to NBFCs. In addition, the authorities introduced a one-time loan restructuring scheme for retail and small loans, and an extension of a previous loan restructuring scheme for MSMEs.

In our analysis, we consider the impact of the following three policy measures. First, the analysis captures a reduction in lending rates because of monetary easing, including through a reduction in the main policy rate by 115 basis points over 2020. Second, we capture a reduction in the debt repayment burden through the loan moratorium. The six-month moratorium on loan repayments were applied to bank and nonbank loans. As reported in the Reserve Bank of India (RBI)'s "Report on Trend and Progress of Banking in India 2019–2020," about 31 percent of corporate customers took advantage of the option to defer loan payments as of the end of August 2020. Third, we consider the impact of debt rollover and access to new credit. Under the on-tap TLTRO scheme, banks could borrow up to Rs1 trillion at a cost linked to the policy rate to purchase corporate bonds, commercial paper, and nonconvertible debt issued by companies in specified sectors. Because the program focused on debt issuances, it primarily benefited large companies.[4] Under the Emergency Credit Line Guarantee Schemes 1.0 and 2.0 totaling Rs3 trillion, eligible MSMEs[5] could obtain additional bank loans (capped at 20 percent of the total debt outstanding as of February 2020) with a one-year moratorium on loan repayments that were fully guaranteed by the government.

We incorporate the three policy measures in our stress testing analysis as follows. For ICR and equity stress tests, the channel through which these policies can impact corporate balance sheets is through lower interest expenses. We decompose interest expenses after the shock, *interest expenses*$_{i,t+1}$ in equations (9.3) and (9.5) as follows:

$$\textit{interest expenses}_{i,t+1|\text{shock}} = (1 - u\% - w\%)*\textit{interest expenses}_{i,t}, \qquad (9.8)$$

where w captures the impact of loan moratorium on interest payments and u captures a change in interest expenses due to lower interest rates. In our policy analysis, we consider the individual impact of the loan repayments and lower lending rates on firm ICR and equity, as well as their combined impact.

For the cash flow-based liquidity stress test, we also consider the impact of the TLTRO and MSME credit guarantee schemes on debt rollover. We rewrite the cash balance after shock, *cash balance*$_{i,t+1}$ in equation (9.4), as follows:

$$\begin{aligned}\textit{cash balance}_{i,t+1|\text{shock}} &= \textit{cash balance}_{i,t} + \textit{retained earnings}_{i,t+1} \qquad (9.9)\\ &+ \textit{current assets}_{i,t+1} - \textit{current liabilities}_{i,t+1} + w\%*(\textit{ST borrowing}_{i,t+1}\\ &+ s\%*(\textit{debt}_{i,t+1} - \textit{ST borrowing}_{i,t+1})) + \eta_L\%*\textit{ST borrowing}_{i,t+1},\end{aligned}$$

where $\textit{debt}_{i,t+1}$ and $\textit{ST borrowing}_{i,t+1}$ stand for total outstanding debt and short-term (one year or less) debt, respectively. The parameter w captures the impact of the loan moratorium on principal payments, and η_L captures debt rollover or additional credit made available through the TLTRO scheme. In the case of MSMEs, we link the amount of credit available through the Emergency Credit Line Guarantee Schemes to the total amount of debt outstanding, consistent with the design of the program. In other words, we replace $\eta_L\%*\textit{ST borrowing}_{i,t+1}$ in equation (9.9) with $\eta_{MSME}\%*\textit{debt}_{i,t+1}$. Finally, the parameter s captures the share of long-term debt ($\textit{debt}_{i,t+1} - \textit{ST borrowing}_{i,t+1}$) due in the current period. Note that the loan moratorium and lower interest rates support cash balances also through lower interest expenses (equations [9.5] and [9.8]). The detailed calibration of policy-related parameters can be found in Annex Table 9.1.3.

---

[4] Earlier long-term refinancing operations programs have also boosted the overall liquidity in the banking system and have contributed to the easing of financial conditions for corporates.

[5] Eligibility criteria changed over time and included caps on annual turnover and total amount of debt outstanding.

Several caveats apply to our policy analysis. Due to a lack of publicly available granular information, we assume a uniform impact of policies on corporate borrowers in different economic sectors. Arguably, companies in the most affected sectors would be likely to take most advantage of policy support. We also assume that firms benefit from these policy measures such as moratorium in full, as detailed and granular data on the uptake by borrowers are not publicly available.

Results

The stress tests highlight that without borrower relief measures and monetary easing, the COVID-19 shock could have led to a sharp increase in debt-at-risk. Based on the ICR stress tests, debt-at-risk could rise from 23 percent to over 34 percent under the baseline scenario and to about 52 percent under the severely adverse scenario. Sectors most affected include construction, manufacturing, and contact-intensive services (trade, transport, and hospitality). The MSME sector entered the COVID-19 pandemic with a weaker liquidity position, and, under the baseline and both adverse scenarios, the share of MSME debt by firms with ICR below 1 increases more than for large firms (Figure 9.5). Similarly, the COVID-19 shock could lead to sharp increases in debt-at-risk based on the cash flow measure in the absence of any policy support measures (Annex Figure 9.2.1). As discussed previously, we have considered robustness checks based on different relationships between sales growth and GVA, and our results are robust to alternative specifications (Annex Figure 9.2.2).

Figure 9.5. Single-Period Stress Test—Impact on ICR by Sector and Size (No Policy)
(Percent of total corporate debt outstanding)

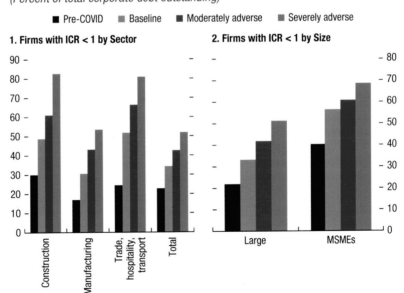

Sources: CMIE Prowess database; and authors' calculations.
Note: ICR = interest coverage ratio; MSMEs = micro, small, and medium enterprises.

Figure 9.6. Single-Period Stress Test—Impact of Policies on Corporate Liquidity

(Percent of corporate debt issued by firms with ICR < 1 or negative cash flows)

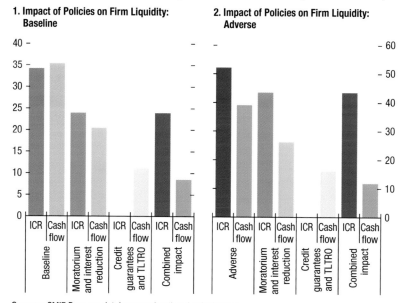

Sources: CMIE Prowess database; and authors' calculations.
Note: ICR = interest coverage ratio; TLTRO = targeted long-term refinancing operations.

Policies including the borrower relief measures and monetary easing provided to firms in 2020 are found to be effective in mitigating the liquidity impact of the COVID-19 shock. For example, the share of debt-at-risk based on ICR in the baseline scenario falls to 24 percent from 34 percent, close to the pre–COVID-19 level.[6] Similarly, the share of debt issued by firms with negative cashflows goes down from about 35 percent to 8.6 percent. The policies also substantially mitigate the impact of the firms' ICR and cash flows also in the moderate and adverse scenarios. For example, the share of debt-at-risk declined from 52 percent to 43 percent in the severely adverse scenario based on ICR, and from 39 percent to 12 percent based on cash flows. By type of policy, the loan moratorium and credit guarantee schemes are found to be most effective in supporting firm liquidity (Figure 9.6 and Annex Figures 9.2.3 and 9.2.4).

---

[6] Under the baseline scenario, the medium ICR stands at 1.7 with policies versus 1.3 without policies. This finding on the mitigating impact of policies is broadly consistent with the latest data from the RBI on corporate financial performances, which would reflect the impact of policies. Specifically, the debt repayment capacity of nongovernment nonfinancial firms increased from 5.2 in the fourth quarter of 2020 to 5.5 in the first quarter of 2021 (from 6.6 in the fourth quarter of 2020 to 7.3 in the first quarter of 2021 for manufacturing firms). Note that the absolute levels of ICR are not comparable between the RBI database and our results (based on the Prowess database) due to differences in sample size, coverage, and aggregation method (aggregate vs. median).

At the same time, the effects of policy measures on corporate solvency are found to be less pronounced, reflecting the focus of the implemented policy measures on supporting corporate liquidity. For example, the share of debt-at-risk declined from 9 percent to 6 percent under the baseline scenario and from 18 percent to 15 percent in the severely adverse scenario (Figure 9.7).

FINANCIAL SECTOR IMPACT

Data

In this section, we analyze how increased credit risk from the corporate loan portfolios could affect the balance sheets of scheduled commercial banks and NBFCs. For this purpose, we apply the results of the three stress scenarios discussed in the previous section on aggregate balance sheets of scheduled commercial banks and NBFCs available from the RBI as of the end of March 2020. We further disaggregate the impact on the scheduled commercial banks by bank type using the aggregate balance sheets of PSBs, private banks, and foreign banks. The balance sheet information we use includes (1) the share of the corporate loan book in the total loan advances; (2) total risk-weighted assets, capital adequacy ratios, and total equity capital; and (3) gross nonperforming loans (NPAs) and total provisions.

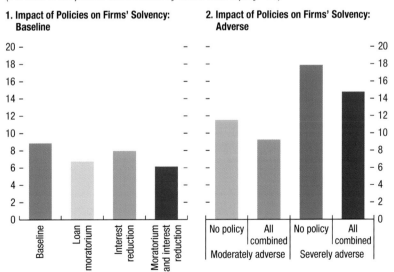

Figure 9.7. Single-Period Stress Test—Impact of Policies on Corporate Solvency
(Percent of corporate debt issued by firms with equity < 0)

Sources: CMIE Prowess database; and authors' calculations.

Figure 9.8 shows the aggregate capital adequacy ratios and the gross NPA ratio by bank type as of March 2020. Prior to the pandemic, PSBs tended to have weaker asset quality compared with other segments of the financial sector with a relatively high gross nonperforming loan ratio of about 10 percent. While having been strengthened with the government's capital injections in previous years, PSBs had a weaker solvency position as of the end of March 2020 with a relatively lower capital adequacy ratio of about 13 percent compared with about 15 percent for the banking sector as a whole and 19 percent for NBFCs. The share of corporate loans in the total loan books was about 60 percent for PSBs and private banks, 87 percent for foreign banks, and 69 percent for NBFCs.

Methodology

To map corporate stress to financial sector stress, we consider a sensitivity analysis that focuses on the credit risk stemming from the corporate credit portfolio to bank and NBFC balance sheets. Our methodology is as follows. First, we compute the debt-at-risk for firms that failed the ICR stress tests, that is, the share of debt of firms with an ICR below 1. We then compare the after-shock debt-at-risk with the pre-shock debt-at-risk. The change in distressed debt can then be translated into an increase in corporate NPAs based on the historical relationship between debt-at-risk and NPA for banks and NBFCs. Specifically, the historical correlation between the annual changes in debt-at-risk and the annual changes in the aggregate NPA ratio

Figure 9.8. Banks and NBFC Balance Sheets Pre–COVID-19
(Percent)

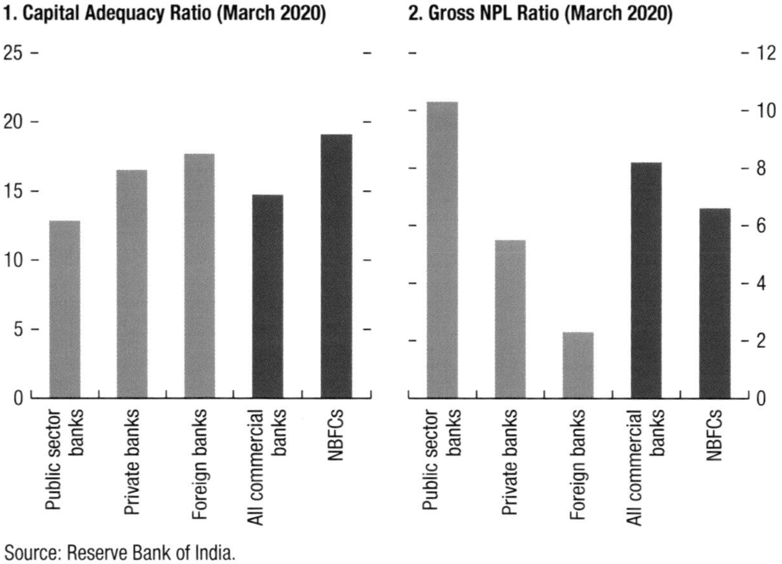

Source: Reserve Bank of India.
Note: NBFCs = nonbanking financial companies; NPL = nonperforming loan.

imply that about 40 percent of the increase in debt-at-risk could potentially translate into NPAs. The loan loss provisions for the NPAs imply lower profits for banks and NBFCs, which in turn leads to a reduction in their after-shock capital ratios (Figure 9.9). The hurdle rate used in our analysis is the regulatory minimum of 9 percent. In other words, if the capital ratio were to be fall below 9 percent, then the regulatory minimum would be breached. Our approach is consistent with other approaches that examine the impact of corporate stress on financial sector balance sheets, including earlier studies on India, such as Oura and Topalova (2009).

Two key caveats apply. First, our analysis is based on publicly available data due to a lack of access to confidential supervisory information. Even though we account for the different composition of corporate and retail exposures for each lender type as an aggregate, there are limited public data on the difference in banks' exposures to various economic sectors by bank type. Similarly, there is no publicly available information on lenders' exposures by firm size or concentration of loans to large borrowers because these data are highly confidential. For example, NBFCs could be more exposed to corporates in the severely hit industries and/or smaller firms, which would imply that the impact on their balance sheets from corporate stress could be higher than reflected. Second, we focus on the results of the ICR stress tests in analyzing the impact on financial balance sheets. ICR is our preferred measure compared with solvency and cash flows because we can estimate and interpret the historical relationship of the NPA ratios more directly. It should be noted that alternative assumptions regarding the distressed debt and NPAs should not matter for the *relative* impact of the shocks on bank and nonbank balance sheets (e.g., by bank type). As a robustness check, we also consider alternative mappings between an increase in debt-at-risk and NPAs in our analysis.

Results

Corporate stress could have a sizable impact on bank and NBFC balance sheets, especially in the two adverse scenarios. In the absence of policy support, for banks, the pre-shock capital adequacy ratio of 14.7 percent could decline to 12.3 percent in the baseline scenario, to 10.3 percent in the moderately adverse scenario, and to 8.4 percent in the severely adverse scenario. Similarly, for NBFCs, the capital ratio would decline from the relatively higher starting level of 19.1 percent to 17.6 percent in the baseline, to 16.6 percent in the moderately adverse scenario, and to 15.3 percent in the severely adverse scenario (Figure 9.10). As mentioned previously, given a lack of access to confidential

Figure 9.9. Mapping Corporate Stress to Financial Sector Balance Sheets

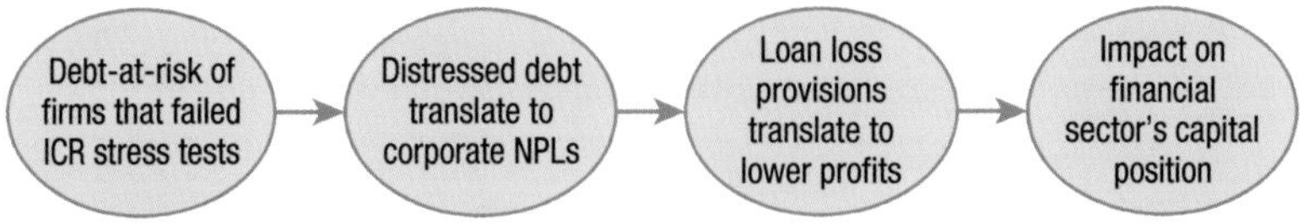

Source: Authors.
Note: ICR = interest coverage ratio; NPLs = nonperforming loans.

Figure 9.10. Impact of Corporate Stress and Policies on Financial Sector Balance Sheets
(Percent)

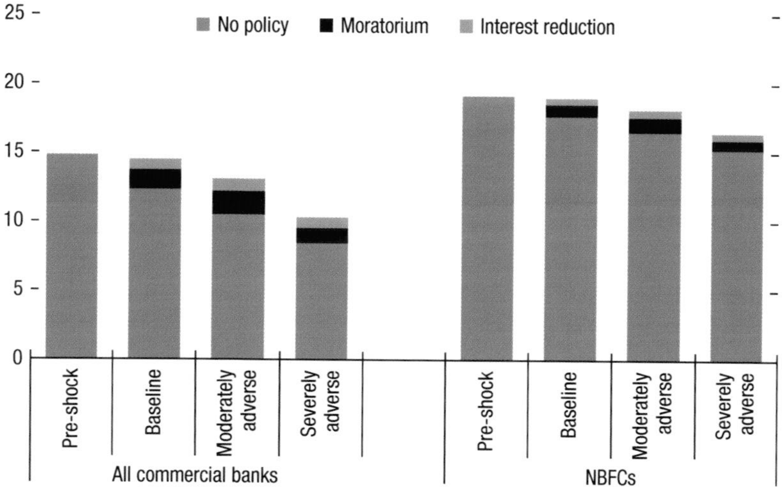

Sources: CMIE Prowess database; Reserve Bank of India; and authors' calculations.
Note: NBFCs = nonbanking financial companies.

supervisory data on the structure of corporate loans, the better performance of the NBFC sector compared with banks is largely driven by their stronger starting capital position.

As we have seen previously in the corporate stress test results, the moratorium is highly effective in cushioning the corporate liquidity stress. Similarly, these policy measures have also provided some buffer to bank and NBFC solvency positions. With policy support, for the banking sector, the capital ratio would only decline to 14.5 percent under the baseline scenario, and to 10.3 percent under the most adverse scenario, which is above the regulatory minimum. Similarly, the capital adequacy for the NBFC sector would only decline to 16.4 percent in the most adverse scenario. Overall, with policy support, the systemwide capital adequacy ratio for the banking sector would remain above the regulatory requirement in the baseline and the most adverse scenario (Figure 9.10). As mentioned previously, we consider different mappings between an increase in debt-at-risk and NPAs as a robustness check and find that our results are robust to alternative specifications (Annex Figure 9.2.5).

We also consider the impact of corporate stress on different segments of the banking sector. Here we present the results with policy support, but the relative performance of the three types of banks is similar in the case without policy support. Under the baseline scenario, all three segments of the banking sector would meet the regulatory minimum with or without policy support. Under the most adverse scenario, PSBs would not meet the regulatory minimum even with policy

Figure 9.11. Impact of Corporate Stress on Bank Balance Sheets by Bank Type
(Percent)

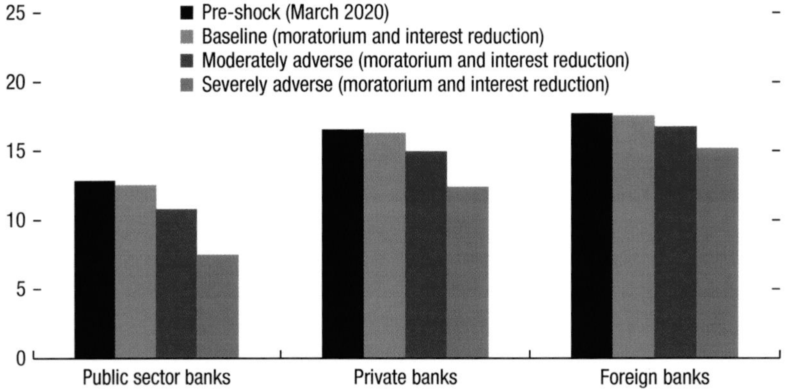

Legend:
- Pre-shock (March 2020)
- Baseline (moratorium and interest reduction)
- Moderately adverse (moratorium and interest reduction)
- Severely adverse (moratorium and interest reduction)

Categories: Public sector banks, Private banks, Foreign banks

Sources: CMIE Prowess database; Reserve Bank of India; and authors' calculations.

support, with the capital adequacy ratio declining from 12.9 percent to 7.5 percent (Figure 9.11). The weaker performance of the PSBs is in part driven by their weaker starting position compared with private banks and foreign banks (Figure 9.8).

MULTIYEAR CORPORATE STRESS TEST

Scenarios

In the multiyear stress tests, we consider two scenarios (by economic sector) over the period 2020–23. The baseline scenario follows the July 2021 *World Economic Outlook* projections. The adverse scenario reflects a more protracted recovery, where the economy experiences persistent low growth for a few years after the initial impact of the pandemic, driven by future waves of the pandemic and consequently a slow recovery in services and industrial sectors.

Figure 9.12 presents the aggregate GDP growth path under the multiperiod baseline and adverse scenarios. The difference between the two growth paths is largest in 2021, when GDP growth experiences a rebound of about 9.5 percent under the baseline scenario versus only 7.5 percent under the adverse path. The two scenarios gradually converge in subsequent years, with growth at about 1 and 0.5 percentage points lower in 2022 and 2023, respectively, under the adverse scenario. At the sectoral level, we assume that the lower growth in the adverse scenario is driven by a slow recovery in services and industrial sectors, particularly in contact-intensive services, construction, and manufacturing sectors.

Figure 9.12. Growth Paths in Multiperiod Scenarios

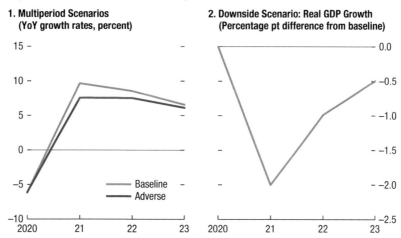

Sources: Flexible System of Global Models simulations; and IMF, July 2021 *World Economic Outlook Update.*
Note: pt = point; YoY = year over year.

Methodology

We apply the ICR and equity stress tests described in the Methodology section under "Single-Year Corporate Stress Tests" and adjust to the multiyear setting by applying sectoral GDP growth as sales shocks for each year in a cumulative manner. We assume that the temporary policy measures, including loan moratorium and interest rate reduction, are reflected in the first year (2020) in both the baseline and adverse scenarios, and a gradual tapering of policy measures in subsequent years. Specifically, we assume that policy measures to ease funding conditions (TLTRO and credit guarantee schemes for MSMEs) are withdrawn after the first year, together with an expiration of loan repayment moratorium, and a normalization of policy rates gradually over the period of the analysis. The end-of-year metric for the first year would, therefore, be the same as the results for the single-year stress tests under the baseline scenario with all policies.

For years 2021–23, we compute the end-of-year ICR and equity using equations (9.3) and (9.7), but using the values computed for the preceding year for $EBIT_{i,t}$, *retained earnings*$_{i,t}$, and *equity*$_{i,t}$. We assume that all borrower-support policies, such as the loan moratorium, have expired by then and have not been reintroduced. Regarding the path of the interest rates, we assume a gradual normalization of interest rates under both the baseline and the adverse scenarios.

Results

The forward-looking multiperiod corporate stress tests suggest that the impact of the COVID-19 shock will depend crucially on the speed of the

Figure 9.13. Multiperiod Analysis—Impact on Corporate Liquidity
(Percent of total corporate debt outstanding)

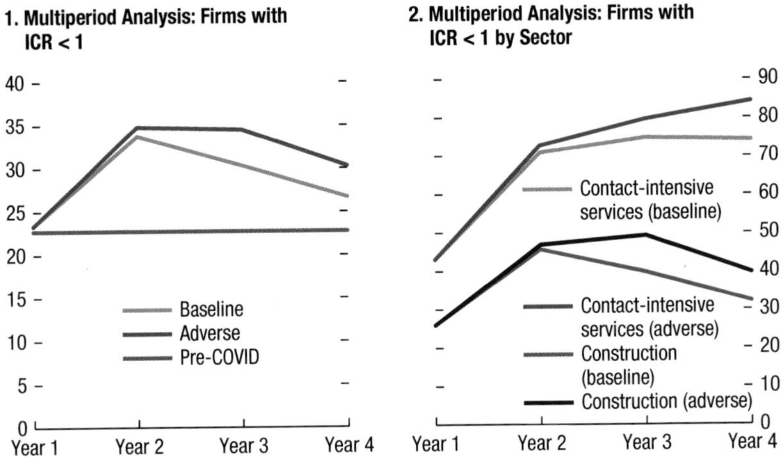

Sources: CMIE Prowess database; and authors' calculations.
Note: ICR = interest coverage ratio.

economic recovery. Under the baseline scenario, overall corporate performance deteriorates in the second year before improving gradually to close to pre–COVID-19 levels by the end of 2023. Specifically, the share of total corporate debt outstanding with an ICR below 1 increased from 22.7 percent to about 33.7 percent in the second year under the baseline scenario, before moderating to 26.7 percent by the end of 2023. However, a slower pace of recovery could lead to persistently high levels of debt-at-risk and a prolonged impact in services and industrial sectors. For example, the share of debt-at-risk would remain at about 30.3 percent by the end of 2023 under the adverse scenario, with more persistent impact on sectors such as contact-intensive services and construction sectors (Figure 9.13).

For the equity stress test, the share of total corporate debt outstanding with an ICR below 1 would rise in both the baseline and adverse scenarios by the end of four-year horizon. The impact on equity is quite persistent, even in the baseline scenario, as it takes time to offset an initial large negative earnings shock on firm equity. It should be noted that those policy measures are intended to provide temporary support to firm liquidity, and, therefore, their mitigating impact on firm equity is quite muted. Under the adverse scenario, the debt-at-risk would rise to about 14.8 percent by the end of the four years. By sector, contact-intensive services and industrial sectors such as manufacturing are also among the most affected sectors (Figure 9.14).

Figure 9.14. Multiperiod Analysis—Impact on Corporate Solvency
(Percent of total corporate debt outstanding)

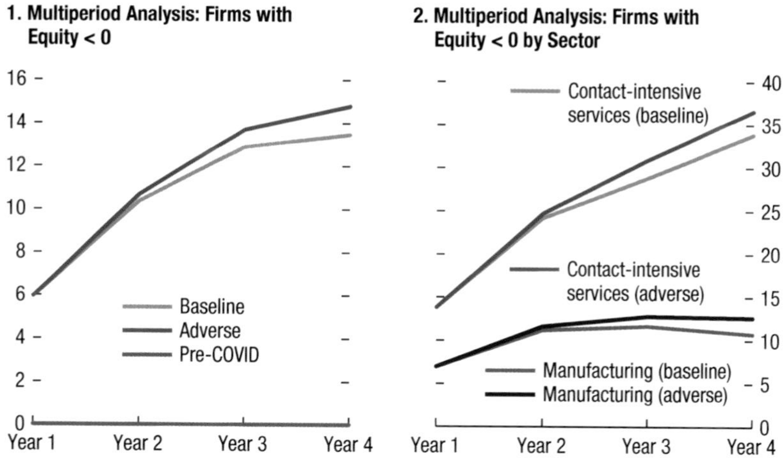

1. Multiperiod Analysis: Firms with Equity < 0

2. Multiperiod Analysis: Firms with Equity < 0 by Sector

Baseline
Adverse
Pre-COVID

Contact-intensive services (baseline)
Contact-intensive services (adverse)
Manufacturing (baseline)
Manufacturing (adverse)

Sources: CMIE Prowess database; and authors' calculations.

CONCLUSION

In this chapter, we conduct a series of stress tests to assess the resilience of India's corporate sector against COVID-19–related shocks. The corporate stress test results reveal a differential impact across sectors with the most severe impact on contact-intensive services, construction, and manufacturing sectors, and on MSMEs. Temporary policy measures have been particularly effective in supporting firm liquidity, but the impact on solvency is less pronounced, in part reflecting the focus of these measures on liquidity relief. On financial sector balance sheets, we found that PSBs are more vulnerable to stress in the corporate sector, partly due to their weaker starting positions. Our results also show that the impact of the COVID-19 shock on the corporate sector will depend on the speed of recovery. Persistent low growth could exacerbate scarring from the pandemic, especially in services and industrial sectors.

These results point to several important policy implications. On corporate sector policies, targeted support to viable corporate sectors should continue, particularly with the heightened uncertainty regarding the future course of the pandemic. Additional targeted support to viable firms in the most vulnerable sectors could be considered, including through additional relief measures. To ensure lenders follow appropriate standards when assessing borrowers' viability, supervisors should apply enhanced monitoring, including collection of more granular data and analyses of a broad range of corporate performance indicators.

At the same time, policies facilitating the exit of nonviable firms are also warranted. The authorities should work proactively in developing a contingency plan to address a potential increase in insolvency cases. Reforms in the existing framework are needed to reduce costs and the time of exit for nonviable firms. For example, introducing hybrid restructuring schemes and a simpler out-of-court restructuring process for MSMEs could facilitate timely resolution of stressed assets. Structural issues, such as existing gaps in access to finance for MSMEs, may need to be addressed in the medium term to minimize scarring, thus enabling a robust recovery.

Financial sector policies need to shift to encourage banks to build capital buffers and to recognize problem loans. To avoid loan evergreening, financial regulators should ensure that the loans benefiting from COVID-19–related restructuring schemes continue to be closely monitored and have proper provisioning. In addition, it would be important to ensure adequate capitalization in the financial system, particularly in PSBs, to deal with a potential rise in corporate insolvencies.

ANNEX 9.1. DATA AND CALIBRATION OF PARAMETERS

ANNEX TABLE 9.1.1.

Variables from the Prowess Database Used in Stress Tests

Variable	Proxy in Prowess	Comments
$EBIT_{i,t}$	interest_cover*total_interest_exp	We derive the EBIT variable from the ICR ratio (*interest_cover*) reported in Prowess by multiplying it by total interest expense (*total_ interest_exp*).
net sales$_{i,t}$	net_sales	
material costs$_{i,t}$	cost_of_goods_sold - 0.7* compensation_to_employees	We compute the material costs from the *cost_ of_goods_sold* variable, which according to the data definition also includes 70 percent of compensation costs.
wage costs$_{i,t}$	compensation_to_employees	
interest expense$_{i,t}$	total_interest_exp	
cash balance$_{i,t}$	cash_bal	
current assets$_{i,t}$	current_assets_incl_st_invest	
current liabilities$_{i,t}$	current_liabilities	
equity$_{i,t}$	total_capital	
tax rate$_{i,t+1}$	exp_total_taxes/(pbit-total_ interest_exp)	We compute the median effective tax rate in the sample as the ratio of total tax expenditure to earnings before taxes but after interest expenses. The value we obtain is equal to 27.5 percent.
ST borrowing$_{i,t}$	short_term_borrowings	Short-term debt: used in policy analysis, see next section
debt$_{i,t}$	debt	Total debt outstanding: used in policy analysis, see next section

Source: Authors' calculations.
Note: EBIT = earnings before interest and taxes ; ICR = interest coverage ratio; ST = short-term.

ANNEX TABLE 9.1.2.

Key Parameters

Parameter	Value (percent) Baseline	Moderate	Adverse	Comments
x	Sector specific	Sector specific	Sector specific	Calibration of the shocks to net sales in each scenario is reported in Figure 9.4.
y	90	100	100	In the baseline scenario, we assume that firms treat the shock as transitory and adjust spending on material costs by less than the decline in net sales. In the moderately adverse and severely adverse scenarios, a decline in material costs is assumed to be proportional to the decline in net sales.
z	0	12.5	25	In the baseline scenario, we assume that firms treat the shock as transitory and do not reduce wages or lay off workers. In the moderately adverse and severely adverse scenarios, compensation costs are assumed to decline by 12.5 and 25 percent, respectively.

Source: Authors' calculations.

ANNEX TABLE 9.1.3.

Key Policy-Related Parameters

Parameter	Value (percent) Baseline	Moderate	Adverse	Comments
u	(0.64*115 bp)/ (total_interest_exp/debt)			The decline in interest expenses is proportional to the decline in the effective interest rate (equal to *total_interest_exp/debt*) due to the reduction in the RBI policy rate (115 bp), where we additionally assume that (1) only 80 percent of the policy rate reduction was passed to lending rates, and (2) the share of variable rate loans (i.e., loans that could benefit from the interest reduction) is 80 percent.
w	15			The share of firm debt and interest payments that could be delayed due to the loan moratorium. We assume that approximately 30 percent of corporates used moratorium and that it applied to half of annual debt and interest payments, because the moratorium lasted for half a year.
s	25			The share of long-term debt due in the current year, based on the average maturity of long-term debt of the firms in the Prowess Database.
η_L	100	90	80	The share of large corporates' short-term borrowings that can be rolled over. In the baseline scenario, large corporates can extend all debt payments due, reflecting easy financial conditions thanks to RBI interventions, and only 80 percent in the adverse scenario, reflecting a negative risk-aversion shock and flight to safety despite policy measures.
η_{MSME}	20			The size of the new lending under the credit guarantee scheme for MSMEs, in percent of the total debt outstanding. We also incorporate an eligibility criterion based on total debt outstanding, which should not exceed Rs500 million.

Source: Authors' calculations.
Note: MSME = micro, small, and medium enterprise; RBI = Reserve Bank of India.

ANNEX 9.2. ADDITIONAL RESULTS AND ROBUSTNESS CHECKS

Annex Figure 9.2.1. Single-Period Stress Test—Impact on Cash Flow by Sector
(Percent of total corporate debt outstanding)

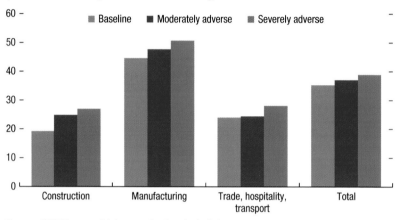

Sources: CMIE Prowess database; and authors' calculations.

Annex Figure 9.2.2. Robustness Checks: Firms with ICR < 1 (Alternative Assumptions on Sales Shocks)
(Percent of total debt outstanding)

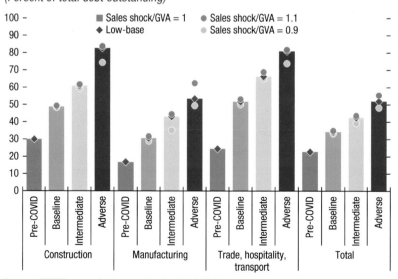

Sources: CMIE Prowess database; and authors' calculations.
Note: GVA = gross value added; ICR = interest coverage ratio.

Annex Figure 9.2.3. Single-Period Stress Test—Detailed Impact of Policies on the ICR
(Percent of total corporate debt outstanding issued by firms with ICR < 1)

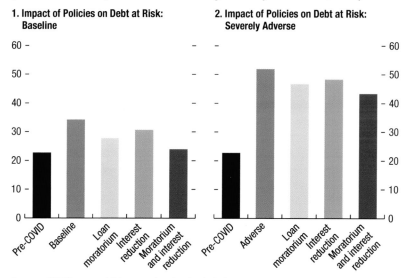

Sources: CMIE Prowess database; and authors' calculations.
Note: ICR = interest coverage ratio.

Annex Figure 9.2.4. Single-Period Stress Test—Detailed Impact of Policies on Cash Flows
(Percent of total corporate debt outstanding issued by firms with cash flow < 0)

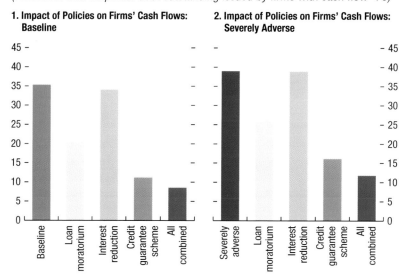

Sources: CMIE Prowess database; and authors' calculations.

Annex Figure 9.2.5. Robustness Checks (Alternative Assumptions on NPA Increase)
(Percent)

**Impact of Corporate Stress on Policies and Financial Sector Capital Ratios
(Delta NPA ratio/delta debt-at-risk = 0.5)**

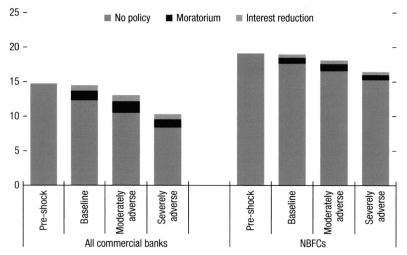

Sources: CMIE Prowess database; and authors' calculations.
Note: NBFCs = nonbanking financial companies; NPA = nonperforming assets.

REFERENCES

Bank of England. 2020. "Financial Stability Report," August 2020.

Bank of Japan. 2020. "Financial System Report," October 2020.

Bank of Japan. 2021. "Financial System Report," April 2021.

Caceres, Carlos, Diego Cerdeiro, Dan Pan, and Suchanan Tambunlertchai. 2020. "Stress Testing U.S. Leveraged Corporates in a COVID-19 World." IMF Working Paper 20/238, International Monetary Fund, Washington, DC.

Core, Fabrizio, and Filippo De Marco. 2021. "Public Guarantees for Small Businesses in Italy During COVID-19." CEPR Discussion Paper DP15799, March 2.

Diez, Federico J., Romain A. Duval, Jiayue Fan, Jose M. Garrido, Sebnem Kalemli-Ozcan, Chiara Maggi, Maria Soledad Martinez-Peria, and Nicola Pierri. 2021. "Insolvency Prospects Among Small-and-Medium-Sized Enterprises in Advanced Economies: Assessment and Policy Options." IMF Staff Discussion Notes 21/002, International Monetary Fund, Washington, DC.

Ebeke, Christian H., Nemanja Jovanovic, Laura Valderrama, and Jing Zhou. 2021. "Corporate Liquidity and Solvency in Europe during COVID-19: The Role of Policies." IMF Working Paper 21/56, International Monetary Fund, Washington, DC.

Elenev, Vadim, Tim Landvoigt, and Stijn Van Nieuwerburgh. 2020. "Can the Covid Bailouts Save the Economy?" NBER Working Paper w27207, National Bureau of Economic Research, Cambridge, MA.

Iorgova, Silvia. 2017. "Corporate and Banking Sector Vulnerabilities in India, India: Selected Issues." IMF Country Report 17/55, International Monetary Fund, Washington, DC.

Lindner, Peter, and Sung Eun Jung. 2014. "Corporate Vulnerabilities in India and Banks' Loan Performance." IMF Working Paper 14/232, International Monetary Fund, Washington, DC.

Oura, Hiroko, and Petia Topalova. 2009. "India's Corporate Sector: Coping with the Global Financial Tsunami, India: Selected Issues." IMF Country Report 09/186, International Monetary Fund, Washington, DC.

Tressel, Thierry, and Xiaodan Ding. 2021. "Global Corporate Stress Tests—Impact of the COVID-19 Pandemic and Policy Responses." IMF Working Paper 21/212, International Monetary Fund, Washington, DC.

CHAPTER 10

Strengthening Private Debt Resolution Frameworks

José M. Garrido and Anjum Rosha

INTRODUCTION

In any vibrant and dynamic economy, companies and households make investment decisions about an uncertain future. Although these investments are critical to foster economic growth, some of them will not yield the expected outcomes, making effective private debt resolution or insolvency frameworks critical to allow for an orderly and efficient resolution of debt overhangs. Such frameworks are particularly important for the financial system to ensure that credit is allocated to the most productive part of the economy.

In the case of India, the legal and business environment applicable to corporate and personal insolvency is complex. The vast majority of businesses in India are micro, small, and medium enterprises (MSMEs) that are not incorporated and that frequently struggle to access credit from the formal banking system (see Chapter 3). At the same time, large and often highly leveraged corporate groups comprise the lion's share of the banking system's loan exposure. Consumer credit from the formal banking system, particularly unsecured credit such as credit card debt, is a relatively new phenomenon in India but has grown exponentially in the last two decades.

Until 2016, corporate insolvency relied on a patchwork of inefficient laws, and personal insolvency was regulated by obsolete procedures from the colonial period. The enactment of the Insolvency and Bankruptcy Code (IBC) in 2016 has been a major milestone establishing an insolvency procedure for both corporates and individuals.[1]

This chapter discusses the strengths of the new Indian legal framework for insolvency and makes recommendations for overcoming some gaps that remain.[2] After introducing the elements of the legal toolkit for private debt resolution, the first section describes the legal reforms in India, the second section analyzes debt restructuring mechanisms, and the third section focuses on corporate resolution and liquidation. The fourth section elaborates on the institutional framework, the

---

[1] The insolvency procedure for individuals has not become effective yet.

[2] As this book went to press, the Ministry of Corporate Affairs had released a proposal to make the insolvency regime significantly more efficient and transparent.

fifth section gives special consideration to MSME insolvency, and the sixth section makes recommendations for further reforms. The final section offers a conclusion.

THE LEGAL TOOLBOX

Frameworks that deal effectively with corporate insolvency are critical, particularly in an emerging market economy like India. A well-functioning insolvency framework can enable financial creditors to assume risks while pricing them appropriately. It can help enhance the value of creditors' claims and help unlock capital that financial institutions can use to support fresh lending and optimize credit availability and growth, as well as lower the cost of such access to credit for entrepreneurs. The predictability fostered by such a system may also serve to exercise considerable discipline on the enterprise sector and on individual debtors themselves. As such, an efficient insolvency framework can increase financial stability, boost both domestic and foreign investment, and raise overall economic growth.

International standards provide the touchstone against which enterprise insolvency regimes can be assessed. International best practice[3] suggests that effective and efficient legal frameworks for enterprise debt resolution promote expeditious restructuring of viable firms and speedy liquidation of nonviable firms. A modern system of insolvency facilitates decision making by creditors in restructuring or liquidating insolvent corporations on a case-by-case basis, depending on whether the preservation of the business offers a better economic outcome than its liquidation. It also supports implementation of those decisions through appropriate and time-bound procedures. The World Bank and United Nations Commission on International Trade Law (UNCITRAL) have recently developed specific guidance for the insolvency of micro and small enterprises (UNCITRAL 2021; World Bank 2021). Unlike in the case of enterprise insolvency, guidance in the area of personal insolvency law is more limited (INSOL 2001, 2011; World Bank 2014), yet lessons can be drawn from an increasingly rich body of cross-country experience in this area. And there is a general consensus that modern personal insolvency frameworks should include a fresh start for overindebted individuals after liquidating the debtor's assets and/or following some period of repayment.

Legal tools to address insolvency can include a variety of procedures and techniques. Formal procedures for debt enforcement, restructuring, and liquidation are typically provided through legislation and entail judicial supervision through an *in-court* process that usually involves all stakeholders—that is, all secured and all unsecured creditors including the state and employees, as well as the debtor. *Out-of-court* debt restructuring frameworks offer greater flexibility, can be cheaper, and involve an informal process that requires voluntary

---

[3] International best practice for enterprise insolvency refers to (1) the UNCITRAL Legislative Guide on Insolvency Law (2004, and successive supplements) and (2) the World Bank Principles for Effective Insolvency and Creditor/Debtor Regimes (2021).

Figure 10.1. Continuum of Legal Instruments

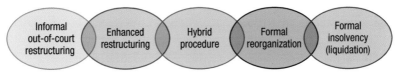

Source: Garrido (2012).

compromises between parties, which typically includes a small subset of the creditor body. *Enhanced* out-of-court procedures use creditor committees and arbitration/mediation (under *ex-ante* framework agreements) to facilitate debt restructuring. *Hybrid* procedures typically provide for negotiations and majority voting to take place out of court and prior to any filing, with a plan submitted for judicial ratification at the final stage of the process. Figure 10.1 illustrates the continuum of instruments provided by modern insolvency systems to address over-indebtedness.

The institutions necessary for the smooth functioning of the insolvency framework also warrant mention. The judiciary, through courts and tribunals, plays a central role, supported by insolvency professionals. An insolvency framework may rely on mediators and, in many cases for consumer insolvency, a dedicated administrative authority. Other institutions support the functioning of the regime, including credit information systems, land and collateral registers, debt counseling services, and legal aid clinics.

In a crisis, the standard market-based toolkit for debt resolution may need to be temporarily supplemented or modified and the state may play a more active role for a time. In the context of general economic shocks such as that caused by the COVID-19 pandemic, debt resolution strategies need to be coordinated with fiscal and financial policies. During such periods, there are three potential phases and key measures for effective corporate and household debt resolution: (1) there might be the need for *interim measures* to halt insolvency and debt enforcement activity; (2) in cases of a severe crisis, *transitional measures* may be required to respond to the wave of insolvency cases, including special out-of-court restructuring mechanisms; and (3) a phase in which countries strengthen their *regular debt resolution tools* to address the remaining debt overhang and support economic growth (Liu, Garrido, and DeLong 2020). In response to the COVID-19 pandemic, the Indian authorities temporarily suspended all insolvency applications under the IBC. The Reserve Bank of India (RBI) also issued COVID-19–specific guidance to banks. These measures are discussed below.

PRIVATE DEBT RESOLUTION REFORMS IN INDIA

The enactment of the IBC was an important milestone aimed at improving the business environment in India and attracting increased domestic and foreign direct investment. Past attempts at reform had faltered for a variety of reasons, including political challenges, multiplicity of authorities, and the prevalence of a sectorial approach to insolvency. Concerns about the rising level of nonperforming loans in public sector banks, a string of high-profile insolvency cases, and the desire to improve the business environment provided much needed impetus for the IBC. Through the reforms, authorities also aim to create a supportive environment for the development of a corporate bond market (see Chapter 5) and to boost the distressed debt market. The Bankruptcy Law Reform Committee was constituted in 2014, submitted its final report in 2015, and the Insolvency and Bankruptcy Code was adopted in 2016 after a relatively uneventful passage through both houses of parliament. The authorities have stated that the IBC "consolidates and amends the laws relating to reorganization and insolvency resolution of corporate persons, partnership firms and individuals in a time bound manner for maximization of the value of assets of such persons, to promote entrepreneurship, availability of credit and balance the interests of all the stakeholders."[4]

Prior to the enactment of the IBC, no clear policy or comprehensive legislation existed for corporate insolvency that aimed to rescue viable businesses and speedily liquidate unviable businesses. Insolvency was dealt with through piecemeal and inadequate legislation including the Companies Act of 1956 and the Sick Industrial Companies (Special Provisions) Act, the Securitization and Reconstruction of Financial Assets and Enforcement of Security Interests Act, and the Recovery of Debts Due to Banks and Financial Institutions Act, to name a few. Under these laws, debt recovery was time consuming, expensive, uncertain, and prone to abuse by debtors. The courts contributed to this outcome with their decisions (van Zwieten 2014). As a result, bank lending tended to be largely secured, quite expensive, and not always readily available for small businesses.

Private debt resolution was plagued with issues before the IBC was enacted. In the past, in case of a default, one of two outcomes was typical—creditors could either "extend and pretend" by "evergreening"[5] loans, or they could immediately enforce collateral without any assessment of the viability of the debtor's business. The RBI's rules for provisioning of nonperforming assets (NPAs) at the time contributed to the extend-and-pretend culture.[6] In addition, public sector bank officials hesitated to write-down loans, including for fear of liability for dissipation of state assets under anticorruption laws. The long delays and severe backlog of cases in the courts also historically made it difficult for creditors to collect on debt in arrears in India. Institutional limitations such as the absence of an insolvency practitioner's profession compounded the weak enforcement and business rescue culture.

---

[4] IBBI website: https://www.ibbi.gov.in/about.

[5] Evergreening of loans refers to banks trying to keep a loan in good standing that is on the verge of default by providing further loans to the same borrower.

[6] For quite some time, the provisioning rules permitted a nonperforming loan to be reclassified as "performing" immediately upon restructuring without requiring a demonstrated period of performance.

The IBC brought about much-needed modernization to this environment. Although the IBC draws inspiration from English law in a few areas, it also includes some novel features. It consolidates the procedures for corporate debt restructuring and liquidation (as well as the yet-to-be effective personal insolvency procedures) in a single piece of legislation. It has a number of features that are consistent with international best practice:

1. *Corporate rescue:* The procedure includes a moratorium on enforcement by secured creditors, procedures that facilitate decision making through a creditors committee, and court confirmation of a debt restructuring plan agreed by a supermajority of creditors.

2. *Time-bound process:* Clear procedural deadlines are specified at every stage in the insolvency process.

3. *Wrongful trading liability for corporate directors:* This concept, similar to English law and recommended by the international standard, assigns liability to directors in cases where no reasonable prospect exists for the company to avoid liquidation and the directors have taken no steps to minimize losses to the company's creditors.

4. *Other features:* As is the trend in many countries, both federal and state taxes do not receive a high priority in the distribution of the proceeds of liquidation. The IBC also includes a personal insolvency procedure, which is not yet implemented. The IBC continues to be refined: eight reforms of the IBC have occurred since its adoption in 2016 based on lessons from experience with the IBC and emerging issues.

The IBC also introduced several important improvements to the institutional framework:

1. *Establishment of an insolvency regulator:* The Insolvency and Bankruptcy Board of India (IBBI) is a unique and powerful body, combining rule-making powers and supervisory and disciplinary powers over participants in the insolvency ecosystem.

2. *Insolvency professionals:* Influenced by the British model, the IBC permits the establishment of insolvency professional agencies that perform the functions of self-regulatory organizations of groups of insolvency professionals under the overall supervision of the IBBI.

3. *Specialized commercial courts (National Company Law Tribunals) for insolvency cases:* The tribunals were established under the Companies Act of 2013, and the IBC provides them with jurisdiction over insolvency cases.

4. *Information utilities and valuers:* The IBC includes other actors in the insolvency ecosystem that go beyond what is found in other countries. Information utilities provide reliable information on defaults and financial claims, whereas valuers perform an important role in corporate resolution.

There are certain aspects of the IBC that could be strengthened. They include:

- *The treatment of operational creditors in corporate resolution:* The IBC distinguishes between financial creditors and operational creditors. Operational creditors are defined in the IBC as those providing goods and services. Although operational creditors are permitted to initiate an insolvency proceeding[7] and may, in certain circumstances, participate in the creditors committee as observers,[8] they may not vote on any of the decisions made by the creditors committee, including on the appointment of insolvency administrators or on the restructuring plan. The lack of rights of operational creditors could raise questions regarding the fairness of corporate resolution.

- *Ambitious timelines for corporate resolution:* The timelines provided for corporate resolution under the IBC have proven quite ambitious: 180 days for ordinary cases (extendable by 90 additional days) and 90 days for fast-track cases (extendable by 45 additional days). These deadlines require significant institutional support, even without taking into account the use and abuse of appeals and challenges: currently, procedures are taking considerably longer.

- *Lack of procedures for MSMEs:* The original design of the IBC included the fast-track procedure, but the procedure includes the same formalities and steps as ordinary resolution, with the deadlines cut by half. This might be inadequate for MSMEs and appears to have motivated the latest reform of the IBC, that is, the introduction of pre-pack insolvency.

The IBC also introduced procedures for personal insolvency, but these have not yet come into effect (Box 10.1). The main objective of these procedures is to provide a fresh start for overindebted individuals by granting them a debt discharge under certain conditions. Due to the social implications of this reform, and the need to develop adequate infrastructure for its application, the effective entry into force of this part of the IBC has not materialized. In the absence of a personal insolvency procedure, the resolution of debts of individuals continues to take place through enforcement procedures.

Financial institutions benefit from a special regime: since 1993, the Recovery of Debts Due to Banks and Financial Institutions Act.[9] The Debt Recovery Tribunals provide a special judicial venue for the recovery of financial claims.

---

[7] An operational creditor can initiate an insolvency proceeding only after it has delivered a demand notice or copy of an invoice demanding payment of the defaulted amount to the corporate debtor and such demand is not repaid or disputed by the corporate debtor within ten (10) days of such notice/invoice. Accordingly, if a corporate debtor delivers a dispute notice to the operational creditor, the operational creditor needs to resort to other remedies available to it under contract, under law, or in equity.

[8] Operational creditors can participate in the creditors committee only if their aggregate claims are not less than 10 percent and through a single observer representing the interests of all operational creditors.

[9] Debt Recovery Tribunals have jurisdiction for claims of at least Rs2 million. For smaller financial debts, financial institutions can resort to the people's courts (Lok Adalats).

> ### Box 10.1. Debt Resolution Process under the IBC
>
> - **The IBC provides for corporate resolution and liquidation.** These procedures are accessible to debtors and creditors on default, incorporate a broad stay of creditor actions, and prioritize reorganization plans over liquidation. Resolution professionals displace the corporate debtor's management, and financial creditors have a decisive influence over the resolution procedure. Originally, the resolution procedure was designed to be concluded within 180 days with a possible extension of 90 days being granted by the court. A fast-track version for low-value cases includes the same process but the timeline is compressed to 90 days, with a possible extension of 45 days. Liquidation is the last resort in the IBC system and has no time limits for its operation.
> - **The IBC introduces procedures for personal insolvency.** The law repeals the outdated laws of the pre-independence period and incorporates personal insolvency procedures influenced by current English law, which include:
>   - (i) A "fresh start" procedure, similar to the United Kingdom's debt relief order. This procedure allows a natural person to obtain a quick discharge, and it only applies to cases where the debtor has low income (Rs60,000 or less), virtually no assets, and limited unsecured debt (Rs35,000).
>   - (ii) An insolvency resolution process for natural persons, which provides for a repayment plan prepared with the assistance of an insolvency professional.
>   - (iii) A traditional bankruptcy procedure based on the liquidation of the debtor's estate.
>
> In all cases, the debtor has the opportunity of discharging its debts on completion of the procedure, with the exception of "excluded debts" (fines, tort claims, alimony, and student loans).
>
> Source: Authors.
> Note: IBC = Insolvency and Bankruptcy Code; Rs = rupees.

Over time, the procedure at the Debt Recovery Tribunals has been streamlined, but a key constraint is the capacity to deal with the elevated number of cases.

Secured credit can be enforced out of court by financial institutions. The Securitisation and Reconstruction of Financial Assets and Enforcement of Security Interest Act, adopted in 2002, includes a system for the creation and registration of charges, and allows financial institutions to enforce those security interests without any court intervention. This remains one of the most efficient tools for the recovery of loans in India.

In response to the pandemic, filings under the IBC were temporarily suspended during March 2020–March 2021 and a six-month moratorium on loan repayments was introduced between March and August 2020. These interim measures aimed to avoid the insolvency of large numbers of enterprises experiencing liquidity problems as a result of the pandemic-related lockdown measures and temporary supply chain issues. The suspension of all filings under the IBC—including voluntary filings—went somewhat beyond the temporary pandemic response measures taken by other countries. Most other countries that introduced similar measures (Australia, Singapore, UK, and others) continued to permit the commencement of insolvency cases by debtor companies seeing such procedures as "protective" of businesses in trouble. Although the suspension of creditor petitions can be justified on the grounds that enterprises experiencing liquidity problems because of the restrictions of the pandemic need breathing room, it might have been beneficial to allow enterprises that need a corporate resolution process to preserve the viability of the business to access insolvency procedures.

DEBT RESTRUCTURING

From a legal perspective, corporate debt restructuring is possible in several different ways. At one end of the spectrum are purely voluntary or informal arrangements that take place fully out of court, whereas at the other end are formal insolvency procedures involving judicial involvement and supervision, with hybrid options falling in between.

Following the adoption of the IBC, formal insolvency procedures have become the preferred tool for corporate debt resolution. It appears that the authorities have now ceased promoting out-of-court restructuring options and have largely focused on formal insolvency procedures in the IBC. The clear preference for formal reorganization procedures and limited use of informal options highlights the deep reliance on the National Company Law Tribunals, which, however, are quickly becoming overwhelmed with the volume of cases.

Informal restructuring options are available, but obstacles to their use persist. Informal restructuring requires close coordination among multiple creditors (particularly financial creditors), which can be challenging when creditors have different positions (e.g., different levels of provisioning in different banks) and diverging expectations on the recovery of the debtor and on the feasibility of providing additional financial support. Because informal restructuring requires unanimity in decision-making, the chances of reaching a restructuring agreement are reduced when multiple actors are involved. An additional challenge for out-of-court restructuring in India is that out-of-court schemes may not provide officials of public banks with the necessary immunity under anticorruption laws to engage in meaningful restructuring that requires the recognition of losses.

Enhanced restructuring refers to any technique that facilitates the agreement of creditors and debtors in an informal setting (for instance, incentives to restructuring, or the use of master restructuring agreements that facilitate majority agreement). The contractual out-of-court debt restructuring mechanism (known as the "CDR") sponsored by the RBI was an example of an enhanced restructuring procedure. It was discontinued and replaced by a myriad of schemes, which were then replaced in February 2018 by a generic framework for resolution of stressed assets.[10] The Supreme Court struck down the February 2018 circular establishing the generic framework for resolution,[11] and later, in June 2019,

---

[10] There is a deadline of 14 days for the admission of application. The average number of days taken for admission of applications is actually 13 days. This is a serious issue, because timely commencement of the process increases the chances for resolution, and severe risk of misconduct by the debtor exists during this period.

[11] Supreme Court of India, judgment of September 13, 2021. https://www.financialexpress.com/economy/sc-asks-insolvency-tribunals-to-stick-to-resolution-deadlines/2329587/.

the RBI put forward a prudential framework for the resolution of distressed assets that remains in place today.

Applicable to various financial institutions,[12] the prudential framework for the resolution of distressed assets sets out a framework for intercreditor collaboration. This RBI guidance encourages early action even before default, intercreditor agreements, agreeing on a resolution plan, and strategies for dealing with delayed implementation of an otherwise viable resolution plan.

However, the success of the RBI's restructuring schemes has been quite limited. The RBI's erstwhile out-of-court frameworks and schemes were not frequently used, likely due to their perceived lack of flexibility and because they suffered from one fundamental limitation—such frameworks operate in the shadow of the law, and they yield best results when they are backed by predictable results under a well-functioning formal insolvency framework. Absent such a formal framework that creditors can resort to, out-of-court techniques offer limited incentives for debtors. Instead, these schemes may have contributed to the practice of financial institutions engaging in the minimal rescheduling necessary for designating the exposure as "performing" from a prudential perspective (evergreening).

Hybrid restructuring has not been widely used in India. The Companies Act enables schemes of arrangement.[13] Similar to schemes under English law and other common law systems, a scheme of arrangement under Indian law is a compromise between the company on the one hand and its creditors and/or shareholders on the other hand. It is considered a hybrid restructuring procedure because it is based on negotiations between creditors and the debtor, with limited court intervention. A scheme can take the form of financial or corporate restructuring. For example, it may include restructuring of debt, and changes to the shareholding structure, sale of assets or the business itself, or a merger with another company. Once approved by the statutory majority of three-fourths in value (on a class basis) and ratified by the court, a scheme of arrangement is binding on all participants (including holdout creditors). Unlike insolvency procedures under the IBC, schemes of arrangement can be used by solvent corporates and can involve a targeted group of interested stakeholders. Although there is no automatic moratorium, the National Company Law Tribunals can grant a limited stay to prevent enforcement actions while a scheme of arrangement is being agreed. Unlike in the UK and Singapore, schemes of arrangement have not been used extensively for debt restructuring in India, but a few high-profile debt restructuring cases, such as *Arvind Mills Limited*, *BPL Limited*, and *Essar Oil Limited*, have demonstrated the usefulness of this process. One reason for the limited popularity of schemes of arrangement for debt restructuring in India could be the complex procedure requiring multiple court hearings, which creates significant scope for delays.

---

[12] The financial institutions covered are the Scheduled Commercial Banks (excluding Regional Rural Banks); all India Term Financial Institutions; Small Finance Banks; Systemically Important Non-Deposit taking Non-Banking Financial Companies; and Deposit taking Non-Banking Financial Companies. See Reserve Bank of India (Prudential Framework for Resolution of Stressed Assets) Directions 2019, para 3, available at https://www.rbi.org.in/Scripts/NotificationUser.aspx?Id=11580.

[13] See section 230(1) of the Companies Act, 2013.

There is thus considerable potential for more intensive use of informal and hybrid restructuring in India. Out-of-court restructuring and hybrid restructuring can achieve results with speed and efficiency and reduce the burden on the already backlogged National Company Law Tribunals. Hybrid restructuring, in particular, could offer a workable solution for many instances of corporate distress where financial restructuring is what is required. The fact that a court confirms the agreement reached by creditors could be instrumental in reducing the personal liability concerns that affect directors and officers of public banks.

CORPORATE RESOLUTION AND LIQUIDATION

Corporate insolvency under the IBC is based on a two-stage process that prioritizes corporate resolution over liquidation. The process potentially has two stages: (1) resolution, where creditors seek to agree on a plan to resolve the debtor's insolvency, and (2) liquidation, in case of failure of an attempted resolution process where parties cannot agree on a resolution plan within the deadlines set by the law.

Corporate resolution has become the most important insolvency proceeding in the new Indian system. Since the entry into force of the IBC, banks have resorted to corporate resolution as the preferred tool to deal with large corporate exposures. Corporate resolution is a creditor-centric process that seeks to promote a speedy outcome to resolve corporate debt distress. In a certain way, several features of corporate resolution appear to be designed in reaction to the problems of the previous insolvency regime in India: the abuse of process by recalcitrant debtors and the unlimited duration of insolvency proceedings being two key examples. To tackle those problems, corporate resolution puts the creditors in control of the procedure and establishes deadlines that increase the pressure to reach an agreement, with the threat of liquidation hanging over the participants.

The corporate resolution process is designed to restructure a company within a short timeline. The creditors must agree on a resolution plan within 180 days, extendable for 90 additional days and should not last more than a maximum of 330 days. To achieve this objective, the procedure follows a clear sequence with a demanding timeline (Box 10.2). This timeline has undergone minor modifications since 2016.

The corporate resolution process is driven by financial creditors. In the past *financial creditors* in India would be more likely to pursue an out-of-court enforcement action against assets they held as security for the debt. But now they are expected to lead the corporate resolution process and control its outcome. The resolution professional requires the approval of the super majority of the creditors' committee for most actions, and the fate of the company is ultimately decided by the financial creditors. Corporate resolution is used as a catalyst for reaching an agreement among creditors. The main effect of corporate resolution is to put pressure on all parties to reach an agreement over a resolution plan, faced with the threat of liquidation if that agreement is not concluded within the prescribed deadline.

Box 10.2. Corporate Resolution: Sequence and Timeline

- A creditor (financial or operational), or the debtor itself, presents an application to the National Company Law Tribunal.
- The National Company Law Tribunal decides on the application within 14 days.
- Once the National Company Law Tribunal opens the case (D0), the countdown of 180 days for the completion of the process starts. A moratorium is imposed for the duration of the process.
- The National Company Law Tribunal will appoint an interim Resolution Professional on the commencement date. In the case of a petition presented by a financial creditor, the court will appoint the professional designated by the creditor. The resolution professional takes control of the debtor's assets and business activity.
- The interim resolution professional will make a public announcement within three days of the appointment (D+3), providing the deadline for the submission of claims (D+14, but now it is possible to submit claims until D+90).
- The interim resolution professional appoints two registered valuers to calculate the liquidation value and the fair value, within seven days of the interim resolution professional's appointment (D+21), and no later than D+47.
- The verification of claims takes place within seven days of the deadline for the submission of claims (D+97 maximum).
- The interim resolution professional constitutes the committee of creditors, after collating the claims and determining the financial situation of the debtor. Report certifying constitution of the committee, two days after verification (D+23).
- The resolution professional files a report certifying the constitution of the committee, within two days from the verification of claims.
- The first meeting of the creditors committee is convened within seven days of the filing of the report (D+30). The creditors can confirm the resolution professional or appoint a new one, by a 66 percent majority.
- The resolution professional will prepare an information memorandum as specified by Insolvency and Bankruptcy Board of India regulations. Two weeks from appointment, no later than D+54.
- The resolution professional sends an invitation for expressions of interest in submitting a resolution plan.
- Financial creditors and resolution applicants can formulate resolution plans based on the information memorandum.
- The resolution professional checks compliance of the proposed resolution plans with the legal requirements and submits the plan to the vote of the Creditors' Committee.
- During the process, the resolution professional will manage the business and can take substantial decisions with the authorization of the Creditors' Committee (by a 66 percent majority).
- A resolution plan must be agreed among the financial creditors within 180 days by a 66 percent majority. If creditors agree, by a 66 percent majority, to continue the process, the resolution professional will submit a petition to the National Company Law Tribunals, and the tribunal may allow the negotiations to be extended for a maximum of 90 additional days.
- If no agreement exists over a resolution plan after 180 days (or after extension granted by the court, up to 330 days, which is the total limit for the conclusion of the process), and the National Company Law Tribunals has not received a plan for its approval, the court "shall order" the liquidation of the company.
- A resolution plan needs to be approved by the National Company Law Tribunal to be effective.

Source: Authors.

Speed is the main objective of the corporate resolution process. The legislative design is that of an extremely fast process, reliant on insolvency professionals and engaged financial creditors.

Initial implementation of corporate resolution focused on large corporate cases. Credit institutions started using the new procedures enthusiastically, prompted by the RBI. Initial practice was tilted toward the use of insolvency proceedings as a tool to acquire large companies. For instance, Essar Steel India Limited was acquired by Arcelor Mittal India Pvt. Ltd. Other high-profile acquisitions include Bhushan Steel Limited, Bhushan Power & Steel Limited, Jaypee Infratech Limited, Alok Industries Limited, and others. The focus on acquisitions appeared to be facilitated by the competitive process to submit resolution plans (Handa 2020). The outcome of the process tends to be a sale of the business rather than a reorganization of the enterprise. Corporate resolution appears much less effective as a tool for operational restructuring.

Experience with the IBC highlighted several issues in practice. Some of these issues have been tackled through amendments to the IBC and regulations, but many challenges remain. A few of them shed light on broader issues and pertain to the roles of creditors and debtors in the process, and limitations in the IBC, such as the treatment of executory contracts, enterprise groups, and cross-border insolvency. Others are of a more technical nature (Box 10.3).

As mentioned previously, corporate resolution relies on the active participation of financial creditors who have the decision-making power over the ultimate fate of the company, but also over practically all significant decisions during the procedure (e.g., appointment of a resolution professional, post-petition financing, sales outside the ordinary course of business). The peculiarity of the process is that financial creditors control it irrespective of their exposure to the debtor or the risk attached to their lending positions (a financial creditor may have provided a small unsecured loan, whereas it is possible that a trade creditor—known as "operational creditors" under the IBC—may have extended more credit, and that credit may be protected by a security interest). This can exacerbate conflicts among creditor classes and foster strategic behavior. The IBC assumes that financial creditors are in the best position to determine the outcome of the process and to take most of the decisions. This seems to be based on a belief that financial creditors have more expertise than other creditor classes[14] and that operational creditors would be more interested in the liquidation of the corporate debtor rather than the resurrection of the firm. In practice, financial creditors have not always responded to the expectations of professionalism placed on them, and, more importantly, their interests are not necessarily aligned with those of the other creditors, or other stakeholders. The proposal to adopt a code of conduct for the committee of creditors seeks to respond to the criticism over the conduct of financial creditors, with

---

[14] The Supreme Court appears to support this argument, stating that "since the financial creditors are in the business of money lending, banks and financial institutions are best equipped to assess viability and feasibility of the business of the corporate debtor" (*Swiss Ribbons v. Union of India*, 4 SCC 17, 2019).

Box 10.3. Technical Issues in the IBC and the Corporate Resolution Regulation

- *Commencement of the insolvency process:* Commencement of corporate resolution is not based on a cash-flow test or balance sheet test of insolvency, as the international standard recommends, but merely on a default of a certain amount (Rs10 million). This may have contributed to the use of insolvency petitions as a pressure mechanism to obtain payment even in situations where there is no insolvency.
- *Appeals and challenges:* The law is designed with the idea that the process must follow its strict deadlines irrespective of any appeal or challenge. However, appeals and challenges do interfere in practice with the strict timeline.
- *Effects of commencement:* It is not clear whether the commencement of resolution accelerates all claims, and whether claims (secured and unsecured) stop generating interest during the process.
- *Treatment of secured creditors:* Secured creditors do not seem to receive any protection against the effects of the moratorium (which may prevent them from enforcing during the whole duration of the resolution process). Secured creditors do not have the possibility to request that the moratorium is lifted.
- *Approval of the resolution plan:* The resolution plan requires a 66 percent majority of claims from the financial creditors' group. However, financial creditors include secured creditors, unsecured creditors, and claims for deficiency in the case of insufficient value of the collateral. These three categories of financial creditors are in different positions in the creditors' hierarchy, yet they are put in the same class to decide on the resolution plan.
- *Valuation and safeguards for creditors:* The baseline for the satisfaction of creditors is the liquidation value of assets, following the international standard, but the resolution procedure does not include the respect of absolute priority among creditor classes (and the concept of a dissenting class is alien to the IBC because only the class of financial creditors has the right to vote). The reform of the corporate resolution regulation included the concept of "fair value" that should also be determined by the valuers, but its main role is informative, and the criteria for determining the fair value are not clear.
- *Types of resolution plan.* The general understanding is that a resolution plan cannot provide for a business transfer, where the legal entity of the debtor is left behind as a shell entity and will therefore need to be dissolved (Ravi 2021).
- *Effects of the resolution plan:* The plan should bind all creditors, but instead, the combined effect of the law and regulations is that the plan results in the immediate payment of the liquidation value to operational creditors, and the payment of the liquidation value to the dissenting financial creditors before the rest receive any payment. In practice, this may complicate the design of plans because it is not possible to predict the amount of cash necessary to make the initial payments.
- *Repeat resolution plans:* The law is not entirely explicit about this point, but it seems that reaching a superficial restructuring agreement would be enough to save the company from liquidation, and that after one year there could be another application to restart the corporate resolution procedure. This diminishes the effectiveness of the threat of liquidation in the insolvency regime.

Source: Authors.
Note: IBC = Insolvency and Bankruptcy Code; Rs = rupees.

the goal of promoting specialization, due diligence, professionalism, and absence of conflicts of interest (Sriram 2021).

In contrast, operational creditors have almost no influence in the process. The IBC does not classify creditors according to the nature of their entitlement (i.e., secured creditors, preferential creditors, unsecured creditors) (see Pryor and Garg 2020). Operational creditors represent a broad category that includes practically all creditors that are not financial institutions. In corporate resolution, no participation mechanisms exist for these creditors: there is no creditors' meeting, and the committee of creditors is only open to financial creditors, as a rule. These creditors are effectively disenfranchised and depend on the actions of financial creditors to satisfy their claims (Mahapatra, Singhania, and Chandna 2020). As indicated, this is irrespective of the amount of their claims and of the legal position of their claims.

Practice has shown that it is not possible to rely on financial creditors to protect the interests of operational creditors, so the courts have insisted on compliance with the legal protections for operational creditors and, over time, some of these legal protections have made their way into the IBC through targeted amendments. In 2019, the IBC was amended to ensure that resolution plans at least offer operational creditors the liquidation value, or the value they would have received if the sums of money under the plan had been distributed according to the general priority order in section 53 of the IBC, whichever is higher.[15] In addition, the lack of recognition of categories of creditors according to the nature of their legal entitlements has led to the peculiar solution of classifying homebuyers as financial creditors (IBC amendment in 2018; see Mohan and Raj 2020). Possibly in recognition of the imbalance in representation of operational creditors through the IBC process, the judiciary has required the committee of creditors to consider the interests of all stakeholders in a resolution.[16] In the same vein, the IBBI proposed a code of conduct for the committee of creditors, which would encourage financial creditors to make decisions in the interest of all stakeholders instead of their own self-interest. This is a remarkable departure from the conventional expectation from creditors in an insolvency (i.e., protecting their own economic interests), and it is possible that this "quasi-fiduciary" role for financial creditors would result in increased litigation and complex case law.

Debtors, and related parties, have limited influence in corporate resolution. The Indian legislator made a conscious policy choice of dispossessing the debtor in corporate resolution. This means that the directors, officials, and shareholders are prevented from using their rights under corporate law to make decisions on behalf of the insolvent company.[17] This is a policy choice entirely admissible

---

[15] See amended section 30 of the IBC (2019).

[16] *Prowess International Pvt. Ltd. v. Parker Hannifin India Pvt. Ltd.* (National Company Law Appellate Tribunal) Company Appeal (AT) (Insolvency) No. 89 of 2017 | 18-08-2017.

[17] As the Supreme Court put it: "Entrenched managements are no longer allowed to continue in management if they cannot pay their debts" (*Innoventive Industries Ltd. v. ICICI Bank and Others*, (2018) 1 SCC 407).

under the international standard, but it has been observed that maintaining the debtor in possession during reorganization represents a powerful incentive that encourages debtors to commence insolvency proceedings at an early stage, maximizing the chances of recovery. A significant motivation for the design of the IBC in this respect is to prevent persons in control of the company ("promoters" or controlling owners) from interfering with corporate resolution, abusing the process, or otherwise deriving a strategic benefit from insolvency. This largely corresponds with bad practices that existed before the IBC. To prevent such abuses, the IBC precludes promoters and parties connected to them from present a resolution plan under a set of specified circumstances (section 29A). Although the policy objective of avoiding abuse is laudable (see Divan and Monga 2021; Gupta 2021; Kamalnath 2020; Mohan and Raj 2021), the prohibition is blunt and possibly unnecessary given the role and involvement of financial creditors, who should be able to accurately assess a resolution plan. The prohibitions on the promoters are complex and can generate litigation, which in turn can delay corporate resolution. Another critical issue affecting promoters is the issue of personal guarantees, which are used extensively in corporate lending in India. The IBC and the courts have affirmed that promoters are liable when they have personally guaranteed corporate debts, and the resolution process does not extinguish such guarantees.[18]

The lack of comprehensive rules for executory contracts reduces the effectiveness of corporate resolution. The IBC allows the continuation of essential goods and services contracts, irrespective of the will of the contracting party. Therefore, these contracts, together with licenses and permits, cannot be terminated during the moratorium. Essential goods and services include electricity, water, telecommunications, and IT services. The law does not include a rule to terminate the contracts that are detrimental to the debtor, specifying the treatment of the claims for breach of contract. This reduces the possibility of using corporate resolution for operational restructuring.

The IBC does not include any rules for the treatment of enterprise group insolvency. Modern enterprises tend to be organized in group structures, rather than concentrating all assets and liabilities in a single corporate entity. This lack of connection between the assumptions of traditional insolvency law and economic reality requires some adjustments, in line with the recommendations issued by UNCITRAL (2010). To tackle the insolvency of an enterprise group, it is necessary to implement *procedural coordination* measures: these can consist, for instance, of the appointment of an insolvency administrator for several insolvent enterprises, the development of coordinated reorganization plans, or even the financing of the continuation of the business with resources of other enterprises in the same group. These procedural coordination measures are absent in the IBC, and this may create severe coordination problems and prevent the restructuring of the group as an

---

[18] See Supreme Court, *Committee of Creditors of Essar Steel India Limited v. Satish Kumar Gupta & Others* (2019) SCC Online SC 1478. In addition, promoters can be liable for corporate debts on account of engaging in wrongful or fraudulent trading.

Figure 10.2. Corporate Resolution Procedures
(Cumulative data)

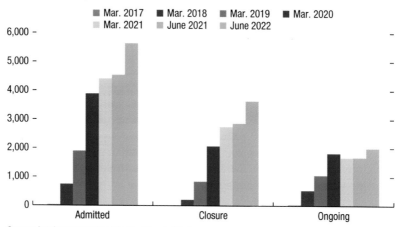

Source: Insolvency and Bankruptcy Board of India.

economic entity.[19] A high degree of flexibility and inventiveness on the side of insolvency professionals and the courts is required to resolve these problems under the current framework, although more ambitious reforms are planned.[20]

Cross-border insolvency is another missing piece in the Indian insolvency regime. Although the lack of cross-border insolvency rules along the lines of the UNCITRAL Model Law (1997) does not cause immediate problems in the operation of corporate resolution, the progressive internationalization of the Indian economy will demand better coordination with foreign insolvency proceedings to give response to the treatment of foreign creditors, improve the possibilities of coordinated rescue of multinational enterprises, and, ultimately, improve the investment climate. Progress has been made with legislative drafts incorporating the UNCITRAL Model Law, and the 2022 budget law has included the adoption of this reform as a priority.

The practical implementation of corporate resolution saw a very promising start, but the performance of corporate resolution has stalled over time. The number of cases has increased, even after the suspension of the IBC for one year during the pandemic (Figure 10.2). The deadlines contemplated in the IBC have proven

---

[19] One of the examples of the difficulties in dealing with enterprise groups under the IBC has been the Videocon case. The resolution of Videocon Industries required a merger of 13 subsidiaries with Videocon Industries as a way of bringing all different economic activities under a single corporate entity to implement resolution. In any event, this has been one of the cases where creditor losses have been highest (it is estimated that creditors took a 96 percent loss).

[20] A special working group on group insolvency was constituted, and its report was published in 2019. The thrust of the framework is "facilitation," "flexibility," and "choice." It envisages an enabling group insolvency framework to be implemented in a phased manner: first, procedural coordination, then cross-border and, finally substantive consolidation (i.e., joint treatment of all assets and liabilities, disregarding separate corporate personality. This is a remedy for exceptional cases of fraud or commingling of assets).

Figure 10.3. Timeline of Ongoing Corporate Resolution Procedures
(As of May 2021)

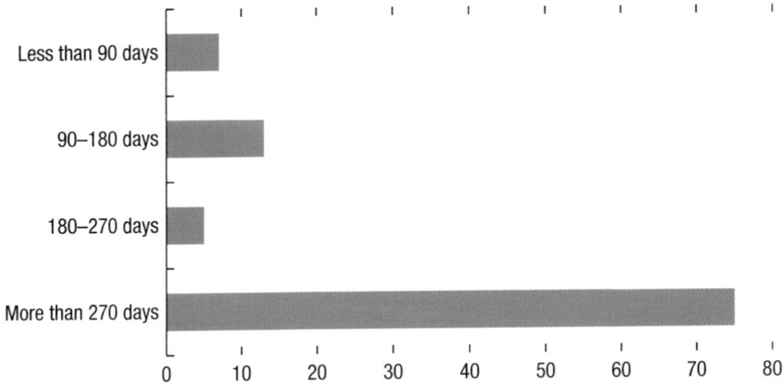

Source: Insolvency and Bankruptcy Board of India.

unattainable in a majority of cases, which is a source of concern (see Shikha and Shahi 2021). Indeed, most insolvency cases last longer than originally foreseen under the IBC (see Figure 10.3). Reports indicate that insolvency resolution takes nearly 593 days on average. Multiple factors may be at play behind this general delay in the completion of cases, but three main reasons seem particularly relevant: insufficient court resources and, especially, an insufficient number of judges; inadequate skills of some insolvency professionals, financial creditors, and other professionals participating in the procedure; and, finally, the fact that the deadlines are rigid and possibly too short for large, complex insolvency cases (see Suyash 2021). Delays also occur in complying with many of the deadlines in corporate resolution, including in the deadline for admission of petitions.[21] The Indian Supreme Court has insisted that the deadlines included in the IBC must be respected.[22]

Statistical analysis of corporate resolution cases reveals interesting insights into the functioning of the process. The IBBI is doing an excellent job collecting statistical information on insolvency. Since the entry into force of the IBC, 4,541 cases have been initiated (as of June 2021). Of these, 2,859 cases had been closed, and 1,682 were ongoing. By June 2021, 47 percent of corporate resolution cases ended in liquidation and 14 percent ended with a resolution plan. In remaining cases, the application was withdrawn,[23] an appeal was made,

---

[21] There is a deadline of 14 days for the admission of application. The average number of days taken for admission of applications is actually 13 days. This is a serious issue, because timely commencement of the process increases the chances for resolution, and severe risk of misconduct by the debtor exists during this period.

[22] Supreme Court of India, judgment of September 13, 2021. https://www.financialexpress.com /economy/sc-asks-insolvency-tribunals-to-stick-to-resolution-deadlines/2329587/.

[23] In general, the number of insolvency petition withdrawals is quite high—this may mean that there is a negotiation with the debtor when a petition is submitted. As of May 31, 2021, the number of withdrawals was 17,631 (out of 32,547 petitions).

Figure 10.4. Closure of Corporate Resolution Procedures
(Cumulative data, 2022)

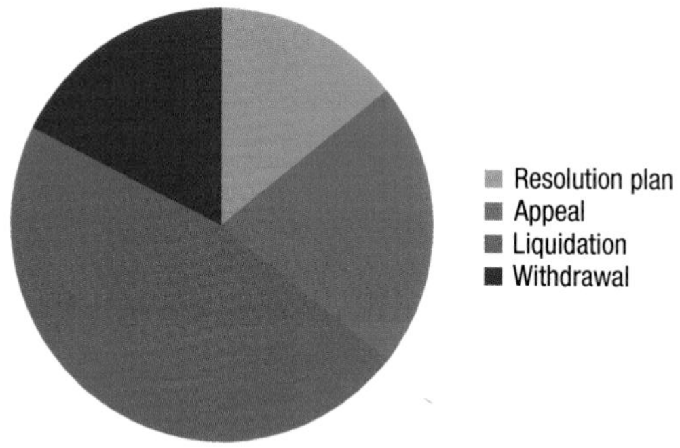

- Resolution plan
- Appeal
- Liquidation
- Withdrawal

Source: Insolvency and Bankruptcy Board of India.

or a settlement was reached (Figure 10.4). These percentages would be even lower considering the global number of petitions: out of 32,547 insolvency petitions, only 365 resolution plans had been concluded (in contrast to 1,318 liquidations). A large number of resolution petitions were withdrawn (17,631), and 1,085 processes were closed midway. There are 1,719 ongoing corporate resolution cases. Financial creditors recovered 167.95 percent of the liquidation value of companies, but this represents only 36 percent of the value of their claims.[24]

Under the IBC, liquidation is the last resort, generally after a failed resolution attempt. International best practice favors the use of reorganization options, but this must be justified by the situation of the firm: if the liquidation value of a firm is higher than its going concern value, the firm should be liquidated. Despite the preference for resolution, liquidations are frequent in practice because resolution attempts often fail (Figure 10.4). When liquidation is postponed, it tends to result in much heavier losses.[25] The average recovery in liquidation cases has been a mere 3.5 percent (Kotak 2021). Contrary to corporate resolution, liquidation does not have a fixed timeline, and it is expected that the time taken to conclude liquidation cases will be substantially longer than for resolution cases (Figure 10.5).

The regulation of the liquidation procedure is concise. Liquidation commences with an order by the National Company Law Tribunals, and the appointment of

---

[24] Of the large 40 accounts referred by order of the RBI in 2017, only 20 had achieved resolution. In those 20 cases, banks recovered 40 percent of their debt; see https://www.bloombergquint.com/business/four-years-on-did-rbis-ibc-gamble-with-40-large-defaulters-work.

[25] In the 37 liquidation cases concluded in December 2019, the average recovery for creditors was 1 percent (Ernst and Young 2019).

Figure 10.5. Duration of Ongoing Liquidations
(As of June 2022)

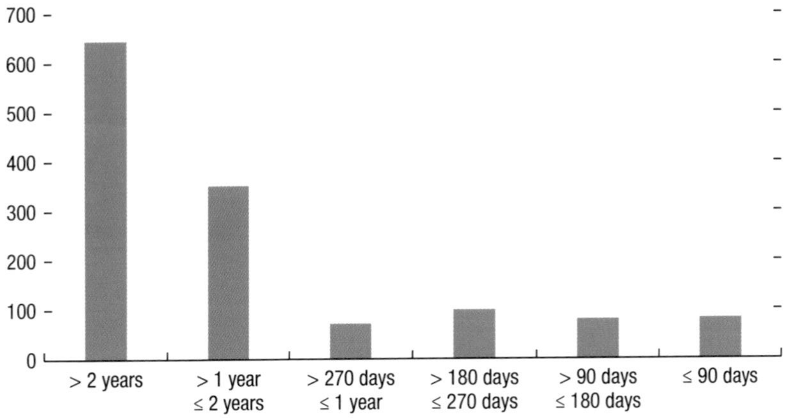

Source: Insolvency and Bankruptcy Board of India.

a liquidator. Rules exist for the formation of the insolvency estate[26] and the verification of claims (the liquidator leads the verification efforts, with a possible appeal to the National Company Law Tribunals).[27] Secured creditors have the option of relinquishing the collateral or realizing the collateral directly. The law ensures that secured creditors pay their share of the liquidation costs and that the residual value after enforcement goes to the liquidation estate.

Liquidation includes a ranking of claims that goes beyond the classification of financial and operational creditors. The ranking of claims recognizes the priority of secured creditors, workers' claims, and it includes a priority for financial unsecured creditors. Tax and public claims rank equally with the unsecured portion of secured loans. This ranking incorporates policy choices that may be influenced by national considerations, but these choices should be closely aligned with the treatment of creditors under corporate resolution.

The participation of secured creditors in the liquidation procedure is optional. If the debtor is to be liquidated, secured creditors have the choice either to relinquish their security to the liquidation estate, and participate in the distribution of proceeds set out under the IBC, or to independently enforce and realize their collateral without participating in the said distribution. In the

---

[26] These rules include exceptions for financial contracts. Similar rules should exist in corporate resolution. Avoidance actions are also contemplated in liquidation, but not in corporate resolution: this can create issues in cases where corporate debt distress is related to a series of previous transactions, even if the company does not end up in a liquidation.

[27] Verification of claims in liquidation should benefit from previous efforts under corporate resolution. In fact, it should be possible to contemplate just an update of the list of claims used in corporate resolution, as the IBBI liquidation regulation recognizes.

latter case, it appears that the secured creditor is required to bear the costs of enforcement, account for the liquidation to the insolvency administrator, and surrender any amount recovered in excess of its claim. It is difficult to understand why a secured creditor would choose to relinquish its security—if a secured creditor does that, the risk is sharing the proceeds realized at *pari passu* with workmen who rank equally in the distribution. The provision allowing the creditor to enforce its collateral outside the insolvency process runs counter to the collective nature of the insolvency proceeding and could make the sale of the business as a going concern virtually impossible. That said, this provision is consistent with the common law tradition, and it reinforces the position of secured creditors.

The work of the insolvency professional is central in the liquidation process. In liquidation, the insolvency professional enjoys ample autonomy, and this includes not only powers to sell assets but also to disclaim contracts. Creditors can provide input and recommendations, and request information through a so-called "stakeholders' consultation committee." This committee is more inclusive than the creditors' committee in corporate resolution, but its role is consultative. The liquidator's fees encourage the prompt realization of assets because those fees decrease over time. Although a scheme of arrangement or the sale of the business as a going concern are possible, the rights given to secured creditors make it extremely challenging in practice.

Overall, the corporate insolvency procedures included in the IBC have improved debt resolution in India, but challenges remain. Legislative and regulatory activity has developed a comprehensive regime for the rehabilitation and liquidation of corporate debtors. Technical issues are still outstanding, but the constant collection of data and the analysis and cooperation with specialists are proof of a strong commitment to improvement of the regime through reforms. The policy issues underlying corporate resolution, however, will need further reflection.

THE INSTITUTIONAL FRAMEWORK

The importance of the institutional framework of the insolvency regime cannot be overstated. In the words of prestigious insolvency experts: "We would opt for bad law and good personnel over good law and bad personnel" (Westbrook and others 2010, 203). The Indian institutional framework is complex and includes the institutions that formulate insolvency policy and the institutions in charge of the application of the regime.

In terms of legislative policy, insolvency stands out as a special matter because of the attention given to it by the office of the prime minister. Insolvency is a cross-cutting subject with multiple ramifications, and for that reason it is necessary to have interdepartmental coordination among the Ministries of Corporate Affairs, Law and Justice, Finance, and MSMEs. In addition, because insolvency performs a fundamental function in tackling NPAs in the banking system, the RBI takes a strong interest in insolvency legislation and has spearheaded initiatives affecting the insolvency system, such as the directions to use corporate resolution given to credit institutions in 2017.[28] Other regulators, such as the Securities and Exchange Board of India (securities markets) and the Competition Commission of India, also contribute to the formulation of insolvency policies. The need to ensure coordination at the policy level, together with the technical complexity of insolvency law, explains why insolvency legislation is frequently the result of delicate trade-offs and compromises.

The institutional framework of the IBC is supported by an elaborate ecosystem. The fundamental institutions for the application of the IBC are the courts, the IBBI, the insolvency professionals (and the insolvency professionals' associations), and the information utilities. These are sometimes referred to as "the four pillars of the ecosystem." In addition, valuators should be included in the analysis of the institutional framework.

The drafters of the IBC were aware of the importance of having specialized courts for the proper application of corporate legislation, which requires ample expertise and knowledge of corporate and commercial law. The IBC attributed exclusive jurisdiction to the National Company Law Tribunals and to the National Company Law Appellate Tribunal. There are 11 National Company Law Tribunals in the country, with 15 benches dedicated to insolvency cases and an additional principal bench in New Delhi.[29]

The caseload for the insolvency tribunals has grown at a steady pace. Most of the cases are resolved without completing the process: Out of the 28,441 cases filed under the IBC until September 2020, 14,884 cases were withdrawn before admission, which suggests that parties negotiate before moving forward with corporate resolution.[30] But the number of cases is nevertheless substantial. During June 1, 2016, to May 31, 2021, the National Company Law Tribunals took 4,283 cases, and they have resolved 3,283. There are 1,000 cases pending resolution, and it is expected that cases will increase after the suspension of the IBC concluded and the consequences of the pandemic over the economy continue. This case workload is in addition to the responsibilities of the National Company Law Tribunals in corporate law litigation.

The court system has not been supported by adequate resources. The delays in corporate resolution are the result of several contributing factors, but one of the main reasons for such delay is the insufficiency of resources at the courts. National Company Law Tribunals and the National Company Law Appellate Tribunal lack

---

[28] With the ordinance of the cabinet in May 2017, amending the Banking Regulation Act 1949, the RBI was empowered to direct banks to use the insolvency process to resolve NPAs. However, in 2019 the Indian Supreme Court ruled that without specific direction from the government, the RBI could not direct banks to use the IBC process, and therefore the court struck down the RBI Circular that set a time limit for restructuring negotiations before commencing the insolvency process.

[29] This includes benches at New Delhi, Ahmedabad, Allahabad, Bengaluru, Chandigarh, Chennai, Guwahati, Jaipur, Hyderabad, Kolkata, Mumbai, Cuttack, Kochi, Amravati, and Indore (https://nclt .gov.in/national-company-law-tribunal-benches).

[30] According to Debroy and Sinha (2021), "There is a need to disseminate the important fact that a large proportion of IBC cases are getting resolved on the way."

human and material resources (Alvarez and Marsal 2017). As of 2021, there were only 15 benches with 19 judicial members and 21 technical members at the National Company Law Tribunals. The National Company Law Appellate Tribunal has two benches with 11 members. Numerous vacancies exist at the National Company Law Tribunals (34 vacancies, including the president, out of a total of 63 members, according to the latest report in August 2021). There have been delays with filling vacancies, inviting further censure from the Indian Supreme Court, following which the authorities have taken steps to increase staffing.[31] A litigious approach with practically any aspect of the insolvency proceedings being contested by parties does not help with these pressures, including when parties present frivolous challenges and appeals unforeseen in the legislation.

The IBBI combines multiple functions as a regulator. The IBBI is a creation of the IBC and represents a critical component of the institutional infrastructure[32] and an invaluable link with policymakers in the executive and legislative powers of the state.

- *Regulation.* The IBBI adopts insolvency regulations. This is a function that sets the IBBI apart from insolvency authorities in other legal systems, which tend to lack the capacity to enact insolvency regulations, despite being informally referred to as "regulators." The IBBI has adopted regulations that specify and develop the provisions of the IBC in multiple areas, including all corporate insolvency proceedings. The regulations must respect the statutory provisions and the rules of procedure established by the IBBI itself (IBBI Mechanism for Issuing Regulations of 2018). The IBBI also has a role in preserving the integrity of the insolvency legislative and regulatory framework; this allows the IBBI to file complaints or appeals with the courts regarding specific decisions or actions. The IBBI is consulted on projected legislative changes to the insolvency legislation and is routinely involved in legal reforms.

- *Supervision.* The IBBI not only regulates the insolvency regime, which includes developing regulations and standards for the qualification and conduct of insolvency professionals and their agencies, but also actively supervises the conduct of insolvency professionals and their agencies. The IBBI seeks to ensure the integrity and quality of the insolvency profession. The IBBI supervises compliance with regulations, with the assistance of the insolvency professional agencies, and punishes irregular conduct of insolvency professionals.

- *Research and dissemination.* The IBBI publishes research on insolvency proceedings, including the collection of comprehensive and accurate data, and conducts training and dissemination activities that support the development of the insolvency system, particularly by providing continuous education to insolvency professionals.

---

[31] https://www.barandbench.com/news/11-judicial-members-10-technical-members-appointed-to-nclt-benches.

[32] In the words of its first chairman, M. S. Sahoo, the IBBI performs executive, quasi-legislative, and quasi-judicial functions. "The IBBI blends the duties of a regulator of professions, a regulator of markets, and a regulator of utilities, though its role is vastly different from that of any of them" (Sahoo 2021, at 3).

Insolvency professional agencies are self-regulatory organizations for insolvency professionals. The agencies complement the activities of the IBBI as regulators for insolvency professionals (see Burman and Roy 2015). This two-tier system is inspired by the English system. Insolvency professional agencies can develop guidelines and recommendations for their members and have competences for the supervision and sanction of insolvency professionals.

Insolvency professionals are tasked with important functions in insolvency proceedings. The ordinary business of insolvency proceedings is conducted by insolvency professionals. Following the international standard, the courts take decisions only on matters litigated by the parties or that require a detailed legal analysis. Insolvency proceedings require numerous routine operations for their smooth functioning (e.g., taking control of the debtor's assets, verifying creditors' claims, examining the debtor's financial statements). To operate seamlessly, it is required that insolvency professionals have adequate expertise. This tends to be a challenge because insolvency professionals should be knowledgeable in varied subjects, including legal, business, and accounting matters relevant to insolvency. India has built a new insolvency profession, applying a degree of flexibility to eligibility requirements.[33] The IBBI oversees the syllabus and the organization of official examinations for insolvency professionals. These professionals also need to complete a training program before registration. The number of insolvency professionals has increased steadily. Per the data on the IBBI website, three insolvency professional agencies and more than 3,600 insolvency professionals and entities have been registered with the IBBI.[34] However, it is not entirely clear that all insolvency professionals have the necessary qualifications, particularly when dealing with large and complex corporate insolvency cases. The rapid growth of the profession has made it difficult to ensure the quality and integrity of all professionals.

Information utilities—another original creation of the IBC—provide infrastructure services to insolvency processes. The idea behind this innovation is to create reliable databases that provide clear evidence for defaults, given the importance that the evidence of default has in the commencement of corporate resolution under the IBC. In addition, information utilities can provide a list of financial claims that can be easily integrated into the resolution process. Although it was envisaged that this would be a competitive industry, in practice there is only one information utility, National e-Governance Services Ltd., active since 2017. The IBBI set the technical standard for the service (Barman 2021). To a certain

---

[33] The eligibility requirements of insolvency professionals have recently been revised to increase flexibility (for management professionals, 10 years' experience is required, after earning a postgraduate degree, or 15 years, after a bachelor's degree; for lawyers, it is 10 years' experience after a bachelor's degree; and for accountants and advocates, 10 years of combined experience) (IBBI regulation, July 2021). The new regulation is also tightening rules on conflicts of interest by barring the possibility of appointing an insolvency professional when another person in the same service firm has acted for any of the parties in the insolvency case.

[34] https://www.taxscan.in/ibbi-to-celebrate-its-5th-annual-day-on-oct-1st/134447/.

extent, the service lends itself to a natural monopoly, but that also means that the supervision of the information utility needs to be rigorous to ensure that the technology is adequate and that no data loss or confidentiality issues occur (Suyash 2021).

The insolvency regime also relies on the work of valuators. "Registered valuers" calculate both the liquidation and the fair value of the assets of companies under corporate resolution. The IBBI has developed a regulatory regime for registered valuers, which is also supported by the establishment of professional organizations for valuers. At present, more than 4,300 valuers and 16 valuers' organizations are registered with the IBBI. However, important gaps exist in the regulation of valuers and of valuation standards (Saini 2021). The Working Group appointed by the Ministry of Corporate Affairs recommended a broader initiative that would consist of the enactment of a Valuers Act, contemplating the establishment of a valuation regulator, the development of valuation standards and the strengthening of the regime of valuers.[35]

In conclusion, reforms have overhauled the institutional framework for corporate insolvency in India, but the judiciary could materially improve. Procedural delays in corporate resolution can be attributed, to a great extent, to the lack of resources at the National Company Law Tribunals and National Company Law Appellate Tribunal.[36] The insolvency profession is in its early stages, and it needs to acquire expertise and further specialization, while valuers would benefit from a comprehensive regulation of their activities.

SPECIAL CONSIDERATIONS FOR MSME INSOLVENCY

When the IBC was adopted in 2016, no special provisions existed for MSMEs. In the design of the IBC, the focus was on large corporates and on the need to address large NPAs on the banks' balance sheets. As a result, the insolvency procedures—notably, corporate resolution—are complex, too sophisticated, and too costly for the needs and resources of MSMEs.

MSMEs are an important part of the Indian economy. They contribute 30 percent of India's gross domestic product and provide jobs for 100 million people. The classification of MSMEs has been recently reformed by the Ministry of MSMEs (July 1, 2020; see Table 10.1). The classification excludes agricultural enterprises, but it now includes unified criteria for manufacturing and service enterprises, based on investment and turnover.

---

[35] See *Report of the Committee of Experts to Examine the Need for an Institutional Framework for Regulation and Development of Valuation Professionals* (2020), available at https://www.mca.gov.in /Ministry/pdf/Notice_14042020.pdf.

[36] See *Implementation of Insolvency and Bankruptcy Code. Pitfalls and Solutions* (2021). 32 report, Lok Sabha, August 2021.

TABLE 10.1.

Classification of Micro, Small, and Medium Enterprises (2020)			
	Micro	**Small**	**Medium**
Manufacturing Enterprises and Enterprises Rendering Services	**Investment in Plant and Machinery or Equipment:** Not more than Rs10 million; and **Annual Turnover:** Not more than Rs50 million.	**Investment in Plant and Machinery or Equipment:** Not more than Rs100 million; and **Annual Turnover:** Not more than Rs500 million.	**Investment in Plant and Machinery or Equipment:** Not more than Rs500 million; and **Annual Turnover:** Not more than Rs2,500 million.

Source: Ministry of Micro, Small, and Medium Enterprises.
Note: Rs = rupees.

Two important peculiarities exist in the MSME sector in India: the prevalence of unincorporated enterprises and the small number of medium enterprises. The share of medium enterprises in India is insignificant (0.05 percent of all MSMEs). Micro enterprises represent 99.5 percent of the whole MSME category.[37] In addition, most MSMEs are unincorporated: 95.98 percent of all MSMEs are proprietary concerns.

The corporate resolution procedure in the IBC is not adequate for the needs of micro enterprises. The lack of adequate legal response to the insolvency of MSMEs is not new (Debroy 2005), and the IBC did not alleviate those problems in 2016. Micro enterprises do not have enough resources or expertise to navigate a sophisticated and costly process such as corporate resolution, and financial creditors are not eager to invest their own resources in seeking the resolution of these businesses: enforcement of collateral, if any, would be the preferred course of action for creditors. The prevalence of micro enterprises in India affects the insolvency debate, because it is estimated that ordinary insolvency proceedings work well for medium enterprises, but micro and small enterprises experience difficulties because of the high costs and complexity of such procedures (Diez and others 2021). Until recently, the IBC included only several special rules and accommodations for the situation of micro and small enterprises. The most notable one is the rule that allows promoters of distressed MSMES to act as resolution applicants in the corporate resolution of their enterprises.[38] This amendment of the IBC allows the promoters of MSMEs to submit resolution plans, and in this way the interests of the owners are protected, but also the interests of creditors are advanced, because it is unlikely that third parties would be interested in proposing resolution plans for a MSME.

---

[37] The absolute numbers are the following: a total of 63,388,000 MSMEs, including 63,530,000 micro enterprises, 331,000 small enterprises, and 5,000 medium enterprises.

[38] Section 240A was introduced in 2018 to provide certain relaxations to MSMEs with respect to the exclusions of eligibility in acting as resolution applicant (section 29A). The intention behind the enactment of this provision was to grant exemptions to corporate debtors which are MSMEs, by permitting a promoter who is not a willful defaulter or covered under any other specific disqualification as provided under the law to bid for the resolution plan of an MSME.

The lack of alignment of the insolvency regime with the needs of MSMEs was highlighted by the COVID-19 pandemic. The pandemic has affected[39] smaller businesses disproportionately. Due to the difficulties of addressing the problems of small businesses through the ordinary insolvency regime, the policy response included a suspension of the IBC, raising the threshold of default for the commencement of corporate resolution, and the introduction of special debt restructuring schemes for MSMEs.

Restructuring schemes for MSME loans have offered an alternative to debt resolution. The RBI adopted the so-called "resolution framework 2.0" to address MSME debt in 2021, raising the threshold for the scheme to Rs500 million. Upon implementation of restructuring plans, banks can set provisions for 10 percent of the residual debt of the borrower, which represents a regulatory incentive to restructure the debt. Loans classified as standard can retain that classification, whereas the accounts that may have slipped into NPA category between April 1, 2021, and date of implementation of the restructuring, may be upgraded.

The introduction of a special insolvency procedure (pre-pack) represents a major development in the regulation of MSME insolvency. The prepackaged insolvency resolution process, specifically designed for MSMEs, was introduced in 2021.[40] The pre-pack, despite the use of this term, is not a variety of expedited reorganization, such as prepackaged reorganization plans in US practice. The design of the procedure resembles a simplified and shortened debtor-in-possession reorganization, with a prearranged plan. At the same time, this procedure also presents similarities with pre-packs in English practice because it assumes an agreement with secured creditors and often with an investor who will take control of the company.

There has been an effort to adapt the pre-packs to the needs of MSMEs. The minimum default necessary to access a pre-pack is Rs1 million, which sets a threshold more in line with the characteristics of MSMEs. The procedure is available to all MSMEs, in principle, but there are certain exclusions for MSMEs that have already used an insolvency procedure in the previous three years, MSMEs undergoing ordinary insolvency procedures, or MSMEs that have been ordered to be liquidated. Connected parties are not allowed to apply for the pre-pack procedure. The procedure can only be accessed by the MSME itself.[41] The application for a pre-pack procedure takes priority over applications for ordinary insolvency.

---

[39] Raising the threshold for default under the IBC to Rs10 million from the previous Rs100,000 can be seen as a measure to protect MSMEs from ordinary insolvency procedures.

[40] The pre-pack procedure was adopted by ordinance on April 4, 2021. The IBC was amended in August 2021 to adapt the code to the new procedure for MSMEs (Insolvency and Bankruptcy Code [Amendment] Act, 2021).

[41] This requires a special resolution (three-fourths majority) adopted by shareholders or at least the agreement of three-fourths of the partners. Financial creditors may request to see evidence of shareholder/partner support, together with the Base Resolution Plan, before agreeing to the commencement of the pre-pack procedure. Parties disqualified from being resolution applicants (section 29A IBC) cannot apply for a pre-pack process.

The procedure assumes the existence of previous out-of-court negotiations between the debtor and its main creditors. Those negotiations rely on a base resolution plan, whose compliance with the legal requirements is verified by a resolution professional.[42] However, these negotiations are not conclusive, because the pre-pack process also offers opportunities for the development of alternative plans.

The debtor-in-possession model can contribute to the success of the pre-pack process. The fact that the debtor remains in control of the business represents a powerful incentive for the use of the procedure, which can assist in tackling distress at an earlier stage. The committee of creditors can apply to the court to remove the debtor's management if there is a 66 percent majority in favor of the removal in cases of fraud or gross mismanagement. In case of removal, the resolution professional takes over the management of the business. In any case, a resolution professional is appointed since the commencement of the procedure, whose duties include, among others, verifying claims, monitoring the management of the business, and preparing an information memorandum for the committee of creditors.

Although the procedure requires agreement over the plan, it is possible to conclude it with a different plan. Since the procedure starts with a plan supported by a majority of creditors, it is foreseen that its duration will be much shorter than that of corporate resolution (120 days, instead of the maximum 330 days that corporate resolution may take) (see Suyash 2021). In theory, the procedure could be shorter, because the majority required for commencement of the procedure is the majority necessary for the adoption of the plan.[43] However, it is always necessary to have a vote at the committee of creditors. If the base resolution plan does not impair the rights of operational creditors, the committee of creditors can approve it and submit it to the National Company Law Tribunals. However, if creditors do not approve the plan or the plan impairs operational creditors' rights, the resolution professional needs to invite competing plans. The "Swiss challenge" allows any third party to present an alternative resolution plan when the original resolution plan does not satisfy operational creditors in full. The original applicant can still match the plan presented by the challenger.

Pre-packs can offer a good option for the resolution of MSMEs in distress (Mehta 2021). In comparison with corporate resolution, the pre-pack procedure is much simpler, the role of the courts is much more limited, and therefore potential is great for achieving a faster and more economical resolution of MSME distress (Box 10.4), although the process is still complex and further streamlining would be possible. In any event, the procedure will need to be tested in practice.

The biggest shortcoming of pre-packs is the lack of coverage of unincorporated MSMEs. Given that more than 95 percent of Indian MSMEs are not incorporated,

---

[42] The resolution professional also verifies that the sufficient majority of shareholders or partners supports the pre-pack petition.

[43] This may not be the case if there are financial creditors related to the corporate debtor, because the majority required for the commencement of the process is required in respect of the financial creditors that are not connected to the corporate debtor.

Box 10.4. "Pre-pack" Insolvency for MSMEs: Sequence and Timeline

- Application with the National Company Law Tribunals by a MSME corporate debtor, naming a resolution professional.
- Unrelated financial creditors, who are not related to the debtor, having a minimum 66 percent of the value of financial debt due, must have approved the filing of the application and proposed the resolution professional (D0).
- National Company Law Tribunal admits the application within 14 days of receiving the petition (D1). A moratorium starts until approval of the plan or termination of the procedure.
- The MSME delivers a list of claims and a preliminary information memorandum to the resolution professional (D+3).
- The MSME submits a "base resolution plan" to the resolution professional (D+2).
- The resolution professional constitutes the committee of creditors (D+7).
- Committee of creditors can approve the resolution plan. Otherwise, the resolution professional can invite resolution applicants to submit alternative resolution plans.
- The resolution professional submits to National Company Law Tribunals a resolution plan approved by the committee of creditors; or informs that the procedure should be terminated (D+90). If the debtor is eligible for ordinary corporate resolution, the committee of creditors can decide to commence that process.
- If a plan has been approved, National Company Law Tribunals decides on the confirmation of the plan within 30 days of receiving it. Confirmation by the court is necessary.
- The procedure should be completed within the statutory deadline (D+120).

Source: Authors.
Note: MSME = micro, small, and medium enterprise.

---

it is clear that the impact of the current pre-pack insolvency procedure will be marginal. The vast majority of MSMEs do not have an insolvency procedure that allows them to reorganize. The challenge is to address the distress situation of enterprises and, at the same time, the effects of distress on individuals and families who own the businesses. To provide a proper response to the problem, the authorities need to further develop a plan to implement a personal insolvency regime.

The treatment of guarantors of MSMEs also needs to be addressed. It is frequent that individuals guarantee the debts of the corporate MSMEs they own. The IBC assigns the competence over the bankruptcy of guarantors of corporate debt to the National Company Law Tribunal, but it must be noted that the problem of promoters guaranteeing debts of large companies is very different from the problem of MSME guarantors. This problem has received the attention of the authorities. A special working group produced a report on this topic.[44] The proposed plan is to implement personal insolvency in phases, first applying bankruptcy to guarantors and, later, introducing personal insolvency law for other categories of debtors (individuals with a business activity first and, as a final step, consumer insolvency).

---

[44] "The Working Group noted that it may be beneficial to have different procedures and frameworks for individuals with business and those without business under Part III of the Code. It was concluded that in personal insolvency, one size may not fit all. Therefore, it shall be appropriate to have separate set of rules and regulations for personal guarantors to corporate debtors, for individuals with business, and for individuals without business" (IBBI 2019).

RECOMMENDATIONS

A series of changes, as part of a concerted initiative, could further increase the effectiveness of private debt resolution. The recommended changes around the main areas covered in this analysis include the following.

Restructuring

- Encourage the use of out-of-court restructuring as an alternative to in-court proceedings. For cases that only require adjustments of debt (and not operational restructuring), informal restructuring is the best option.
- To increase debt restructuring activity, preconditions need to be met. Banks must be adequately capitalized, guidelines or codes of conduct are needed for cooperation among financial creditors, and bankers that follow prescribed procedures and enter into agreements that benefit the interests of their entities must face no risk of liability.
- The use of hybrid restructuring tools, such as schemes of arrangement—which would need to be reformed to be made more efficient—would contribute to the development of the restructuring practice.
- Hybrid restructuring could also be promoted by legislative reforms, adapting lessons from the pre-pack insolvency procedure for MSMEs. This would reduce the use of scarce judicial resources.
- The judicial procedure under the IBC should become a deterrent that encourages the negotiation between debtors and creditors, and its use should be reserved for cases where such agreements are not possible, or the company cannot be restructured without heavy judicial involvement.

Corporate Resolution and Liquidation

- The corporate resolution process should include mechanisms for the participation of operational creditors[45] and ensure that creditors are classified according to their position in the hierarchy of claims. These changes would also result in improved decision-making over resolution plans and safeguards for dissenting minorities.
- The process should include comprehensive rules for the continuation, rejection, and assignment of executory contracts. This would improve the possibility of restructuring the operations of businesses in corporate resolution, instead of opting for the sale of the business as the usual outcome.

---

[45] Participation of operational creditors requires structural changes to the scheme of the IBC by giving them the right to vote on a resolution plan and other governance rights. It has been argued that even incremental changes, such as giving them a right to give their objections on proposed resolution plans, may reduce litigation, improve decision making, and increase trust in the process (see Prakash 2021).

- Corporate resolution should commence as soon as possible after a petition is submitted to the courts. Any delays should be avoided, and courts should be ready to adopt provisional measures to protect the interests of creditors.

- Liquidation rules should find a compromise between the respect of the rights of secured creditors and a realistic possibility of a going concern sale, which can offer higher recoveries for all classes of creditors.

- In both corporate resolution and liquidation, appeals should be discouraged. Courts should favor consensual solutions to conflicts. Frivolous appeals should result in costs and damages being paid by the appealing party.

- Corporate resolution and liquidation should include procedural coordination mechanisms for enterprise group insolvency. Substantive consolidation should also be possible in cases of fraud or commingling of assets.

- The system of the IBC would benefit from the adoption of the UNCITRAL Model Law on cross-border insolvency and the model law on cross-border insolvency of enterprise groups.

Institutional Framework

- The main priority is strengthening the courts in charge of insolvency litigation. It is necessary to cover vacancies at the National Company Law Tribunals and at the National Company Law Appellate Tribunal and increase the number of insolvency judges (plans exist to double the National Company Law Tribunals benches). An evaluation of the needs in human and material resources should precede a plan to ramp up the court infrastructure, including full digitalization of the courts and specialized training for judges and court officials. The courts specializing in insolvency law will benefit from the plans of the Indian government to reinforce the judicial system (National Institution for Transforming India [NITI] action agenda).

- Information utilities could increase their functions by becoming early warning systems. Information utilities could integrate data from other sources, beyond the financial sector (for instance, information on tax liabilities or commercial claims).

- Continue developing expertise and specialization of insolvency professionals, particularly in management and restructuring of distressed enterprises.

- A platform for the sale of distressed assets would be a welcome addition to the insolvency ecosystem. An electronic platform could perform several functions: it can leverage finance for distressed companies, provide a competitive environment for the analysis and formulation of resolution plans, and serve as a venue for electronic auctions of enterprises and assets.

MSME Insolvency

- The latest reform, the pre-pack insolvency process for MSMEs, represents a notable attempt to adapt the corporate resolution process to the needs of smaller enterprises. Pre-packs will need to be tested in practice, although they show considerable promise and could inspire reforms for the general resolution framework.

- However, the pre-pack process will probably be too costly and complex for micro and small enterprises, and further simplification should be studied— including by using out-of-court mechanisms more widely to reduce the costs of restructuring and avoid overloading the courts.

- Most important, the pre-pack insolvency process is not available for unincorporated MSMEs, which represent the overwhelming majority of enterprises in India. It is necessary to offer flexible and economical procedures that can apply to both legal and natural persons.

CONCLUSION

In the past five years, private debt resolution in India has been substantially transformed, mostly thanks to the introduction of the IBC. The IBC has redesigned the insolvency regime with corporate resolution and liquidation processes, and the development of a full ecosystem where the IBBI is the central institution. Targeted amendments and reforms are building over the foundations of the code; among these, the pre-pack insolvency process for MSMEs is probably the most consequential.

At the same time, RBI has been active in developing out-of-court restructuring solutions. The evolution of the RBI schemes for debt restructuring has occurred in several stages with the overarching goal of preventing the rise of NPAs. RBI moved from recognizing multiple restructuring schemes to a unified framework for resolution of stressed assets in 2019. However, to mitigate the economic impact of the pandemic over Indian businesses, RBI has developed a number of special schemes targeted at the specific debt distress problems induced by COVID-19.

Despite all improvements in restructuring and insolvency, India needs to step up efforts to improve private debt resolution to face the challenge of widespread distress. The economic consequences of the pandemic have worsened the situation of Indian businesses, particularly MSMEs. The private debt resolution system will be subject to increased pressure, particularly after changes in monetary and economic policy revert to a normal stance.

After more than five years of operation, an examination of the performance of the IBC, and of the private resolution regime in general, seems appropriate. The comprehensive data collected by the IBBI shows that corporate resolution is facing challenges, and to a great extent these are due to the lack of institutional support. Legislative and regulatory activity need to go hand in hand with supporting institutional reforms, building on the remarkable progress since 2016.

ANNEX 10.1.

ANNEX TABLE 10.1.1.

Financial Soundness Indicators
(Percent, unless indicated otherwise)

	2015/16	2016/17	2017/18	2018/19	2019/20	2020/21	2021/22
I. Scheduled Commercial Bank							
Risk-Weighted Capital Adequacy Ratio (CAR)	**13.3**	**13.6**	**13.8**	**14.3**	**14.7**	**16.0**	**16.8**
Public sector bank	11.8	12.1	11.7	12.2	12.9	14.0	14.6
Private sector bank	15.7	15.5	16.4	16.3	16.5	18.4	18.8
Foreign bank	17.1	18.7	19.1	19.4	17.7	19.5	19.8
Number of Institutions Not Meeting 9 Percent CAR	**1**	**0**	**1**	**1**	**3**	**0**	**N/A**
Public sector bank	0	0	1	0	1	0	N/A
Private sector bank	1	0	0	1	1 (LVB only)	0	N/A
Foreign bank	0	0	0	0	0	0	N/A
Net Nonperforming Assets (percent of outstanding net advances)	**4.4**	**5.3**	**5.9**	**3.7**	**2.8**	**2.4**	**1.7**
Public sector bank	5.7	6.9	7.8	4.8	3.8	3.1	2.3
Private sector bank	1.4	2.2	2.4	2.0	1.5	1.4	1.0
Foreign bank	0.8	0.6	0.4	0.5	0.5	0.6	0.6
Gross Nonperforming Assets (percent of outstanding advances)[1]	**7.5**	**9.6**	**11.2**	**3.1**	**8.2**	**7.3**	**5.9**
Public sector bank	9.3	12.5	14.6	11.6	10.3	9.1	7.3
Private sector bank	2.8	4.1	4.6	5.3	5.5	4.9	3.8
Foreign bank	4.2	4.0	3.8	3.0	2.3	2.4	2.8
Return on Assets[2]	**0.4**	**0.4**	**−0.2**	**−0.1**	**0.1**	**0.7**	**0.9**
Public sector bank	−0.1	−0.1	−0.9	−0.7	−0.2	0.3	0.5
Private sector bank	1.5	1.3	1.1	0.6	0.4	1.2	1.4
Foreign bank	1.5	1.6	1.3	1.5	1.5	1.6	1.4
Balance Sheet Structure of All Scheduled Banks							
Total assets (percent of GDP)	95.3	92.3	89.2	87.3	88.6	99.2	N/A
Loan/deposit ratio	78.2	73.0	78.6	79.9	78.1	73.1	N/A
Investment in government securities/deposit ratio	26.8	26.3	27.9	26.5	27.8	29.5	N/A
II. Nonbanking Financial Companies[3]							
Total assets (percent of GDP)	...	13.5	14.3	15.1	16.6	17.6	N/A
Risk-weighted CAR	24.3	22.1	22.8	22.5	23.7	25.0	26.6
Gross nonperforming assets (percent of outstanding net advances)	4.5	6.1	5.8	6.1	6.8	6.4	6.4
Net nonperforming assets (percent of outstanding net advances)[1]	2.5	4.4	3.8	3.5	3.4	2.7	2.5
Return on assets[2]	2.1	1.8	1.7	1.2	1.2	1.8	2.0

Sources: Bankscope; Reserve Bank of India; and IMF staff estimates.
[1] Gross nonperforming assets less provisions.
[2] Net profit (+) / loss (−) in percent of total assets.
[3] Data are based on sample of 300 nonbanking financial companies of total asset size Rs 43.9 lakh crore, comprising about 94 percent of total assets of the sector.

ANNEX TABLE 10.1.2.

Asset Quality/CRARs of NBFCs							
(Percent of assets/RWA)							
	2016	2017	2018	2019	2020	2021	2022
GNPA ratio	4.5	6.1	5.8	6.1	6.8	6.4	6.4
NNPA ratio	2.5	4.4	3.8	3.3	3.4	2.7	2.5
CRAR	24.3	22.1	22.8	22.5	23.7	25.0	26.6

Source: June 2022 *Financial Stability Report.*
Note: CRAR = capital-to-risk weighted average ratio; GNAP = ross nonperforming asset; NBFCs = nonbanking financial companies; RWA = risk-weighted asset.

REFERENCES

Alvarez & Marsal (India). 2017. *The National Company Law Tribunal (NCLT) Readiness.* https://www.alvarezandmarsal.com/sites/default/files/restructingindia_nclt.pdf.

Barman, R. B. 2021. "Role of Information Utility in Insolvency Resolution." *Quinquennial of Insolvency and Bankruptcy Code, 2016.* Insolvency and Bankruptcy Board of India, New Delhi, 153.

Burman, Anirudh, and Shubho Roy. 2019, "Building an Institution of Insolvency Practitioners in India", 5 Bus. & Bankr. L.J. 118.

Debroy, Bibek. 2005. "An Economic and Legal Analysis." In *Small Scale Industry in India. Large Scale Exit Problems*, edited by Bibek Debroy and Laveesh Bhandari. Academic Foundation, New Delhi, 111.

Debroy, Bibek, and Aditya Sinha. 2021. "IBC: Liberalising Exit." *Quinquennial of Insolvency and Bankruptcy Code, 2016.* Insolvency and Bankruptcy Board of India, New Delhi, 121.

Diez, Federico J., Romain A. Duval, Jiayue Fan, José Garrido, Sebnem Kalemli-Ozcan, Chiara Maggi, Maria Soledad Martinez Peria, and Nicola Pierri. 2021. "Insolvency Prospects Among Small-and-Medium-Sized Enterprises in Advanced Economies: Assessment and Policy Options." IMF Staff Discussion Note 2021/002, International Monetary Fund, Washington, DC.

Divan, Madhavi, and Sahil Monga. 2021. "Promoter's Paradise Lost." *Quinquennial of Insolvency and Bankruptcy Code 2016.* Insolvency and Bankruptcy Board of India, New Delhi, 179.

Ernst and Young India. 2019. *Evolving Landscape of Corporate Stress Resolution.* https://assets .ey.com/content/dam/ey-sites/ey-com/en_in/topics/transaction-advisory-services/pdfs/evolving -landscape-of-corporate-stress-resolution.pdf?download.

Garrido, José. 2012. *Out-of-court Debt Restructuring.* World Bank, Washington, DC.

Gupta, Akhil. 2021. "Section 29A of IBC: A Key Feature." *Quinquennial of Insolvency and Bankruptcy Code 2016.* Insolvency and Bankruptcy Board of India, New Delhi, 175.

Handa, Ankit. 2020. "An Analysis of the Corporate Insolvency Resolution Process as a Route for Acquisitions in India." *International Insolvency Review* 29 (2): 234–53.

INSOL International. 2001. *Consumer Debt Report: Report of Findings and Recommendations,* London, UK.

INSOL International. 2011. *Consumer Debt Report II: Report of Findings and Recommendations,* London, UK.

Insolvency and Bankruptcy Board of India (IBBI). 2019. "Report on Bankruptcy Process: Proposing Rules and Regulations for Personal Guarantors to Corporate Debtors." IBBI Working Group on Individual Insolvency. https://www.ibbi.gov.in/uploads/resources/ e6153215c43ebfcd00b29f946d8005bc.pdf.

Kamalnath, A. 2020. "Corporate Insolvency Resolution Law in India—A Proposal to Overcome the 'Initiation Problem.'" *UMKC Law Review* 88 (3): 631.

Kotak, Uday. 2021. "IBC: How Do We Reach the Promised Land?" *Quinquennial of Insolvency and Bankruptcy Code, 2016.* Insolvency and Bankruptcy Board of India, New Delhi, 205.

Liu, Yan, José Garrido, and Chanda DeLong. 2020. "Private Debt Resolution in the Wake of the Pandemic." IMF Special Series on COVID-19, International Monetary Fund, Washington, DC.

Mahapatra, Sudip, Pooja Singhania, and Misha Chandna. 2020. "Operational Creditors in Insolvency: A Tale of Disenfranchisement." *NALSAR Student Law Review* 14: 78–92.

Mehta, Sunil. 2021. "Pre-pack: A Great Enabler for Resolution of Stress in MSMEs." *Quinquennial of Insolvency and Bankruptcy Code, 2016.* Insolvency and Bankruptcy Board of India, New Delhi, 371.

Mohan, M. P. Ram, and Vishakha Raj. 2020. "Apartment Buyers as Financial Creditors: Pushing the Conceptual Limits of the Indian Insolvency Regime." *Columbia Journal of Asian Law* 33 (2): 219–63.

Mohan, M. P. Ram, and Vishakha Raj. 2021. "Section 29A of India's Insolvency and Bankruptcy Code: An Instance of Hard Cases Making Bad Law?" Indian Institute of Management Ahmedabad Working Paper.

Prakash, Shreya. 2021. "Increasing Participation of Non-Financial Creditors while Approving Resolution Plans." *Quinquennial of Insolvency and Bankruptcy Code, 2016.* Insolvency and Bankruptcy Board of India, New Delhi, 233.

Pryor, C. Scott, and Risham Garg. (2020). "Differential Treatment among Creditors under India's Insolvency and Bankruptcy Code, 2016: Issues and Solutions." *American Bankruptcy Law Journal* 94 (1): 123–54.

Ravi, Aparna. 2021. "Easing the Resolution Process." *Quinquennial of Insolvency and Bankruptcy Code, 2016.* Insolvency and Bankruptcy Board of India, New Delhi, 211.

Sahoo, M. S. 2021. "Insolvency and Bankruptcy Board of India: A Regulator Like No Other." *Quinquennial of Insolvency and Bankruptcy Code, 2016.* Insolvency and Bankruptcy Board of India, New Delhi, 1.

Saini, Navrang. 2021. "Valuation Profession in India: Organisational Evolution, Institutional Importance and Way Forward." *Quinquennial of Insolvency and Bankruptcy Code, 2016.* Insolvency and Bankruptcy Board of India, New Delhi, 501.

Shikha, Neeti, and Urvashi Shahi. 2021. "Timely Resolution of Insolvency in India: Assessing the Roadblocks." *Quinquennial of Insolvency and Bankruptcy Code, 2016.* Insolvency and Bankruptcy Board of India, New Delhi, 217.

Sriram, B. 2021. "A Code of Conduct for Committee of Creditors." *Quinquennial of Insolvency and Bankruptcy Code, 2016.* Insolvency and Bankruptcy Board of India, New Delhi, 295.

Suyash, Ashu. 2021. "IBC: Coding a Seismic Shift." *Quinquennial of Insolvency and Bankruptcy Code, 2016.* Insolvency and Bankruptcy Board of India, New Delhi, 37.

United Nations Commission on International Trade Law (UNCITRAL). 1997. *Model Law on Cross-Border Insolvency.* United Nations, New York.

United Nations Commission on International Trade Law (UNCITRAL). 2004. *Legislative Guide on Insolvency Law, Part 3.* United Nations, New York.

United Nations Commission on International Trade Law (UNCITRAL). 2010. *Legislative Guide on Insolvency Law, Part 3* (Enterprise Group Insolvency). United Nations, New York.

United Nations Commission on International Trade Law (UNCITRAL). 2021. *Draft Legislative Guide on Insolvency Law for Micro- and Small Enterprises.* http://undocs.org/en/A/CN.9/WG.V/WP.174.

van Zwieten, Kristin. 2014. *"Corporate Rescue in India: The Influence of the Courts."* Oxford Legal Studies Research Paper 37/2014. https://ssrn.com/abstract=2466329.

Westbrook, Jay Lawrence, Charles D. Booth, Christoph G. Paulus, and Harry Rajak. 2010. *A Global View of Business Insolvency Systems.* World Bank, Washington, DC.

World Bank. 2021. *Principles for Effective Insolvency and Creditor/Debtor Regimes, 2021 Edition.* World Bank, Washington, DC.

World Bank, Insolvency and Creditor/Debtor Regimes Task Force. 2014. *Report on the Treatment of the Insolvency of Natural Persons.* World Bank, Washington, DC.

CHAPTER 11

Monetary Policy Communication and Financial Markets in India

Faisal Ahmed, Mahir Binici, and Jarkko Turunen

INTRODUCTION

Forward-looking monetary policy communication has become a key element of flexible inflation targeting regimes adopted across advanced and emerging market economies. The Reserve Bank of India (RBI) implemented a flexible inflation targeting framework in 2016, which has been associated with improved anchoring of inflation expectations (Blagrave and Lian 2020). The flexible inflation targeting framework is supported by a set of communication tools, including monetary policy statements and minutes, press releases, and the governor's press conference. These tools have provided directional guidance on policy rates, enhancing the predictability of monetary policy.

The RBI has undertaken important innovations in monetary policy communication in recent years. Starting in October 2019 in the aftermath of the non-banking financial company shock of 2019 and during a growth slowdown that preceded the COVID-19 outbreak, the RBI introduced forward guidance that focused on reviving growth and providing state-contingent direction on the duration of accommodative monetary policy. In October 2020, amid the unprecedented uncertainties stemming from the pandemic, the RBI introduced time-based forward guidance, committing to an accommodative stance for "at least during the current financial year and into the next financial year." Amid elevated macro and inflation uncertainties, the central bank returned to its state-contingent forward guidance in April 2021 while also introducing forward guidance on asset purchases.

From a policy design perspective, it is important to understand how monetary policy communication affects policy transmission, including market outcomes. Although disentangling the impact of communication on financial market outcomes

We thank Elif Arbatli, Alfred Schipke, and TengTeng Xu for useful comments and suggestions, and Nimarjit Singh and Ankita Goel for excellent help with the data.

can be challenging, market participants have highlighted that forward-looking communication reduced market uncertainty and helped better anchor market expectations in India during the pandemic. For example, even with inflation outside the RBI's target band, and amid a sizeable increase in pandemic-related public sector borrowing, the volatility of 10-year government bond yields remained moderate during 2020, aided by the guidance on the direction and duration of monetary policy support.

The impact of monetary policy communication is ultimately an empirical question. Given recent innovations in communication, including on forward guidance, the natural questions that arise include: Does communication have a quantitatively significant impact on financial markets in India? How can the impact be measured? What do asset price movements suggest about the impact of monetary policy communication? These questions are addressed in the chapter. In particular, the chapter is structured as follows: The first section briefly reviews related literature. The second section reviews the RBI's monetary policy communication framework since the adoption of flexible inflation targeting. The third section discusses narrative analysis of recent RBI communication and its implications for financial markets, with focus on asset prices. The fourth section presents data and methodology and key results from an empirical analysis of communication and its impact on asset prices. The final section summarizes results and policy recommendations.

LITERATURE

A large share of the literature on monetary policy communication focuses on advanced economies, particularly on the impact channels, including on uncertainty. The evidence suggests that communication can be a powerful component of the central bank's toolkit—it can meaningfully impact asset prices and enhance the predictability of monetary policy decisions even if the channels through which this occurs are not often clear (see Blinder and others 2008; Boukus and Rosenberg 2006; Carvalho, Hsu, and Nechio 2016; Gürkaynak, Sack, and Swanson 2005).

Using theoretical models, Nakamura and Steinsson (2018) showed that monetary policy shocks transmit information about economic fundamentals that affect long-run market expectations of economic conditions, called "the information effect." The information effect impacts beliefs not only about monetary policy but also about other economic fundamentals, playing an important role in the overall causal effect of monetary policy shocks on output. Communications can also affect market expectations. Hansen, McMahon, and Tong (2019), using data from the Bank of England's Inflation Report, focused on the "uncertainty channel" and showed that central bank communication affects market beliefs about long-term uncertainty. Coenen and others (2017) argued in a related point that announcements of the asset purchase programs of the European Central Bank (ECB) have lowered market uncertainty, particularly when accompanied by a contextual release of implementation details such as the envis-aged size of the programs. Furthermore, evidence suggests that forward guidance reduces uncertainty more effectively when it is state-contingent or when it pro-vides guidance about a long horizon, as opposed to when it is open-ended or covers only a short horizon. Analyzing asset prices, Altavilla and others (2019) showed the existence of perceived policy target, timing, forward guidance, and quantitative easing, which influences short-, medium-, and long-term segments of the yield curve. This is consistent with earlier evidence that central bank com-munication may lead to substantial revisions in expectations of monetary policy and can impact interest rates at longer maturities (Brand, Buncic, and Turunen 2010; Gürkaynak, Sack, and Swanson 2005). Altavilla and others (2019) also found that the market response to monetary policy surprises depends on whether the announcements are perceived to reveal information about the state of the economy.

In the emerging market context, recent analyses have looked at how mon-etary policy communication affects asset prices. McMahon, Schipke, and Li (2018) assessed the impact of People's Bank of China monetary policy com-munication on financial markets using various types of communication, including (1) the quarterly monetary policy executive report, (2) monetary policy committee (MPC) minutes, (3) press conferences and speeches by governors and deputy governors, and (4) open market operations notices. The results show that communication innovations, such as open market operation information notices, reduced volatility and improved monetary policy effec-tiveness. In Chile, Pescatori (2018) found that the predictability of policy decisions has been relatively high and has increased over time. Furthermore, the efficacy of statements at times of monetary policy surprises is quite high and monetary policy surprises significantly affect the medium and long end of the yield curve, and communication has helped the predictability of the monetary policy. Forward guidance from statements is found to shift the entire yield curve, whereas surprise actions tend to tilt the short end of the curve rather than shift the whole curve. Ahokpossi and others (2020) focused on the transparency, clarity, predictability, and impact of monetary policy communication on financial markets in Indonesia by examining two channels of communication—monetary policy press releases and reports. They found that monetary policy surprises have a significant impact on money market rates up to maturities of one month, but they have no significant impact on the bond market and the exchange rate. Also, monetary policy press releases and monetary policy reports themselves do not have a significant impact on market rates.

On India, Patnaik and Pandey (2020) reviewed the institutional framework supporting inflation targeting and conclude that, aided by the specification of the inflation target and the central bank's communication framework, the institutional framework has been largely successful in keeping headline inflation within the target range. Mathur and Sengupta (2020), based on quantitative analyses of the monetary policy statements of the RBI during 1998–2018, found a persistent semantic shift in RBI's monetary policy communication since the adoption of inflation targeting. They found that the RBI's communication is linguistically complex on average, but the length of monetary policy statements has gone down, and readability has improved significantly recently. Lengthier statements are found to be associated with higher volatility in equity and currency markets but not in bond markets. Lakdawala and Sengupta (2021) analyzed official statements and the corresponding media narrative from RBI announcement dates to assess the markets' response to such announcements and how they update their expectations. The research findings suggest that bond and stock markets react strongly to monetary policy shocks but exhibit notable heterogeneity across regimes across governors. They also found some evidence of the conventional transmission of monetary policy to prices. Finally, RBI (2021a) found that the overnight interest rate swap (OIS) rates in India are good predictors of the direction of monetary policy, if not the exact timing of policy changes.

MONETARY POLICY COMMUNICATION FRAMEWORK IN INDIA

The RBI's monetary policy framework and communication have evolved significantly over time (see Box 11.1). With the adoption of flexible inflation targeting in 2016, forward-looking monetary policy communication has become a key element of the framework to anchor inflation expectations and thus ensure price stability. In addition to setting a medium-term inflation target (4 percent with a 2 percent tolerance band), the monetary policy communications strategy was also designed such that the MPC decisions are published after the conclusion of every meeting and the minutes of the proceedings released on the 14th day following the meeting. The minutes provide background information on the decision, including the statement of each MPC member.

The RBI also publishes a monetary policy report every six months explaining the sources of inflation. The report forecasts inflation for a period between six and 18 months from the date of publication of the document. Finally, if the inflation target is not met, the RBI is required to submit a report providing reasons for the failure and proposing remedial actions as well as an estimate of when the inflation target is meant to be met.

The flexible inflation targeting framework is supported by other communication tools, including the governor's addresses and statements that are released following each MPC meeting, other press releases, and the governor's press conferences. As with other inflation targeting central banks, the information content of the resolution of the MPC meetings may be more substantive than the change to the benchmark policy rate, because it may entail important information about the direction of policy actions to support the predictability of monetary policy and to anchor inflation expectations.

Cross-country evidence suggests that implementation of the flexible inflation targeting framework has contributed to improvements in monetary policy

Box 11.1. Evolution of Monetary Policy Framework and Communication

India's monetary policy framework has evolved over the recent decades. This evolution was also accompanied by changes in monetary policy communication. Initially, the focus of monetary policy centered around expanding the access and availability of credit for development. Subsequently, following the inflationary pressures during the 1970s, inflation control was largely based on price controls by the government and selective credit controls and moral suasion by the Reserve Bank of India (RBI) (Das 2022).

During the 1980s, amid high inflation and fiscal dominance, a rule-based monetary targeting framework was adopted. In this framework, reserve money was used as the operating target and broad money as the intermediate target for controlling inflation by regulating monetary expansion consistent with inflation and growth objectives. In the late 1990s, following the trade and financial sector reforms in the early 1990s and growing financial integration and innovation, the monetary targeting framework that rested on the assumption of a stable relationship among money, output, and prices came under pressure.

Consequently, the RBI adopted a multiple-indicators approach in 1998, which placed greater emphasis on the interest rate vis-à-vis money supply for monetary policy formulation, with policy emphasis shifting to price of credit rather than its quantity. Accordingly, short-term interest rates were the key instruments in signaling the monetary policy stance and the liquidity operations of the RBI were geared to align market rates with the policy stance. One challenge of monetary policy communication under the multiple-indicators approach was that the approach, with its focus on a large set of indicators, did not provide a clearly defined nominal anchor for monetary policy.

Subsequently, an expert committee set up by the RBI (2014) recommended headline inflation as the nominal anchor for monetary policy. Since the formal adoption of the flexible inflation targeting framework in June 2016, monetary policy communication has focused on this streamlined objective.[1] In its communication, the RBI has referred to the target band of 4 ± 2 percent as the tolerance band. The amended Act states the role of the RBI in monetary policy as follows: "The primary objective of monetary policy is to maintain price stability while keeping in mind the objective of growth."

As mentioned previously, the shifts in the monetary policy frameworks were reflected in the way the RBI communicated its policy stance. Recent analysis of the monetary policy communication of the RBI and its evolution over a 20-year period by Mathur and Sengupta (2020) showed that the move toward an inflation targeting regime is reflected in the monetary policy statements of the RBI. With the adoption of inflation targeting, RBI's monetary policy communication appears to highlight its focus on inflation. Using text analysis, they show that during the period that the multiple-indicators approach was used, the words *inflation* or *price* did not have much prominence in communication, whereas words such as *financial market*, *credit*, etc., were used more frequently. Consistent with the streamlined objective, during the flexible inflation targeting period, select words—*inflation, price, growth*—featured more prominently instead.

---

[1] A recent Bank for International Settlements study highlighted that monetary policy communication is important for financial market development and stability (BIS 2020).

credibility in India, reflected in lower frequency of monetary policy surprises since 2016 (Figure 11.1). This suggests that monetary policy communication is important in anchoring expectations and thus reducing uncertainties. It should be noted that the increase in size of the surprises in recent years (2016–21) captures the pandemic-related easing in the context of increased certainty.

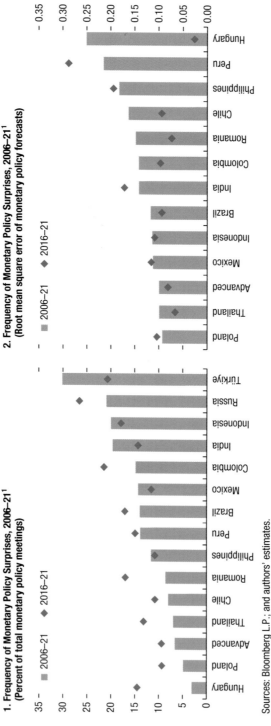

Figure 11.1. Monetary Policy Surprises: Cross-Country Evidence

1. Frequency of Monetary Policy Surprises, 2006–21[1]
(Percent of total monetary policy meetings)

2. Frequency of Monetary Policy Surprises, 2006–21[1]
(Root mean square error of monetary policy forecasts)

■ 2006–21   ◆ 2016–21

Sources: Bloomberg L.P.; and authors' estimates.
Note: "Advanced" includes average for Australia, Canada, Czech Republic, Korea, New Zealand, Norway, United Kingdom, and United States.
[1]Monetary policy surprise is the difference between the central bank's rate decision and analysts' expected rate.

The RBI has also introduced important communication innovations over the past few years. A key innovation is the introduction of forward guidance on the monetary policy stance since October 2019. Specifically, after the nonbank financial company stress of 2019 and amid the pre–COVID-19 growth slowdown, in October 2019, the RBI introduced state-contingent forward guidance that provided additional clarity on the stance of monetary policy (Table 11.1). The forward guidance was preceded by a series of policy rate cuts in 2019 as growth and inflation were subdued. Following the introduction of forward guidance in October 2019 and accompanying its subsequent innovations amid the unprecedented uncertainties stemming from the COVID-19 pandemic, both conventional and unconventional tools were used actively. Importantly, the design of the forward guidance explicitly cited growth, with implications for the relative weights of inflation and growth in the RBI's reaction function. Along with two policy rate cuts, in March and May 2020, the RBI embarked on a series of extended lending and term-funding facilities, asset purchases, and operation twist programs to ensure proper market functioning. As uncertainty increased further due to macro and inflation developments during the COVID-19 pandemic, the RBI recalibrated its forward guidance to both a state and time-contingent setting in October 2020, including a commitment to keep inflation within the target. The RBI returned to its state-contingent setting in April 2021 while introducing additional forward guidance on its asset purchase program. As discussed in the narrative analysis of the

TABLE 11.1.

RBI Forward Guidance Evolution

Meeting	Statement	Context
Aug 2019	35 bps easing, maintain the accommodative stance	NBFC shock, growth slowdown
Oct 2019	. . . an accommodative stance as long as it is necessary to revive growth, while ensuring that inflation remains within the target.	Continued growth slowdown and inflation expected to remain below target
Dec 2019		Inflation above target
Feb 2020		COVID-19 shock
Mar 2020	'ABOVE' and mitigate the impact of COVID-19 on the economy.	. . .
May 2020	. . .	Rise in inflation due to temporary supply shock
Aug 2020	. . .	. . .
Oct 2020	. . . at least during the current financial year and into the next financial year – to revive growth on a durable basis . . ., while ensuring that inflation remains within the target going forward.	. . .
Dec 2020	. . .	Moderating inflation
Feb 2021	. . .	. . .
Apr 2021	. . . accommodative stance as long as necessary to sustain growth on a durable basis and continue to mitigate the impact of COVID-19 on the economy, while ensuring that inflation remains within the target going forward.	COVID-19 second wave

Source: Reserve Bank of India.
Note: bps = basis points; NBFC = nonbanking financial company; RBI = Reserve Bank of India.

next section, in the context of a stable policy rate and other unconventional policies, forward guidance on the monetary policy stance has become the central component of monetary policy communication. The RBI has also communicated the timing and volume of its Government Securities Acquisition Programme in April 2021 and its subsequent discontinuation of the program in October 2021.

A NARRATIVE ANALYSIS OF COMMUNICATION AND ASSET PRICES

The innovations in forward guidance, especially since the pandemic shock in March 2020, allow exploration of how monetary policy communication can affect transmission, particularly through asset prices. That said, careful selection of the communication innovations and events is important to analyze the impact of forward guidance, given the size and types of monetary and financial sector measures introduced during the pandemic amid significant policy rate easing and liquidity injections (Figures 11.2 and 11.3). The impacts of these measures on different asset prices varied.

An event study around select important policy announcement dates during the recent easing cycle is conducted using announcement dates from December 2019 to October 2020, which cover the important monetary policy communication innovations since the pandemic.

By analyzing the behavior of the overnight indexed swap curve (OIS rates for maturities ranging from the day before, on the day of the MPC decision, and the day after), we can observe how various announcements impacted market expectations for interest rates.[1] Figure 11.4 shows that during the early phase of the easing cycle (e.g., December 2019, March and May 2020), the OIS curve displays a U shape, implying that markets expected additional policy easing. By the summer of 2020, with significant liquidity measures announced by the RBI, markets formed the view that the easing cycle of the policy rates was largely complete, as reflected in the upward-sloping OIS curve. The dynamics of the OIS curve around the March and May 2020 MPC dates, when the RBI demonstrated its commitment to monetary easing through policy rate easing and various financial sector measures, the OIS curves shifted downward. Amid elevated inflation in October, due to supply shocks that were perceived to be transitory, the MPC provided explicit time-based forward guidance by specifying that the accommodative stance would continue (". . .this fiscal year and next. . ."), thus addressing market uncertainty about the duration of the accommodative policy stance (Nomura 2020). The October 9, 2020 event is instructive in that the observation serves as a controlled experiment of communication impact, with relatively minimal changes in other policy measures. As seen in Figure 11.4, the explicit time-based forward guidance led to a downward pivot

---

[1] We use the OIS rates up to the 10-year maturity—while the liquid segment is mostly up to five-year maturity, and price changes from any changes in expectations or policy measures are well reflected.

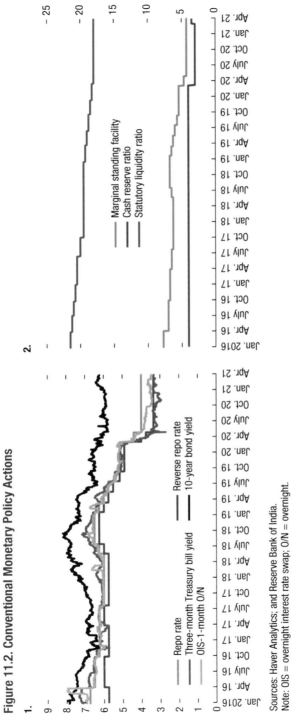

Figure 11.2. Conventional Monetary Policy Actions

Sources: Haver Analytics; and Reserve Bank of India.
Note: OIS = overnight interest rate swap; O/N = overnight.

Figure 11.3. Liquidity Operations
(Billions of rupees)

1. LAF Repo and Targeted Operations and OMO

2. Reverse Repo

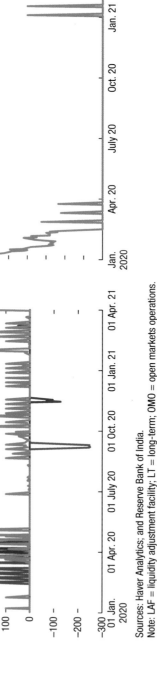

Sources: Haver Analytics; and Reserve Bank of India.
Note: LAF = liquidity adjustment facility; LT = long-term; OMO = open markets operations.

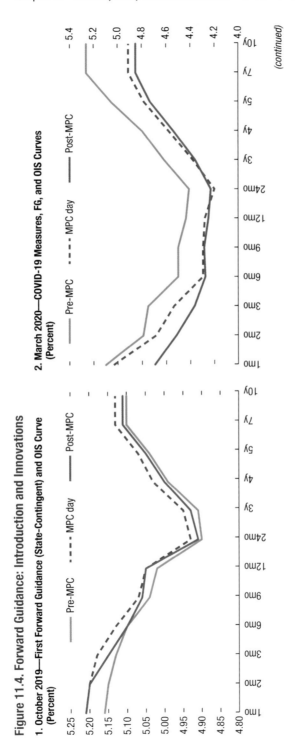

Figure 11.4. Forward Guidance: Introduction and Innovations

1. October 2019—First Forward Guidance (State-Contingent) and OIS Curve
(Percent)

2. March 2020—COVID-19 Measures, FG, and OIS Curves
(Percent)

(continued)

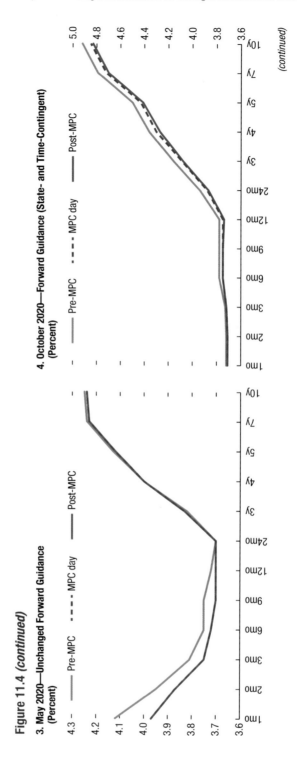

Figure 11.4 *(continued)*

(continued)

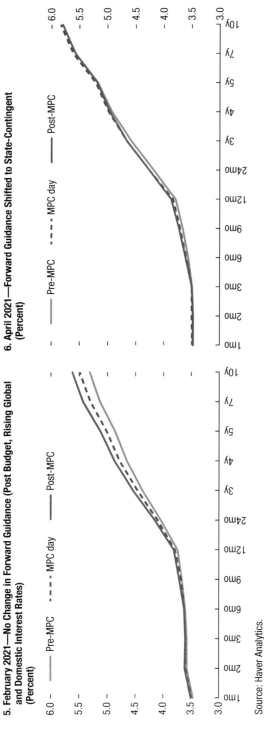

5. February 2021—No Change in Forward Guidance (Post Budget, Rising Global and Domestic Interest Rates)
(Percent)

6. April 2021—Forward Guidance Shifted to State-Contingent
(Percent)

Pre-MPC   MPC day   Post-MPC

Source: Haver Analytics.
Note: FG = forward guidance; mo = month; MPC = monetary policy committee; OIS = overnight interest rate swap; y = year.

of the OIS curve, likely a reflection of some reduction in uncertainties. Although inflation increased and remained elevated throughout 2020, the RBI's monetary policy measures accompanied by liquidity measures and forward guidance throughout the year appear to have contributed to the reduction in volatility of yields for government securities (Figure 11.5).

To analyze the impact of communication on asset prices, the focus is on the 10-year government securities' yield, given the relative liquidity of both the OIS curve and government securities at this maturity. Figure 11.6 displays how risk-free asset prices (10-year government bond yield, before and after the monetary policy announcement) behaved when monetary policy communication innovation (forward guidance) included an explicit time-based guidance during the October 9, 2020 monetary policy decision. The time-contingent forward guidance appears to have resulted in a decline in risk-free interest rates (10-year government securities yields).

Notably, during the easing cycle, RBI communication also included announcements on asset purchase programs, special monetary operations ("operation twists"), and long-term repo operations. The RBI also conducted an event study analysis around announcement days and found that (1) government securities yield generally reacts to monetary policy surprises, and (2) operation twists and long-term repo operations had significant impact on government securities yields of some maturities (RBI 2020).

Figure 11.5. Impact of RBI Policy Measures: Reduced Volatility
(10-year G-SEC, 2019–21)

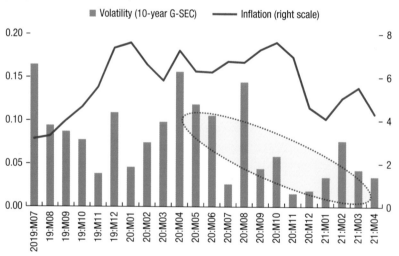

Sources: Haver Analytics; Reserve Bank of India; and authors' estimates.
Note: The shaded oval area represents moderation inflation volatility of the 10-year yield.
G-SEC = Government Securities Asset Purchase Program; RBI = Reserve Bank of India.

Figure 11.6. Forward Guidance in October 2020: Intraday Impact on 10-Year Government Bond Yield
(Percent; India Standard Time)

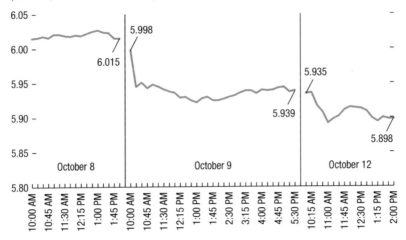

Source: Bloomberg Finance L.P.

THE IMPACT OF MONETARY POLICY ANNOUNCEMENTS ON ASSET PRICES

Methodology

To measure the impact of monetary policy surprises on asset prices, the following regression is used:

$$\Delta y_t = \alpha + \beta \Delta x_t + \gamma z_t + \varepsilon_t \qquad (11.1)$$

where Δy_t denotes the change in government security yields across different maturities, long-term (10-year) corporate bond yields, exchange rate, or stock market index on the day of monetary policy announcements; Δx_t denotes the surprise component of monetary policy changes; z_t denotes other policy announcements from the RBI on the day of MPC meetings, or other major changes in macro or financial market indicators globally; and ε_t is an error term. Ideally, high-frequency (i.e., intraday) data are needed to estimate the equation (11.1) that may have Δx_t as a single control variable. However, due to limited availability of intraday data in India, daily data are used to measure changes in asset prices and surprise components of monetary policy announcements following, for instance, Kuttner (2001). Thus, daily data from MPC meeting days (Table 11.2) are used to conduct the event study. Estimation of equation (11.1) using daily data could be subject to bias stemming from simultaneity (the possibility that movements in asset prices and monetary policy surprises could be jointly determined) and omitted variables (the possibility that variables that

TABLE 11.2.

Decisions at the MPC Meetings		
Meeting	**Decision on Policy Rate**	**Stance**
Oct. 4, 2016	Reduce by 25 basis points from 6.5% to 6.25%	Accommodative
Dec. 7, 2016	Unchanged at 6.25%	Accommodative
Feb. 8, 2017	Unchanged at 6.25%	Neutral
Apr. 6, 2017	Unchanged at 6.25%	Neutral
Jun. 7, 2017	Unchanged at 6.25%	Neutral
Aug. 2, 2017	Reduce by 25 basis points from 6.25% to 6.0%	Neutral
Oct. 4, 2017	Unchanged at 6%	Neutral
Dec. 4, 2017	Unchanged at 6%	Neutral
Feb. 7, 2018	Unchanged at 6%	Neutral
Apr. 5, 2018	Unchanged at 6%	Neutral
Jun. 6, 2018	Increase by 25 basis points from 6% to 6.25%	Neutral
Aug. 1, 2018	Increase by 25 basis points from 6.25% to 6.5%	Neutral
Oct. 5, 2018	Unchanged at 6.5%	Calibrated tightening
Dec. 5, 2018	Unchanged at 6.5%	Calibrated tightening
Feb. 7, 2019	Reduce by 25 basis points from 6.5% to 6.25%	Neutral
Apr. 4, 2019	Reduce by 25 basis points from 6.25% to 6%	Neutral
Jun. 6, 2019	Reduce by 25 basis points from 6% to 5.75%	Accommodative
Aug. 7, 2019	Reduced by 35 basis points from 5.75% to 5.40%	Accommodative
Oct. 4, 2019	Reduced by 25 basis points from 5.40% to 5.15%	Accommodative
Dec. 5, 2019	Unchanged at 5.15%	Accommodative
Feb. 6, 2019	Unchanged at 5.15%	Accommodative
Mar. 27, 2020	Reduced by 75 basis points from 5.15% to 4.40%	Accommodative
May 22, 2020	Reduced by 40 basis points from 4.40% to 4%	Accommodative
Aug. 6, 2020	Unchanged at 4%	Accommodative
Oct. 9, 2020	Unchanged at 4%	Accommodative
Dec. 4, 2020	Unchanged at 4%	Accommodative
Feb. 5, 2021	Unchanged at 4%	Accommodative
Apr. 7, 2021	Unchanged at 4%	Accommodative

Source: Reserve Bank of India.
Note: MPC = monetary policy committee.

determine movements if asset prices are excluded from the equation, thus incorrectly attributing their impact to monetary policy surprises). Simultaneity is a potential problem when a major macro data announcement (such as the release of GDP growth data) is made on the same day and prior to the MPC meeting. This does not seem to be a concern in the case of the RBI because no major macro news announcements take place on MPC days. To address potential omitted variable bias, other policy announcements such as RBI's decisions on forward guidance, operation twists, asset purchases, or liquidity ratios are controlled for.[2] At daily frequency, asset prices might also be responding to external factors such as global risk appetite or major swings in commodity prices. To account for these, the change in the volatility index (VIX) and oil prices in the specification (11.1) is added. Both the relatively small sample size and challenges associated with using daily data to identify the impact of monetary policy surprises on asset

---

[2] Liquidity ratios are cash reserve requirement and statutory liquidity ratio. See Figure 11.2 for the evolution of these ratios since the adoption of flexible inflation targeting.

prices suggest that the results from the regression analysis should be interpreted with caution.

To measure the monetary policy surprises, three approaches are used. First, the change in the OIS rates at short maturity (one month) is used. Studies (e.g., Lloyd 2018) showed that OIS rates represent market-based measures of monetary policy expectations reasonably well in comparison to the earlier strand of the literature using federal funds futures for US monetary policy expectations. Altavilla and others (2019) relied on OIS rates for their study measuring ECB monetary policy. In India, the market is dominated by Mumbai interbank offer rate (MIBOR)-OIS, with a large increase in activities across different maturities in recent years (RBI 2021a).

Even though the change in OIS rates at a short maturity by itself is a useful proxy for monetary policy surprises, variation in other short-term OIS rates and longer-term treasury securities could entail further information about the direction of monetary policy. As a second approach, following Gürkaynak, Sack, and Swanson (2005) and the related literature since, a principal component analysis of the OIS and treasury securities to extract monetary policy surprises from the unobserved factors is performed. The factor structure is presented as follows:

$$X = F\Lambda + \eta \qquad (11.2)$$

where X is a $T \times n$ matrix, with rows corresponding to monetary policy announcements, columns corresponding to asset prices, and each element of X reporting the change in the corresponding asset price; F is a $T \times k$ matrix of unobserved factors (with $k < n$), Λ is a $k \times n$ matrix of factor loadings, and η is a $T \times n$ matrix of white noise disturbances. Unobserved factor matrix F is estimated using the standard method of principal components applied to the data matrix X, which includes changes in OIS (one-month, three-month, six-month) and treasury securities (two-year, five-year, and 10-year). All variables are standardized to have zero mean and unit variance.[3]

The principal component analysis shows that the first two components explain about 94 percent of variation, but these unobserved factors do not offer any structural interpretation. Gürkaynak, Sack, and Swanson (2005) addressed this by doing a factor rotation so that the first factor corresponds to surprise changes in the current policy rate and the second factor corresponds to moves in interest rate expectations over a longer term, which are then called "target" and "path factor." This approach and the two factors in specification (11.2) are used to assess their impact on the asset prices. Gürkaynak, Sack, and Swanson (2005) associated the target factor with changes in policy interest rates and the path factor with forward-looking monetary policy communication. Brand, Buncic, and Turunen (2010) confirmed this interpretation using intraday data and separate time windows for ECB announcement of the policy rate decision and forward-looking communication.

---

[3] In construction of matrix X, we follow the approach taken in Ho and Karagedikli (2021), which looks at the effects of monetary policy communication in Malaysia.

For the third approach, survey data are used to construct the monetary policy surprises. Bloomberg conducts a survey of market analysts within the 24-hour window prior to the MPC meeting in which analysts report their anticipated policy rate from the forthcoming meeting. In this setting, the difference between the observed policy rate (realized after the MPC meeting) and analysts' anticipated rate constitutes a policy surprise, which could be written as (Ahokpossi and others 2020; Pescatori 2018),

$$\Delta i_t = (i_t - E_{t-1} i_t) + (E_{t-1} i_t - i_{t-1}) = \Delta i_t^u + \Delta i_t^a \tag{11.3}$$

where i_t denotes the central bank policy rate, $E_{t-1} i_t$ is analysts' anticipated policy rate, and Δi_t^u and Δi_t^a are the unanticipated (surprise) and anticipated changes in policy rate, respectively. As shown in Figure 11.1, monetary policy surprises in India have become less frequent but remain sizeable.

To perform the analysis discussed above, daily data from October 2016 through April 2021 for MPC meeting days (listed in Table 11.1) are used for the event analysis. Table 11.1 also shows the decision on policy rate on respective dates, and also the committee's decision on the monetary policy stance, which recently has been geared toward forward guidance. The main data sources are Haver Analytics, the RBI's monetary policy statements, and press releases. RBI's actions on conventional or unconventional policy tools enter the regression specification (11.1) either in continuous form (such as change in cash reserve ratio and the statutory liquidity ratio) or as an indicator variable (for the targeted longer-term refinancing operation, asset purchases, operation twists, or forward guidance) if any announcements are made as part of the resolution of the MPC or statement by the governor. The impact of these policy actions may already be reflected in OIS rate changes, but we control for them and for the other macro variables to address omitted variable bias problem and to test for a plausible independent impact, if any, on the asset prices.

Results

At a first pass, the scatter plot of one-month OIS rate changes (on the x-axis) and change in government and corporate securities across different maturities, and other asset prices (exchange rate and stock index), is presented in Figure 11.7. The results show that the association between monetary policy surprises and government security and corporate yields across all maturities is positive and strong, whereas this is less evident for the exchange rate and stock prices in the Indian case.

Moving to the results from the regression analysis using specification (11.1), first relying on OIS rate changes as a proxy for the policy surprise, Table 11.3 presents results from the reduced form, and Table 11.4 shows results from the model including additional control for other monetary actions.[4] The results for

---

[4] Announcements of major macroeconomic data such as GDP, inflation, industrial production, or purchasing managers' index, among others, do not seem to overlap with the MPC dates during our sample.

Figure 11.7. Overnight Index Swap and Asset Price Correlations

(Percent or basis point change)

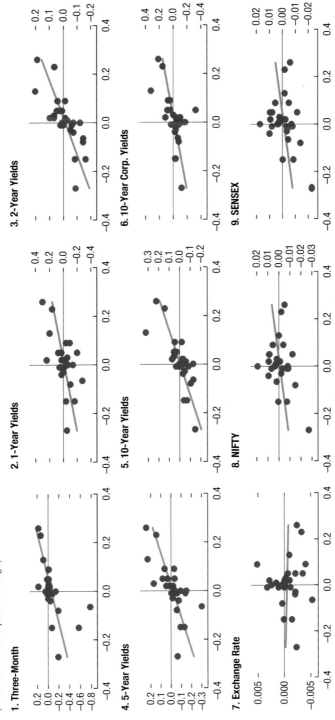

Sources: Haver Analytics; Reserve Bank of India; and authors' estimates.

Note: Scatter plot for daily change in one-month overnight interest rate swap rates (x-axis) and asset prices (y-axis). Corp. = corporate.

TABLE 11.3.

Response of Asset Prices to Changes in OIS Spread								
	(1)	**(2)**	**(3)**	**(4)**	**(5)**	**(6)**	**(7)**	**(8)**
	Government Securities					**Corporate**	**Exchange**	**NIFTY**
Variables	**3-Month**	**1-Year**	**2-Year**	**5-Year**	**10-Year**	**10-Year**	**Rate**	**Index**
ΔOIS spread	1.09***	0.68***	0.65***	0.76***	0.75***	0.65***	−0.00	0.03
	(0.32)	(0.22)	(0.14)	(0.19)	(0.14)	(0.17)	(0.00)	(0.02)
Other controls	No	No	No	No	No	No	No	No
Constant	−0.06*	−0.01	−0.01	−0.02	−0.00	−0.02	−0.00	−0.00
	(0.03)	(0.02)	(0.01)	(0.02)	(0.01)	(0.02)	(0.00)	(0.00)
Observations	28	28	28	28	28	28	28	28
R^2	0.33	0.31	0.56	0.47	0.58	0.30	0.00	0.10

Source: Authors' estimates.
Note: Robust standard errors are in parentheses. OIS = overnight interest rate swap.
*$p < .10$; **$p < .05$; ***$p < .01$.

TABLE 11.4.

Response of Asset Prices to Changes in OIS Spread								
	(1)	**(2)**	**(3)**	**(4)**	**(5)**	**(6)**	**(7)**	**(8)**
	Government Securities					**Corporate**	**Exchange**	**NIFTY**
Variables	**3-Month**	**1-Year**	**2-Year**	**5-Year**	**10-Year**	**10-Year**	**Rate**	**Index**
ΔOIS spread	0.89**	0.67**	0.63***	0.69***	0.70***	0.75***	−0.00	0.02
	(0.38)	(0.24)	(0.14)	(0.17)	(0.17)	(0.20)	(0.01)	(0.02)
Other controls	Yes	Yes	Yes	Yes	Yes	Yes	Yes	Yes
Constant	−0.04	−0.00	−0.01	0.00	0.01	−0.01	−0.00	−0.00
	(0.03)	(0.02)	(0.01)	(0.02)	(0.02)	(0.02)	(0.00)	(0.00)
Observations	28	28	28	28	28	28	28	28
R^2	0.67	0.45	0.71	0.73	0.64	0.43	0.31	0.28

Source: Authors' estimates.
Note: Robust standard errors are in parentheses. Other controls include the Reserve Bank of India's forward guidance, long-term repo operation, asset purchase announcements, and change in federal fund rate; 10-year US yields; oil price; and the Chicago Board Options Exchange Volatility Index (VIX). OIS = overnight interest rate swap.
*$p < .10$; **$p < .05$; ***$p < .01$.

government security yields imply that, on average, a 1 percent surprise tightening in the policy rate leads to an increase of 109 basis points (89 basis points when controlling for the other announcements) in the three-month yield and an increase of 75 (70) basis points in the 10-year yield. Both estimates are highly statistically significant. Tables 11.3 and 11.4 also suggest that the estimated coefficients, on average, become smaller as we move toward the longer end of the yield curve (and for long-term corporate bonds), but the differences are not statistically different. The impact on exchange rate and stock prices is not statistically significant at the conventional confidence level.

Tables 11.5 and 11.6 report results using the target and path factors for the analysis. Results for the target factor are broadly consistent with the change in the OIS rates shown above, with statistically significant impact throughout rates with different maturities. The impact is largest for the three-month rate, consistent with the interpretation that the target factor measures the surprise component associated with the near-term policy rate decision. Table 11.5 shows that the estimates of the effect of the path factor is statistically significant and large for yields of one year and longer. The impact on three-month yields is not

TABLE 11.5.

Response of Asset Prices to Target and Path Factors

	(1)	(2)	(3)	(4)	(5)	(6)	(7)	(8)
	Government Securities					Corporate	Exchange	NIFTY
Variables	3-Month	1-Year	2-Year	5-Year	10-Year	10-Year	Rate	Index
Target factor	1.16***	0.75***	0.66***	0.80***	0.77***	0.67***	0.00	0.03
	(0.33)	(0.14)	(0.05)	(0.07)	(0.07)	(0.12)	(0.00)	(0.02)
Path factor	0.72	0.73***	0.73***	1.03***	0.77***	0.72***	0.00	−0.03
	(0.49)	(0.23)	(0.06)	(0.13)	(0.15)	(0.22)	(0.01)	(0.02)
Other controls	No	No	No	No	No	No	No	No
Constant	−0.05*	−0.01	−0.01	−0.01*	0.00	−0.01	−0.00	−0.00
	(0.03)	(0.02)	(0.01)	(0.01)	(0.01)	(0.02)	(0.00)	(0.00)
Observations	28	28	28	28	28	28	28	28
R^2	0.43	0.55	0.89	0.92	0.89	0.49	0.00	0.13

Source: Authors' estimates.
Note: Robust standard errors are in parentheses.
*$p < .10$; **$p < .05$; ***$p < .01$.

TABLE 11.6.

Response of Asset Prices to Target and Path Factors

	(1)	(2)	(3)	(4)	(5)	(6)	(7)	(8)
	Government Securities					Corporate	Exchange	NIFTY
Variables	3-Month	1-Year	2-Year	5-Year	10-Year	10-Year	Rate	Index
Target factor	0.84***	0.77***	0.70***	0.75***	0.80***	0.84***	−0.00	0.02
	(0.29)	(0.17)	(0.06)	(0.07)	(0.09)	(0.14)	(0.01)	(0.02)
Path factor	0.68**	0.82***	0.73***	0.93***	0.90***	1.04***	−0.00	−0.02
	(0.28)	(0.26)	(0.08)	(0.12)	(0.15)	(0.20)	(0.01)	(0.02)
Other controls	Yes	Yes	Yes	Yes	Yes	Yes	Yes	Yes
Constant	−0.04	−0.01	−0.01**	−0.00	−0.00	−0.02	−0.00	−0.00
	(0.03)	(0.02)	(0.01)	(0.01)	(0.01)	(0.02)	(0.00)	(0.00)
Observations	28	28	28	28	28	28	28	28
R^2	0.67	0.62	0.93	0.94	0.94	0.69	0.32	0.29

Source: Authors' estimates.
Note: Robust standard errors are in parentheses. See Table 11.4 for additional notes.
*$p < .10$; **$p < .05$; ***$p < .01$.

significant. Beyond one year, on average, the estimated impact on yields is much greater than the change in the policy rate itself, meaning that the forward-looking monetary policy communication captured in the path factors conveys important information about the future direction of monetary policy. With much larger R^2 statistics, Table 11.6 suggests that, including other potential policy actions, monetary policy communication does play an important role for the asset prices because the variation in yields seems to be largely explained by the two-factor model. These results confirm the importance of the information content of the MPC decision and governor's statements as key monetary policy communication tools. As presented in Table 11.1, during the sample period, the key policy rate was changed at only 11 of 28 MPC meetings. In particular, the main source of information on the monetary policy stance more recently stems from the forward guidance on the monetary policy stance, which was included for the first time in the October 2019 MPC statement as "state" contingent guidance (". . . as long as it is necessary . . ."). Further, the October 2020 statement included explicit time-based guidance to address market uncertainty about the duration of the stance (". . .this fiscal year and next. . .") of monetary policy. Intraday data give further evidence on the impact of policy communication from the October 9, 2020, event (Figure 11.6), which is instructive in that the observation serves as a controlled experiment with almost no changes in other policy measures.

To complement the cross-country evidence on the monetary policy surprises from Figure 11.1, Table 11.7 presents the results in using the unanticipated and anticipated policy changes constructed from analysts' surveys. The results are broadly consistent with those from Tables 11.3 and 11.4 and Tables 11.5 and 11.6. The monetary policy surprises, unanticipated changes in the policy rate, on average, have statistically significant impact on the government security and corporate yields, and no effect on the exchange rate and stock market. In their exercise for Indonesia, Ahokpossi and others (2020) showed that the monetary policy surprises have significant impact on the money market rates but not on the bond

TABLE 11.7.

Response of Asset Prices to Anticipated and Unanticipated Policy Change

	(1)	(2)	(3)	(4)	(5)	(6)	(7)	(8)
	Government Securities					Corporate	Exchange	NIFTY
Variables	3-Month	1-Year	2-Year	5-Year	10-Year	10-Year	Rate	Index
MP surprise	0.50***	0.44*	0.37***	0.42***	0.35***	0.46***	−0.00*	0.02*
	(0.10)	(0.22)	(0.09)	(0.10)	(0.12)	(0.15)	(0.00)	(0.01)
Anticipated change	0.05	−0.14	−0.06	−0.11	−0.23**	−0.13	−0.00	0.01
	(0.10)	(0.17)	(0.09)	(0.08)	(0.09)	(0.17)	(0.00)	(0.01)
Other controls	No	No	No	No	No	No	No	No
Constant	−0.01	−0.02	−0.02	−0.02	−0.02	−0.03*	−0.00	−0.00
	(0.01)	(0.02)	(0.01)	(0.02)	(0.01)	(0.02)	(0.00)	(0.00)
Observations	24	24	24	24	24	24	24	24
R^2	0.62	0.42	0.47	0.55	0.54	0.39	0.09	0.12

Source: Authors' estimates.
Note: Robust standard errors in parentheses. MP = monetary policy.
*$p < .10$; **$p < .05$; ***$p < .01$.

TABLE 11.8.

Response of Asset Prices to Anticipated and Unanticipated Policy Change

	(1)	(2)	(3)	(4)	(5)	(6)	(7)	(8)
	Government Securities					Corporate	Exchange	NIFTY
Variables	3-Month	1-Year	2-Year	5-Year	10-Year	10-Year	Rate	Index
MP surprise	0.48***	0.48*	0.40***	0.44***	0.37**	0.44**	−0.01	0.02*
	(0.12)	(0.23)	(0.09)	(0.10)	(0.14)	(0.20)	(0.00)	(0.01)
Anticipated change	0.04	−0.17	−0.09	−0.11	−0.24*	−0.09	−0.00	0.01
	(0.10)	(0.20)	(0.09)	(0.11)	(0.12)	(0.22)	(0.00)	(0.01)
Other controls	Yes	Yes	Yes	Yes	Yes	Yes	Yes	Yes
Constant	−0.01	−0.02	−0.02	−0.01	−0.01	−0.02	−0.00	−0.00
	(0.01)	(0.03)	(0.01)	(0.01)	(0.01)	(0.02)	(0.00)	(0.00)
Observations	24	24	24	24	24	24	24	24
R^2	0.66	0.47	0.69	0.73	0.64	0.44	0.31	0.47

Source: Authors' estimates.
Note: Robust standard errors in parentheses. See Table 11.4 for additional notes. MP = monetary policy.
*$p < .10$; **$p < .05$; ***$p < .01$.

yields, attributing this to a shallow financial market and incomplete yield curve. However, the findings here suggesting that monetary policy surprises impact yields at all maturities are similar to Pescatori (2018), which examined the impact of unanticipated monetary policy changes in Chile.

Figures 11.8 and 11.9 summarize results from alternative approaches. Scatter plots of estimated target and path factors and the change in one-month OIS spreads are presented. A close association between target factor and OIS change reflects that these two indicators capture similar information about shorter-term changes in markets, whereas the path factor has additional information, which could be attributed to forward-looking communication. Finally, the summary of estimated coefficients from regression tables above using three alternative approaches across the different segments of the yield curve are presented in Figure 11.9. Consistent with the scatter plots (Figure 11.8), the impacts of OIS changes and target factors are similar and larger for the shorter end of the yield curve (including both for the government and for corporate securities); the path factor explains larger changes at the longer end, while the unanticipated change in monetary policy has a smaller and uniform effect across different maturities.

Among the additional control variables, a significant effect of forward guidance from October 2020, and the extended lending/term-funding (long-term repo operations/targeted long-term refinancing operations) facilities particularly on the middle segment of the yield curve (two-year and five-year bonds) are found. Additional analyses are also done to examine the impact of outright asset purchases and the operation twists. While outright purchases had limited impact on government bond yields, operation twists had some impact on the term spread (measured by the change in spread between 10-year and one-year yields), consistent with the RBI (2020, 2021b) findings.

Figure 11.8. OIS Spread, Target, and Path Factors

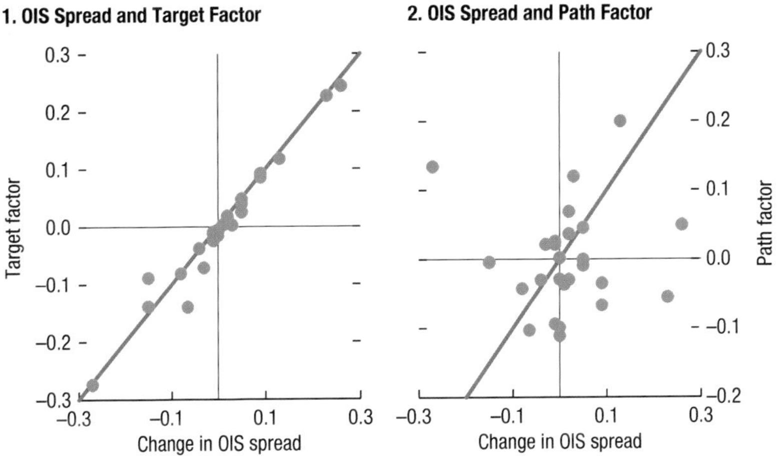

Source: Authors' estimates.
Note: OIS = overnight interest rate swap.

Figure 11.9. Reaction of Asset Prices to MP Surprises

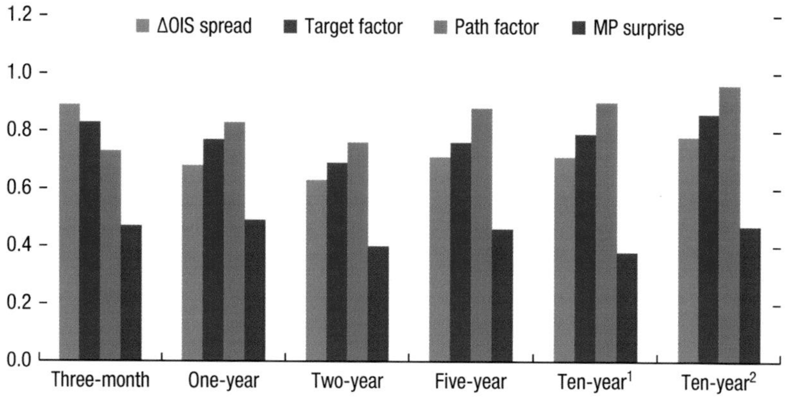

Source: Authors' calculations.
Note: MP = monetary policy; OIS = overnight interest rate swap.
[1]Indicates ten-year treasury yield responses.
[2]Indicates ten-year corporate yield responses.

CONCLUSION

The RBI's monetary policy communication has evolved since the introduction of flexible inflation targeting in 2016. This includes a set of communication tools, including monetary policy statements and minutes, press releases, and the governor's press conference, and an increasing role for explicit forward-looking communication about the policy stance and asset purchases, as observed when the pandemic-related monetary and financial sector measures were unveiled in 2020. The chapter highlights that forward guidance announcements in India influenced asset prices and have facilitated a reduction in financial market uncertainty amid increased inflationary pressures. Furthermore, quantitatively, the announcement impacts of asset purchases in India are estimated to be broadly in line with those in other emerging markets. Specifically, a review of the recent innovations of monetary policy communications suggests that forward guidance likely played a key role in moderating uncertainty and supporting some asset prices during the pandemic. We also find that the relationship between monetary policy surprises and yields for government and corporate securities across all maturities are positive and statistically significant in India, but are less so for exchange rate and equity prices, which is broadly in line with what is observed in other emerging markets. The chapter finds that monetary policy communication, including forward guidance, impacts longer-term yields for government securities, consistent with the interpretation that monetary policy communication conveys important information about the future direction of monetary policy. This is confirmed by a narrative analysis of the intraday data, which suggests that specific forward guidance announcements facilitated a reduction in market uncertainty and helped guide longer-term interest rates. For example, the RBI's decision on October 9, 2020 and the governor's statement on forward guidance were more specific about the duration of the RBI's accommodative stance, contributing to a decline in 10-year rates on the same day. The results support an important role for monetary policy communication in guiding market expectations about the monetary policy stance, including the likely path of policy interest rates.

For communication to be useful as an independent policy tool, it has to be consistent and credible with the overall macroeconomic context. For example, the degree to which forward guidance can moderate long-term rates is impacted by overall liquidity conditions, inflation expectations, and accumulated monetary policy credibility. In the future, RBI monetary policy communication has an important role to play in providing guidance on the likely path of policy normalization, including durable liquidity and the relative sequencing of phased absorption of excess liquidity and future policy rate actions. In this context, communication of any change in the policy reaction function as the recovery strengthens can help guide market expectations, especially amid elevated global and domestic inflationary pressures and the expected tightening in monetary policy in advanced economies.

REFERENCES

Ahokpossi, Calixte, Agnes Isnawangsih, M. Shah Naoaj, and Ting Yan. 2020. "The Impact of Monetary Policy Communication in an Emerging Economy: The Case of Indonesia." IMF Working Paper 20/109, International Monetary Fund, Washington, DC.

Altavilla, Carlo, Luca Brugnolini, Refet S. Gürkaynak, Roberto Motto, and Giuseppe Ragusa. 2019. "Measuring Euro Area Monetary Policy." *Journal of Monetary Economics* 108: 162–79.

Bank for International Settlements (BIS). 2020. "Financial Market Development, Monetary Policy and Financial Stability in Emerging Market Economies." BIS Papers 113.

Blagrave, Patrick, and Weicheng Lian. 2020. "India's Inflation Process before and after Flexible Inflation Targeting." IMF Working Paper 20/251, International Monetary Fund, Washington, DC.

Blinder, Alan S., Michael Ehrmann, Marcel Fratzscher, Jakob De Haan, and David Jan Jansen. 2008. "Central Bank Communication and Monetary Policy: A Survey of Theory and Evidence." *Journal of Economic Literature* 46 (4): 910–45.

Boukus, Ellyn, and Joshua V. Rosenberg. 2006. "The Information Content of FOMC Minutes." Federal Reserve Bank of New York.

Brand, Claus, Daniel Buncic, and Jarkko Turunen. 2010. "The Impact of ECB Monetary Policy Decisions and Communication on the Yield Curve." *Journal of the European Economic Association* 8 (6): 1266–98.

Carvalho, Carlos, Eric Hsu, and Fernanda Nechio. 2016. "Measuring the Effect of the Zero Lower Bound on Monetary Policy." Federal Reserve Bank of San Francisco Working Paper 16/06. https://www.frbsf.org/wp-content/uploads/sites/4/wp2016-06.pdf.

Coenen, Gunter, Michael Ehrmann, Gaetano Gaballo, Peter Hoffmann, Anton Nakov, Stefano Nardelli, Eric Persson, and Georg Strasser. 2017. "Communication of Monetary Policy in Unconventional Times." ECB Working Paper Series 2080. European Central Bank, Frankfurt, Germany.

Das, Shaktikanta. 2022. "Monetary Policy and Central Bank Communication." Address delivered at the National Defense College, New Delhi.

Gürkaynak, Refet S., Brian Sack, and Eric T. Swanson. 2005. "Do Actions Speak Louder Than Words? The Response of Asset Prices to Monetary Policy Actions and Statements." *International Journal of Central Banking* 1 (1).

Hansen, Stephen, Michael McMahon, and Matthew Tong. 2019. "The Long-Run Information Effect of Central Bank Communication." *Journal of Monetary Economics* 108: 185–202.

Ho, Sui-Jade, and Özer Karagedikli. 2021. "Effects of Monetary Policy Communication in Emerging Market Economies: Evidence from Malaysia." CAMA Working Paper 67/2021.

Kuttner, Kenneth N. 2001. "Monetary Policy Surprises and Interest Rates: Evidence from the Fed Funds Futures Market." *Journal of Monetary Economics* 47 (3): 523–44.

Lakdawala, Aeimit, and Rajeswari Sengupta. 2021. "Measuring Monetary Policy Shocks in India." Working Paper 21/21, Indira Gandhi Institute of Development Research, Mumbai, India.

Lloyd, Simon. 2018. "Overnight Index Swap Market-Based Measures of Monetary Policy Expectations." Working Paper 709, Bank of England, London.

Mathur, Aakriti, and Rajeswari Sengupta. 2020. "Analysing Monetary Policy Statements of the Reserve Bank of India." Working Paper HEIDWP08-2019, Graduate Institute of International and Development Studies.

McMahon, Michael, Alfred Schipke, and Xiang Li. 2018. "China's Monetary Policy Communication: Frameworks, Impact, and Recommendations." IMF Working Paper 18/244, International Monetary Fund, Washington, DC.

Nakamura, Emi, and Jón Steinsson. 2018. "High-Frequency Identification of Monetary Non-Neutrality: The Information Effect." *Quarterly Journal of Economics* 133 (3, August 2018): 1283–330.

Nomura. 2020. "RBI Makes Policy Palatable with Extra-Dovish Guidance." Global Market Research Report, October 9, 2020.

Patnaik, Ila, and Radhika Pandey. 2020. "Four Years of the Inflation Targeting Framework." Working Paper 20/325, National Institute of Public Finance and Policy, New Delhi.

Pescatori, Andrea. 2018. "Central Bank Communication and Monetary Policy Surprises in Chile." IMF Working Paper 18/156, International Monetary Fund, Washington, DC.

Reserve Bank of India. 2014. "Report of the Expert Committee to Revise and Strengthen the Monetary Policy Framework." January.

Reserve Bank of India. 2020. "Monetary Policy and Financial Markets: Twist and Tango." *RBI Bulletin*, August.

Reserve Bank of India. 2021a. "Assessing the Markets' Expectations of Monetary Policy in India from Overnight Indexed Swap Rates." *RBI Bulletin*, February.

Reserve Bank of India. 2021b. "Unconventional Monetary Policy in Times of COVID-19." *RBI Bulletin*, March.

Index